Collins

English for Exams

PRACTICE TESTS FOR THE TOEIC® TEST

Collins

HarperCollins Publishers
77-85 Fulham Palace Road
Hammersmith
London W6 8JB

First edition 2013

Reprint 10 9 8 7 6 5 4 3 2 1 0

© HarperCollins Publishers 2013

ISBN 978-0-00-749971-7

Collins® is a registered trademark of
HarperCollins Publishers Limited.

www.collinselt.com

A catalogue record for this book is available from the British Library.

Typeset by Davidson Publishing Solutions, Glasgow

Printed in China by South China Printing Co. Ltd

Contents

Introduction

Practice Tests for the TOEIC® Test offers a comprehensive guide to the TOEIC® (Test of English for International Communication). If you use these four complete practice tests to prepare for the test, you will be able to improve your score and demonstrate your skills in using English in a business setting.

This book has four complete practice tests for TOEIC Listening and Reading sections as well as TOEIC Speaking and Writing. It includes all four sections of the TOEIC test to give you the opportunity you to experience the full exam as part of your study and preparation.

In addition to complete practice tests, the Overview section offers useful and practical information on the test. Additionally there are guides to each of the four sections of the test so that you are fully prepared for what to expect from each part of the exam.

To help you succeed in the TOEIC test, the Challenges & Solutions sections point out common problems and concerns of test takers and offer solutions and strategies to overcome these difficulties. This resource can help you feel confident about tackling the many tasks you will encounter on the TOEIC test.

At the back of the book you will find a mini-dictionary, the answer keys to the practice tests, including an audio script for the Listening tests, and sample answers for all the Writing tasks and Speaking questions.

Specifically the book contains:

- Tips for success – Essential advice for success on your exam and an overview of the TOEIC Test.

- A TOEIC Test overview – Use this as a quick reference to the TOEIC test whenever you need to remind yourself of what to expect on test day.

- Quick guides – A brief summary of the question types in an easy-to-read format, making it simple for you to quickly understand what it is important to know in order to answer the questions correctly.

- Challenges and solutions sections – These sections offer strategy and skill reviews to help you learn how to overcome the most common challenges in each part of the test.

- Practice tests for Listening & Reading and Speaking & Writing – Realistic test questions, showing you the types of questions you can expect to find in the test. Knowing what to expect is an important part of preparing for the test.

- Audio script and Answer keys – Found at the back of this book, these tools will help you practice and check your answers as you prepare for the TOEIC test. You will find sample answers for the Writing and Speaking tests.

- CD – The CD included with this book provides you with all of the Listening passages for the practice tests. You will also find sample answers for the Speaking test.

- Mini-Dictionary – Definitions and examples are provided to help you understand all the high-level words that appear in *Practice Tests for the TOEIC® Test* and help you build your vocabulary. All definitions are from Collins COBUILD dictionaries.

Studying with *Practice Tests for the TOEIC® Test* gives you the unique advantage of taking complete TOEIC practice tests as you prepare for this important test.

Tips for Success

Start getting ready to take the TOEIC® test by following these tips.

» **Find out where you can take the test.** Begin by asking the organization requiring the test information if the TOEIC test can be administered on its premises. There are also test sites around the world with specific test dates available. Finally, if neither of these options is available in your country, you or your organization can contact ETS to find out how the test can be made available. Visit the ETS website for information: www.ETS.org/TOEIC.

» **Find out the score requirements for your organization.** Your organization will decide how to use the score you receive on the TOEIC test.

» **Start to study early.** The more you practice, the more you will improve your skills. Try to spend at least one hour a day studying. Remember, by using this book, you are on your way to good scores on the TOEIC test!

» **Time yourself.** When you do the Practice Tests in this book, track the time used to match TOEIC test requirements. By practicing in a timed setting, you will feel more comfortable with the time limits of the actual test.

» **Listen to the audio.** When you do the Listening and Speaking Practice Tests, stay with the audio and listen only once. You cannot go back in the actual test, so this will help you get used to the process.

Overview of the TOEIC® Test

The TOEIC test measures your proficiency in the type of English used in business settings around the world. The test does not evaluate your knowledge of the English language. Rather, it measures your ability to <u>use</u> English in a variety of business settings.

The TOEIC test is divided into two smaller, timed tests: Listening and Reading, and Speaking and Writing. The Listening and Reading Test is a paper and pencil test. The Speaking and Writing Test is administered on a computer. Each test evaluates key skills that you will need in order to use English in a business setting, regardless of where in the world this might be. You can choose to take either test first and the other second. You may also opt to take only the test that is needed to gauge your skills in a specific area, listening and reading or speaking and writing.

Listening and Reading

The TOEIC Listening and Reading Test takes approximately 2.5 hours to complete.

• Listening Section = 45 minutes

• Reading Section = 75 minutes

• Filling out forms = approximately 30 minutes

For the Listening and Reading Test, you will receive an answer sheet and a test booklet. The TOEIC test for Listening and Reading is a multiple-choice test. You will mark each answer by filling in the circle on your answer sheet, <u>not by marking the test booklet</u>.

You must fill in the circle completely. Look at the example. This test taker has marked (B) as the answer.

You <u>must</u> use a #2 pencil to mark your answers on the answer sheet. For security reasons, you may <u>not</u> use a mechanical pencil. You may <u>not</u> use a pen, either.

You can erase an answer if you decide a different answer is the correct one. If you change your mind, be sure to erase the answer completely. <u>Never</u> cross out an answer. The machine that scores the test will count that as two answers, and two answers are always wrong.

You may <u>not</u> mark your answers in the test booklet.

Listening Section

The Listening Test is first on the TOEIC paper and pencil test. The Listening Test consists of four parts and 100 questions total. The Listening Test lasts approximately 45 minutes. You cannot go back during any of the four parts and listen again, and you cannot go back between the parts or at the end.

Part 1: Photographs	10 questions
Part 2: Question-Response	30 questions
Part 3: Conversations	30 questions (10 conversations with 3 questions each)
Part 4: Talks	30 questions (10 talks with 3 questions each)

Reading Section

The Reading Test is second on the TOEIC paper and pencil test. The Reading Test consists of three parts and 100 questions total. The Reading Test lasts 75 minutes.

Because the reading material is in the test booklet, you can go back to check or adjust your answers during the Reading Test.

Part 5: Incomplete Sentences	40 questions
Part 6: Text Completion	12 questions
Part 7: Reading Comprehension	
Single Reading Passages	28 questions (7–10 passages with 2–5 questions each)
Double Reading Passages	20 questions (4 pairs of passages with 5 questions per pair)

Scoring for the Listening and Reading Test

You will receive a score for each part of the Listening and Reading Test. A raw score—the actual number of correct answers—is converted to a scaled score by the testing center using statistical analysis. The scores for the Listening and Reading Test are all done by computer. The raw score ranges per section are as follows.

Listening 0–100

Reading 0–100

Speaking and Writing

The Speaking and Writing sections of the TOEIC test takes approximately 2 hours to complete.

- Speaking Section = 20 minutes

- Writing Section = 60 minutes

- Filling out forms = approximately 30 minutes

For the Speaking and Writing Test, you will be tested on a computer. You will complete each task by responding into a microphone or typing your response on-screen. You cannot go back and rerecord or retype most task responses.

Speaking Section

The Speaking Test is first on the TOEIC Speaking and Writing test. The Speaking Test consists of 11 tasks total and lasts about 20 minutes.

Questions 1–2: Read a Text Aloud

Question 3: Describe a Picture

Questions 4–6: Respond to Questions

Questions 7–9: Respond to Questions Using Information Provided

Question 10: Propose a Solution

Question 11: Express an Opinion

You will wear a headset with both earphones and a microphone during the test. You should speak clearly and carefully to be sure your speech is heard correctly by the scorers. You will be given the opportunity before you start to check that your microphone is in the best position and at the best levels to record your responses. Should you have any technical issues before or during the test, you will be able to call an administrator for help.

You will be expected to speak for a specific amount of time on some of the tasks and will be given a specific amount of time to prepare for some of the tasks. The audio program will indicate when preparation and speaking times begin and end. An on-screen timer may also be used to help you gauge how much time you've used and how much time you have left to speak.

Writing Section

The Writing Test is last on the computer-based Speaking and Writing Section of the TOEIC test.

The Writing Test consists of 8 tasks total and lasts about one hour.

Questions 1–5: Write a Sentence Based on a Picture

Questions 6–7: Respond to a Written Request

Question 8: Write an Opinion Essay

The test is given on a standard English-language keyboard. You should therefore practice typing and working with this type of keyboard (called a QWERTY keyboard) if possible to ensure that you will be able to perform well on the test day. A QWERTY keyboard is the most common English keyboard layout, and you can check to see if you have this version by looking at the first six letters that are located at the top left edge of the keyboard. The letters should read Q-W-E-R-T-Y. If you do not have a QWERTY keyboard, you may wish to find one on which you can practice before you take the test.

In the Writing Test, you will be expected to complete specific tasks in a certain amount of time. When your time is over, a pop-up window will notify you that your time is finished and that you need to move to the next question. As with the Speaking Section, the on-screen timer may also be used to help you gauge how much time you've used and how much time you have left to write.

If at any given point during the test you are unsure how to do a task, you can click on the "Help" button to get information about how to do the test. You can also call an administrator for help with technical issues.

Scoring for Speaking and Writing

You will receive a score for each section of the Speaking and Writing Test. Each score is based on a scale of 1–200, given in increments of 10. The individual task scores, which are most often referenced in this book, are rated based on performance and range from 0–5 for the task types listed below.

Speaking

Questions 1–2: Score range 0–3

Question 3: Score range 0–3

Questions 4–6: Score range 0–3

Questions 7–9: Score range 0–3

Question 10: Score range 0–5

Question 11: Score range 0–5

Writing

Questions 1–5: Score range 0–3

Questions 6–7: Score range 0–4

Question 8: Score range 0–5

In addition to this scaled score, you will receive an indication of your general skills and abilities in the skills. The Speaking Test has 8 levels of proficiency, and the Writing Test has 9 levels of proficiency. These proficiency levels are based on common general English skills for speaking and are assigned according to the total scaled scores a test taker receives.

General Test Information

On the day of the test, you must present an original, valid photo ID with a signature. The ID must be current, and the photo must be a recent one. Other types of ID may be required as well. You may <u>not</u> bring any personal items, food, cell phones, or other electronic devices into the testing room. You may <u>not</u> bring in any books or paper, either.

Score Report

All test takers receive a TOEIC® Score Report, which lists the test taker's name, birth date, identification number, test date and location, individual scores and total score, score descriptions, abilities measured, and so on. It can also include a photo of the test taker, if requested. If you take the test through an organization or employer, a report will be sent directly to that organization or employer and it will report the score to you.

Certificate of Achievement

Test takers in some parts of the world can request a TOEIC® Certificate of Achievement, which lists the test taker's name, test date and location, individual scores and total score, and administering organization.

Listening Section

The first section of the TOEIC Listening and Reading Test is the Listening Section. It consists of four parts with a total of 100 questions. It is a test of your ability to understand spoken English in a business context. You will listen to audio recordings and answer questions.

QUICK GUIDE

Definition	The Listening Section tests your comprehension of English statements, questions, conversations, and talks. There are four parts to this section. You will choose the best descriptions of photos and the best responses to questions, and you will answer comprehension questions about conversations and talks.
Targeted Skills	In order to do well on the Listening Section, you must be able to: • understand basic vocabulary pertaining to business and everyday activities. • identify objects and activities in photographs of common business and everyday scenes. • respond to common questions and statements in business and everyday conversation. • understand the main ideas and details of conversations and talks. • make inferences about information you hear in conversations and talks. • keep pace with the audio recordings and answer questions within the time given.
The Parts of the Listening Section	**Part 1:** You will see photographs and hear statements about them. **Part 2:** You will hear questions and statements and possible responses to them. **Part 3:** You will hear conversations and answer comprehension questions about them. **Part 4:** You will hear talks and answer comprehension questions about them. (See below for more detailed descriptions of each part of the Listening Section.)
Question Types	Each part of the Listening Section has different types of questions. **Part 1:** Choose the statement that best describes the photo. **Part 2:** Choose the most appropriate response to the question or statement. **Part 3:** Answer main idea, detail, and inference questions about a conversation. **Part 4:** Answer main idea, detail, and inference questions about a talk.
Timing	The Listening Section of the TOEIC test takes a total of 45 minutes. After you hear each question, you will have a short time to choose your answer. Then you will hear the next question. You have five seconds to choose each answer in Part 1 and Part 2 and eight seconds to choose each answer in Part 3 and Part 4. No part of the audio will be repeated. You cannot control the audio, and you must keep pace with the audio.

Parts of the Listening Section

Part 1

In Part 1 of the Listening Section, you will see photos and hear statements about them. There are a total of ten photos. For each photo, you will hear four statements about the photo. One of the statements gives true information about the photo. The other three statements are incorrect in some way. These incorrect answer options are called distracters. You must choose the statement that gives the correct information. You will see the photos, but you will only hear the statements. The statements are not written anywhere on the page, so you must listen to them carefully.

The photos show scenes of everyday life in places such as:

- Offices
- Restaurants
- Airports and airplanes
- Train stations and trains

- Hotels
- Stores
- Streets
- Parks

The photos may focus on objects and their location or on people and their activities. Photos of people show them involved in everyday and business activities, such as:

- Meetings and conferences
- Desk work
- Phone conversations
- Eating

- Shopping
- Traveling
- Checking into a hotel
- Playing sports

Part 2

There are a total of 30 items in Part 2 of the Listening Section. For each item, you will hear a question or statement followed by three possible responses. You must choose the most appropriate response to the question or statement. You will not read the questions or statements or the responses; you will only hear them. They are not written anywhere on the page, so you must listen carefully.

The questions and statements are things you would hear in normal business or everyday situations, such as:

- Requests for information (*Wh-* and *yes-no* questions)
- Requests for help (polite requests)

- Statements of opinion
- Statements about problems

The questions and statements deal with topics such as:

- Personal information
- Office procedures
- Weather
- Everyday objects

- Schedules
- Plans
- Preferences, needs, and wants

Part 3

In Part 3 you will hear conversations and answer questions about them. You will hear a total of ten conversations and will answer three comprehension questions about each one, for a total of 30 questions in this part of the test. Each conversation is between two people and is fairly short, usually with four lines of dialog. Unlike Parts 1 and 2, in Part 3 you will see the questions and answer options written on the test page. The questions ask about the main ideas and details of the conversations and may require you to make inferences, or logical guesses, about the information you hear.

The conversations are about things you would hear in normal business or everyday contexts in places such as:

- Offices
- Stores
- Hotels
- Restaurants
- Theaters
- Banks
- Post offices

The conversations are about normal business and everyday topics, such as:

- Office issues
- Travel plans
- Making purchases
- Ordering in a restaurant
- Planning events
- Ordering supplies
- Giving directions to a place
- Giving instructions
- Making appointments
- Leaving messages

Part 4

In Part 4 you will hear short talks and answer questions about them. You will hear a total of ten talks and will answer three comprehension questions about each one, for a total of 30 questions in this part of the test. Each talk is fairly short, lasting approximately 30 seconds. As in Part 3, in Part 4 you will see the questions and answer options written on the test page. The questions ask about the main ideas and details of the talks and may require you to make inferences about the information you hear.

The talks are about things you would hear in normal business or everyday situations, such as:

- Announcements
- Speeches
- Tours
- Advertisements
- Reports
- Voicemail messages
- Lectures
- Introductions

The talks deal with topics such as:

- Travel information
- Tourism
- Weather
- News
- Business advice
- Store information
- Appointments and schedules
- Meeting agendas
- Office procedures

Challenges and Solutions

»CHALLENGE 1: "Some of the words I hear on the test are completely unfamiliar to me."

SOLUTION: Listen to English as much as possible—including in advertisements, notices, and instructions—to get used to the language. TV and radio programs and podcasts are good places to hear English. Internet sites, such as video hosting sites and various news sites, are also good places to find listening material. Watching movies in English will also help you improve your general listening vocabulary. When you are watching by yourself, replay parts you don't understand.

SOLUTION: Learn vocabulary related to common topics found on the TOEIC test, including words associated with specific business tasks, occupations, travel and transportation, banking, sports and entertainment, dining out, hotels, and so on. Make a list of these common topics and words often associated with them to help you study. Here is an example.

Topics	Associated Words
Business tasks	submit, review, evaluate, supervise, duplicate, organize, project
Occupations	accountant, lawyer, dentist, engineer, physician, event planner
Travel and transportation	reservation, transfer, luggage, fare, passenger, gate, boarding pass
Banking	deposit, withdraw, account, teller, loan, mortgage, interest rate, percentage, balance
Sports and entertainment	player, tickets, performance, program, applaud, musician, entertainer
Dining out	reservation, waiter, server, appetizer, beverage, menu, course, chef, check, tip
Hotels	reservation, check in, check out, front desk, room service, bellhop, concierge

SOLUTION: Remember that you don't have to understand every word to understand the audio or to answer all the questions. Focus on what you do understand and on getting the overall meaning.

SOLUTION: Recognizing homonyms (words that are spelled differently but sound alike) is key to finding correct answers in the TOEIC Listening Test. Look for lists of common homonyms and learn to distinguish among them. Here are a few examples.

Homonyms	
Words	**Examples**
by buy	She is waiting by the car. Where did you buy that computer?
billed build	Have you billed the client? The company plans to build a new mall.
blew blue	The wind blew the roof off the building. A room painted in blue can be calming.
read red	The assistant read the report yesterday. The light on the machine is flashing red.
know no	Do you know what time it is? I have no idea.
knew new	He knew the answer. Several new employees were hired.
hear here	The workers didn't hear the alarm. When did they get here?

» CHALLENGE 2: "I sometimes have no idea what answer option to choose!"

SOLUTION: Answer options are often paraphrased, or reworded, versions of words and phrases from the audio.

SOLUTION: Quickly eliminate answer options you know aren't correct. Every answer option you can eliminate improves your chances of choosing the correct answer.

SOLUTION: If you really don't know what the answer is—guess! On the TOEIC test, incorrect answers are simply not totaled with your score. You do NOT lose points for wrong answers.

» CHALLENGE 3: "Listening is really difficult for me. I just can't understand everything that the speakers say."

SOLUTION: Understanding varieties of native-speaker pronunciation is often part of the problem. You can use the scripts at the end of this book as you listen to the audio. This will help you connect sound and meaning. Get used to native-speaker English by listening to news reports from different English-speaking countries. Watch movies and TV programs from different English-speaking countries while you're at home or online. Have conversations with native speakers as much as possible.

SOLUTION: As you read the scripts and listen to the audio, mark words with unusual pronunciation. Look up words you don't know and keep a vocabulary log—it will increase your vocabulary.

SOLUTION: Listen to the audio from the practice activities and repeat what you hear. This will help your pronunciation and help you get used to native-speaker pronunciation.

SOLUTION: Try to listen selectively, and don't panic! Remember, it's also a matter of knowing what to listen for. You don't have to understand every word; you just need to be able to understand the most important information in order to answer the questions.

SOLUTION: Watching English-language movies and TV shows is especially good for improving listening comprehension because you can also see what is happening. Seeing gives you extra clues about the context. You can find many of these listening opportunities on the Internet. Practice watching and listening to English as much as you can to improve your listening skills.

» CHALLENGE 4: "Sometimes I have no problem answering the first questions, but then I have trouble answering the last ones."

SOLUTION: As you take the test, you'll discover that the questions generally get harder as you progress through each section. Be sure to move quickly through test questions that you consider easy, saving time for the more difficult ones that follow.

SOLUTION: DON'T spend a lot of time on any one question if you can't think of the answer. It's much more important to keep up with the audio recordings. First, answer the questions that you can. Then, if you have time, go back and try to answer the questions you couldn't do while listening.

SOLUTION: DON'T leave any questions unanswered. Guess or just fill in an answer if you are really stuck.

» CHALLENGE 5: "I forget what the people said when it's time to answer the questions!"

SOLUTION: You'll need to boost your short-term memory skills to overcome this problem. One way to do this is to listen to the audio in this book and try to remember as much as you can. After you listen, quickly write down everything you remember. Include the main idea and details. Then check the audio scripts at the back of the book. How well did you do? Did you remember the facts correctly?

SOLUTION: For some people, answering the questions while listening can be distracting. If this doesn't work for you, focus on listening. What's happening? What are the people saying? Why are they saying it? Then answer the questions.

SOLUTION: Focus on the context. Every conversation and every talk tells a little story. Ask yourself the following questions: Who is talking? What are they talking about and why? Where are they? What do they want or need? Keeping the context in mind will help you remember what was said.

» CHALLENGE 6: "I forget what the answer options are when they're on the recordings!"

SOLUTION: In Listening Test Part 1, you'll hear <u>four</u> answer options, which do not appear on the page. In Listening Test Part 2, you'll hear a question followed by <u>three</u> answer options, which also do not appear on the page. Some students have a hard time remembering all this information. A good technique is to make a mental note of only the possible answer options when you hear them. If something does not make sense or seems completely irrelevant, it's probably not the correct option. Select the best option from the possible ones and wait for the next question to begin.

SOLUTION: Anticipate the answer. When you see a photograph in Listening Test Part 1, think of some phrases or words that describe it. When you hear a statement or question in Listening Test Part 2, think of how someone might respond to it. This will help you be ready to recognize the correct response when you hear it. The correct response is the only one you have to remember.

» CHALLENGE 7: "I do well in class and when I take practice tests, but when it comes to taking the real test, I feel so nervous that I have difficulty answering the questions."

SOLUTION: Learn stress-reducing techniques, such as deep breathing and visualizing. Before you enter the exam room, take a few deep breaths. Do this again before you begin each section of the test and whenever you start feeling nervous. This will help you relax and focus.

SOLUTION: When you take practice tests, simulate the conditions of the real test as much as you can. You should be in a quiet room without a phone or other distractions. Don't replay any part of the audio; you will not be able to do this in the real test. Keep going and complete the entire Listening Section before taking a break. The more you practice under realistic conditions, the more confidence you will have when you take the real test.

SOLUTION: Get plenty of sleep the night before you take the test, and then eat a good breakfast. You will be in top condition to take the exam.

» CHALLENGE 8: "I miss questions sometimes because I'm still thinking about my answer to the last question."

SOLUTION: Stay with the audio. <u>No part of it is ever repeated</u>. If you miss a question or part of a conversation because you were thinking about something else, you won't have a chance to hear it again. If you spend too much time trying to decide on an answer, you may miss part of the audio. That hurts your chances of answering the next question. When you're unsure of an answer, try to narrow down the options or guess. Then mark an answer and move on with the audio. Remember, you won't lose points for wrong answers.

More Tips for Doing Well on the Listening Section of the TOEIC® Test

1. **Become familiar with the format of the test.**

   If you know what to expect in each part of the TOEIC test, you won't have to worry about not understanding what you are supposed to do. You'll be able to focus your energy on answering the questions. This book will help you become familiar with the format of the test. As you work through the sections, you will learn what the TOEIC test contains. You'll become familiar with the directions for each part of the test, and you'll learn about the types of questions you'll encounter in each part.

2. **Develop a regular study plan.**

   It's best to schedule time to study every day, but if you can't do that, try to make time at least every other day, and try to make it at the same time. You're more likely to follow a study plan if you make it into a regular habit. It's a good idea to write out your study schedule on a piece of paper or on your computer. This will help you commit to the plan. If you study every day or every other day, this will help you stay focused on practicing for the TOEIC test and keep your mind prepared for the test.

3. **Do exercises and take practice tests.**

   Practice answering TOEIC test questions as much as possible. This will improve your test-taking skills. It will also help you identify your areas of weakness by showing which questions you get incorrect. Then you can concentrate on improving in these areas.

4. **Develop your vocabulary.**

   You need both everyday and business vocabulary for the TOEIC test, so build your vocabulary in these areas. You can do this by reading and listening to English. Choose articles and programs with content related to the topics that appear on the TOEIC test, such as:

   - Personal finance
   - Business advice
   - Restaurant reviews
   - Vacation information
   - Weather information
   - Shopping

   Make a vocabulary log and divide it into categories such as the ones above. You can add to the log and your categories as you practice and build your vocabulary.

Reading Section

The second section of the TOEIC Listening and Reading Test is the Reading Section. It consists of three parts with a total of 100 questions. It is a test of your ability to comprehend written English in a business context. You will complete sentences and answer comprehension questions about reading passages.

QUICK GUIDE

Definition	The Reading Section tests your comprehension of written English and your ability to identify correct language use. There are three parts to this section. You will choose the correct words or phrases to complete sentences and answer comprehension questions about a variety of types of reading passages.
Targeted Skills	In order to do well on the Reading Section, you must be able to: • understand vocabulary pertaining to business and everyday activities. • identify correct grammatical forms. • identify correct word usage. • understand the main idea and details in a variety of types of reading passages. • make inferences about information you read. • read and answer questions within the time given.
The Parts of the Reading Section	**Part 5:** You will choose the best words or phrases to complete sentences. **Part 6:** You will read passages with incomplete sentences and choose the best words or phrases to complete these sentences. **Part 7:** You will read passages of varying types and lengths and answer comprehension questions about them. You will also read double passages and answer questions about both. (See below for more thorough descriptions of each part of the Reading Section.)
Question Types	**Parts 5 and 6:** Choose the correct grammatical form, word form, or vocabulary word to complete each sentence. **Part 7:** Answer main idea, detail, audience, and inference questions about a variety of reading passages.
Timing	The Reading Section of the TOEIC test lasts approximately 75 minutes. Because the content is printed in your test booklet, you can go back and check or adjust your answers as long as it's within the time allowed.

Parts of the Reading Section

Part 5

In Part 5 of the Reading Test, you will read sentences and complete them. There is a total of 40 items in this part of the test. For each sentence, you will choose among four answer options to complete the sentence. The sentence topics focus on common business and everyday themes. The sentences focus on different types of language issues.

Part 5 sentences may deal with themes such as:

- Office issues
- Financial issues
- Sales and marketing
- Business transactions
- Schedules

- Transportation
- Tourism
- Dining out
- Entertainment
- Weather

Part 5 items may focus on grammar issues such as:

- Verb tense
- Verb form
- Subject-verb agreement
- Pronouns
- Prepositions

- Transition words
- Comparative adjectives
- Adverbs
- Time clauses
- Conditionals

Part 5 items may focus on vocabulary issues such as:

- Word families (related words)
- Parts of speech

- Word meaning
- Commonly confused words

Part 6

Part 6 of the Reading Test consists of four reading passages. Three sentences in each passage are incomplete. For each of these incomplete sentences, you will choose among four answer options. There is a total of 12 questions in this part of the test.

The reading passages include a variety of types like those you might see in common business or everyday contexts. They may be of the following types:

- E-mails
- Memos
- Notices
- Advertisements

- Letters
- Instructions
- Articles

The incomplete sentences in Part 6 are similar to the incomplete sentences in Part 5. The difference is that they are presented within the context of a passage, or text. To complete some of the items, you may have to look at the surrounding sentences in order to choose the correct answer option.

Part 7

In Part 7 of the Reading Test, you will read passages of varying types and lengths and answer comprehension questions about them. The reading passages include types you might see in common business and everyday situations.

The passages may be of the following types:

- E-mails
- Letters
- Memos
- Agendas
- Advertisements
- Notices
- Articles
- Reports
- Forms
- Charts, tables and graphs
- Schedules

There is a total of 48 questions in Part 7. You will answer a variety of types of comprehension questions. Comprehension question types will include the following:

- Main Idea: *What is this report mainly about?*
- Detail: *Where does Ms. Kim work?*
- Purpose: *Why did Mr. Jones write the letter?*
- Audience: *Who is this article for?*
- Inference: *What can we infer about the writer of this e-mail?*
- Vocabulary: *The word "insight" in line 10 is closest in meaning to*

Part 7 begins with 7–10 single passages, each one followed by 2–5 comprehension questions, for a total of 28 questions. The single passages are followed by a series of double passages. Double passages are sets of two related reading passages followed by five comprehension questions for each set, for a total of 20 questions. Some of the questions require looking at the information in both passages and making the appropriate connections in order to answer correctly. The question types are the same as for the single passages, except that you normally won't see vocabulary questions for the double passages.

Here are some examples of double passage types:

- A train schedule and an e-mail about making travel arrangements
- A help-wanted ad and a letter asking for employment
- A page of course descriptions and a class registration form
- An invoice and a letter disputing the charges
- A meeting agenda and a meeting report

Challenges & Solutions

» CHALLENGE 1: "The vocabulary in the Reading Test is even harder than in the Listening Test!"

SOLUTION: The Reading Test does include higher-level vocabulary than the Listening Test, so it's important to become comfortable reading in English. Practice by reading advertisements, business letters (a "how-to guide" for writing business letters is a great source), newspaper articles, and business journals. There are many sources of reading material on the Internet. Most major business journals have websites, and you can learn a lot of vocabulary by reading the articles. Websites with information about tourism, shopping, restaurants, and so on will also expose you to many vocabulary words that are useful for the TOEIC test.

SOLUTION: Underline words you don't know as you go through the readings and questions in this book. Then look them up in a dictionary. (You might want to try *Collins COBUILD Key Words for the TOEIC® Test* or *Collins COBUILD Advanced Dictionary of American English*.) This will help you get used to some of the language you may find on the test. (See also the Quick Guide to the TOEIC Test Listening Section for more vocabulary expansion hints.)

SOLUTION: Learn common suffixes and prefixes to help you find the meanings of new words. Suffixes, or word endings, often indicate the part of speech of a word. Prefixes, or word beginnings, often add a specific meaning to a word. Learning the function and meaning of different suffixes and prefixes will help you expand your vocabulary. Here are some examples.

Suffixes	Parts of Speech	Meanings	Examples
-ation -tion -sion	nouns	refers to a state or process, or to an instance of that process	examination, inflammation, protection, information, permission, confusion
-ment	nouns	refers to the process of making or doing something, or to the result of this process	replacement, government, environment, document, assessment
-er -or	nouns	refers to a person who performs a particular action, often because it's his or her job	carpenter, teacher, copier, vendor, inspector
-ize	verbs	refers to the process by which things or people are brought into a new state	civilize, modernize, realize
-ify	verbs	refers to making something or someone different in some way	beautify, glorify, terrify, signify
-en	verbs	refers to the process of putting someone or something into a particular state, condition, or place	brighten, enlighten, frighten
-ate	verbs	refers to becoming or changing into	educate, eradicate, obliterate
-able	adjectives	indicates what someone or something can have done to them	readable, reliable, believable, adorable
-ive	adjectives	refers to a state of being related to something, or to having certain qualities	creative, decisive, objective
-al	adjectives	indicates what something is connected with	regional, grammatical, magical, national

Prefixes	Parts of Speech	Meanings	Examples
de-	verbs	forms words that have the opposite meaning of the root word	defrost, decompress, deform, decompose
dis-	various	forms words that have the opposite meaning of the root word	dishonest, disagree, displease, disorder, discomfort
e-	nouns; verbs	refers to electronic	e-mail, e-business, e-commerce, e-news
fore-	nouns; verbs	refers to something being or coming before	foretell, forefather, forethought

il- im- in- ir-	various	forms words that have the opposite meaning of the root word	inconsiderate, incapable, impossible, immoral, illiterate, illegal, irresponsible, irregular
inter-	adjectives	refers to things that move, exist, or happen between two or more people or things	international, interact, intermingle, interdependent
mis-	nouns; verbs	refers to something being done badly or incorrectly	misspell, misquote, misunderstanding, mistreatment
re-	nouns; verbs	refers to an action or process being repeated	reread, redo, rebuild, rework
sub-	nouns; adjectives	**nouns:** refers to things that are part of a larger thing or that are below something **adjectives:** refers to people or things that are at a lower standard or level	**nouns:** subgroup, subtotal, submarine, subway, subzero **adjectives:** substandard, subtropical
un-	various	forms words that have the opposite meaning of the root word	uninteresting, unlawful, unpopular, unprofessional

» CHALLENGE 2: "There seems to be a big focus on grammar in the Reading Test, and I'm not that good at grammar."

SOLUTION: When you finish Part 5 of the practice tests, note which types of questions you got wrong (e.g., Did you miss a lot of questions about verb tenses? Did you have trouble choosing the right verb forms?). This will help narrow down problem areas where you need more practice. When you have identified your weak areas, you can then look for exercises in grammar books to help you practice and strengthen your skills in these areas.

SOLUTION: Read a lot, especially business-related materials. Seeing language and grammar in context will help you become more familiar with structure and word forms.

» CHALLENGE 3: "I can't always find important information in the reading passages."

SOLUTION: Before reading the passage, always read the questions first. This will give you an idea of what to look for in the passages.

SOLUTION: Know how to spot specific question types, such as main idea, detail, vocabulary, or inference questions. Knowing the question type will help you know what sort of information to look for in the passage.

SOLUTION: Practice skimming texts. Skimming means reading over a text very quickly to get a general understanding of the main ideas, how the passage is organized, and what types of information it contains. Being able to skim well will help you more quickly answer main idea, detail, and general questions.

» CHALLENGE 4: "The passages can be pretty long! There's no way I can read them all and still have time to complete the questions."

SOLUTION: Here again you can use your skimming skills. You can practice skimming with any reading text. Before reading, skim the text to get a general idea of the content. Make a guess about the main idea and some of the details. Then read the entire text more thoroughly to see how close your guesses came.

SOLUTION: Practice reading short texts about common TOEIC test topics and time yourself. You can read the text again later and try to do it in less time, or you can try to read texts of about the same length in the same amount of time or less. This will get you used to reading in a timed situation and help you read more quickly.

SOLUTION: When you're taking the test, quickly look for key words in the questions and answer options. Then go back to the passage and look for these key words in the text. The answer to the question will often be found in the general part of the text where the key words appear.

» CHALLENGE 5: "The wording in the answer options doesn't match the wording in the passage."

SOLUTION: The answer options on the reading comprehension section of Part 7 are often paraphrased, or reworded from the information in the passage. You can practice paraphrasing when you read texts in English. After you read a sentence, write the idea again using your own words. This will help you get used to different ways of expressing the same idea.

SOLUTION: Quite often, some of the answer options do have the exact wording found in the text. Be sure to look very closely at these answer options and compare them to the information presented in the text. These answer options often contain factual information, but they do not actually answer the question.

» CHALLENGE 6: "I can never decide what the correct answer option is!"

SOLUTION: The questions after the passages are presented in the same order as the information in the passage. This will help you narrow down the possible places where an answer can be found.

SOLUTION: You'll probably notice that one or two of the answer options are clearly not the correct answers. Many students find that they can effectively narrow down the possible answers to two answer options. Carefully consider these two answer options, and if you still can't decide on the correct answer option, guess between the two. A fifty percent chance of getting the correct answer is always better than a twenty-five percent or thirty-three percent chance. On the TOEIC test, incorrect answers are simply not totaled with your score. You do not lose points for wrong answers.

SOLUTION: Don't spend too much time thinking about an answer. If you find yourself being indecisive, go with the answer you chose first. Often your first instinct is the right one.

» CHALLENGE 7: "I'm very tired by the time I get to the last section of the test, so I don't do as well on that part."

SOLUTION: Pace yourself. Try to work at a steady pace and avoid spending too much time worrying over any one question. If you find that you are lingering too long over a question, just make a guess and move on. Working at a steady pace will help you maintain your energy throughout the test.

SOLUTION: Do the test backward. Some students find it useful to start with the last, most difficult part of the test so that they can tackle those questions with greater energy. However, this solution doesn't work for everyone. The problem is that you may end up spending too much time on the last part, leaving yourself too little time for the earlier parts. You can try this out with the practice tests and see if it works for you.

» CHALLENGE 8: "I always worry that I won't be able to finish."

SOLUTION: Again, pace yourself. When you practice at home, time yourself. Make sure you allow enough time to get through all the parts of the Reading Test. In the actual Reading Test, you <u>can</u> go back to the earlier parts, so leave enough time to go back to questions you weren't sure of.

Speaking Test

About the Speaking Test

The Speaking Test consists of a total of 11 questions. Each question presents you with a different type of speaking task. You will read out loud, give a description, use information provided to answer questions, and talk about your own experiences and opinions.

QUICK GUIDE

Definition	The Speaking Test evaluates your ability to speak clearly and correctly and to convey a variety of types of everyday information and ideas in a way that is easily comprehensible to the listener. You will demonstrate this by responding to a variety of question types and prompts.
Targeted Skills	In order to do well on the Speaking Test you must be able to: • speak with correct pronunciation and intonation. • use appropriate vocabulary when speaking. • use correct grammatical structures when speaking. • provide information in response to specific questions. • express and explain your opinion. • talk about your ideas.
Parts of the Speaking Test	**Questions 1–2:** You will read a text out loud. **Question 3:** You will describe a photo. **Questions 4–6:** You will answer questions about familiar topics. **Questions 7–9:** You will answer questions using information provided. **Question 10:** You will propose a solution to a problem. **Question 11**: You will talk about your opinion on a particular topic. (See below for more thorough descriptions of each part of the Speaking Test.)
Timing	The Speaking Test takes approximately 20 minutes to complete.

Parts of the Speaking Test

Questions 1–2: Read a Text Aloud

For Questions 1 and 2, you will read a text aloud. A short text will appear on the screen. You will then have 45 seconds to look it over and get ready to speak. After that, you will have 45 seconds to read the text aloud. Each text is written in common everyday language and is the type of thing that is normally spoken, such as:

- Announcements
- Advertisements
- Introductions
- News reports
- Phone messages

Texts may be about such topics as:

- Office issues
- News
- Cultural events

- Sales
- Shopping
- Housing issues

- Education
- Transportation

You will be evaluated on:

- Pronunciation
- Intonation and stress

Question 3: Describe a Picture

For Question 3, you will describe a photo with as much detail as possible. A photo will appear on the screen. You will have 30 seconds to look it over and get ready to respond. Then you will have 45 seconds to talk about the photo. You will describe the people, objects, and activities that you see. The photo for Question 3 will focus on some type of everyday activity in a common context, such as:

- Leisure time
- Dining and entertainment

- Shopping
- Travel

- Home
- Sports

You will be evaluated on:

- Pronunciation
- Intonation and stress

- Vocabulary
- Grammar

- Cohesion of ideas

Questions 4–6: Respond to Questions

For Questions 4–6, you will be asked to imagine that you are taking part in a survey. You will be asked a series of three related questions. The questions will appear on the screen, and you will also hear them spoken. After each question is spoken, you will hear a beep. You will then need to begin speaking right away. There will be no preparation time. You will have 15 seconds to respond to Questions 4 and 5 and 30 seconds to respond to Question 6. Questions 4–6 will be about familiar topics, such as:

- Holidays and travel
- Dining and entertainment
- Friends and family

- Shopping
- News
- Health and sports

- Housing

You will be evaluated on:

- Pronunciation
- Intonation and stress
- Vocabulary

- Grammar
- Cohesion of ideas
- Completeness of content

- Relevance of content

Questions 7–9: Respond to Questions Using Information Provided

For Questions 7–9, you will answer three questions about information that will be provided to you. The information will be in the form of a schedule, agenda, or travel itinerary. The information will appear on the screen, and you will have 30 seconds to look it over. Then you will hear the questions. The questions will only be spoken. They will not appear on the screen. After each question, you will hear a beep and you will need to begin speaking right away. You will have 15 seconds to respond to Questions 7 and 8 and 30 seconds to respond to Question 9. Questions 7 and 8 ask for specific details on the schedule. They may be in the form of embedded questions, such as:

- *Can you tell me where the event will be?*
- *I was wondering if I could buy my ticket later.*

- *Do you know how many speakers there are?*
- *I don't remember what time the event begins.*

Question 9 asks you to connect pieces of information from different parts of the schedule. For example:

- *What topics do the workshops cover?*
- *Who will the speakers be?*
- *Will there be any special events in the afternoon?*
- *What special exhibits will be on display?*

The information provided will be about topics such as:

- Conferences
- Travel
- Theater
- Business meetings
- Tours

You will be evaluated on the same criteria as Questions 4–6.

Question 10: Propose a Solution

For Question 10, you will hear a voicemail message about a problem and you will be asked to propose a solution in a voicemail reply. You will only hear the problem; it will not appear on the screen. After you hear the problem, you will have 30 seconds to get ready, and then you will have 60 seconds to respond. You will have to understand the problem the speaker is describing, come up with a reasonable solution, and then describe your solution out loud. The problem will usually be in the form of a complaint or request. It will deal with familiar topics, such as:

- Travel and transportation
- Health
- Purchases
- Housing
- Office issues
- Dining

You will be evaluated on the same criteria as Questions 4–9.

Question 11: Express an Opinion

For Question 11, you will be asked to express your opinion about a particular topic. The question will appear on the screen, and you will also hear it spoken. After you hear the question, you will have 15 seconds to get ready, and then you will have 60 seconds to speak. You will need to make a clear statement of your opinion about the topic and provide details and examples to support your opinion. Question 11 will include a brief description of a situation or commonly held opinion. Then you will be asked about your thoughts and feelings on the issue, your preferences, or whether or not you agree. The question may be presented in one of these ways:

- *Which do you prefer?*
- *Are you in favor of this plan?*
- *What is your preference / opinion?*
- *Do you agree or disagree with this statement?*
- *Do you support or oppose this plan?*
- *What do you think about this issue?*

Question 11 will be about familiar topics, such as:

- Money and work
- Personal relationships
- Sports
- Shopping
- Transportation
- Education and community

You will be evaluated on the same criteria as Questions 4–10.

Challenges and Solutions

» **CHALLENGE 1:** "I have problems with things like stress, rhythm, pacing, and vocabulary in the speaking tasks."

SOLUTION: English can be difficult because it gives stress to some words and not others. Here are some simple stress rules to remember.

Stress content words. Content words are the words that carry meaning in a sentence. Content words can be:

- Nouns
- Negative auxiliary verbs
- Adverbs
- Main verbs
- Adjectives

Don't stress function words. Function words help form the grammatical structure of a sentence. Even though they are necessary, they are not normally stressed. Function words can be:

- Prepositions
- Articles
- Auxiliary verbs
- Pronouns
- Conjunctions

Stress words to give emphasis. A speaker may want to emphasize a word for a particular reason. For example, the speaker may want to contrast two things.

> **This** one is easy, but **that** one is not.

Stress can also be used to emphasize words when correcting misinformation.

> **A:** They both contributed to the report.

> **B:** Yes, but **he** did most of the work.

SOLUTION: Practice paying attention to the way English speakers use stress. You can use the audio and scripts in this book to do that. Follow along in the script as you listen to the audio. Notice which words are stressed and which words are not. Mark them in the script. Then practice reading aloud. Record yourself. Compare your stress to the audio. Do this as many times as possible.

SOLUTION: In one part of the Speaking Test, you will have to read short texts aloud. It is very easy to practice this using short newspaper and magazine articles or paragraphs from books. Record yourself as you read. Then listen to the recording. Practice reading at least one short text a day.

SOLUTION: Try singing along with English music to improve your rhythm and pacing. Singing along can often help non-native English speakers get used to the rhythm of natural English.

SOLUTION: If you can't remember a word you want to use, explain around it using vocabulary you know and are comfortable using. There are several possible ways to do this. You can quickly explain your meaning by classifying things, saying how something is used, or comparing it to something else.

- *It's a type of* tool.
- *It's used for* fixing things.
- *It's similar to* a knife.

SOLUTION: Build your speaking vocabulary through practice. The tasks on the Speaking Test deal with common everyday activities and ideas. As you go through your day, try speaking to yourself in English about what you are doing and thinking. Practice describing photos in books and magazines. Note where you have difficulty finding the right words. Then look up those words in a bilingual dictionary and learn them.

» **CHALLENGE 2:** "I don't have a chance to speak to native speakers of English, so I get nervous."

SOLUTION: Look for opportunities to make English-speaking friends. There may be English speakers in your city who are studying your language, and you could offer to help them in return for helping you with English. You can sometimes meet English speakers at language schools, universities, and tourist areas.

SOLUTION: Practice recording yourself. Then play back your recording to evaluate your speaking style. This will also help you get used to the TOEIC test style of being recorded while speaking so you won't be so nervous.

» CHALLENGE 3: "My pronunciation is bad. I'm afraid that the test graders won't even understand me!"

SOLUTION: A good place to start is by recording your voice using the scripts at the back of this book. You can then listen to the audio program and compare your recordings to the recorded passages. That way, you can compare your pronunciation with the pronunciation of a native speaker.

SOLUTION: Four (or more) ears are better than two. Play your recordings from the tasks in this book for a friend who is studying English or for a teacher. What about your speaking do they have difficulty understanding? Ask them to help you determine which sounds or combinations of sounds are especially problematic for you. Practice those parts until your speech becomes more easily understandable.

SOLUTION: Don't try to hide the problem by speaking too softly. You can't get a good score if the grader can't hear you. Practice speaking English at the same volume you speak your own language.

SOLUTION: Listen to English as much as you can. Listening to English-speaker pronunciation will help you become accustomed to the way the language sounds. Look on the Internet for movies, videos, radio programs, news broadcasts, and podcasts in English. Listen and repeat after the speakers.

SOLUTION: When you learn a new word, learn its pronunciation. Learn to read dictionary symbols used to show pronunciation and stress. Be aware that stress makes a big difference in some words. Certain words become a different part of speech depending which syllable is stressed. Here are some common ones.

First syllable stressed = noun
Second syllable stressed = verb

Noun	Verb	Noun	Verb
address	address	protest	protest
combat	combat	rebel	rebel
conduct	conduct	record	record
contrast	contrast	refund	refund
convert	convert	reject	reject
insult	insult	survey	survey
permit	permit	suspect	suspect

First syllable stressed = adjective
Second syllable stressed = verb

Adjective	Verb
absent	absent
frequent	frequent
perfect	perfect

» CHALLENGE 4: "I know some of the responses in the Speaking Test are timed. I'm afraid I'll still have time left after I've run out of things to say!"

SOLUTION: You will naturally speak at a pace that is slower than a native English speaker. It is better to be clear and evenly paced than to speak quickly and make errors. This will also help you use more time.

SOLUTION: Learn common English expressions to introduce ideas and transition from one idea to the next. These help you expand your answers. You will find lists of expressions for adding information, giving examples, offering details, and so on throughout this book. Here are some expressions that are commonly used in spoken English.

To Give Examples	To Add Information	To Explain	To Express an Opinion
For example,	*As well as*	*In fact,*	*To be honest,*
As an example,	*In addition,*	*As a matter of fact,*	*Honestly,*
For instance,	*Additionally,*	*The fact of the matter is*	*To tell the truth,*
	Furthermore,	*Actually,*	*Truthfully,*
	too / also		*As I see it,*

SOLUTION: Practice speaking with a timer. This will help you get used to the amount of time you need to speak. Make a chart like the one below and practice giving responses to questions. That way you can track your progress.

Question #	Time (first try)	Time (second try)	Time (third try)

» CHALLENGE 5: "I know that the Speaking Test also requires good reading and listening skills. What can I do to help improve my understanding?"

SOLUTION: You'll need to read quickly, or scan, texts to find specific information during the test. Practice scanning schedules, menus, price lists, advertisements, invoices, and similar things in English for specific information. You can switch your Internet search engine to the English version. Then do searches for texts like these. Scanning the search results for links in English is also good practice. Then time yourself as you scan to find specific types of information. Go back and check your answers by reading more slowly and carefully. This will help you learn how to find information quickly and report it accurately. Here's a list of things to find to help get you started.

1. For a restaurant menu, find:
- the most expensive item on the menu.
- the least expensive item.
- two kinds of dessert.
- a seafood dish.
- the restaurant's opening and closing times.

2. For a train schedule, find:
- the departure time of the earliest train.
- the departure time of the latest train.
- the names of three cities on a route.
- information about how to purchase tickets.

3. For a theater schedule, find:
- the times for performances on a particular date.
- the types of performances scheduled.
- the name of the star performer.
- information about how to purchase tickets.

4. For a conference schedule, find:
- the titles of the workshops to be given at a particular time.
- the dates of the conference.
- the cost to attend the conference.
- information about exhibits.

SOLUTION: In one part of the Speaking Test, you will need to listen to a phone message in English, then briefly summarize and respond to it. Practice for this by looking on the Internet for short podcasts, radio programs, or news programs. Listen and summarize what you heard aloud. Record it if possible. Then listen to the original piece again to see if you forgot or misunderstood any parts of it.

SOLUTION: A good way to practice listening skills is to listen to songs in English. As you listen, try to write down the words. Listen as many times as you need to. You can find the lyrics to most popular songs online, so it is easy to check your work.

Writing Test

About the Writing Test

The Writing Test consists of a total of eight questions in which you are presented with different types of writing tasks. In response to various prompts, you will compose sentences using the words provided, respond to written requests, and write an essay.

QUICK GUIDE

Definition	The Writing Test evaluates your ability to convey information and to express your ideas in written English in a comprehensible manner using appropriate vocabulary and grammar forms. You will demonstrate this by responding to a variety of question types and prompts.
Targeted Skills	In order to do well on the Writing Test, you must be able to: • write simple, compound, and complex sentences. • use appropriate vocabulary. • use correct grammar. • respond to requests in writing. • explain problems and ask questions in writing. • express and explain your opinion in writing. • organize and write an essay.
Parts of the Writing Test	**Questions 1–5:** You will write sentences about photos. **Questions 6–7:** You will respond to e-mails. **Question 8:** You will write about your opinion on a particular topic. (See below for more thorough descriptions of each part of the Writing Test.)
Timing	The Writing Test takes approximately 60 minutes to complete.

Parts of the Writing Test

Questions 1–5: Write a Sentence Based on a Picture

For each of Questions 1–5, you will see a photo accompanied by two words or phrases. You will write a sentence about the photo using the two words or phrases provided. You will have a total of eight minutes to complete all of Questions 1–5. In this section, you <u>can</u> go back to previous questions by clicking the "Back" button. The photos show people involved in common everyday activities, such as:

• Meeting with colleagues

• Doing office work

• Cooking

• Eating at home or at a restaurant

• Using public transportation

• Traveling

• Enjoying leisure time

• Banking

• Shopping

Word combinations you may see in Questions 1–5 may include:

- Noun / noun
- Noun / verb
- Noun / preposition
- Verb / preposition
- Noun / coordinating conjunction
- Verb / coordinating conjunction
- Noun / adjective
- Noun / adverb
- Noun / subordinating conjunction
- Verb / subordinating conjunction

In Questions 4–5, one word or phrase of the pair will always be a subordinating conjunction. Therefore, to respond to these questions, you will have to write a sentence with a subordinate clause. Types of subordinating conjunctions you may see in Questions 4–5 include:

- Time: *when, while, after, before, until*
- Location: *where*
- Cause and effect: *because, as, since, so, so that*
- Contrast: *although, even though, though, in spite of the fact*
- Condition: *if, even if, unless*

For Questions 1–5, you will be evaluated on:

- Grammar
- Appropriate use of both provided words or phrases
- Relevancy of the sentence to the picture

Questions 6–7: Respond to a Written Request

For Questions 6–7, you will read an e-mail and write a response to it in which you address the tasks you are given. For each of the e-mails, you will be given two or more tasks to address in your response. You will have ten minutes to read each e-mail and write a response to it. The e-mails in Questions 6–7 deal with common scenarios in everyday business and personal life, such as:

- Making appointments
- Scheduling meetings
- Ordering supplies
- Explaining problems with shipments
- Requesting repairs
- Organizing events
- Solving office problems
- Making travel plans
- Applying for jobs
- Advertising employment opportunities

You will be asked to address tasks such as the following:

- Making suggestions
- Asking questions
- Making requests
- Giving information
- Explaining reasons for problems
- Describing problems
- Making statements about specific things

For Questions 6–7, you will be evaluated on:

- Organization and cohesion of ideas
- Appropriate tone
- Use of a variety of correct sentence structures
- Appropriate use of vocabulary

Question 8: Write an Opinion Essay

For Question 8, you will be asked a question and will respond with a written essay in which you explain and support your opinion. You will have a total of 30 minutes to read the question, plan your response, and write your essay. Question 8 asks your opinion on a topic such as:

- Workplace issues
- Family
- Friendships
- Career choices
- Education

- Transportation issues
- City issues
- Shopping
- Leisure time

You will be asked to state your opinion on the topic in one of the following ways:

- Agree or disagree with a statement
- State your preference for something
- Describe the advantages and disadvantages of a situation
- Explain the importance of something

You will be evaluated on:

- Organization and cohesion of ideas
- Use of reasons and examples to support your opinion
- Relevancy to the topic
- Appropriate use of vocabulary and grammar

Challenges and Solutions

» CHALLENGE 1: "I never write this type of material in English. I don't even know where to start."

SOLUTION: Practice writing as often as you can. One way to do this is to keep a journal in English. You can write about your daily activities, thoughts, and plans. This will help you get used to expressing your ideas in written English.

SOLUTION: Expand your vocabulary by learning the English words and phrases for things you most commonly write about in your own language. You can practice by translating e-mails that you've recently written to friends, colleagues, or customers into English. This is another way to get used to expressing your ideas in written English.

SOLUTION: Become familiar with business English. Go online and look for companies with English language websites. Many of these websites allow people to write in with questions. Write e-mails and notice the language of the responses. Some companies even have social networking sites where you can practice interacting personally with others in writing. This will help you get used to using written business English.

SOLUTION: Look for employment ads online and practice writing e-mails in response to them. This will help you develop the language you will need for responding to written requests on the test.

SOLUTION: Look for photos in magazines that show people in a variety of situations. Practice writing sentences that describe what is happening in the pictures. This will help you write sentences about photos on the test.

» CHALLENGE 2: "My grammar and spelling are weak, so I'm afraid I'll make a lot of mistakes."

SOLUTION: Review and practice useful grammatical structures. Pay attention to the grammar used in this book. What you see on the test will be very similar. Make a note of any grammatical structures that are difficult for you. Find a good English grammar book, and practice the things you find most problematic.

SOLUTION: Do practice activities to keep your grammar and spelling skills sharp. Check online sources for free grammar and spelling practice activities. There are dozens of tests online that have answer keys. Some also offer explanations about grammar or spelling. This will help you become familiar with correct grammar forms and spelling.

SOLUTION: Learn about different types of sentences, and practice writing different sentence types as often as possible. This will help you use correct sentence structure when you write during the test. It will also help you become more comfortable with a variety of sentence types—something that can improve your score on the test.

> **Sentence Types:** Sentences are made up of clauses. A clause is a part of a sentence that contains a subject and a verb. An independent clause can stand alone. A dependent clause must be part of a sentence with an independent clause.
>
> A **simple sentence** consists of one independent clause.
>
> > The clerk answered the phone.
>
> A **compound sentence** consists of two independent clauses joined by a coordinating conjunction, such as *and, but, or,* or *so.*
>
> > <u>The man dropped the box,</u> and <u>the computer broke</u>.
> > (independent clause)   (independent clause)
>
> A **complex sentence** consists of an independent clause and one or more dependent clauses. A dependent clause is one that begins with a subordinating conjunction, such as *because, after, before, although, if, while,* or *when.*
>
> > <u>If we get the contract,</u> <u>we will need to hire some people</u>.
> > (dependent clause)   (independent clause)
>
> A **compound-complex sentence** consists of three or more clauses. At least two are independent clauses, and one is a dependent clause.
>
> > <u>The conference was interesting,</u> but <u>not many people attended</u> <u>because it was so expensive</u>.
> > (independent clause)   (independent clause)   (dependent clause)

» CHALLENGE 3: "I can handle the short sentences, but I have a hard time writing a long essay."

SOLUTION: A long essay is basically just a lot of well-written sentences organized in a logical way. If you can write good sentences, you just need to learn to become comfortable combining them in interesting ways to produce paragraphs and longer essays.

SOLUTION: Learn how essays are developed by studying basic organizational structures used in the essays and templates in this book. Look on university websites for examples of student essays and study how the essays are organized. Looking at a lot of sample essays will help you understand different ways to organize your ideas in writing.

SOLUTION: Practice writing essays. The more you practice essay writing, the easier it will be for you. You can use the sample essay questions in this book. Write about each topic twice. Take a different point of view each time.

SOLUTION: Study other written pieces to see how other writers do it. Look online for editorials and other opinion pieces to see how writers present opinions. After you read an editorial, think about your own opinion on the topic, then write an essay expressing your opinion.

» CHALLENGE 4: "I just can't think of anything to say when I have to answer a written request."

SOLUTION: Begin by focusing on just one thing. Practice writing e-mails about a single topic. For example, write an e-mail apologizing for missing a meeting, an e-mail requesting a day off, an e-mail offering advice to a co-worker about a raise, or an e-mail explaining a problem.

SOLUTION: Practice brainstorming. This will help you come up with a lot of different ideas. When you come up with a lot of ideas, you can choose the best ones. This will make your writing much easier. Think about any topic, and brainstorm ideas. You can do this while riding on the bus, waiting for a doctor's appointment, or eating lunch by yourself. You can start with the e-mails in the exercises in this book. For each task, brainstorm a list of at least ten possible ways you could address the task. Some of the ideas you come up with may be silly, but it doesn't matter. The point is to loosen up your mind. If you have trouble coming up with ideas, think about different people you know and how they might respond to the situation presented in the e-mail. Practicing in this way will help you get used to coming up with ideas when you need them on the test.

» CHALLENGE 5: "I never have a chance to write to native English speakers."

SOLUTION: Join an online forum. Post your thoughts on different subjects that interest you. This will give you a chance to practice writing English in a situation of real communication.

SOLUTION: Take advantage of free online resources and read native speaker texts. Even if you don't have the chance to write to someone in English, you can learn a lot by reading correspondence in English. Look at how the responses are structured. Look at some of the words and phrases used. The more you read, the more examples you will see and the more accustomed you will become to the ways the language is used.

» CHALLENGE 6: "By the time I think about what to write and then write it, I'm out of time."

SOLUTION: For the Writing Test, you will need to be comfortable using a computer for writing. Practice typing on a computer using a word-processing program. Also, be sure to practice editing what you write because you will be able to change what you write during the test. You should be comfortable cutting and pasting text.

SOLUTION: You will also need to be very comfortable using an English keyboard. It is extremely important that you know where all of the letters are on the keyboard, how to make capital letters, and where the punctuation marks are. You do not want to waste time figuring these things out during the test. See page 8 for more about typing practice needs.

SOLUTION: Practice working within a time limit. Use the timing suggestions in this book, and practice writing to meet time limits. Do this frequently. This will help you learn to use your time more efficiently.

SOLUTION: Write simply. Don't make things overly complex. A good simple piece will get a better grade than a poorly written complex one. It will also take less time.

SOLUTION: Don't spend a lot of time trying to figure out what your opinion really is or what the most interesting response to a task might be. Just think of something that you can write about and that is relevant to the given task. When you answer the questions, you must respond to the tasks, but other than that, the content is not as important as your ability to demonstrate good writing skills.

TOEIC® TEST 1

Listening Answer Sheet

1. (A) (B) (C) (D)	26. (A) (B) (C)	51. (A) (B) (C) (D)	76. (A) (B) (C) (D)
2. (A) (B) (C) (D)	27. (A) (B) (C)	52. (A) (B) (C) (D)	77. (A) (B) (C) (D)
3. (A) (B) (C) (D)	28. (A) (B) (C)	53. (A) (B) (C) (D)	78. (A) (B) (C) (D)
4. (A) (B) (C) (D)	29. (A) (B) (C)	54. (A) (B) (C) (D)	79. (A) (B) (C) (D)
5. (A) (B) (C) (D)	30. (A) (B) (C)	55. (A) (B) (C) (D)	80. (A) (B) (C) (D)
6. (A) (B) (C) (D)	31. (A) (B) (C)	56. (A) (B) (C) (D)	81. (A) (B) (C) (D)
7. (A) (B) (C) (D)	32. (A) (B) (C)	57. (A) (B) (C) (D)	82. (A) (B) (C) (D)
8. (A) (B) (C) (D)	33. (A) (B) (C)	58. (A) (B) (C) (D)	83. (A) (B) (C) (D)
9. (A) (B) (C) (D)	34. (A) (B) (C)	59. (A) (B) (C) (D)	84. (A) (B) (C) (D)
10. (A) (B) (C) (D)	35. (A) (B) (C)	60. (A) (B) (C) (D)	85. (A) (B) (C) (D)
11. (A) (B) (C)	36. (A) (B) (C)	61. (A) (B) (C) (D)	86. (A) (B) (C) (D)
12. (A) (B) (C)	37. (A) (B) (C)	62. (A) (B) (C) (D)	87. (A) (B) (C) (D)
13. (A) (B) (C)	38. (A) (B) (C)	63. (A) (B) (C) (D)	88. (A) (B) (C) (D)
14. (A) (B) (C)	39. (A) (B) (C)	64. (A) (B) (C) (D)	89. (A) (B) (C) (D)
15. (A) (B) (C)	40. (A) (B) (C)	65. (A) (B) (C) (D)	90. (A) (B) (C) (D)
16. (A) (B) (C)	41. (A) (B) (C) (D)	66. (A) (B) (C) (D)	91. (A) (B) (C) (D)
17. (A) (B) (C)	42. (A) (B) (C) (D)	67. (A) (B) (C) (D)	92. (A) (B) (C) (D)
18. (A) (B) (C)	43. (A) (B) (C) (D)	68. (A) (B) (C) (D)	93. (A) (B) (C) (D)
19. (A) (B) (C)	44. (A) (B) (C) (D)	69. (A) (B) (C) (D)	94. (A) (B) (C) (D)
20. (A) (B) (C)	45. (A) (B) (C) (D)	70. (A) (B) (C) (D)	95. (A) (B) (C) (D)
21. (A) (B) (C)	46. (A) (B) (C) (D)	71. (A) (B) (C) (D)	96. (A) (B) (C) (D)
22. (A) (B) (C)	47. (A) (B) (C) (D)	72. (A) (B) (C) (D)	97. (A) (B) (C) (D)
23. (A) (B) (C)	48. (A) (B) (C) (D)	73. (A) (B) (C) (D)	98. (A) (B) (C) (D)
24. (A) (B) (C)	49. (A) (B) (C) (D)	74. (A) (B) (C) (D)	99. (A) (B) (C) (D)
25. (A) (B) (C)	50. (A) (B) (C) (D)	75. (A) (B) (C) (D)	100. (A) (B) (C) (D)

Reading Answer Sheet

101. (A) (B) (C) (D)	126. (A) (B) (C) (D)	151. (A) (B) (C) (D)	176. (A) (B) (C) (D)
102. (A) (B) (C) (D)	127. (A) (B) (C) (D)	152. (A) (B) (C) (D)	177. (A) (B) (C) (D)
103. (A) (B) (C) (D)	128. (A) (B) (C) (D)	153. (A) (B) (C) (D)	178. (A) (B) (C) (D)
104. (A) (B) (C) (D)	129. (A) (B) (C) (D)	154. (A) (B) (C) (D)	179. (A) (B) (C) (D)
105. (A) (B) (C) (D)	130. (A) (B) (C) (D)	155. (A) (B) (C) (D)	180. (A) (B) (C) (D)
106. (A) (B) (C) (D)	131. (A) (B) (C) (D)	156. (A) (B) (C) (D)	181. (A) (B) (C) (D)
107. (A) (B) (C) (D)	132. (A) (B) (C) (D)	157. (A) (B) (C) (D)	182. (A) (B) (C) (D)
108. (A) (B) (C) (D)	133. (A) (B) (C) (D)	158. (A) (B) (C) (D)	183. (A) (B) (C) (D)
109. (A) (B) (C) (D)	134. (A) (B) (C) (D)	159. (A) (B) (C) (D)	184. (A) (B) (C) (D)
110. (A) (B) (C) (D)	135. (A) (B) (C) (D)	160. (A) (B) (C) (D)	185. (A) (B) (C) (D)
111. (A) (B) (C) (D)	136. (A) (B) (C) (D)	161. (A) (B) (C) (D)	186. (A) (B) (C) (D)
112. (A) (B) (C) (D)	137. (A) (B) (C) (D)	162. (A) (B) (C) (D)	187. (A) (B) (C) (D)
113. (A) (B) (C) (D)	138. (A) (B) (C) (D)	163. (A) (B) (C) (D)	188. (A) (B) (C) (D)
114. (A) (B) (C) (D)	139. (A) (B) (C) (D)	164. (A) (B) (C) (D)	189. (A) (B) (C) (D)
115. (A) (B) (C) (D)	140. (A) (B) (C) (D)	165. (A) (B) (C) (D)	190. (A) (B) (C) (D)
116. (A) (B) (C) (D)	141. (A) (B) (C) (D)	166. (A) (B) (C) (D)	191. (A) (B) (C) (D)
117. (A) (B) (C) (D)	142. (A) (B) (C) (D)	167. (A) (B) (C) (D)	192. (A) (B) (C) (D)
118. (A) (B) (C) (D)	143. (A) (B) (C) (D)	168. (A) (B) (C) (D)	193. (A) (B) (C) (D)
119. (A) (B) (C) (D)	144. (A) (B) (C) (D)	169. (A) (B) (C) (D)	194. (A) (B) (C) (D)
120. (A) (B) (C) (D)	145. (A) (B) (C) (D)	170. (A) (B) (C) (D)	195. (A) (B) (C) (D)
121. (A) (B) (C) (D)	146. (A) (B) (C) (D)	171. (A) (B) (C) (D)	196. (A) (B) (C) (D)
122. (A) (B) (C) (D)	147. (A) (B) (C) (D)	172. (A) (B) (C) (D)	197. (A) (B) (C) (D)
123. (A) (B) (C) (D)	148. (A) (B) (C) (D)	173. (A) (B) (C) (D)	198. (A) (B) (C) (D)
124. (A) (B) (C) (D)	149. (A) (B) (C) (D)	174. (A) (B) (C) (D)	199. (A) (B) (C) (D)
125. (A) (B) (C) (D)	150. (A) (B) (C) (D)	175. (A) (B) (C) (D)	200. (A) (B) (C) (D)

Test 1: Listening

The Listening section evaluates how well you understand spoken English. The Listening test has four sections and will take approximately 45 minutes. You <u>must</u> mark your answers on the answer sheet not in the test book.

🎧 PART 1: PHOTOGRAPHS
01

> **Directions:** For each item in Part 1, you will hear four statements about a photograph in the test book. You must listen carefully to the statements in order to select the statement that best describes the photograph. Mark the corresponding letter (A), (B), (C), or (D) on the answer sheet.

Example

Listen to the statements and select the one that best describes the picture.

(A) They're drinking orange juice.
(B) They're turning on a computer.
(C) They're looking at a screen.
(D) They're putting on formal clothes.

Statement **(C), "They're looking at a screen."** best describes the picture, so you should choose answer (C) and mark it on your answer sheet.

Sample Answer

(A) (B) ● (D)

Go on to the next page ➔

🎧
02

1.

2.

3.

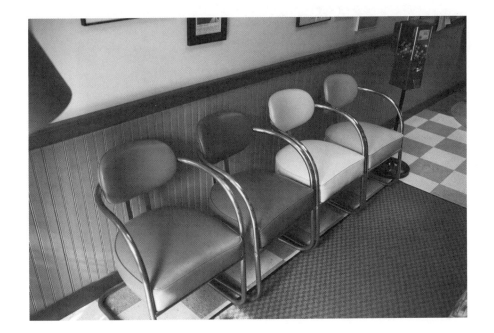

4.

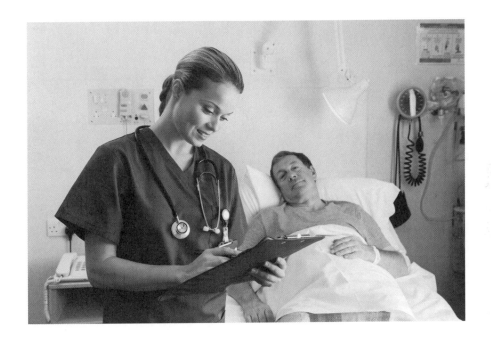

Go on to the next page →

5.

6.

7.

8.

Go on to the next page ➔

9.

10.

This is the end of Part 1.

Look at the next page to start Part 2 ➔

PART 2: QUESTION–RESPONSE

03

Directions: For each item in Part 2, you will hear a statement or a question followed by three responses. Listen and choose the best response. Then mark the corresponding letter (A), (B), or (C) on the answer sheet.

Example

Have you met the new Managing Director?

(A) Actually I talked with him in the lobby just now.
(B) Yes, I took the call.
(C) No, he takes the subway to work.

The best response to the question "Have you met the new Managing Director?" is answer choice **(A), "Actually I talked with him in the lobby just now."** You should mark answer (A) on your answer sheet.

Sample Answer

04

11. Listen and choose the best response.

12. Listen and choose the best response.

13. Listen and choose the best response.

14. Listen and choose the best response.

15. Listen and choose the best response.

16. Listen and choose the best response.

17. Listen and choose the best response.

18. Listen and choose the best response.

19. Listen and choose the best response.

20. Listen and choose the best response.

21. Listen and choose the best response.

22. Listen and choose the best response.

23. Listen and choose the best response.

24. Listen and choose the best response.

25. Listen and choose the best response.

26. Listen and choose the best response.

27. Listen and choose the best response.

28. Listen and choose the best response.

29. Listen and choose the best response.

30. Listen and choose the best response.

31. Listen and choose the best response.

32. Listen and choose the best response.

33. Listen and choose the best response.

34. Listen and choose the best response.

35. Listen and choose the best response.

36. Listen and choose the best response.

37. Listen and choose the best response.

38. Listen and choose the best response.

39. Listen and choose the best response.

40. Listen and choose the best response.

This is the end of Part 2.

Go on to the next page to start Part 3 →

05

PART 3: CONVERSATIONS

> **Directions:** You will hear conversations with two speakers. Then you will answer three questions about each conversation. Listen and select the best response to each question. Mark the corresponding letter (A), (B), (C), or (D) on the answer sheet.

41. What is the woman doing?

    (A) Inviting a friend to a dinner

    (B) Making a reservation

    (C) Cooking dinner

    (D) Changing an appointment

42. What is the woman requesting?

    (A) A recipe

    (B) A dinner

    (C) A table

    (D) Attendance at a party

43. What should the woman do next?

    (A) Call her friends

    (B) Cancel an appointment

    (C) Book a table online

    (D) Give the man her contact details

44. Where most likely are the two people?

    (A) In an office

    (B) In a gallery

    (C) In a shop

    (D) In a station

45. Why is the man in New York?

    (A) He is attending a meeting.

    (B) He has an interview.

    (C) He is studying art.

    (D) He is visiting his sister.

46. What does the woman recommend the man do?

    (A) Move to New York

    (B) Go to a station

    (C) Study art

    (D) Visit a tourist attraction

47. Who most likely is the man?

    (A) A customer

    (B) A post office clerk

    (C) A secretary

    (D) A real estate agent

48. What is the purpose of the woman's call?

    (A) To book a flight

    (B) To send some mail

    (C) To ask for a phone number

    (D) To inquire about a parcel

49. What is the woman going to do?

    (A) Send a document

    (B) Go to the post office

    (C) Talk to a friend

    (D) Issue a delivery notice

50. What is the man asking for?

    (A) To open an account

    (B) To book an appointment

    (C) To deposit some money

    (D) To arrange a vacation

51. What does the woman give the man?

    (A) A business card

    (B) A phone number

    (C) Account details

    (D) An application form

52. What should the man do?

    (A) Get a credit card

    (B) Make a phone call

    (C) Drop by next week

    (D) Cancel his business trip

53. Who most likely is the woman?

(A) A recruiter

(B) A tour guide

(C) A hotel receptionist

(D) A property manager

54. Why is the man calling?

(A) To get a new job

(B) To rent an apartment

(C) To book a trip

(D) To reschedule a meeting

55. What is the woman asking about?

(A) The man's schedule

(B) The man's personal details

(C) The man's address

(D) The man's job

56. Why is the man calling?

(A) His report is not ready.

(B) His phone is not working.

(C) He has to cancel a meeting.

(D) He won't be on time.

57. When will the woman call the IT Department?

(A) Right away

(B) During lunch

(C) After the meeting

(D) This afternoon

58. What does the woman say about the IT Department?

(A) They were at work.

(B) They found all her numbers.

(C) They are experienced.

(D) They have old computers.

59. What does the woman ask the man to do?

(A) Check a folder

(B) Sign a contract

(C) Reschedule a meeting

(D) Write some reports

60. When is the man going to complete the work?

(A) Now

(B) Thursday

(C) Next Monday

(D) In two days

61. What is the man's concern?

(A) The woman may not catch her flight.

(B) The woman may forget about the reports.

(C) The woman has lost her files.

(D) The woman is not working.

62. Why is the woman calling?

(A) To return an old car

(B) To talk about a car sale

(C) To find out if her car is ready for pick-up

(D) To request a rental car

63. What is the problem?

(A) The price of a repair

(B) Transportation for a family member

(C) The cost of a rental car

(D) Opening times

64. What is the man's offer?

(A) To give a discount on a purchase

(B) To repair a car immediately

(C) To open a business early

(D) To provide a free car

Go on to the next page ➜

65. What are the speakers mainly talking about?

(A) Fixing a car

(B) Completing a project

(C) Becoming a real estate agent

(D) Finding a house

66. What problem does the man mention?

(A) Low salaries

(B) Transportation around downtown

(C) Commuting time

(D) Property prices

67. Why is the woman fortunate?

(A) Roads were repaired.

(B) Rent prices decreased.

(C) Her salary was increased.

(D) She found a house.

68. How many applicants will the speakers interview?

(A) Two

(B) Three

(C) Four

(D) Five

69. What will the speakers do on Wednesday?

(A) Look at job applications

(B) Write a sales presentation

(C) Meet with interviewees

(D) Hire new staff

70. What does the man think is important?

(A) Having studied management

(B) Having an educational background

(C) Having previous experience

(D) Having certificates

This is the end of Part 3.

Look at the next page to start Part 4 ➔

PART 4: TALKS

06

Directions: You will hear several talks, each with one speaker. Then you will answer three questions about the talk. Listen and select the best response to each question. Mark the corresponding letter (A), (B), (C), or (D) on the answer sheet.

71. What does the report say is unusual about the current weather?

(A) Storms

(B) Warm weather

(C) Low temperatures

(D) Severe flooding

72. What does the government advise people to do?

(A) Drive carefully

(B) Take lots of water

(C) Wear snowboots

(D) Stay near home

73. When will the weather improve?

(A) On Wednesday

(B) On Thursday

(C) On Sunday

(D) On Tuesday

74. Who mostly likely is the speaker?

(A) A car engineer

(B) A TV reporter

(C) A telecommunications company employee

(D) An accountant

75. What is the problem?

(A) The Internet is not running in part of the city.

(B) Engineers are sick.

(C) A research project has been turned down.

(D) Bad weather is causing traffic congestion.

76. When is the problem going to be resolved?

(A) By 9:00 a.m.

(B) By 1:00 p.m.

(C) By 1:30 p.m.

(D) By 5:00 p.m.

77. What is the purpose of the message?

(A) To offer a special discount

(B) To make an online order

(C) To confirm an order

(D) To increase shipping costs

78. What kind of business does the woman probably work for?

(A) A delivery company

(B) A food supplier

(C) A phone company

(D) A website design company

79. What does the woman ask Mr. Jones to do?

(A) Give her his e-mail address

(B) Order a product

(C) Return the telephone call

(D) Place an online order

80. What is the purpose of the speech?

(A) To welcome a new manager

(B) To say farewell to a retiring colleague

(C) To celebrate the company's anniversary

(D) To open a new regional office

81. What did Mike Smith do?

(A) He founded an overseas office.

(B) He moved to New York.

(C) He became president.

(D) He worked at a Chinese bank.

82. How long has Mike Smith worked at the company?

(A) 5 years

(B) 15 years

(C) 20 years

(D) 35 years

83. Who is the audience?

(A) Students

(B) Researchers

(C) New employees

(D) Mechanics

84. What does the speaker say that Green Enterprises produces?

(A) Helmets

(B) Cars

(C) Safety clothing

(D) Solar panels

85. What does the speaker ask the listeners to do?

(A) Produce helmets

(B) Wear safety hats

(C) Design clothing

(D) Enter the building

86. What is being promoted?

(A) A new book

(B) A radio show

(C) A website

(D) A new phone

87. How can listeners contribute an opinion?

(A) By writing to the host

(B) By visiting a website

(C) By going to the studio

(D) By calling a number

88. What is available on the website?

(A) More information

(B) A show

(C) Short stories

(D) Cell phones

89. Who is Gavin Sanders?

(A) A taxi driver

(B) A radio host

(C) A weather reporter

(D) A marketing manager

90. What is causing a lot of traffic?

(A) Weather conditions have deteriorated.

(B) There has been a traffic accident.

(C) There are fewer trains.

(D) Bus services have been cut.

91. When is the next traffic report?

(A) In 5 minutes

(B) In 15 minutes

(C) In 20 minutes

(D) In 30 minutes

92. What is the main purpose of the talk?

(A) To introduce new employees

(B) To describe a tour

(C) To teach history

(D) To promote a vacation

93. What does the speaker say the listeners are permitted to do?

(A) Eat inside the church

(B) Teach a course

(C) Take photographs

(D) Leave children unaccompanied

94. What does the speaker ask the audience to do?

(A) Sell some food

(B) Find a restaurant

(C) Take a bus

(D) Be quiet

95. Where most likely is the announcement being made?

(A) At an art exhibit

(B) At a music concert

(C) At a sports competition

(D) At a school auditorium

96. What is the main purpose of the talk?

(A) To announce a performer

(B) To welcome the audience

(C) To introduce a piece of music

(D) To request appropriate behavior

97. What does the man say the audience may pick up at the exit?

(A) Information brochures

(B) Food and drinks

(C) Music recordings

(D) Photographs

98. Who is the man talking to?

(A) Shop attendants

(B) Flight crew

(C) Airline passengers

(D) Pedestrians

99. From which country is the flight departing?

(A) United States

(B) Argentina

(C) Chile

(D) Mexico

100. What does the speaker say will be provided?

(A) Food and beverages

(B) Free handsets

(C) Magazines

(D) Toothbrushes

This is the end of Part 4.

Go on to the next page to start Part 5 ➔

Test 1: Reading

The Reading section evaluates how well you understand written English. The Reading test has three sections and will take approximately 75 minutes. You must mark your answers on the answer sheet not in the test book.

PART 5: INCOMPLETE SENTENCES

Directions: One or more words is missing from each of the following sentences. Choose the best answer choice to complete the sentence. Mark the corresponding letter (A), (B), (C), or (D) on the answer sheet.

101. If I could decide, I _____ prices in order to win interest from our customers.

   (A) would decrease
   (B) decreased
   (C) is decreasing
   (D) was decreasing

102. Customers must visit the website before their password _____ 28 days after the order.

   (A) expiry
   (B) expired
   (C) expiration
   (D) expires

103. The president gave a speech of _____ to all the staff before the picnic began.

   (A) encourage
   (B) encouraged
   (C) encouraging
   (D) encouragement

104. A new _____ for working with customers has been created by Mr. Minelli and will be distributed shortly.

   (A) proceedings
   (B) procedure
   (C) proceed
   (D) procedurally

105. The current balance of your savings account is _____ on your online statement.

   (A) indicated
   (B) labeled
   (C) foreseen
   (D) announced

106. The Advertising Department will hold their weekly staff meeting over lunch at a restaurant _____ to the office.

   (A) close
   (B) closely
   (C) closened
   (D) closen

107. The Sales Director set up a consulting company and started working for _____.

   (A) he
   (B) him
   (C) his
   (D) himself

108. Because Ms. Porter often arrived late for work, her co-workers _____ assumed that she was going through a family crisis.

   (A) inaccurately
   (B) precisely
   (C) coincidentally
   (D) carefully

109. Roy Garcia left his job as Head of Accounts to move up to an executive position at a _____ firm.

    (A) brother
    (B) recession
    (C) rival
    (D) head-hunted

110. The product is expected to appeal _____ young girls and women, who appreciate bright colors and delicate design.

    (A) for
    (B) at
    (C) with
    (D) to

111. The most _____ transformation last year came with the introduction of the new production system, which we believe increased our efficiency.

    (A) distinct
    (B) remarkable
    (C) minor
    (D) surprising

112. Because of the severe overnight rain, it was _____ to walk on the sidewalk all day.

    (A) recommended
    (B) unsafe
    (C) disabled
    (D) unlikely

113. When choosing which of two similar products to buy, an _____ number of people name ethical issues as the main concern.

    (A) increase
    (B) increases
    (C) increased
    (D) increasing

114. Ms. Nakamura briefed staff at the meeting that she had received a number of positive reviews _____ excellent service.

    (A) with
    (B) onto
    (C) about
    (D) into

115. Their product is priced favorably in contrast _____ products made by other manufacturers.

    (A) with
    (B) for
    (C) by
    (D) from

116. They have _____ approved our proposal but are yet to reach a consensus.

    (A) hopefully
    (B) instead of
    (C) tentatively
    (D) inevitably

117. Mr. Wooding contacted the Sales Executive _____ to learn about promotional tactics for his team's new product.

    (A) repeatedly
    (B) repeated
    (C) repetition
    (D) repetitive

118. Dennison Services was _____ for dealing with the outsourcing of all manufacturing processes.

    (A) responsibility
    (B) response
    (C) responsible
    (D) responsibly

Go on to the next page ➜

119. We will invest over $500,000 _____ marketing next quarter.

(A) from

(B) in

(C) to

(D) for

120. Mr. Karanoff's efforts went _____ unnoticed by the manager until he launched a new project.

(A) principally

(B) largely

(C) consequently

(D) sufficiently

121. Mr. Blake has lived here _____ he was 18 years old.

(A) when

(B) since

(C) until

(D) from

122. Jose's Kitchen has received _____ acclaim for its homemade Mexican dishes as well as its use of the healthiest ingredients.

(A) critique

(B) critical

(C) critic

(D) criticize

123. Please make sure that you _____ any errors in the essay before sending the final version.

(A) correct

(B) correction

(C) correctly

(D) corrected

124. The Recruiting Team maintain a _____ preference for graduates from private schools.

(A) favorable

(B) big

(C) strong

(D) wholehearted

125. Following _____ consideration, Ms. Lamant decided to take the promotion offer.

(A) careful

(B) painful

(C) easy

(D) normal

126. The company increased its productivity _____ developing and strengthening its manufacturing system.

(A) in

(B) by

(C) instead of

(D) rather than

127. Hopefully, we will _____ reschedule our flights free of charge if the conference is delayed.

(A) be likely to

(B) be happy to

(C) be likely to

(D) be able to

128. Ms. Soulani is being transferred to the Brazil office to direct our _____ into South America.

(A) beginning

(B) expansion

(C) subjection

(D) collaboration

129. _____ the application is ready by Friday morning, we'll have to postpone our conference presentation.

(A) Unless

(B) Instead of

(C) Regardless of

(D) In spite of

130. The deal has not yet been finalized as we are still engaged in _____ discussions with the customer over the terms of the contract.

(A) heated

(B) vocal

(C) critical

(D) lengthy

131. Sales over the winter were considerable but, _____, annual profits are likely to go down.

    (A) in spite of
    (B) although
    (C) even so
    (D) despite

132. _____ the Director and the most senior manager announced their resignation.

    (A) Either
    (B) Neither
    (C) Both
    (D) As well as

133. Mr. Collinson _____ his investors by bringing the business back into profit.

    (A) silence
    (B) silenced
    (C) silent
    (D) silently

134. We have recruited some of the best hardware _____ from all over the country.

    (A) engineer
    (B) engineering
    (C) engineered
    (D) engineers

135. Sales revenues are rising more _____ now, but the outlook remains negative.

    (A) quickly
    (B) quick
    (C) quicken
    (D) quickened

136. The vice president is currently composing his _____, which will be published next month.

    (A) autograph
    (B) autopsy
    (C) automobile
    (D) autobiography

137. To show customers how to wash the fabrics, _____ care instructions are printed on the labels.

    (A) crafted
    (B) produced
    (C) detailed
    (D) made

138. The Lincoln Institute is a pioneer in the field of cancer research, for which work it _____ multiple prizes over the past 30 years.

    (A) has won
    (B) is winning
    (C) is won
    (D) would win

139. The company's share price _____ last week after the CEO announced his resignation.

    (A) will drop
    (B) drops
    (C) has dropped
    (D) dropped

140. The secretary is going to _____ a proposal to the management to hire an extra staff member.

    (A) put in
    (B) make up
    (C) set in
    (D) get up

This is the end of Part 5.

Go on to the next page to start Part 6 ➔

PART 6: TEXT COMPLETION

Directions: The following texts have sentences with some words and phrases missing. Read the answer choices given to complete the sentences. Choose the best answer choice to complete the sentence. Mark the corresponding letter (A), (B), (C), or (D) on the answer sheet.

Questions 141–143 refer to the following notice.

❧ The Nutcracker ❧

The City Ballet presents its annual holiday extravaganza in the Ventura Center at 7:30 on Saturday, December 14. This year's event will feature a world-class solo _____ from Viviana Tratson, so don't miss out!

141. (A) assurance
(B) performance
(C) significance
(D) insurance

_____ the show refreshments will be served

142. (A) When
(B) After
(C) Frequently
(D) From

courtesy of our caterers, Sweet Things. An entry fee of $15 will be charged at the venue. This money will be _____ to one of our company's

143. (A) to send
(B) send
(C) sending
(D) sent

nominated charities. The Ventura Center has a limited capacity, so please arrive early to secure your seats.

Questions 144–146 refer to the following letter.

Rent-4-U Property Management
104 Coastal Avenue, New York, NY

Dear Ms. Johnson,

Many thanks for your phone call this afternoon _____

144. (A) regardless
(B) regard
(C) regarded
(D) regarding

your wish to rent apartment 11 at Harris Court. Your move-in date will be June 21. I am attaching a rental agreement for you to sign and e-mail back to us. Please remember to pay the deposit by bank transfer or by check by June 15 _____

145. (A) in
(B) at
(C) by
(D) to

the latest.

Upon receipt of your signed contract and deposit, you will receive an inventory of furnishings in the apartment. The inventory will note any damage currently affecting any of the furniture. Please be advised that you will be charged for any additional damage to furniture or to the property itself. Any damage or maintenance issues that may occur during your tenancy should be reported to us without delay.

We wish to take this opportunity to thank you for _____

146. (A) choosing
(B) seeing
(C) asking
(D) purchasing

us as your rental agent.

Kind regards,
Edward Redford
Rental Agent Rent-4-U Property Management

Go on to the next page →

Questions 147–149 refer to the following letter.

October 6

Patricia Damon
Dallus Pharma
108 London Street
Sydney

Dear Ms. Damon,

Many thanks for your letter offering me the _____ of

147. (A) position
(B) recommendation
(C) place
(D) spot

Sales Director at Dallus Pharma. I regret to inform you that after much deliberation I have decided _____ your offer.

148. (A) to decline
(B) decline
(C) declined
(D) declining

I greatly enjoyed meeting you and your team, and found the position extremely attractive. However, I felt that another offer that was subsequently made to me, from a global manufacturer of surgical equipment, was better suited to my expertise and background.

I want to wish you and your company the best of _____

149. (A) luck
(B) well
(C) best
(D) regardless

in future endeavours, and thank you once again for considering my application.

Yours sincerely,
George Shepherd

Questions 150–152 refer to the following e-mail.

To: All employees, design team
Date: Friday, March 10
Subject: Revised agenda

Dear all,

I'm writing to inform you that we _____ the agenda for

150. (A) will be modified
(B) modify
(C) are modifying
(D) have modified

Monday's design team meeting slightly. Please see the attached revised version now. As some of you may know, I had discussions last week with two of our main clients and I'd like to explain to you some issues that were raised during those meetings. Both clients asked that _____ add new features to their

151. (A) we
(B) them
(C) ourselves
(D) they

websites on a number of levels. Above all, they have asked us to create a _____ user interface, as some customers have commented

152. (A) shorter
(B) lighter
(C) simpler
(D) closer

that the websites are not easy to use. We need to come up with some more straightforward designs that are easier for users to understand. This is added as a priority item to the agenda for our team meeting, so please bring new ideas to share with the team. I look forward to discussing this with you all next Monday.

Best wishes,
Ruby Styles

Go on to the next page →

PART 7: READING COMPREHENSION

Directions: This section includes a variety of texts. You will read each one and answer questions about it. Choose the best answer and mark the corresponding letter (A), (B), (C), or (D) on the answer sheet.

Questions 153–154 refer to the following article.

Financial news

January 13, Paris – The first new bank to launch in France in more than 50 years plans to expand beyond the capital, its chairman announced this morning. Jean-Marie Bertland told reporters at a press conference that the bank aims to launch 15 new branches in other parts of the country. The plan marks the beginning of the global expansion of the Bank du Paris, whose online products and European branches have significantly expanded its share of the global market since it was founded three years ago.

The Bank du Paris was created with the purpose of appealing to customers dissatisfied with the level of service offered by the major banks. Bertland stressed this aim during this morning's announcement, saying that "Europeans want a bank that is focused on customer service, and we can provide them with that." However, some analysts warn that the bank's range of insurance and savings products seem less competitive than those available at local banks. Shareholders will be looking toward next year to see whether Bertland's strategy pays off.

153. What is suggested about the Bank du Paris?

(A) It doesn't have branches in other parts of France.

(B) It will fire some of its employees.

(C) It will launch next year.

(D) It is the largest bank in the country.

154. According to the article, what is the goal of the Bank du Paris?

(A) To open overseas branches

(B) To provide high-quality customer service

(C) To get more shareholders

(D) To offer insurance plans

Questions 155–156 refer to the following advertisement.

Forbidden Palace

Chinese Take-Out and Restaurant

25 Tucson Avenue

Tel : 555-2134

Specialists in Regional Sichuan Cuisine

Restaurant opening hours

Monday, Wednesday, and Thursday 12PM–10PM
Friday–Saturday 1PM–11:30PM
Sunday 12PM–5PM
Closed Tuesdays

Take-out hours (pick-up or delivery)

Monday, Wednesday, and Thursday 6PM–11PM
Friday–Saturday 7:30PM–Midnight
Sunday 5:30PM–10PM
Closed Tuesdays

10% off orders on presentation of a student ID (eat-in only)

155. How can students get a discount?

(A) By ordering on the phone

(B) By visiting the restaurant on Tuesdays

(C) By showing a student ID

(D) By spending more than $10

156. According to the advertisement, what is NOT true about the service?

(A) It is closed on Tuesdays.

(B) Customers can eat in or take out.

(C) It serves authentic Sichuan food.

(D) It delivers food in the morning.

Go on to the next page ➔

Questions 157–159 refer to the following announcement.

The Secrets Of Persia

A special exhibition of the recently discovered paintings and ceramics of the ancient empire of Persia which uncovers one of the world's most mystical cultural histories.

Westlake Museum
54 Church Avenue
July 17–September 20

Exhibition sponsored by the Cultural Society

An opening event will be held on the evening of July 16 featuring a talk by Mari Souyani, professor of Near Eastern Studies at the University of Washington. Tickets will be on sale in the ticket office from July 1. Admission price will include priority entry to the exhibition and a guidebook.

157. What is the purpose of the announcement?

(A) To promote a charity event

(B) To advertise a career fair

(C) To celebrate the opening of a gallery

(D) To publicize a new exhibition

158. What will most likely happen on September 20?

(A) An exhibition will close.

(B) A ceramic course will begin.

(C) An opening event will be held.

(D) A guidebook will be launched.

159. Who is Mari Souyani?

(A) A ceramic artist

(B) An academic

(C) A writer

(D) A sculptor

Questions 160–161 refer to the following invoice.

Apex Office Supplies

1100 World Boulevard, Los Angeles, California
Tel: 429-555-3148

INVOICE

Invoice Date: April 20
Order No.: 75612Q
Delivery Address: Rosa Ximenez, ACT Automotive, 400 Tucson Street, Irvine, CA
Delivery Method: Next Day Delivery

Black toner cartridge (pack of 5)	$410.92
Recycled color copy paper 500 sheets (box of 10)	88.79
Yellow adhesive notes 50 sheets (pack of 20)	15.99
Subtotal	**$515.70**
Returning Customer Discount (5%)	-25.78
Delivery Charge	3.99
Total	**$493.91**

Thank You For Your Order!

160. What is suggested about Rosa Ximenez?

(A) She needs the delivery immediately.
(B) She works at a delivery control center.
(C) She went back to her former company.
(D) She sent the invoice.

161. How much discount is given on the invoice?

(A) $3.99
(B) $15.99
(C) $25.78
(D) $88.79

Go on to the next page ➜

Questions 162–164 refer to the following advertisement.

TCB VENUES
HARDWICK HOUSE

One of our most famous venues, Hardwick House, is only 30 minutes from downtown Chicago, and only ten minutes from Hardwick Train Station. The venue is a perfect place for your seminar, business training, or professional meeting. While other companies charge an extra fee for Internet access, we offer wifi free of charge throughout the building. All rooms are comfortably furnished and have ample work space. Guests can also use the venue's extensive spa, gym, and swimming pool facilities, available at a small additional charge.

For your events, Hardwick House offers a wide range of room capacity suitable for any needs. We can also cater for 10, 20, 30, and up to 100 people, making us the perfect choice whatever your event. All business event and meeting rooms include microphones, projectors, and numerous electrical outlets. Laptops and printers are also available in the printing room next to the reception.

To reserve this venue, please call our reservation services at 987-555-1252, or e-mail reserve@tcbvenues.com. Alternatively, visit our website, www.tcbvenues.com, where you will find maps and additional information about all our venues.

162. What can the guests use for an extra fee?

(A) Printing

(B) Room services

(C) Internet access

(D) Fitness facilities

163. What is true about Hardwick House?

(A) It is in downtown.

(B) It can cater for large groups of people.

(C) It offers training sessions.

(D) It is a resort.

164. According to the advertisement, where are the directions to Hardwick House available?

(A) The reservation center

(B) The train station

(C) The website

(D) The gym

Questions 165–167 refer to the following notice.

PASSENGER NOTICE

On July 10, East-West Trains will launch wireless Internet access on all mainline services. All passengers, whether in first or regular class cars, will be able to connect to the wifi from their laptops or mobile devices. This service will be free of charge.

To log onto our Internet service on one of our trains, simply search for the East-West Trains wireless signal while onboard. The first time you log on, you need to register for the service by providing some personal information. You will be asked to do this only once, after which time your personal details will be valid on all East-West Train services.

Please do not use the onboard Internet service to download large files or stream video content, as this will slow down connection speeds for all passengers, especially during rush hours. You may use the service only for checking and sending e-mails, and for regular Web browsing.

You can access technical support at any time by sending an e-mail to **wireless@e-wtrains.com**. We aim to respond to all e-mails within a day. We regret that telephone support is not available at this time.

---

165. What does this notice aim to promote?

(A) A new train line

(B) A new service

(C) A new battery

(D) An assistance program

166. According to the notice, what can passengers do?

(A) Download large files

(B) Check e-mails

(C) Watch live videos

(D) Travel late at night

167. What should the passengers do if they have questions?

(A) Go to the train office

(B) Send an e-mail

(C) Check the website

(D) Provide personal details

Go on to the next page ➜

Questions 168–171 refer to the following document.

 # Alpha Software Development

The following agreement is made between Alpha Software Development (hereinafter the Employer) and the undersigned party (hereinafter the Employee) who agrees to the following.

1. Based on the Employee's employment by the Employer, the Employee may acquire information that is confidential to and the exclusive property of the Employer, including, without limitation, personal details, methods and processes, source codes and current and potential business clients of the Employer. The Employee will not disclose such information during and after the period of employment.

2. During his/her period of employment with the Employer, and for three (3) years subsequent to the termination of the contract, the Employee will not, whether directly or indirectly, assist another employee or contractor of the Employer in terminating their employment with the Employer.

3. All patents and intellectual properties invented by the Employee during the employment will be the property of Alpha Software Development.

I have read and understood this agreement.

Signed: Rob Marchant
Title: Assistant Software Manager
Date: August 5

---

168. What is the purpose of this document?

(A) To make an offer of a contract
(B) To agree on pension plans
(C) To terminate a period of employment
(D) To detail an agreement

169. What is NOT described as a confidential issue?

(A) Personal information
(B) Future business contacts
(C) Patents and intellectual property rights
(D) Methods and processes

170. According to the document, what should Mr. Marchant NOT do?

(A) Help other employees leave the company
(B) Take sick leave
(C) Produce patents
(D) Sign the agreement

171. The word "exclusive" in paragraph 2, is closest in meaning to

(A) limited
(B) sole
(C) lonely
(D) elitist

Questions 172–175 refer to the following memo.

To: All staff
From: Management Board
Date: October 15
Re: Important announcement for all staff

As we all know, Bensons is well-known for producing the highest quality ice cream in the business. However, trading conditions this year, even for us, have deteriorated significantly. Like so many of our competitors, we are struggling with increasing production and manufacturing costs due to price increases affecting some of our key raw ingredients on international markets.

For over three months we have searched for a number of ways of tackling this problem. A suggestion was made to continue our recent policy of raising the price of our products, but the Senior Management Board, after discussion with the sales teams, feels that such increases will no longer appeal to the markets.

We have therefore come to a conclusion: We intend to improve profitability by developing our advertising spending and restructuring the Research and Development Department to focus on specific areas of market need and, consequently, produce products with greater sales potential. A detailed plan will be formed to begin actioning this over the coming weeks.

---

172. What is stated about Bensons?

(A) It is well recognized in its industry.

(B) It manufactures beverages.

(C) It reduced the price of some ingredients.

(D) It is not competing with other companies.

173. According to the memo, what are Bensons's problems?

(A) Its advertisements do not attract customers.

(B) Its competitors sell cheaper products.

(C) Its staff costs have increased.

(D) Its ingredients have become more expensive.

174. What has the Senior Management Board decided to do?

(A) Raise prices

(B) Discuss with sales staff

(C) Cut the marketing budget

(D) Restructure a department

175. The word "focus" in paragraph 3, is closest in meaning to

(A) attract

(B) concentrate

(C) photograph

(D) look at

Go on to the next page →

Questions 176–180 refer to the following e-mail.

Subject: Crafts Depot catalog
Date: November 21

Dear Ms. Newman,

Many thanks for your interest in Crafts Depot, and for your inquiry about having your products promoted in our catalog.

The Crafts Depot catalog has the largest circulation of any crafts-based catalog, reaching over 3 million homes across the country. It includes handmade accessories, art, ceramics and pottery, jewelry, paper goods, and toys, among many other categories. All items in our catalog must be handmade and be supplied to us directly by manufacturers. We do not deal with third-party suppliers. The minimum product price is $0.99, and the maximum is $200. Manufacturers receive 70% of sales revenue for their products, while we keep the remaining 30% to cover our sales and advertising costs.

Next year the Crafts Depot catalog will enter into the digital age with the launch of an online store. We expect the introduction of an online presence to have a drastic effect on sales, and we are delighted to offer the usual 70%/30% revenue share policy.

To become one of the thousands of happy manufacturers with whom we work, please fill in the application form informing us about you and your products. We will also need to see representative samples of the items. We are afraid that we do not accept photographs of your samples. Please be assured that we will treat any samples you send us with absolute care, and will return them to you free of charge after evaluating them for inclusion in our product offering. Please see the attached form for more details.

We look forward to hearing from you.

Kind regards,
Annabel Nichols
Producer Liaison, Crafts Depot

---

176. What is the purpose of the e-mail?

(A) To apply for an exhibition
(B) To arrange a business deal
(C) To advertise some handmade goods
(D) To circulate a catalog

177. What most likely does Ms. Newman do?

(A) She conducts market research.
(B) She examines samples.
(C) She designs catalogs.
(D) She makes items.

178. What is Crafts Depot's plan for next year?

(A) To set up to a new office
(B) To increase the circulation of catalogs
(C) To launch a website
(D) To increase sales by 30%

179. The word "presence" in paragraph 3, is closest in meaning to

(A) existence
(B) presentation
(C) continuation
(D) nuisance

180. What is Ms. Newman likely to do next in order to work with Crafts Depot?

(A) Fill in a form
(B) Send a photograph
(C) Sell an item
(D) Visit a website

Questions 181–185 refer to the following advertisement and e-mail.

VERIN OUTSOURCING ⟫ ⟫ ⟫ ⟫ ⟫ ⟫ ⟫ ⟫ ⟫ ⟫

Verin Outsourcing will set up a new Business Process Management (BPM) Center in the vibrant and cosmopolitan city of New Delhi, India, on November 12. The Center will be part of our network of South Asian offices, and be a new adddition to our highly successful company.

As a result of the new launch, we are looking for senior staff to fill a number of top-level positions in the New Delhi center.

Verin Outsourcing offers an intellectually stimulating environment in which inventive minds gather. We provide high-quality benefits and extensive promotion opportunities.

Applicants should e-mail a cover letter and résumé with a recent photograph to the recruiter of their chosen department. Applications are due on July 28. Interviews will start the week beginning August 15, and hiring decisions will be communicated on September 1. Visa sponsorship will be available for exceptional international candidates.

To submit your application, or for further information, please get in touch with a recruiter at the e-mail addresses indicated below.

Please note that we will only contact successful applicants by e-mail. If you haven't heard from us by September 1, you should consider that your application has been unsuccessful on this occasion.

AVAILABLE POSITIONS

RESEARCH AND DEVELOPMENT	QUALITY AND TESTING	SYSTEMS INTEGRATION	SYSTEMS ENGINEERING
Research and Development Assistant	Junior Testing Engineer	Systems Integration Test Director	Junior Systems Assistant
Junior Researcher		Junior Data Integrity Analyst	Senior Systems Engineer
CONTACT: Rupert Cooper rfield@verinout.com	CONTACT: Yash Kapoor ykapoor@verinout.com	CONTACT: Glenn Badger gbadger@verinout.com	CONTACT: Jennifer Yang jyang@verinout.com

---

To: Glenn Badger <gbadger@verinout.com>
From: Ellie Meaton <ellie.meaton@my-messenging.com>
Subject: Job application
Date: July 10

Dear Mr. Badger,

I am writing with reference to your advertisement in the Outsourcing Newsletter regarding vacancies at your new process management center in New Delhi. I am very interested in working with you, and believe that I have qualifications and experience that may interest you. I wish to apply for the managerial position. I studied computer science and have six years of experience in the industry. This has given me excellent knowledge of various software packages as well as good commercial awareness. I also worked as an accomplished project manager, with superior communication skills and good attention to detail. My first language is English and I speak French and Portuguese fluently. Please see my attached résumé for further details of my background.

Please feel free to contact me should you require any further information. I look forward to hearing from you.

Yours sincerely,
Ellie Meaton

Questions on next page ➔

181. When will the succcessful candidates be notified?

(A) In July

(B) In August

(C) In September

(D) In November

182. What is NOT accurate about Ms. Meaton?

(A) She speaks three languages

(B) She has managed projects.

(C) She has good knowledge of technology.

(D) She has invented software packages.

183. In the advertisement, the word "inventive" in paragraph 3, is closest in meaning to

(A) innovative

(B) talkative

(C) productive

(D) efficient

184. For which position is Ms. Meaton most likely applying?

(A) Research and Development Assistant

(B) Systems Integration Test Director

(C) Junior Testing Engineer

(D) Senior Systems Engineer

185. If Mr. Badger is interested in hiring Ms. Meaton, what will he most likely do?

(A) Call her

(B) Send her an e-mail

(C) Talk to her current employer

(D) Contact her supervisor

Questions 186–190 refer to the following form and e-mail.

Application for Building Permit
City of Carlston

The applicant named herein hereby gives notice of his/her intention to commence building work as described below. The applicant confirms that the following details are true and correct.

Details of applicant: Name: Ramon Alvaro
Address: 15 Leslie Circle, Carlston
Telephone: 243-555-4865
E-mail: ramonalvaro@mail-tome.com

Details of building to which building work relates: Address:15 Leslie Circle, Carlston

Description of proposed work: Construction of deck at rear of property

The above named applicant has indicated the following in consideration of his/her application:
• Detailed plans of the proposed construction
• An Environmental Impact Assessment (EIA) covering the proposed construction, composed and confirmed by a licensed provider
• Permit processing fee of $200; Optional $10 not provided

The applicant confirms that the above statements are accurate and that he or she will comply with Building Regulation 14(1a) if and when a permit is issued resulting from this application. The application is submitted on the date indicated below.

Signature of applicant: Ramon Alvaro
Date: May 2

To: Ramon Alvaro <ramonalvaro@mail-tome.com>
From: no-reply <permitresponse@cityofcarlston.gov>
Date: May 5, 10:16 a.m.
Re: Confirmation of your application

Dear Applicant,

Thanks for your recent application to the City of Carlston for a building permit. Your application is being processed. This e-mail is to inform you that you will hear from a member of our Inspections Department shortly by telephone to arrange a visit to the property in question. Please note the following inspection dates:

Receipt of application	Inspection visit
April 1–20:	May
April 21–30:	June
May 1–17:	July
May 18–31:	August

We usually issue permits within two weeks of inspection visits. Please be available and punctual at the time and date specified by the Inspections Department. Failure to do so may result in your inspection date delayed until the following month.

Please note that we will only return original copies of documents submitted with applications upon receipt of the optional $10 fee.

City of Carlston

Questions on next page ➔

186. Why did Mr. Alvaro complete the form?

(A) He is moving to a new city.

(B) He wants to add an extension to his home.

(C) He is filing taxes.

(D) He was charged a fee.

187. What is NOT mentioned on the form?

(A) A fee

(B) Building regulations

(C) Application deadlines

(D) Contact information

188. What is the purpose of the e-mail?

(A) To arrange an inspection date

(B) To make payment

(C) To charge Mr. Alvaro for a fee

(D) To cancel an appointment

189. When will Mr. Alvaro most likely meet a city official?

(A) In May

(B) In June

(C) In July

(D) In August

190. According to the form and the e-mail, what will NOT occur?

(A) All documents will be returned.

(B) A permit will be issued after an inspection.

(C) An application will be processed.

(D) A phone call will be made.

Questions 191–195 refer to the following advertisement and e-mail.

THOMSON'S COMPUTING

Back to School Promotion

To welcome the academic year, we will have special deals on our full range of computers from September 1st through 15th. And what's more, we are offering free delivery on our bestselling laptops listed below.

Praxa XA300-S

The popular Praxa XA300-S is perfect for those who like to work and study on the go. Measuring just 10.1", you can take it anywhere, and its eight-hour battery life makes this laptop extra portable. Two-year manufacturer's warranty. **$592**

Praxa R97-L

The large screen is ideal for reading and producing documents. Comes fitted with the latest FRK processor for excellent performance. Connects to the Internet quickly. **$750**

LeKlux ZD29

The ZD29 is our bestselling model in the LeKlux range. It features a special graphics card which enhances your satisfaction like never before when playing games. Suitable for both work and play! **$699**

Ace 1000

New Japanese manufacturer Ace is gaining critical acclaim among computer users thanks to the 1000 model. This model features the Ace matte screen, which makes it easier to use in sunlight. Perfect for studying in the park! **$710**

* Unless stated otherwise, one-year warranties are included on all computers.

To: Customer Service <customerservice@thomsonscomputing.com>
From: Charlie Burson <cburson@anbe-mail.com>
Date: September 12, 14:29:06
Re: Order number 81431717B

Dear Sir/Madam:

I recently ordered a laptop from you, which I received yesterday (September 11). Although your "back to school" advertisement says that all delivery is free during the promotional period, I paid $10 for the delivery. Since I placed an order on the second day of the promotion, I assume that this charge has been applied to my order by mistake.

Also, I did not receive the two-year warranty certificate. I have searched through the box and user's manual, but I can't find it anywhere. I would greatly appreciate if you could send me the certificate as soon as possible.

Thanks in advance for your assistance in these matters.

Charlie Burson

Questions on next page ➜

191. What is being advertised?

(A) A special offer

(B) A computer course

(C) A college program

(D) A welcome party

192. What is the advantage of the Praxa XA300-S?

(A) It has a large screen.

(B) It is affordable.

(C) It has a long-lasting battery.

(D) It connects to the Internet very quickly.

193. Which product did Mr. Burson most likely buy?

(A) Praxa XA300-S

(B) Praxa R97-L

(C) LeKlux ZD29

(D) Ace 1000

194. When did Mr. Burson place his order?

(A) September 1

(B) September 2

(C) September 12

(D) September 15

195. What does Mr. Burson want?

(A) Cancellation of the order

(B) Warranty certification

(C) A receipt

(D) A replacement product

Questions 196–200 refer to the following e-mails.

To: Julie Mendle <jm2@lanklater-corp.com>
From: Robert Fawcett <rf@lanklater-corp.com>
Date: February 17
Subject: French business culture

Hi Julie,

I dropped by your office this morning but your secretary told me you're on vacation at the moment. I hope you don't mind me writing you like this, but I'd like to pick your brains if possible. I'm leaving for Marseille later this week to meet with a new French client for the first time. I know you worked for a French company for many years, so I'd be grateful for any tips you could give me. Although I've worked in Portugal before, I'm not familiar with French business protocols. As you may have guessed, this is my first trip since I was promoted to Area Sales Manager for Europe so I really want the trip to go well.
Hope everything's going well with you.

Best wishes,
Robert

To: Robert Fawcett <rf@lanklater-corp.com>
From: Julie Mendle <jm2@lanklater-corp.com>
Date: February 22
Subject: Re: French business culture

Hi Robert,

Many thanks for your e-mail. I'm currently stranded in Oslo due to heavy snow. All the flights out of here are delayed. So, plenty of time to catch up on e-mails!

Of course, I'm happy to offer a few tips on doing business in France. Firstly, you should keep in mind the importance of business suits in France. If you want to be taken seriously, you should dress professionally at all times, especially when dealing with French clients. Marseille is slightly more relaxed. You can usually go without a jacket there. Another main feature of working in France is the significance of drinks, which can last up to four hours. Business meetings are often held at restaurants over wine, and I'd say that these occasions are extremely important in forming a good working relationship. Probably the key difference between our company and French companies relates to briefings. French companies don't have a briefings culture, so they don't happen often. When they do take place, it's usually senior staff members who give orders and instructions. Open discussions are rare. They hardly have an agenda for a meeting, and when there is an agenda it isn't necessarily followed.

Well, I think that's all for now, but I'm happy to discuss further with you in person when I get back to the office. I hope the trip goes well, and I'll hopefully see you at the policy group meeting next week.

Best wishes,
Julie

Questions on next page ➜

196. What is the purpose of Mr. Fawcett's e-mail to Ms. Mendle?

(A) To schedule a business trip together

(B) To hear about a French company

(C) To request information about her trip to Norway

(D) To get advice about a business trip

197. What is implied about Ms. Mendle?

(A) Her return trip has been delayed.

(B) Her secretary works in France.

(C) She recently got promoted.

(D) She dresses very formally.

198. What is NOT suggested by Ms. Mendle?

(A) French companies do not have briefings frequently.

(B) French business people discuss business matters while drinking at restaurants.

(C) Agendas are always required in French companies.

(D) It is important to dress appropriately when doing business in France.

199. According to the e-mails, what is probably unnecessary for Mr. Fawcett to do when he meets his client next week?

(A) Drink wine

(B) Look professional

(C) Have a business discussion

(D) Wear a formal jacket

200. In the first e-mail, the phrase "familiar with" in paragraph 1, is closest in meaning to

(A) knowledgeable about

(B) friends with

(C) disappointed in

(D) working with

This is the end of the Reading Test.

Look at the next page to start the Speaking Test ➜

Test 1: Speaking

This speaking test includes 11 questions that evaluate your ability to speak English. This test will take approximately 20 minutes.

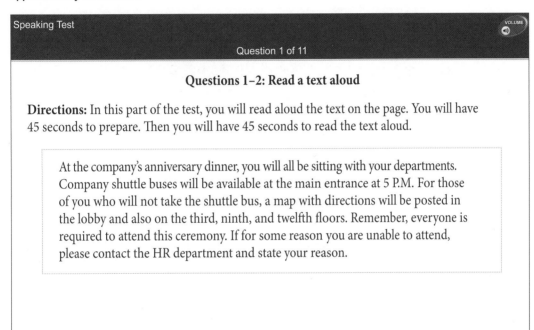

Speaking Test   VOLUME

Question 1 of 11

Questions 1–2: Read a text aloud

Directions: In this part of the test, you will read aloud the text on the page. You will have 45 seconds to prepare. Then you will have 45 seconds to read the text aloud.

> At the company's anniversary dinner, you will all be sitting with your departments. Company shuttle buses will be available at the main entrance at 5 P.M. For those of you who will not take the shuttle bus, a map with directions will be posted in the lobby and also on the third, ninth, and twelfth floors. Remember, everyone is required to attend this ceremony. If for some reason you are unable to attend, please contact the HR department and state your reason.

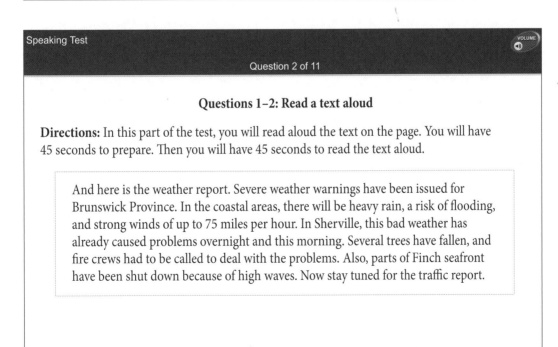

Speaking Test   VOLUME

Question 2 of 11

Questions 1–2: Read a text aloud

Directions: In this part of the test, you will read aloud the text on the page. You will have 45 seconds to prepare. Then you will have 45 seconds to read the text aloud.

> And here is the weather report. Severe weather warnings have been issued for Brunswick Province. In the coastal areas, there will be heavy rain, a risk of flooding, and strong winds of up to 75 miles per hour. In Sherville, this bad weather has already caused problems overnight and this morning. Several trees have fallen, and fire crews had to be called to deal with the problems. Also, parts of Finch seafront have been shut down because of high waves. Now stay tuned for the traffic report.

Go on to the next page →

Speaking Test

VOLUME

Question 3 of 11

Question 3: Describe a picture

Directions: You will describe a photograph as completely as you can. The photograph is in the test book. You will have 30 seconds to prepare what you will say, and then you will have 45 seconds to describe the picture in as much detail as possible.

Speaking Test

VOLUME

Question 4 of 11

Questions 4–6: Respond to questions

Directions: You will be asked three questions. After each question you will hear a beep. Begin speaking your answer immediately after the beep. You will not have any time to prepare your answer. For Questions 4 and 5 you will have 15 seconds to respond. For Question 6 you will have 30 seconds.

Imagine that a British marketing firm is doing research in your country. You have agreed to participate in a telephone interview about exercising.

Question 4: How often do you exercise?

Questions 4–6: Respond to questions

Directions: You will be asked three questions. After each question you will hear a beep. Begin speaking your answer immediately after the beep. You will not have any time to prepare your answer. For Questions 4 and 5 you will have 15 seconds to respond. For Question 6 you will have 30 seconds.

_____

Imagine that a British marketing firm is doing research in your country. You have agreed to participate in a telephone interview about exercising.

Question 5: What kinds of exercise do you do?

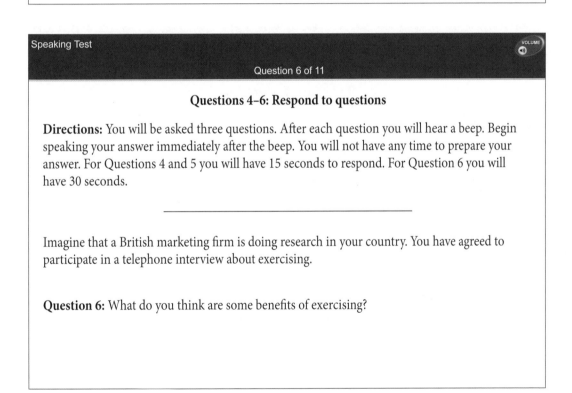

Questions 4–6: Respond to questions

Directions: You will be asked three questions. After each question you will hear a beep. Begin speaking your answer immediately after the beep. You will not have any time to prepare your answer. For Questions 4 and 5 you will have 15 seconds to respond. For Question 6 you will have 30 seconds.

_____

Imagine that a British marketing firm is doing research in your country. You have agreed to participate in a telephone interview about exercising.

Question 6: What do you think are some benefits of exercising?

Go on to the next page ➔

Questions 7–9: Respond to questions using information provided

Directions: You will read a short text and then answer three questions based on the information in the text. You will have 30 seconds to read the text before the first question. After each question you will hear a beep. Begin speaking immediately after the beep. You will not have any extra time to prepare your answer. For Questions 7 and 8 you will have 15 seconds to respond. For Question 9 you will have 30 seconds.

TRAVEL EXPERTS

Round Trip	**Travel Dates**
Departure: New York, NY (JFK)	Departing: 09/10
Destination: Las Vegas, NV (LAS)	Returning: 09/15

FLIGHTS

Virgo America $593
Departure 8:00 a.m., New York
Arrival 10:50 a.m., Las Vegas
Nonstop flight

Peak $451
Departure 7:40 a.m., New York
Arrival 4:26 p.m., Las Vegas
Connect in Pittsburgh

USA Air $467
Departure 11:28 p.m., New York
Arrival 6:14 p.m., Las Vegas
Connect in Charlotte

Unified Airlines $610
Departure 10:00 p.m., New York
Arrival 12:45 a.m., Las Vegas
Nonstop flight

12

Question 10: Propose a solution

Directions: You will hear about a problem and be asked to propose a solution. You will have 30 seconds to prepare your solution, and then 60 seconds to speak.

Respond as if you work at the store.

In your response, make sure to

• show that you understand the situation, and

• suggest a way to handle the problem.

13

Question 11: Express an opinion

Directions: You will hear about a specific topic and then give your opinion about it. Make sure you say as much as you can about the topic in the time allowed. You will have 15 seconds to prepare, and then 60 seconds to speak.

This is the end of the Speaking Test.

Go on to the next page to start the Writing Test ➔

Test 1: Writing

This writing test includes 8 questions that evaluate your ability to write English. This test will take approximately 1 hour.

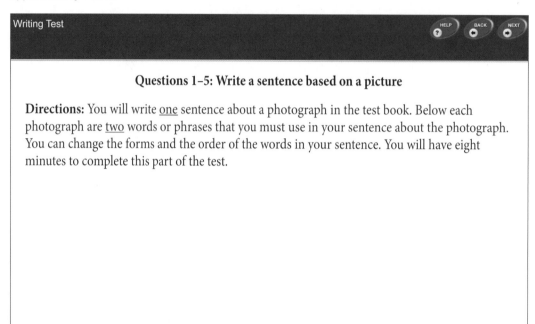

Questions 1–5: Write a sentence based on a picture

Directions: You will write <u>one</u> sentence about a photograph in the test book. Below each photograph are <u>two</u> words or phrases that you must use in your sentence about the photograph. You can change the forms and the order of the words in your sentence. You will have eight minutes to complete this part of the test.

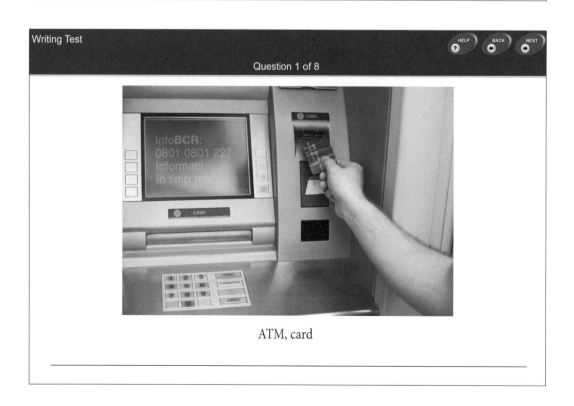

ATM, card

_____

family, breakfast

_____

tiger, fire

_____

Go on to the next page ➜

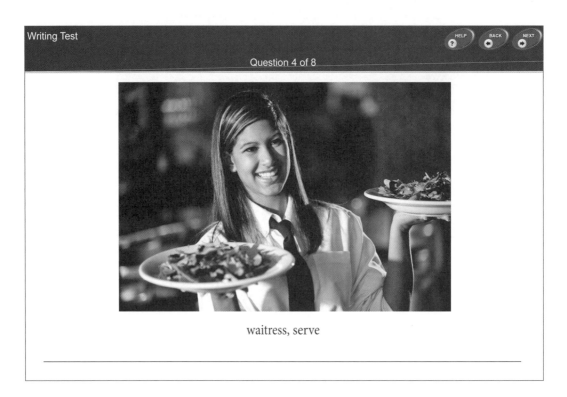

waitress, serve

_____

subway, passenger

_____

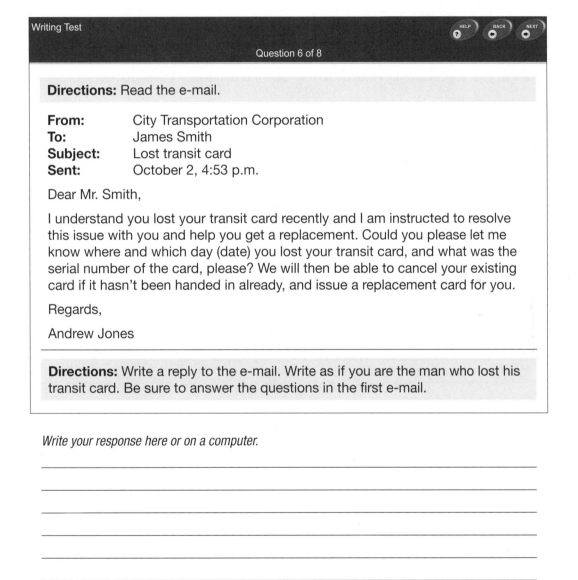

Questions 6–7: Respond to a written request

Directions: You will write responses to two e-mails. Your essay will be evaluated on

- sentence quality
- grammar
- vocabulary
- organization

You will have 10 minutes to read and respond to each e-mail.

Directions: Read the e-mail.

From: City Transportation Corporation
To: James Smith
Subject: Lost transit card
Sent: October 2, 4:53 p.m.

Dear Mr. Smith,

I understand you lost your transit card recently and I am instructed to resolve this issue with you and help you get a replacement. Could you please let me know where and which day (date) you lost your transit card, and what was the serial number of the card, please? We will then be able to cancel your existing card if it hasn't been handed in already, and issue a replacement card for you.

Regards,

Andrew Jones

Directions: Write a reply to the e-mail. Write as if you are the man who lost his transit card. Be sure to answer the questions in the first e-mail.

Write your response here or on a computer.

_____

_____

_____

_____

_____

_____

_____

_____

_____

_____

Go on to the next page →

Directions: Read the e-mail.

From:	Silvestri & Sons
To:	Valerie Gardener
Subject:	Jacuzzi catalog
Sent:	May 10, 9:38 a.m.

Dear Ms. Gardener,

Attached is the new catalog you requested for our latest in-home Jacuzzis. Please feel free to look through the catalog and tell me which models you like the best. I can then get back to you with further information, and we can arrange a convenient time for us to visit your home to give you a quote.

Warm regards,

Paul Silvestri

Directions: Write a reply to the e-mail. Write as if you are the person who will choose a Jacuzzi. Explain what kind of Jacuzzi you want, and when is convenient for the company to visit your home.

Write your response here or on a computer.

_____

_____

_____

_____

_____

_____

_____

_____

_____

_____

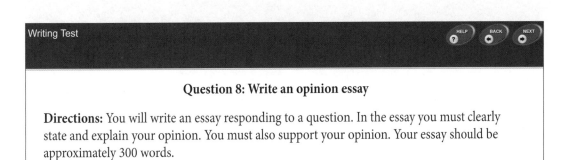

Question 8: Write an opinion essay

Directions: You will write an essay responding to a question. In the essay you must clearly state and explain your opinion. You must also support your opinion. Your essay should be approximately 300 words.

Your essay will be evaluated on

- including supporting reasons and/or examples
- grammar
- vocabulary
- organization

You will have 30 minutes to plan, write, and review your essay.

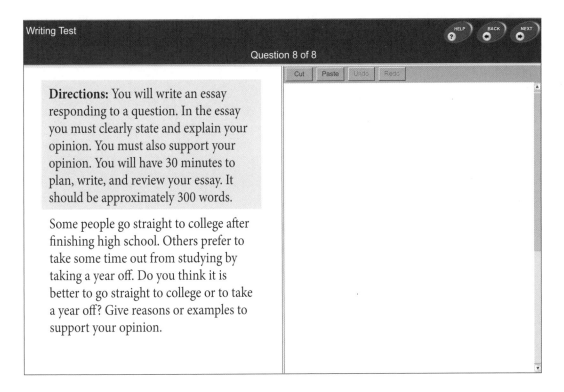

Directions: You will write an essay responding to a question. In the essay you must clearly state and explain your opinion. You must also support your opinion. You will have 30 minutes to plan, write, and review your essay. It should be approximately 300 words.

Some people go straight to college after finishing high school. Others prefer to take some time out from studying by taking a year off. Do you think it is better to go straight to college or to take a year off? Give reasons or examples to support your opinion.

Write your essay on a separate piece of paper or on a computer.

This is the end of Test 1.

TOEIC® TEST 2

PRACTICE TEST 2 ANSWER SHEET

Listening Answer Sheet

1. Ⓐ Ⓑ Ⓒ Ⓓ   26. Ⓐ Ⓑ Ⓒ   51. Ⓐ Ⓑ Ⓒ Ⓓ   76. Ⓐ Ⓑ Ⓒ Ⓓ
2. Ⓐ Ⓑ Ⓒ Ⓓ   27. Ⓐ Ⓑ Ⓒ   52. Ⓐ Ⓑ Ⓒ Ⓓ   77. Ⓐ Ⓑ Ⓒ Ⓓ
3. Ⓐ Ⓑ Ⓒ Ⓓ   28. Ⓐ Ⓑ Ⓒ   53. Ⓐ Ⓑ Ⓒ Ⓓ   78. Ⓐ Ⓑ Ⓒ Ⓓ
4. Ⓐ Ⓑ Ⓒ Ⓓ   29. Ⓐ Ⓑ Ⓒ   54. Ⓐ Ⓑ Ⓒ Ⓓ   79. Ⓐ Ⓑ Ⓒ Ⓓ
5. Ⓐ Ⓑ Ⓒ Ⓓ   30. Ⓐ Ⓑ Ⓒ   55. Ⓐ Ⓑ Ⓒ Ⓓ   80. Ⓐ Ⓑ Ⓒ Ⓓ

6. Ⓐ Ⓑ Ⓒ Ⓓ   31. Ⓐ Ⓑ Ⓒ   56. Ⓐ Ⓑ Ⓒ Ⓓ   81. Ⓐ Ⓑ Ⓒ Ⓓ
7. Ⓐ Ⓑ Ⓒ Ⓓ   32. Ⓐ Ⓑ Ⓒ   57. Ⓐ Ⓑ Ⓒ Ⓓ   82. Ⓐ Ⓑ Ⓒ Ⓓ
8. Ⓐ Ⓑ Ⓒ Ⓓ   33. Ⓐ Ⓑ Ⓒ   58. Ⓐ Ⓑ Ⓒ Ⓓ   83. Ⓐ Ⓑ Ⓒ Ⓓ
9. Ⓐ Ⓑ Ⓒ Ⓓ   34. Ⓐ Ⓑ Ⓒ   59. Ⓐ Ⓑ Ⓒ Ⓓ   84. Ⓐ Ⓑ Ⓒ Ⓓ
10. Ⓐ Ⓑ Ⓒ Ⓓ   35. Ⓐ Ⓑ Ⓒ   60. Ⓐ Ⓑ Ⓒ Ⓓ   85. Ⓐ Ⓑ Ⓒ Ⓓ

11. Ⓐ Ⓑ Ⓒ   36. Ⓐ Ⓑ Ⓒ   61. Ⓐ Ⓑ Ⓒ Ⓓ   86. Ⓐ Ⓑ Ⓒ Ⓓ
12. Ⓐ Ⓑ Ⓒ   37. Ⓐ Ⓑ Ⓒ   62. Ⓐ Ⓑ Ⓒ Ⓓ   87. Ⓐ Ⓑ Ⓒ Ⓓ
13. Ⓐ Ⓑ Ⓒ   38. Ⓐ Ⓑ Ⓒ   63. Ⓐ Ⓑ Ⓒ Ⓓ   88. Ⓐ Ⓑ Ⓒ Ⓓ
14. Ⓐ Ⓑ Ⓒ   39. Ⓐ Ⓑ Ⓒ   64. Ⓐ Ⓑ Ⓒ Ⓓ   89. Ⓐ Ⓑ Ⓒ Ⓓ
15. Ⓐ Ⓑ Ⓒ   40. Ⓐ Ⓑ Ⓒ   65. Ⓐ Ⓑ Ⓒ Ⓓ   90. Ⓐ Ⓑ Ⓒ Ⓓ

16. Ⓐ Ⓑ Ⓒ   41. Ⓐ Ⓑ Ⓒ Ⓓ   66. Ⓐ Ⓑ Ⓒ Ⓓ   91. Ⓐ Ⓑ Ⓒ Ⓓ
17. Ⓐ Ⓑ Ⓒ   42. Ⓐ Ⓑ Ⓒ Ⓓ   67. Ⓐ Ⓑ Ⓒ Ⓓ   92. Ⓐ Ⓑ Ⓒ Ⓓ
18. Ⓐ Ⓑ Ⓒ   43. Ⓐ Ⓑ Ⓒ Ⓓ   68. Ⓐ Ⓑ Ⓒ Ⓓ   93. Ⓐ Ⓑ Ⓒ Ⓓ
19. Ⓐ Ⓑ Ⓒ   44. Ⓐ Ⓑ Ⓒ Ⓓ   69. Ⓐ Ⓑ Ⓒ Ⓓ   94. Ⓐ Ⓑ Ⓒ Ⓓ
20. Ⓐ Ⓑ Ⓒ   45. Ⓐ Ⓑ Ⓒ Ⓓ   70. Ⓐ Ⓑ Ⓒ Ⓓ   95. Ⓐ Ⓑ Ⓒ Ⓓ

21. Ⓐ Ⓑ Ⓒ   46. Ⓐ Ⓑ Ⓒ Ⓓ   71. Ⓐ Ⓑ Ⓒ Ⓓ   96. Ⓐ Ⓑ Ⓒ Ⓓ
22. Ⓐ Ⓑ Ⓒ   47. Ⓐ Ⓑ Ⓒ Ⓓ   72. Ⓐ Ⓑ Ⓒ Ⓓ   97. Ⓐ Ⓑ Ⓒ Ⓓ
23. Ⓐ Ⓑ Ⓒ   48. Ⓐ Ⓑ Ⓒ Ⓓ   73. Ⓐ Ⓑ Ⓒ Ⓓ   98. Ⓐ Ⓑ Ⓒ Ⓓ
24. Ⓐ Ⓑ Ⓒ   49. Ⓐ Ⓑ Ⓒ Ⓓ   74. Ⓐ Ⓑ Ⓒ Ⓓ   99. Ⓐ Ⓑ Ⓒ Ⓓ
25. Ⓐ Ⓑ Ⓒ   50. Ⓐ Ⓑ Ⓒ Ⓓ   75. Ⓐ Ⓑ Ⓒ Ⓓ   100. Ⓐ Ⓑ Ⓒ Ⓓ

Reading Answer Sheet

101. (A) (B) (C) (D)	126. (A) (B) (C) (D)	151. (A) (B) (C) (D)	176. (A) (B) (C) (D)
102. (A) (B) (C) (D)	127. (A) (B) (C) (D)	152. (A) (B) (C) (D)	177. (A) (B) (C) (D)
103. (A) (B) (C) (D)	128. (A) (B) (C) (D)	153. (A) (B) (C) (D)	178. (A) (B) (C) (D)
104. (A) (B) (C) (D)	129. (A) (B) (C) (D)	154. (A) (B) (C) (D)	179. (A) (B) (C) (D)
105. (A) (B) (C) (D)	130. (A) (B) (C) (D)	155. (A) (B) (C) (D)	180. (A) (B) (C) (D)
106. (A) (B) (C) (D)	131. (A) (B) (C) (D)	156. (A) (B) (C) (D)	181. (A) (B) (C) (D)
107. (A) (B) (C) (D)	132. (A) (B) (C) (D)	157. (A) (B) (C) (D)	182. (A) (B) (C) (D)
108. (A) (B) (C) (D)	133. (A) (B) (C) (D)	158. (A) (B) (C) (D)	183. (A) (B) (C) (D)
109. (A) (B) (C) (D)	134. (A) (B) (C) (D)	159. (A) (B) (C) (D)	184. (A) (B) (C) (D)
110. (A) (B) (C) (D)	135. (A) (B) (C) (D)	160. (A) (B) (C) (D)	185. (A) (B) (C) (D)
111. (A) (B) (C) (D)	136. (A) (B) (C) (D)	161. (A) (B) (C) (D)	186. (A) (B) (C) (D)
112. (A) (B) (C) (D)	137. (A) (B) (C) (D)	162. (A) (B) (C) (D)	187. (A) (B) (C) (D)
113. (A) (B) (C) (D)	138. (A) (B) (C) (D)	163. (A) (B) (C) (D)	188. (A) (B) (C) (D)
114. (A) (B) (C) (D)	139. (A) (B) (C) (D)	164. (A) (B) (C) (D)	189. (A) (B) (C) (D)
115. (A) (B) (C) (D)	140. (A) (B) (C) (D)	165. (A) (B) (C) (D)	190. (A) (B) (C) (D)
116. (A) (B) (C) (D)	141. (A) (B) (C) (D)	166. (A) (B) (C) (D)	191. (A) (B) (C) (D)
117. (A) (B) (C) (D)	142. (A) (B) (C) (D)	167. (A) (B) (C) (D)	192. (A) (B) (C) (D)
118. (A) (B) (C) (D)	143. (A) (B) (C) (D)	168. (A) (B) (C) (D)	193. (A) (B) (C) (D)
119. (A) (B) (C) (D)	144. (A) (B) (C) (D)	169. (A) (B) (C) (D)	194. (A) (B) (C) (D)
120. (A) (B) (C) (D)	145. (A) (B) (C) (D)	170. (A) (B) (C) (D)	195. (A) (B) (C) (D)
121. (A) (B) (C) (D)	146. (A) (B) (C) (D)	171. (A) (B) (C) (D)	196. (A) (B) (C) (D)
122. (A) (B) (C) (D)	147. (A) (B) (C) (D)	172. (A) (B) (C) (D)	197. (A) (B) (C) (D)
123. (A) (B) (C) (D)	148. (A) (B) (C) (D)	173. (A) (B) (C) (D)	198. (A) (B) (C) (D)
124. (A) (B) (C) (D)	149. (A) (B) (C) (D)	174. (A) (B) (C) (D)	199. (A) (B) (C) (D)
125. (A) (B) (C) (D)	150. (A) (B) (C) (D)	175. (A) (B) (C) (D)	200. (A) (B) (C) (D)

Test 2: Listening

The Listening section evaluates how well you understand spoken English. The Listening test has four sections and will take approximately 45 minutes. You <u>must</u> mark your answers on the answer sheet not in the test book.

PART 1: PHOTOGRAPHS

14

> **Directions:** For each item in Part 1, you will hear four statements about a photograph in the test book. You must listen carefully to the statements in order to select the statement that best describes the photograph. Mark the corresponding letter (A), (B), (C), or (D) on the answer sheet.

Example

Listen to the statements and select the one that best describes the picture.

(A) They're drinking orange juice.
(B) They're turning on a computer.
(C) They're looking at a screen.
(D) They're putting on formal clothes.

Statement **(C), "They're looking at a screen."** best describes the picture, so you should choose answer (C) and mark it on your answer sheet.

Sample Answer

Go on to the next page ➜

🎧
15

1.

2.

3.

4.

Go on to the next page ➜

5.

6.

7.

8.

Go on to the next page ➔

9.

10.

This is the end of Part 1.

Look at the next page to start Part 2 →

PART 2: QUESTION–RESPONSE

16

Directions: For each item in Part 2, you will hear a statement or a question followed by three responses. Listen and choose the best response. Then mark the corresponding letter (A), (B), or (C) on the answer sheet.

Example

Have you met the new Managing Director?

(A) Actually I talked with him in the lobby just now.
(B) Yes, I took the call.
(C) No, he takes the subway to work.

The best response to the question "Have you met the new Managing Director?" is answer choice **(A)**, "**Actually I talked with him in the lobby just now.**" You should mark answer (A) on your answer sheet.

Sample Answer

17

11. Listen and choose the best response.

12. Listen and choose the best response.

13. Listen and choose the best response.

14. Listen and choose the best response.

15. Listen and choose the best response.

16. Listen and choose the best response.

17. Listen and choose the best response.

18. Listen and choose the best response.

19. Listen and choose the best response.

20. Listen and choose the best response.

21. Listen and choose the best response.

22. Listen and choose the best response.

23. Listen and choose the best response.

24. Listen and choose the best response.

25. Listen and choose the best response.

26. Listen and choose the best response.

27. Listen and choose the best response.

28. Listen and choose the best response.

29. Listen and choose the best response.

30. Listen and choose the best response.

31. Listen and choose the best response.

32. Listen and choose the best response.

33. Listen and choose the best response.

34. Listen and choose the best response.

35. Listen and choose the best response.

36. Listen and choose the best response.

37. Listen and choose the best response.

38. Listen and choose the best response.

39. Listen and choose the best response.

40. Listen and choose the best response.

This is the end of Part 2.

Go on to the next page to start Part 3 →

PART 3: CONVERSATIONS

18

> **Directions:** You will hear conversations with two speakers. Then you will answer three questions about each conversation. Listen and select the best response to each question. Mark the corresponding letter (A), (B), (C), or (D) on the answer sheet.

41. What is the purpose of the call?

    (A) To discuss delivery options

    (B) To process handling fees

    (C) To check on an order

    (D) To give the number of a product

42. What items are the speakers talking about?

    (A) Cameras

    (B) Office desks

    (C) Phones

    (D) Copy machines

43. What does the woman want to do?

    (A) Order more products

    (B) Call the main factory

    (C) Schedule a delivery

    (D) Get a discount

---

44. What does the man ask the woman to do?

    (A) Get a package for some fabrics

    (B) Take him to the post office

    (C) Have lunch with him

    (D) Call the office

45. What is the woman's plan in the afternoon?

    (A) To go to the office

    (B) To make a lunch appointment

    (C) To meet a client

    (D) To cancel a staff meeting

46. What is the man going to do next?

    (A) Get some fabric samples

    (B) Order a phonebook

    (C) Post some packages

    (D) Search for a co-worker on a list

47. Where are the speakers?

    (A) In a school

    (B) In an office

    (C) In a building

    (D) In a hospital

48. When most likely will the machine start working?

    (A) This morning

    (B) This afternoon

    (C) Tomorrow morning

    (D) Tomorrow afternoon

49. What does the woman want the man to do?

    (A) Call a mechanic

    (B) Reschedule an appointment

    (C) Call a doctor

    (D) Close a window

---

50. When is the party?

    (A) This Thursday

    (B) This Friday

    (C) Next Monday

    (D) Next Tuesday

51. What does the man need to do?

    (A) Finish a report

    (B) Organize a party

    (C) Set up a new project

    (D) Postpone a meeting

52. What is the woman going to do later?

    (A) Host a party

    (B) Write a report

    (C) Order some invitation cards

    (D) Go to the man's office

53. What is the topic of discussion?

    (A) Safety regulations
    (B) Office purchases
    (C) New employees
    (D) Changes to an office

54. How far ahead of schedule is the renovation?

    (A) One week
    (B) Two weeks
    (C) Four weeks
    (D) Five weeks

55. What does the woman ask the man to do?

    (A) Give a training course
    (B) Pack up his belongings
    (C) Move to a new office
    (D) Ask someone else

56. What is the man's request?

    (A) To open a new account
    (B) To take out a loan
    (C) To buy a train ticket
    (D) To call a phone number

57. What is the problem?

    (A) He got lost.
    (B) He cannot pay back his loan.
    (C) He can't see the manager.
    (D) He missed his lunch.

58. What does the woman ask the man to do?

    (A) Come back again
    (B) Wait for the manager
    (C) Leave his contact number
    (D) Leave a business card

59. What is the main topic of the conversation?

    (A) A honeymoon
    (B) The weather
    (C) A change of plan
    (D) A client

60. What is the problem?

    (A) Marketing failures
    (B) Flight cancellations
    (C) A broken computer
    (D) Severe weather

61. What does the woman advise the man to do?

    (A) Book a flight
    (B) Attend a conference
    (C) Speak to the marketing manager
    (D) Move to Tokyo

62. What is the woman searching for?

    (A) A report
    (B) A letter
    (C) A phone book
    (D) A folder

63. Who is the woman going to meet tomorrow?

    (A) An assistant
    (B) A doctor
    (C) Job applicants
    (D) A new manager

64. What is the man going to do?

    (A) Go to the doctor
    (B) E-mail résumés
    (C) Find a co-worker
    (D) Open the cabinet

Go on to the next page ➜

65. Where most likely are the speakers?

(A) At a bank

(B) At a gym

(C) At an accountant's office

(D) At a café

66. What does the woman show the man?

(A) A bag

(B) A photograph

(C) A phone number

(D) An identification document

67. What is the man going to do next?

(A) Print some documents

(B) Return a license

(C) Make a photocopy

(D) Mail a letter

68. What are the speakers discussing?

(A) The new food service

(B) The company's holiday party

(C) The arrangements for a seminar

(D) The location of a show

69. What is the woman concerned about?

(A) Not having enough food

(B) Having few people

(C) Arranging a banquet

(D) Booking the wrong room

70. What does the woman ask for?

(A) An office address

(B) Directions to a building

(C) A telephone number

(D) A dinner menu

This is the end of Part 3.

Look at the next page to start Part 4 ➔

PART 4: TALKS

19

Directions: You will hear several talks, each with one speaker. Then you will answer three questions about the talk. Listen and select the best response to each question. Mark the corresponding letter (A), (B), (C), or (D) on the answer sheet.

71. What is the main content of the report?

(A) International news

(B) A traffic update

(C) Bus times

(D) Construction projects

72. What is causing problems near City Hall?

(A) Street musicians

(B) Protests

(C) Traffic

(D) Road construction

73. What is the next program?

(A) A weather report

(B) A book reading

(C) An interview

(D) A music show

74. What is the message about?

(A) An order

(B) A printer

(C) A co-worker

(D) Office furniture

75. Why is the speaker calling?

(A) A product was not returned.

(B) A product is not available.

(C) A product has been misplaced.

(D) A faulty item was dispatched.

76. What does the caller want Ms. Gernin to do?

(A) Call back

(B) Cancel an order

(C) Order a different item

(D) Visit her office

77. Who most likely is making the announcement?

(A) A tour guide

(B) A flight attendant

(C) A waitress

(D) A train driver

78. What does the speaker recommend the listeners do?

(A) Eat a meal on the bus

(B) Go to a cathedral

(C) Get a dinner menu

(D) Order traditional food

79. When are the listeners supposed to leave the city?

(A) At 1:00 p.m.

(B) At 2:00 p.m.

(C) At 7:00 p.m.

(D) At 9:00 p.m.

80. Who most likely are the listeners?

(A) Travel agents

(B) Students

(C) Shoppers

(D) Airline passengers

81. What weather conditions does the speaker mention?

(A) High waves

(B) High winds

(C) Heavy rain

(D) A hurricane

82. According to the speaker, what will happen next?

(A) An airplane will land.

(B) Movies will be shown.

(C) Free drinks will be served.

(D) Snacks will be sold.

Go on to the next page →

83. Who most likely is the speaker?

   (A) A government official
   (B) A leisure park spokesperson
   (C) A gym instructor
   (D) A news reporter

84. When will the new building open?

   (A) In two years
   (B) In three years
   (C) In four years
   (D) In five years

85. What will the listeners hear next?

   (A) Commercials
   (B) Business news
   (C) A weather forecast
   (D) A music program

86. Where is the speech taking place?

   (A) In a classroom
   (B) In a bookstore
   (C) In a shopping mall
   (D) In a meeting room

87. According to the speaker, what was Ms. Tenison's first job?

   (A) Teacher
   (B) Writer
   (C) Photographer
   (D) Sales assistant

88. What will happen after the speech?

   (A) A sale will begin.
   (B) A senior manager will talk.
   (C) A new strategy will be presented.
   (D) A book will be read out.

89. What kind of event is being advertised?

   (A) A basketball game
   (B) An annual sale
   (C) A trade show
   (D) A garage sale

90. What will be 30% cheaper?

   (A) Electrical products
   (B) Fashion jewelry
   (C) Ladies' glasses
   (D) Men's shoes

91. When will the event start?

   (A) On Thursday
   (B) On Friday
   (C) On Saturday
   (D) On Sunday

92. What does the company make?

   (A) Plants
   (B) Safety clothing
   (C) Phones
   (D) Cars

93. Who are the listeners?

   (A) New employees
   (B) Mechanics
   (C) Farmers
   (D) Recruiters

94. What does the speaker ask the listeners to do?

   (A) Produce safety glasses
   (B) Turn off their phones
   (C) Check some equipment
   (D) Design a helmet

95. What industry does Ms. Peterson work in?

(A) Education

(B) Finance

(C) Retail

(D) Publishing

96. What was Ms. Peterson's first position in the company?

(A) Trainee

(B) Professor

(C) Manager

(D) Editor

97. What is Ms. Peterson going to do next?

(A) Start a publishing company

(B) Go back to the tax department

(C) Return to university

(D) Write about her life

98. What is being advertised?

(A) Short-term jobs

(B) Vacation packages

(C) Camping workshops

(D) Leadership training

99. Who is the advertisement for?

(A) Young people

(B) International students

(C) Tourists

(D) Teachers

100. According to the advertisement, where is information available?

(A) From an office

(B) On a bulletin board

(C) At a camp site

(D) On a website

This is the end of Part 4.

Go on to the next page to start Part 5 ➜

Test 2: Reading

The Reading section evaluates how well you understand written English. The Reading test has three sections and will take approximately 75 minutes. You must mark your answers on the answer sheet not in the test book.

PART 5: INCOMPLETE SENTENCES

Directions: One or more words is missing from each of the following sentences. Choose the best answer choice to complete the sentence. Mark the corresponding letter (A), (B), (C), or (D) on the answer sheet.

101. We gave the product special features _____ differentiate it from competitor products.

(A) because of

(B) rather than

(C) in order to

(D) as opposed to

102. It's the same woman _____ gave a lecture at last year's conference.

(A) who

(B) which

(C) what

(D) how

103. I'm going to be unavailable _____ meetings for at least the next week while I set up the new project.

(A) for

(B) to

(C) with

(D) of

104. Please see the _____ file for a detailed itinerary of the tour.

(A) attachment

(B) attach

(C) attached

(D) attaching

105. The number of visitors to traditionally popular tourist _____ has diminished this year.

(A) trips

(B) locations

(C) positions

(D) destinations

106. Before we get started, our recently appointed Sales Director, Ted Ottmeier, would like to introduce _____.

(A) he

(B) himself

(C) him

(D) his

107. The new office furniture looks very nice _____ it's costing a lot of money to source.

(A) but

(B) however

(C) whereas

(D) provided that

108. There is talk at Nomadic Inc. that job losses will result from the _____ of the company with Teen Tours.

(A) merger

(B) buyer

(C) flight

(D) connector

109. Our customers won't _____ any further defects in our products.

    (A) tolerate
    (B) tolerant
    (C) tolerance
    (D) tolerating

110. _____ the economy grow, the group suggested the construction of new roads and affordable housing.

    (A) Make
    (B) To make
    (C) Being made
    (D) Have made

111. There were _____ increases in production costs across all our models.

    (A) basic
    (B) significant
    (C) crucial
    (D) fair

112. In spite of being an outstanding project manager in all other ways, he lacks _____ skills.

    (A) manage
    (B) managed
    (C) manager
    (D) managerial

113. We _____ need new advertising staff to promote the new products that will be released next year.

    (A) urgent
    (B) urgency
    (C) urgently
    (D) urging

114. As agreed last year, EST _____ some of the key elements for our new model.

    (A) will supply
    (B) was supplied
    (C) having supplied
    (D) had been supplied

115. We could save time by using other people, who could do the work _____.

    (A) quick
    (B) quicker
    (C) most quick
    (D) more quickly

116. If you want to apply for any of the available positions, please _____ a résumé.

    (A) send
    (B) sends
    (C) sending
    (D) sent

117. The shareholders expect the new CEO to be capable _____ making the company more profitable.

    (A) with
    (B) by
    (C) of
    (D) to

118. The news staff worked under my _____ for the first three months of their contracts.

    (A) guidance
    (B) advice
    (C) occasion
    (D) advancement

Go on to the next page →

119. In order to get approval to develop a new product, it is important to _____ a presentation to the approval committee.

    (A) devise

    (B) get

    (C) make

    (D) see

120. The annual seminar for all employees will _____ in July next year.

    (A) take place

    (B) make up

    (C) hold on

    (D) give up

121. The vice president announced yesterday that he would be leaving his job, _____ the rumors that he had fallen out with the chairman.

    (A) verify

    (B) verified

    (C) verifying

    (D) verification

122. _____ many employees were leaving the company, the human resources manager held an emergency meeting.

    (A) Because

    (B) Consequently

    (C) Due to

    (D) As a result

123. You need to remember that the occasional overseas trip is a _____ of the job.

    (A) necessary

    (B) needed

    (C) needing

    (D) necessity

124. If we had started preparing for this presentation earlier, we _____ have done it much better.

    (A) will

    (B) do

    (C) should

    (D) would

125. I'm looking forward to _____ the client's feedback at the meeting next week.

    (A) receive

    (B) received

    (C) receiving

    (D) will receive

126. Don't forget to consult a legal specialist before _____ the form.

    (A) fill in

    (B) fills in

    (C) filled in

    (D) filling in

127. The decline _____ the birth rate may be due to longer working hours.

    (A) in

    (B) at

    (C) to

    (D) with

128. All staff must have worked no _____ than seven hours by the end of each day.

    (A) most

    (B) rather

    (C) fewer

    (D) little

129. Our ability to employ new staff relies _____ our profits.

    (A) of

    (B) to

    (C) on

    (D) for

130. As far as I _____, the engineer came yesterday and fixed the boiler.

(A) know

(B) known

(C) to know

(D) knew

131. In spite of our company's difficulties last year, we now have an _____ new group of products.

(A) impress

(B) impressed

(C) impressive

(D) impressively

132. Even though the restaurant was crowded, we _____ find a free table.

(A) can

(B) may

(C) were able to

(D) would be able to

133. Sales have been improved by the marketing department's new advertising _____.

(A) elevation

(B) strategy

(C) distribution

(D) motion

134. Due to low demand in developed countries, industrial _____ was disappointing this quarter.

(A) rules

(B) survey

(C) output

(D) reliance

135. All the old _____ from the 19th floor offices will be picked up today.

(A) furnishing

(B) furnished

(C) furniture

(D) furnish

136. I saw Mr. Kwan at the trade show, _____ to the rest of his team.

(A) both

(B) as well

(C) either

(D) in addition

137. You _____ bring your notebook to the conference, as paper is not available at the venue.

(A) need to

(B) needn't

(C) would

(D) oughtn't to

138. Her flight took off on time, so she _____ be in Rome by now.

(A) can

(B) will

(C) could

(D) is going to

139. Ms. Nguyen didn't pick up her phone, but that doesn't _____ mean that she's not in the office.

(A) necessary

(B) necessarily

(C) necessity

(D) necessitate

140. If you don't like the transportation provided, you are more than welcome to travel to the center _____ you like, as long as the cost is under $100.

(A) however

(B) whoever

(C) whatever

(D) whichever

Go on to the next page ➔

PART 6: TEXT COMPLETION

> **Directions:** The following texts have sentences with some words and phrases missing. Read the answer choices given to complete the sentences. Choose the best answer choice to complete the sentence. Mark the corresponding letter (A), (B), (C), or (D) on the answer sheet.

Questions 141–143 refer to the following e-mail.

To: cathy.j.king@genmail.com
From: j.hall@cristiensen-hotels.com

Dear Ms. King,

Many thanks for your recent message _____ about

141. (A) inquiries
    (B) inquiry
    (C) inquiring
    (D) inquired

membership of our hotel's fitness club. I am glad that you are interested in joining the club. As you may know, the club is currently not open as we are in the process of renovating its facilities. It _____ at

142. (A) will open again
    (B) opened again
    (C) could open again
    (D) had opened again

the end of October. The renovated fitness club will have high-tech gym equipment, an Olympic-size swimming pool, and a modernized spa.
We hope you will be _____ with these new facilities.

143. (A) happily
    (B) happiness
    (C) being happy
    (D) happy

We will be accepting membership applications beginning in September, so please contact me again then for further information. In the meantime, please let me know if you have any questions.

Kind regards,

Joseph Hall
Manager

Questions 144–146 refer to the following e-mail.

Dear Mr. Gifford,

Many thanks for applying _____ the position of Project Coodinator

144. (A) from
(B) for
(C) by
(D) at

at MK Sloane. We are grateful for your interest in our company.

I am sorry to inform you that your application has not been _____

145. (A) success
(B) succeeding ⟵
(C) successful
(D) successfully ✗

on this occasion. I apologize if this is disappointing for you. We received a large number of applications, and, upon reviewing the candidates' résumés, our selection committee decided that other candidates were more _____

146. (A) suitable
(B) advantageous
(C) advanced
(D) capable

for the job.

Please do not hesitate to apply for any future positions with us that may interest you.

We wish you every success for your future.

Yours sincerely,

Julia Fraser
HR Officer

Go on to the next page ➜

Questions 147–149 refer to the following e-mail.

In spite of the difficult economic conditions, Standard Electronics announced a 25% _____ in its third-quarter income on Tuesday. The company

147. (A) increase
     (B) decrease
     (C) cost
     (D) contribution

exceeded investor assumptions with the help of improvement in its mobile technology business and rapidly growing _____ in developing markets.

                148. (A) orders
                     (B) desires
                     (C) demand
                     (D) concerns

Income increased to $2.4 million, up from $1.9 million in the same period a year ago. Standard CEO Ryan C. Stowe said that the company has "a creative product range and an outstanding distribution network." These factors, he said, resulted in "the outstanding performance in the third quarter."

Investors received the announcement enthusiastically as shares went up _____ 1.6%. Standard Electronics' main competitors will

149. (A) as
     (B) for
     (C) at
     (D) by

release their results next week, starting with EcoTech, the Seattle-based cell phone specialist, on Monday.

Questions 150–152 refer to the following report.

To: All employees

The Technical Team will start upgrading all PCs on the weekend of July 8 and 9. They will install new software and a new operating system. We expect that the upgrade _____ the many problems we have

    150. (A) resolved
          (B) would resolve
          (C) will resolve
          (D) would have resolved

had over recent months with our IT systems.

Before the upgrade takes place, please make sure that you save all of your files to the company server. Any files remaining on your PC will be erased. Please also remove any hardware that personally belongs to you from the office. Also, please _____ that your desk is clean and

    151. (A) insure
          (B) assure
          (C) sure
          (D) reassure

tidy, as IT staff may have to directly access your PC. Please complete these procedures by the end of Friday, July 7 at the latest.

By now all employees should have attended training in the new operating system. If you haven't, please contact Joan Birkby to arrange _____ training as soon as possible. It is important

152. (A) you
     (B) your
     (C) yours
     (D) yourself

that we are all familiar with the new software so that we can resume business as usual on Monday July 10.

Go on to the next page ➔

PART 7: READING COMPREHENSION

> **Directions:** This section includes a variety of texts. You will read each one and answer questions about it. Choose the best answer and mark the corresponding letter (A), (B), (C), or (D) on the answer sheet.

Questions 153–155 refer to the following memo.

MEMO

To: All employees
From: Robert Thomas, Managing Director, Principa Accountants
Re: Ron Fernandez
Date: Monday, November 10

I wish to thank you all for cooperating so enthusiastically with Ron Fernandez over the past two months. As you know, Ron was recruited as a consultant to help us plan how we can improve our working practices and our corporate culture. Ron's work is now complete, and he has submitted his report, which I will be sharing with you all at the next monthly meeting. Before the meeting, however, I wish to communicate Ron's main suggestions to you so that you can start thinking about them right away.

Ron suggests that we aim to:
- better understand our customer profile
- be the company that people want to work for in the accounting field
- be a more environmentally responsible firm

Now that Ron has proposed these objectives, it is our task to find ways of accomplishing them. Over the coming months, we will be organizing three working groups. These groups will meet regularly to discuss each of the objectives. You will be invited to join the group that suits your interests best. I will talk more about this at next month's company briefing.

I trust I will continue to have your support as we bring change to our organization, and as we move forward into a challenging yet exciting future.

---

153. What is the purpose of the memo?

(A) To share recommendations

(B) To arrange a meeting

(C) To introduce a new employee

(D) To organize a consultation

154. What is NOT stated about the company?

(A) It should care more about the environment.

(B) It should recruit younger people.

(C) It should do more research on its customers.

(D) It should be an interesting place for people to work.

155. According to the memo, what is planned for the future?

(A) New staff will be selected.

(B) Meetings will be held.

(C) A party will be organized.

(D) An environmental plan will be presented.

Questions 156–157 refer to the following memo.

MEMO

Companies Weekly

Entrepreneurs

Rosanne Rawley started her company, Beta Web Solutions, ten years ago while a senior at Northern University in Newark, NJ. Within four years, the company, which has created customized websites for large multinational corporations such as ABD Electronics and Clio Pharmaceuticals, was producing around $700,000 in annual revenue. However, the more websites that Beta Web Solutions built, the more employees Rawley had to hire. Instead of making an expensive move to larger office space, Rawley was interested in a way to serve more clients without having to take on more staff.

Rawley's opportunity came in 2008, when she took part in a financial services conference in Chicago. Inter Life Insurance hired her company, headquartered in Santa Cruz, CA, to produce a system that would enable customers to easily purchase and manage insurance policies online. Rawley hoped that if the system was a success, it could be sold to other insurance companies without much extra work. Eight months later, Rawley launched a brand name for the system—EasyChoice—and advertized it to the insurance industry as "the world's premier Web-based policy purchasing system." Contracts with three other major insurance groups were soon sealed. Rawley didn't stop there. She invested the profits in inventing new software, this time developing a system for opening bank accounts online. Before the system was even complete, Rawley had already made deals with some of the major banks around the world, from New York to Tokyo.

The decision to create software solutions rather than continue focusing on website design was a significant triumph for Rawley. Beta Web Solutions gets $5 for each insurance policy purchased, and $10 for each bank account opened. This has resulted in a large increase in profits. The company now generates revenue of around $15 million, a figure that is rising yearly. Not surprisingly, the company's success has led to a move to a larger office after all. Rosanne Rawley can now be seen in her office on the 11th floor of Beta Tower, in the heart of Santa Cruz's business district.

156. Where is the company's headquarters?

(A) Chicago

(B) New York

(C) Tokyo

(D) Santa Cruz

157. What is stated about the company?

(A) It was founded by a university.

(B) It belongs to a bank.

(C) It changed the aim of its business.

(D) It transferred to a different city.

Go on to the next page →

Questions 158–159 refer to the following e-mail.

To: Frances Jepsen fjepsen@bookhouse.com
From: Paul Gordon pgordon@bookhouse.com

Subject: Product Development Meeting, November 18

Hi Frances,

Thanks for letting me know that you can't attend the Product Development Meeting next week. Could you provide me with an update from your department that I can present at the meeting? As you know, we have to know the estimated sales figures for the product before we decide whether or not to proceed with development. I'd be grateful to have your input ahead of the meeting.

Best wishes,

Paul

158. What is the purpose of the e-mail?

(A) To write a report
(B) To hold a meeting
(C) To request new information
(D) To advertise the latest products

159. In which department does Ms. Jepsen most likely work?

(A) Advertising
(B) Security
(C) Marketing
(D) Sales

Questions 160–162 refer to the following advertisement.

The Vietnam Lotus
Savor the flavors of the East

Open 12:00–3:00 p.m. for lunch   6:00–11:00 p.m. for dinner
Tuesday through Sunday

The newly refurbished Vietnam Lotus offers a sophisticated dining atmosphere and an amazing new menu! The revised menu contains all your old favorites, plus new modern recipes that will surely become future favorites. But don't take our word for it. Vietnamese cuisine expert Suchika Yonchanam has recently given our chef's menu five stars in the *Glendale Food Review!*

Of course, the Vietnam Lotus offers more than just great food. Our new, stylishly designed dining area is ideal for business lunches, romantic dinners, and celebration, parties, and events, and our location makes us a perfect choice for post-theater dining. Plus, our professional wait staff are always ready to accommodate your every need. All our servers dress in traditional Vietnamese costume, so that that you'll feel like you're in Vietnam, right in the heart of Glendale!

Visit the Vietnam Lotus this month to enjoy our re-opening offers:

Special three-course lunch for just $14.99

Free appetizer for parties of four and over ordering from the main menu

---

160. What is new about the Vietnam Lotus?

(A) The kitchen

(B) The menu

(C) The location

(D) The opening times

161. Who most likely is Suchika Yonchanam?

(A) A restaurant owner

(B) A qualified cook

(C) An experienced waiter

(D) A food critic

162. What is NOT stated about the Vietnam Lotus?

(A) It is open all day.

(B) It cooks Asian food.

(C) It can host a number of events.

(D) It is near a theater.

Go on to the next page ➜

Questions 163–164 refer to the following notice.

Severe Weather Conditions

In light of the bad weather that is expected for the coming weeks, the Senior Management Team has decided to implement a new policy regarding severe weather conditions. This will take effect from Monday, January 15.

From January 15, any staff member who is concerned about their safety and journey home due to weather conditions must consult his or her manager. The manager will review the weather conditions and the personal circumstances of the employee before deciding whether to permit the employee to go home early. If the employee is allowed to go home early, he or she must take the time off as unpaid leave or vacation.

Likewise, an employee who thinks that his or her commute in the morning will be hazardous or impossible because of extreme weather is allowed to decide to take the day off as unpaid leave or vacation. The employee must notify his or her manager of this decision before 9:00 a.m. on the day in question.

---

163. What will happen on January 15?

(A) Severe weather is predicted.
(B) Senior staff will have a meeting.
(C) An analyst will be hired.
(D) A new rule will be introduced.

164. According to the notice, what may happen during bad weather?

(A) Business trips may be canceled.
(B) Staff may leave the office early.
(C) Staff may be allowed to work at home.
(D) Roads may become hazardous.

Questions 165–168 refer to the following e-mail.

To: Sue Barnett suebarnett84@mail22u.com
From: Frank Paul paulf@dlf.uk.com
Subject: Assessment day

Dear Ms. Barnett,

Thank you for taking part in this morning's telephone interview for a trainee position at Dasbrough Lasatti Foster. The managers were very impressed with your performance in the interview, and would like you to attend an assessment day from 9:00 a.m. to 4 p.m. on March 17. The assessment day will involve mathematical and verbal reasoning tests, in addition to a face-to-face interview with one of our senior partners. The event will be held at our offices in London, directions to which are provided below. Please keep any receipts for travel costs, which we will be happy to reimburse you for.

I'd greatly appreciate it if you could call my assistant, Jonathan Summers, at 623-555-9233 to confirm your attendance.

We look forward to seeing you on March 17.

Kind regards,

Frank Paul
Human Resources Administrator

Directions to Dasbrough Lasatti Foster London: take Northern Line 1 or 2 to Fenchurch Station. Take Exit 3 from the station and turn right onto Horningsey Road. Walk three blocks, then turn left onto Kewes Avenue. When you reach the Royal Museum of Art, turn right. Walk two more blocks along Fenchurch Street, past the Court of Justice and Health ministries, and you will see our offices on your right, next to the London University administration block. Please notify reception on arrival.

165. What is the purpose of this e-mail?

(A) To invite a candidate for another interview

(B) To arrange a business trip

(C) To explain the reasons for promotion

(D) To help organize a vacation

166. What does the e-mail indicate about Ms. Barnett?

(A) She has met Mr. Paul before.

(B) She lacks mathematical skills.

(C) She always travels by train.

(D) She is inexperienced.

167. The word "taking" part in in paragraph 1, is closest in meaning to

(A) following

(B) going

(C) participating

(D) taking care of

168. What will Ms. Barnett see on Fenchurch Street before she reaches the destination?

(A) A library

(B) A bus stop

(C) University laboratories

(D) Government buildings

Go on to the next page →

Questions 169–172 refer to the following letter.

PTC Bank
1 Elizabeth Drive, Ottawa, ON

Ms. E. Evans
120 East Circle
Ottawa, ON

September 14

Dear Ms. Evans,

I am pleased to enclose your Annual Personal Statement. This new statement—unavailable from any other bank—is part of PTC's commitment to being the nation's number one bank. Your statement shows you an analysis of all the accounts and transactions that you made with PTC Bank over the last 12 months.

We hope that the Annual Personal Statement will help you understand and plan your finances better. For this reason, we have added some advice on how we could help you make even better use of your money. And in case you have any questions, we have included a frequently asked questions section on the back of this statement. If you have any further questions, or if you wish to discuss your finances with one of our specialized financial advisors, please drop by your local branch to arrange an appointment, or call our Customer Care Department at 148-555-4243. We are always here to help you reach your financial goals, whatever they may be.

Finally, we would greatly appreciate your feedback on the Annual Personal Statement. Please tell us what you think by filling in the enclosed questionnaire. By doing so, you will help us improve this service in the future, and you will be entered into a prize drawing to win $3,000 of interest-free credit. You can also enter the drawing by sending an e-mail to APSdraw@PTCBank.com.

Yours sincerely,

Christopher Martin
Annual Personal Statement Team
PTC Bank

---

169. What is the purpose of the letter?

(A) To attract customers from other banks

(B) To reschedule a financial planning meeting

(C) To explain a new service

(D) To answer an inquiry

170. What is NOT provided in the statement?

(A) A list of financial aims

(B) A survey of data

(C) Suggestions for change

(D) Answers to common questions

171. According to the letter, what should Ms. Evans do to get more information?

(A) Fill in a form

(B) E-mail her local bank

(C) Call customer service

(D) Visit a website

172. The word "specialized" in paragraph 2, is closest in meaning to

(A) interested

(B) expert

(C) useful

(D) well-known

Questions 173–175 refer to the following telephone message.

WHILE YOU WERE OUT

For: Crystal Lim
Date: June 4

You have received calls from the following people while you were out of the office:

From: Angelo Ticas   **Of:** XX Recording Studio   **Time:** 10:15
Number: 953-555-1418
Message: You will be able to re-record the sentences that were inaccurately recorded for the audio book. Please call back to confirm dates and other details. He is free from 2:00 to 3:30 p.m., then working in the studio for the rest of the afternoon.

From: Kendra Smiley   **Of:** IT Department   **Time:** 10:45
Number: Ext. 259
Message: We have now completed the software update that you requested last week. Any issues, please call the IT Department helpline. If you need training in the new software, please get in touch with Kendra directly and she will visit your office to give you a demonstration.

From: Fred Harvey   **Of:** Pelican Editorial Services   **Time:** 11:20
Number: (341) 555-8930
Message: Needs to discuss with you about the archeology book project. The editor working on it is ill so the deadline may need to be extended.

From: Natalie Lafranc   **Of:** Finance   **Time:** 12:10
Number: Ext. 193
Message: Has returned your March expenses form. You have to use the new 20% sales tax rate on the form. Natalie has e-mailed you the guidelines and instructions.

---

173. What did Ms. Lim do last week?

(A) Bought some software

(B) Gave a demonstration on how to use some software

(C) Requested software installation

(D) Tested new software

174. What is the purpose of Ms. Lafranc's call?

(A) To begin a new business

(B) To send back a purchased item

(C) To request an alteration

(D) To notify her of a sale

175. In which industry does Ms. Lim work most likely?

(A) Banking

(B) Publishing

(C) Manufacturing

(D) Music

Go on to the next page →

Questions 176–180 refer to the following press release.

PRESS RELEASE

McCarthur Hooke and Parker Advertising agree to merger, producing global advertising giant. Companies expect annual cost savings of $10 million.

McCarthur Hooke Advertising Corporation and Parker Advertising announced today that they have agreed to merge. The new company, to be called McCarthur Hooke Parker Corporation, will provide one of the advertising industry's most extensive sets of advertising services and products. The merger combines McCarthur Hooke's global leadership in traditional media channels with Parker's dominance of new media to produce a worldwide advertising leader.

In addition to bringing together the different advertising media, the companies hope that the merger will produce combined cost savings of approximately $10 million through knowledge and resource sharing. The new, merged company will operate in 110 countries and comprise more than 27,000 people.

Sam Lemon, the McCarthur Hooke chairman who conducted the merger negotiations on behalf of the company, will become chairman of the new company. Melissa Foxley, 2010 AdExec Prize winner and currently CEO of Parker Advertising, will serve as president and CEO. The headquarters will be located in New York City, at McCarthur Hooke's current offices.

"This is a wonderful moment for the company," said Lemon. "The combined experience and capabilities of both companies will create clear strategic advantages, allowing us to provide our clients with a unique level of service. No other company has the range of products that we can now put at the disposal of our clients."

Foxley added, "We are aware this is a challenging time for the industry as a whole. This merger places us as undisputed market leaders, and also generates substantial cost savings and significant value for shareholders of both organizations."

The agreement between the two companies, approved by both Boards of Directors at meetings held late on March 16, was received well by shareholders and industry analysts.

---

176. What is the purpose of the press release?

(A) To introduce a new service

(B) To congratulate the winner of an award

(C) To announce the joining of two companies

(D) To suggest cost saving methods

177. What is indicated about Parker Advertising?

(A) It specializes in newspaper advertising.

(B) It has offices in 110 countries.

(C) It was founded in New York City.

(D) It is not a traditional company.

178. According to the press release, what did Melissa Foxley do?

(A) She received an award.

(B) She got a pay raise.

(C) She transferred to New York.

(D) She began working in 2010.

179. What does Sam Lemon say about his company?

(A) It has a number of products to offer.

(B) It produces innovative products.

(C) It transferred to a different location.

(D) It gained new clients.

180. What did company directors do on March 16?

(A) They analyzed cost savings.

(B) They discussed the winner of an award.

(C) They approved a deal.

(D) They rejected a merger.

Questions 181–185 refer to the following e-mail and schedule.

To: Helen Spencer h.spencer@symonds-wyatt.com
From: Julian Magliocco jmagliocco@tachotraining.com
Subject: Training Seminar for Managers
Attachment: managers training seminar plan.doc

Dear Helen Spencer,

Please find the enclosed schedule for the residential management training seminar beginning on October 1. Your room will be ready by 2:00 p.m. on the first day of the seminar. If you need accommodation for the night before the seminar begins (Sunday), please contact me immediately. The room will be charged separately from the seminar.

Seminar participants should arrive at the venue at 9:30 a.m. on the first day. Please be on time so that you can meet the seminar leader and your fellow participants before the seminar begins at 10:00 a.m. On the second day of the seminar participants will be asked to demonstrate a case study from their own fields. As you can see on the attached schedule, your presentation is scheduled at 4:30 p.m. There will be time to prepare for this.

We look forward to meeting you at the seminar.

Regards,

Julian Magliocco
Seminar Coordinator

Questions on next page ➔

Management Training Seminar
The Kennedy Center, Baltimore
October 1–3

<u>Monday, October 1</u>
9:30	Arrival
10:00–11:45	Seminar opening: What is management?
11:45–13:00	The role of manager; Case study introduction
13:00	Lunch
14:00–16:00	Making the change from "manager" to "leader"
16:00	Break
16:30–18:30	Creating and leading teams 1
19:00	Dinner

<u>Tuesday, October 2</u>
9:30–11:45	Financial management
11:45–13:00	Preparation for case study
13:00	Lunch
14:00–16:00	Case study presentation—technology
16:00	Break
16:30–18:30	Case study presentation—engineering
19:00	Dinner

<u>Wednesday, October 3</u>
9:30–11:45	Creating and leading teams 2
11:45–13:00	Performance review and objective setting
13:00	Lunch
14:00–16:00	Harnessing your staff's emotions
16:00	Closing session
16:30	End

---

181. In which field does Ms. Spencer probably work?

(A) Engineering

(B) Teaching

(C) Technology

(D) Hospitality

182. What is NOT suggested about the training course?

(A) It is intended for managers.

(B) It ends earlier on the final day.

(C) It has time for meals.

(D) It offers Sunday night accommodation.

183. In the e-mail, the word "participants" in paragraph 2, is closest in meaning to

(A) Managers

(B) Competitors

(C) Candidates

(D) Attendees

184. When is Ms. Spencer going to discuss finance?

(A) On Sunday

(B) On Monday

(C) On Tuesday

(D) On Wednesday

185. When will Ms. Spencer give a presentation?

(A) On September 30

(B) On October 1

(C) On October 2

(D) On October 3

Questions 186–190 refer to the following advertisement and review.

DUFFY'S GOES ONLINE!

The world-famous academic publisher Duffy's has made its bestselling books and journals available online! Now you don't have to wait for your book to arrive. Just visit Duffy's Online and you can begin reading it in seconds on your computer or handheld device.

And what's more, for a limited time we are providing the following special deals to celebrate the launch of Duffy's Online:

→ **5% off your first purchase from Duffy's Online**

→ **25% off all books in the University Editions series**

→ **Free electronic book reader for all orders over $200**

→ **Free printed journals for all annual subscribers to academic journals**

Offer expires November 1

Duffy's Online is also available to libraries and academic institutions worldwide through adjustable and attractive sales packages. Please visit the website or call your local Duffy's sales representative for more details.

The Publishing Review
January Edition

Duffy's Online launches, disappoints

Last month witnessed the long-awaited launch of Duffy's Online, an online store for electronic versions of Duffy's titles. The launch was originally scheduled for May, but technical problems resulted in a lengthy delay. So, after the long wait, how good is it?

The site is beautifully designed, and navigation is simple. Books are classified clearly by category, and there is a different site for academic journals. Once you find the book or journal you want to purchase, payment is easy and accomplished within three mouse clicks. User registration is not necessary.

As the company's advertising says, you can indeed begin reading your chosen book on your computer screen within seconds—but only on your computer screen. Because, problems emerge when you try to download a book to your cell phone or electronic book reader. Duffy's has decided to provide its electronic books in the rare IPUB format only, which is compatible with just a few devices. Other setbacks of the site concern the limited selection of available titles, and the lack of user-generated content—it is not even possible to leave comments about the books on sale.

Questions on next page →

186. What is being publicized?

(A) An online store

(B) A delivery service

(C) A tourist destination

(D) A handheld device

187. What is implied about Duffy's?

(A) It hosts school events.

(B) It publishes educational books.

(C) It constructed a public library.

(D) It altered a delivery method.

188. What is a problem with Duffy's Online?

(A) It's unattractive.

(B) It's disorganized.

(C) It's difficult to download books.

(D) It's more expensive to order books.

189. What is mentioned in the review?

(A) Some phones are unreliable.

(B) Buying items is difficult.

(C) The launch was postponed.

(D) Products were left in the wrong categories.

190. In the review, the word "provide" in paragraph 3, is closest in meaning to

(A) remain

(B) purchase

(C) reserve

(D) supply

Questions 191–195 refer to the following letter and advertisement.

Dear Mr. Ferdinand,

Following up on my phone conversation with your assistant this morning, I am writing to you to point out some errors that I have noticed in the invoice you sent us dated October 16.

We submitted an order to you on October 15 for you to supply catering for a business breakfast for our Board of Directors at our offices on October 16. As usual, we were very pleased with the food provided, but when I saw the invoice I noticed that you had added an extra charge of 18%. I do not know why this charge has been added. Would you please explain?

As you know, we have been regular customers of yours for over five years now, which makes these extra charges all the more confusing.

I look forward to hearing from you soon.

Sincerely,
Sophia Hart

CORPORATE CATERING STRAIGHT TO YOUR OFFICE

For any business occasion, The Chefs can meet your catering needs. We offer: fresh fruits, pastries, and juices for morning meetings; light, buffet, or full selections for working lunches, including our award-winning burgers; complete, three-course dinner services for evening events. All our food is prepared daily and delivered to your office or venue direct from our kitchens. In a recent customer satisfaction survey, 98% of companies who rated our services commented that they were "very good to excellent."

To order, simply complete the three-step process below:

1. Choose your menu. Complete our online order form, notifying us of your choice of food and accompaniments, the number of people in your party, any special dietary requirements, etc.

2. Place your order. Orders must be submitted by 4:00 p.m. at least two days before the event to take advantage of standard menu prices. Orders submitted after this time may be possible and an 8% short notice fee will be applied.

3. Payment. New customers need to pay a 10% deposit. Returning customers will be sent an invoice when the order is delivered.

Questions on next page →

191. What is the purpose of Ms. Hart's letter?

(A) To raise an issue

(B) To qualify for a discount

(C) To request an item

(D) To return some food

192. According to the letter, what did Ms. Hart do before writing to Mr. Ferdinand?

(A) She had some food.

(B) She talked on the telephone.

(C) She sent a bill.

(D) She delivered an order.

193. What did Ms. Hart's company probably request?

(A) A three-course lunch

(B) A buffet dinner

(C) Bread and cereals

(D) Beverages and light snacks

194. What is implied about The Chefs?

(A) It caters only for morning breakfasts.

(B) It offers online ordering.

(C) It cooks food in customers' offices.

(D) Its customers are often dissatisfied with its services.

195. What will Mr. Ferdinand most likely give Ms. Hart?

(A) An 8% refund

(B) A 10% refund

(C) An 18% refund

(D) A 98% refund

Questions 196–200 refer to the following announcement and form.

Sweeney Books celebrates
10th anniversary of *Easy English Grammar*
at International Language Learning Conference

This year marks the 10th anniversary of the world's number one English grammar book, *Easy English Grammar* by Liz McEllis. To celebrate, Sweeney Books would like to offer a special 5% discount on all English language learning books purchased during the week of the International Language Learning Conference (February 1–4). In addition those customers belonging to academic institutions receive an extra 5% off! You can browse our extensive selection of books and download an order form on our website: www.sweeneybooks.com. Here are just a few of our popular discounted books:

Skills
962-85-1296—Wong, *Talk Like a Native*—$17.43
962-45-2548—Peters, *Power Listening*—$17.10

Grammar
962-54-4596—McEllis, *Easy English Grammar*—$19.10
962-48-2562—Simms, Sweeney *English Grammar for Beginners*—$16.43
962-78-1597—Martin, *Classroom Grammar for All*—$15.10

Teaching guides
962-84-7287—McEllis, *Let's Teach English*—$23.58
962-45-4598—Sonenberg, *How to Teach Multi-Level Classes*—$21.22

And remember, Liz McEllis will be signing copies of her book at the conference. To meet Liz and get a signed book, drop by the Sweeney Books stand between 2 and 3:30 p.m. on February 3.
Everyone is invited!

Sweeney Books Order Form

Please complete your order and details, then print the form and mail or fax it to Sweeney Books Orders Department.

Quantity	Product number
30	962-85-1296
1	962-84-7287
1	962-45-4598

Name: Rosie Thompson
Department/Faculty: English Language Institute
Company/University: Beyreuth University
Address: 19 Gustav Strabe
City: Berlin
ZIP/Postal Code: 85774
Telephone: (987) 555-2326
E-mail: rosie.thompson@uni-beyreuth.de

Questions on next page ➔

196. What is being announced?

(A) The launch of a website

(B) The publication of a new book

(C) Details of a conference

(D) Plans for a celebration

197. In the announcement, the word "browse" in paragraph 1, is closet in meaning to

(A) buy

(B) write

(C) view

(D) find

198. What is NOT indicated about Liz McEllis?

(A) She published a bestselling book.

(B) She knows how to teach.

(C) She studies at a university.

(D) She will attend an event.

199. What most likely will Ms. Thompson receive?

(A) An autograph

(B) A 5% discount

(C) An copy of a press release

(D) A textbook

200. What is the cost of the third product that Ms. Thompson ordered?

(A) $17.10

(B) $19.10

(C) $21.22

(D) $23.58

This is the end of the Reading Test.

Look at the next page to start the Speaking Test ➔

Test 2: Speaking

This speaking test includes 11 questions that evaluate your ability to speak English. This test will take approximately 20 minutes.

Questions 1–2: Read a text aloud

Directions: In this part of the test, you will read aloud the text on the page. You will have 45 seconds to prepare. Then you will have 45 seconds to read the text aloud.

> If you have been planning your dream vacation, there is no better place than Crystal Beach Resort on beautiful Jewel Island. At Ruby Sands Beach Resort, our convenient facilities, friendly staff, and wonderful location are sure to provide the best vacation of your life. We have 100 private villas along the beach, all of which are designed in an elegant contemporary style. This is a place where anything is possible, and your days will be filled with moments of magic!

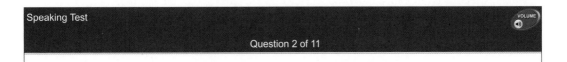

Questions 1–2: Read a text aloud

Directions: In this part of the test, you will read aloud the text on the page. You will have 45 seconds to prepare. Then you will have 45 seconds to read the text aloud.

> Hello, you have reached the Customer Service Department at Neo Industries Incorporated. Our customer service center is temporarily unavailable due to technical difficulties with our computer system. We are currently working on the problem, and we hope to have the system up and running again within the hour. If you're calling to find out about your order status, our new products, or any other information, please visit our website and click on the appropriate link. We apologize for any inconvenience, and thank you for calling Neo Industries Incorporated.

Go on to the next page ➜

Question 3: Describe a picture

Directions: You will describe a photograph as completely as you can. The photograph is in the test book. You will have 30 seconds to prepare what you will say, and then you will have 45 seconds to describe the picture in as much detail as possible.

Questions 4–6: Respond to questions

Directions: You will be asked three questions. After each question you will hear a beep. Begin speaking your answer immediately after the beep. You will not have any time to prepare your answer. For Questions 4 and 5 you will have 15 seconds to respond. For Question 6 you will have 30 seconds.

Imagine that a Canadian marketing firm is doing research in your country. You have agreed to participate in a telephone interview about going to the movies.

Question 4: How often do you go to the movies, and who do you go with?

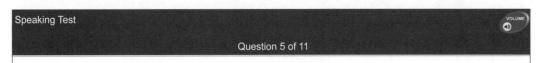

Questions 4–6: Respond to questions

Directions: You will be asked three questions. After each question you will hear a beep. Begin speaking your answer immediately after the beep. You will not have any time to prepare your answer. For Questions 4 and 5 you will have 15 seconds to respond. For Question 6 you will have 30 seconds.

––––––––––––––––––––––––––––

Imagine that a Canadian marketing firm is doing research in your country. You have agreed to participate in a telephone interview about going to the movies.

Question 5: What kind of food or snacks do you get when you go to the movies?

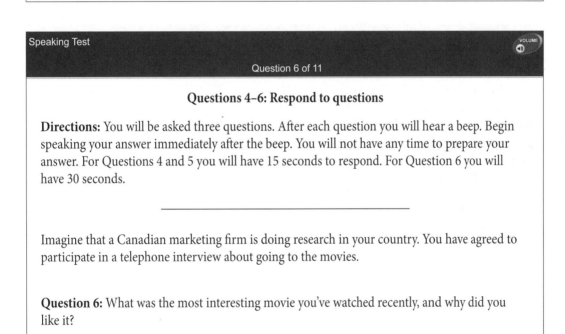

Questions 4–6: Respond to questions

Directions: You will be asked three questions. After each question you will hear a beep. Begin speaking your answer immediately after the beep. You will not have any time to prepare your answer. For Questions 4 and 5 you will have 15 seconds to respond. For Question 6 you will have 30 seconds.

––––––––––––––––––––––––––––

Imagine that a Canadian marketing firm is doing research in your country. You have agreed to participate in a telephone interview about going to the movies.

Question 6: What was the most interesting movie you've watched recently, and why did you like it?

Go on to the next page ➔

Questions 7–9: Respond to questions using information provided

Directions: You will read a short text and then answer three questions based on the information in the text. You will have 30 seconds to read the text before the first question. After each question you will hear a beep. Begin speaking immediately after the beep. You will not have any extra time to prepare your answer. For Questions 7 and 8 you will have 15 seconds to respond. For Question 9 you will have 30 seconds.

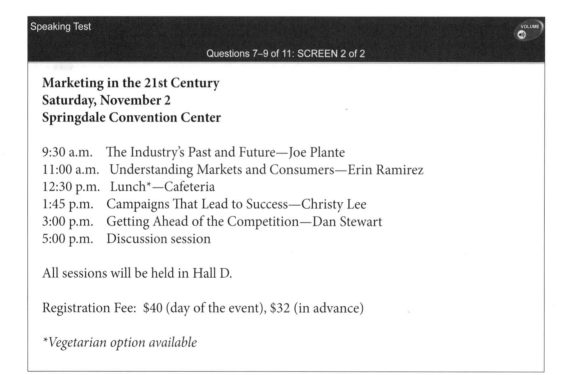

Marketing in the 21st Century
Saturday, November 2
Springdale Convention Center

9:30 a.m.   The Industry's Past and Future—Joe Plante
11:00 a.m.   Understanding Markets and Consumers—Erin Ramirez
12:30 p.m.   Lunch*—Cafeteria
1:45 p.m.   Campaigns That Lead to Success—Christy Lee
3:00 p.m.   Getting Ahead of the Competition—Dan Stewart
5:00 p.m.   Discussion session

All sessions will be held in Hall D.

Registration Fee: $40 (day of the event), $32 (in advance)

Vegetarian option available

25

Speaking Test

Question 10: Propose a solution

Directions: You will hear about a problem and be asked to propose a solution. You will have 30 seconds to prepare your solution, and then 60 seconds to speak.

Respond as if you work at the store.

In your response, make sure to

• show that you recognize the problem, and

• propose a way of dealing with the problem.

Now listen to the voice message.

26

Speaking Test

Question 11: Express an opinion

Directions: You will hear about a specific topic and then give your opinion about it. Make sure you say as much as you can about the topic in the time allowed. You will have 15 seconds to prepare, and then 60 seconds to speak.

This is the end of the Speaking Test.

Go on to the next page to start the Writing Test ➔

Test 2: Writing

This writing test includes 8 questions that evaluate your ability to write English. This test will take approximately 1 hour.

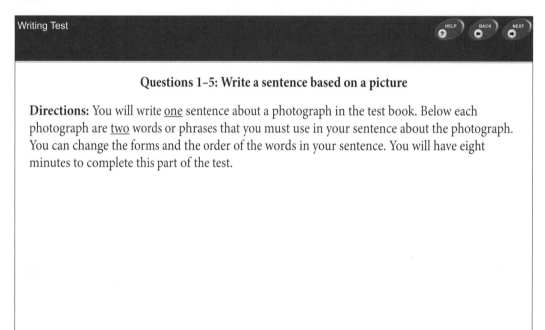

Questions 1–5: Write a sentence based on a picture

Directions: You will write one sentence about a photograph in the test book. Below each photograph are two words or phrases that you must use in your sentence about the photograph. You can change the forms and the order of the words in your sentence. You will have eight minutes to complete this part of the test.

interview, job

_____

Writing Test

crowd, street

_____

Writing Test

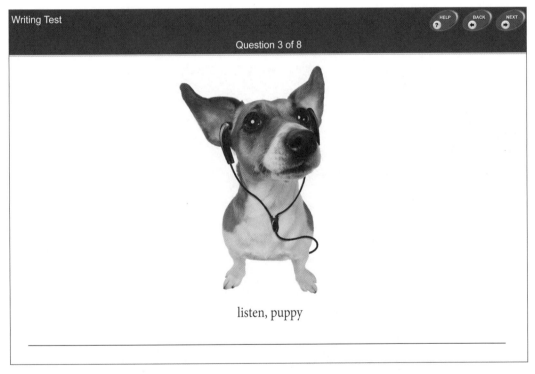

listen, puppy

_____

Go on to the next page →

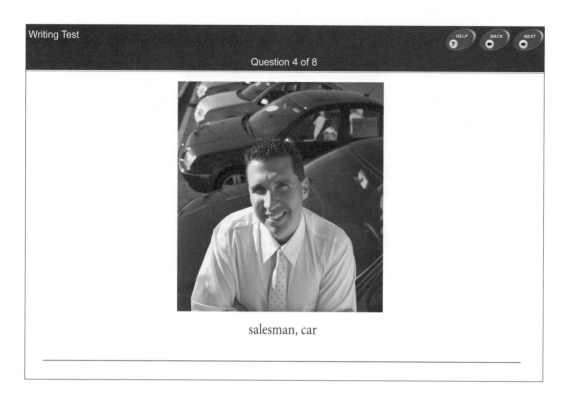

salesman, car

grass, bicycle

Questions 6–7: Respond to a written request

Directions: You will write responses to two e-mails. Your essay will be evaluated on

- sentence quality
- grammar
- vocabulary
- organization

You will have 10 minutes to read and respond to each e-mail.

Directions: Read the e-mail.

From:	Steve Lutz
To:	Sara Lee
Subject:	Class reunion parties
Sent:	April 4, 3:55 p.m.

Hi Sara!

It was great to hear from you after so long! The reunions are going to be amazing!

There are going to be two separate reunions, one on Friday the 25th of this month, that'll be for the first year students, and the second reunion will be the next day, Saturday the 26th. Both start at around 8 p.m. Since we were second year students, I guess you want to be on the list for the 26th? The first year students are inviting second year students (I don't think many first year students want to go, so they need more people), so you can go to both if you want.

Also, if you want to help us set up any or both of the reunions, let me know. They will begin setting up around 6 p.m., putting up decorations, preparing tables and chairs, etc. Oh, and don't forget to bring a dish for the buffet table, anything you like!

Let me know what you plan to do.

Yours excitedly,
Stevie

Directions: Write a reply to the e-mail. Write as if you are excited about the reunion and willing to help out with set up. Explain that you will attend the reunion on the 26th. Tell what dish you cook well and that you'll bring it to share.

Write your response here or on a computer.

_____

_____

_____

_____

_____

_____

_____

_____

Go on to the next page →

Directions: Read the e-mail.

From:	High Street Cleaners
To:	Customer Patty Sprague
Subject:	Order #75-98
Sent:	June 16, 2:34 p.m.

Dear Patty Sprague,

Thank you for your order, we will treat your articles with quality and care as always. We understand you need them dry cleaned by Tuesday, June 30, so could you please let us know the following information:

How many articles do you have to be dry cleaned?

Will you be dropping them off at our center or do you want us to pick them up?

If you want to use our express pick-up service, what time on Tuesday best suits you? Please remember that there is an additional charge of $3.50 for this service.

We look forward to hearing from you. Please don't forget to quote your order number above.

Sincerely,

Toby Le Rone, Manager

Directions: Write a reply e-mail. Write as if you are the customer. Describe the items you want to have cleaned, when they can be picked up at your home, and ask about a drop-off service after the clothes are cleaned.

Write your response here or on a computer.

_____

_____

_____

_____

_____

_____

_____

_____

_____

_____

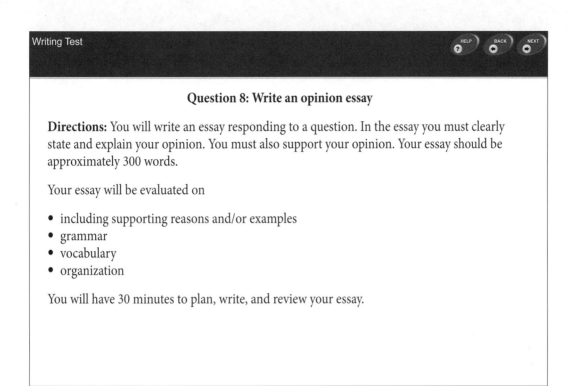

Question 8: Write an opinion essay

Directions: You will write an essay responding to a question. In the essay you must clearly state and explain your opinion. You must also support your opinion. Your essay should be approximately 300 words.

Your essay will be evaluated on

- including supporting reasons and/or examples
- grammar
- vocabulary
- organization

You will have 30 minutes to plan, write, and review your essay.

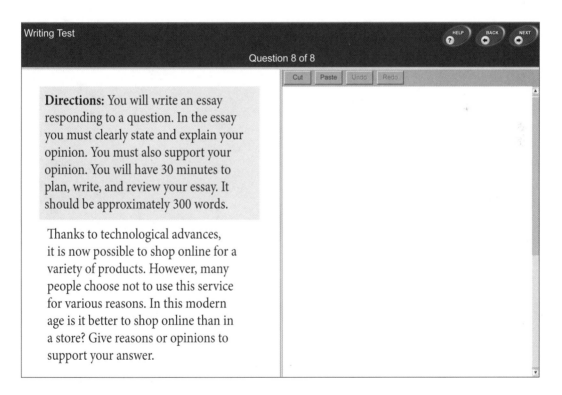

Cut | Paste | Undo | Redo

Directions: You will write an essay responding to a question. In the essay you must clearly state and explain your opinion. You must also support your opinion. You will have 30 minutes to plan, write, and review your essay. It should be approximately 300 words.

Thanks to technological advances, it is now possible to shop online for a variety of products. However, many people choose not to use this service for various reasons. In this modern age is it better to shop online than in a store? Give reasons or opinions to support your answer.

Write your essay on a separate piece of paper or on a computer.

This is the end of Test 2.

TOEIC® TEST 3

Listening Answer Sheet

1. (A) (B) (C) (D)   26. (A) (B) (C)   51. (A) (B) (C) (D)   76. (A) (B) (C) (D)
2. (A) (B) (C) (D)   27. (A) (B) (C)   52. (A) (B) (C) (D)   77. (A) (B) (C) (D)
3. (A) (B) (C) (D)   28. (A) (B) (C)   53. (A) (B) (C) (D)   78. (A) (B) (C) (D)
4. (A) (B) (C) (D)   29. (A) (B) (C)   54. (A) (B) (C) (D)   79. (A) (B) (C) (D)
5. (A) (B) (C) (D)   30. (A) (B) (C)   55. (A) (B) (C) (D)   80. (A) (B) (C) (D)

6. (A) (B) (C) (D)   31. (A) (B) (C)   56. (A) (B) (C) (D)   81. (A) (B) (C) (D)
7. (A) (B) (C) (D)   32. (A) (B) (C)   57. (A) (B) (C) (D)   82. (A) (B) (C) (D)
8. (A) (B) (C) (D)   33. (A) (B) (C)   58. (A) (B) (C) (D)   83. (A) (B) (C) (D)
9. (A) (B) (C) (D)   34. (A) (B) (C)   59. (A) (B) (C) (D)   84. (A) (B) (C) (D)
10. (A) (B) (C) (D)   35. (A) (B) (C)   60. (A) (B) (C) (D)   85. (A) (B) (C) (D)

11. (A) (B) (C)   36. (A) (B) (C)   61. (A) (B) (C) (D)   86. (A) (B) (C) (D)
12. (A) (B) (C)   37. (A) (B) (C)   62. (A) (B) (C) (D)   87. (A) (B) (C) (D)
13. (A) (B) (C)   38. (A) (B) (C)   63. (A) (B) (C) (D)   88. (A) (B) (C) (D)
14. (A) (B) (C)   39. (A) (B) (C)   64. (A) (B) (C) (D)   89. (A) (B) (C) (D)
15. (A) (B) (C)   40. (A) (B) (C)   65. (A) (B) (C) (D)   90. (A) (B) (C) (D)

16. (A) (B) (C)   41. (A) (B) (C) (D)   66. (A) (B) (C) (D)   91. (A) (B) (C) (D)
17. (A) (B) (C)   42. (A) (B) (C) (D)   67. (A) (B) (C) (D)   92. (A) (B) (C) (D)
18. (A) (B) (C)   43. (A) (B) (C) (D)   68. (A) (B) (C) (D)   93. (A) (B) (C) (D)
19. (A) (B) (C)   44. (A) (B) (C) (D)   69. (A) (B) (C) (D)   94. (A) (B) (C) (D)
20. (A) (B) (C)   45. (A) (B) (C) (D)   70. (A) (B) (C) (D)   95. (A) (B) (C) (D)

21. (A) (B) (C)   46. (A) (B) (C) (D)   71. (A) (B) (C) (D)   96. (A) (B) (C) (D)
22. (A) (B) (C)   47. (A) (B) (C) (D)   72. (A) (B) (C) (D)   97. (A) (B) (C) (D)
23. (A) (B) (C)   48. (A) (B) (C) (D)   73. (A) (B) (C) (D)   98. (A) (B) (C) (D)
24. (A) (B) (C)   49. (A) (B) (C) (D)   74. (A) (B) (C) (D)   99. (A) (B) (C) (D)
25. (A) (B) (C)   50. (A) (B) (C) (D)   75. (A) (B) (C) (D)   100. (A) (B) (C) (D)

Reading Answer Sheet

101. Ⓐ Ⓑ Ⓒ Ⓓ	126. Ⓐ Ⓑ Ⓒ Ⓓ	151. Ⓐ Ⓑ Ⓒ Ⓓ	176. Ⓐ Ⓑ Ⓒ Ⓓ
102. Ⓐ Ⓑ Ⓒ Ⓓ	127. Ⓐ Ⓑ Ⓒ Ⓓ	152. Ⓐ Ⓑ Ⓒ Ⓓ	177. Ⓐ Ⓑ Ⓒ Ⓓ
103. Ⓐ Ⓑ Ⓒ Ⓓ	128. Ⓐ Ⓑ Ⓒ Ⓓ	153. Ⓐ Ⓑ Ⓒ Ⓓ	178. Ⓐ Ⓑ Ⓒ Ⓓ
104. Ⓐ Ⓑ Ⓒ Ⓓ	129. Ⓐ Ⓑ Ⓒ Ⓓ	154. Ⓐ Ⓑ Ⓒ Ⓓ	179. Ⓐ Ⓑ Ⓒ Ⓓ
105. Ⓐ Ⓑ Ⓒ Ⓓ	130. Ⓐ Ⓑ Ⓒ Ⓓ	155. Ⓐ Ⓑ Ⓒ Ⓓ	180. Ⓐ Ⓑ Ⓒ Ⓓ
106. Ⓐ Ⓑ Ⓒ Ⓓ	131. Ⓐ Ⓑ Ⓒ Ⓓ	156. Ⓐ Ⓑ Ⓒ Ⓓ	181. Ⓐ Ⓑ Ⓒ Ⓓ
107. Ⓐ Ⓑ Ⓒ Ⓓ	132. Ⓐ Ⓑ Ⓒ Ⓓ	157. Ⓐ Ⓑ Ⓒ Ⓓ	182. Ⓐ Ⓑ Ⓒ Ⓓ
108. Ⓐ Ⓑ Ⓒ Ⓓ	133. Ⓐ Ⓑ Ⓒ Ⓓ	158. Ⓐ Ⓑ Ⓒ Ⓓ	183. Ⓐ Ⓑ Ⓒ Ⓓ
109. Ⓐ Ⓑ Ⓒ Ⓓ	134. Ⓐ Ⓑ Ⓒ Ⓓ	159. Ⓐ Ⓑ Ⓒ Ⓓ	184. Ⓐ Ⓑ Ⓒ Ⓓ
110. Ⓐ Ⓑ Ⓒ Ⓓ	135. Ⓐ Ⓑ Ⓒ Ⓓ	160. Ⓐ Ⓑ Ⓒ Ⓓ	185. Ⓐ Ⓑ Ⓒ Ⓓ
111. Ⓐ Ⓑ Ⓒ Ⓓ	136. Ⓐ Ⓑ Ⓒ Ⓓ	161. Ⓐ Ⓑ Ⓒ Ⓓ	186. Ⓐ Ⓑ Ⓒ Ⓓ
112. Ⓐ Ⓑ Ⓒ Ⓓ	137. Ⓐ Ⓑ Ⓒ Ⓓ	162. Ⓐ Ⓑ Ⓒ Ⓓ	187. Ⓐ Ⓑ Ⓒ Ⓓ
113. Ⓐ Ⓑ Ⓒ Ⓓ	138. Ⓐ Ⓑ Ⓒ Ⓓ	163. Ⓐ Ⓑ Ⓒ Ⓓ	188. Ⓐ Ⓑ Ⓒ Ⓓ
114. Ⓐ Ⓑ Ⓒ Ⓓ	139. Ⓐ Ⓑ Ⓒ Ⓓ	164. Ⓐ Ⓑ Ⓒ Ⓓ	189. Ⓐ Ⓑ Ⓒ Ⓓ
115. Ⓐ Ⓑ Ⓒ Ⓓ	140. Ⓐ Ⓑ Ⓒ Ⓓ	165. Ⓐ Ⓑ Ⓒ Ⓓ	190. Ⓐ Ⓑ Ⓒ Ⓓ
116. Ⓐ Ⓑ Ⓒ Ⓓ	141. Ⓐ Ⓑ Ⓒ Ⓓ	166. Ⓐ Ⓑ Ⓒ Ⓓ	191. Ⓐ Ⓑ Ⓒ Ⓓ
117. Ⓐ Ⓑ Ⓒ Ⓓ	142. Ⓐ Ⓑ Ⓒ Ⓓ	167. Ⓐ Ⓑ Ⓒ Ⓓ	192. Ⓐ Ⓑ Ⓒ Ⓓ
118. Ⓐ Ⓑ Ⓒ Ⓓ	143. Ⓐ Ⓑ Ⓒ Ⓓ	168. Ⓐ Ⓑ Ⓒ Ⓓ	193. Ⓐ Ⓑ Ⓒ Ⓓ
119. Ⓐ Ⓑ Ⓒ Ⓓ	144. Ⓐ Ⓑ Ⓒ Ⓓ	169. Ⓐ Ⓑ Ⓒ Ⓓ	194. Ⓐ Ⓑ Ⓒ Ⓓ
120. Ⓐ Ⓑ Ⓒ Ⓓ	145. Ⓐ Ⓑ Ⓒ Ⓓ	170. Ⓐ Ⓑ Ⓒ Ⓓ	195. Ⓐ Ⓑ Ⓒ Ⓓ
121. Ⓐ Ⓑ Ⓒ Ⓓ	146. Ⓐ Ⓑ Ⓒ Ⓓ	171. Ⓐ Ⓑ Ⓒ Ⓓ	196. Ⓐ Ⓑ Ⓒ Ⓓ
122. Ⓐ Ⓑ Ⓒ Ⓓ	147. Ⓐ Ⓑ Ⓒ Ⓓ	172. Ⓐ Ⓑ Ⓒ Ⓓ	197. Ⓐ Ⓑ Ⓒ Ⓓ
123. Ⓐ Ⓑ Ⓒ Ⓓ	148. Ⓐ Ⓑ Ⓒ Ⓓ	173. Ⓐ Ⓑ Ⓒ Ⓓ	198. Ⓐ Ⓑ Ⓒ Ⓓ
124. Ⓐ Ⓑ Ⓒ Ⓓ	149. Ⓐ Ⓑ Ⓒ Ⓓ	174. Ⓐ Ⓑ Ⓒ Ⓓ	199. Ⓐ Ⓑ Ⓒ Ⓓ
125. Ⓐ Ⓑ Ⓒ Ⓓ	150. Ⓐ Ⓑ Ⓒ Ⓓ	175. Ⓐ Ⓑ Ⓒ Ⓓ	200. Ⓐ Ⓑ Ⓒ Ⓓ

Test 3: Listening

The Listening section evaluates how well you understand spoken English. The Listening test has four sections and will take approximately 45 minutes. You <u>must</u> mark your answers on the answer sheet not in the test book.

🎧 PART 1: PHOTOGRAPHS

27

Directions: For each item in Part 1, you will hear four statements about a photograph in the test book. You must listen carefully to the statements in order to select the statement that best describes the photograph. Mark the corresponding letter (A), (B), (C), or (D) on the answer sheet.

Example

Listen to the statements and select the one that best describes the picture.

(A) They're drinking orange juice.
(B) They're turning on a computer.
(C) They're looking at a screen.
(D) They're putting on formal clothes.

Statement **(C), "They're looking at a screen."** best describes the picture, so you should choose answer (C) and mark it on your answer sheet.

Sample Answer

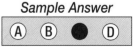

Go on to the next page ➜

🎧
28

1.

2.

3.

4.

Go on to the next page ➜

5.

6.

7.

8.

Go on to the next page ➔

9.

10.

This is the end of Part 1.

Look at the next page to start Part 2 ➔

PART 2: QUESTION–RESPONSE

29

Directions: For each item in Part 2, you will hear a statement or a question followed by three responses. Listen and choose the best response. Then mark the corresponding letter (A), (B), or (C) on the answer sheet.

Example

Have you met the new Managing Director?

(A) Actually I talked with him in the lobby just now.
(B) Yes, I took the call.
(C) No, he takes the subway to work.

The best response to the question "Have you met the new Managing Director?" is answer choice **(A), "Actually I talked with him in the lobby just now."** You should mark answer (A) on your answer sheet.

Sample Answer

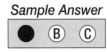

30

11. Listen and choose the best response.

12. Listen and choose the best response.

13. Listen and choose the best response.

14. Listen and choose the best response.

15. Listen and choose the best response.

16. Listen and choose the best response.

17. Listen and choose the best response.

18. Listen and choose the best response.

19. Listen and choose the best response.

20. Listen and choose the best response.

21. Listen and choose the best response.

22. Listen and choose the best response.

23. Listen and choose the best response.

24. Listen and choose the best response.

25. Listen and choose the best response.

26. Listen and choose the best response.

27. Listen and choose the best response.

28. Listen and choose the best response.

29. Listen and choose the best response.

30. Listen and choose the best response.

31. Listen and choose the best response.

32. Listen and choose the best response.

33. Listen and choose the best response.

34. Listen and choose the best response.

35. Listen and choose the best response.

36. Listen and choose the best response.

37. Listen and choose the best response.

38. Listen and choose the best response.

39. Listen and choose the best response.

40. Listen and choose the best response.

This is the end of Part 2.

Go on to the next page to start Part 3 ➔

🎧 PART 3: CONVERSATIONS
31

> **Directions:** You will hear conversations with two speakers. Then you will answer three questions about each conversation. Listen and select the best response to each question. Mark the corresponding letter (A), (B), (C), or (D) on the answer sheet.

41. What is the purpose of the call?

   (A) To arrange a business lunch
   (B) To inquire about a special offer
   (C) To reserve a room
   (D) To organize a conference

42. What does the woman offer the man?

   (A) A free dinner buffet
   (B) A taxi service
   (C) A conference package
   (D) A discount on a gym

43. What does the man ask about?

   (A) Check-in time
   (B) A place to work out outdoors
   (C) Suitcase storage
   (D) A restaurant menu

44. Where does the conversation most likely take place?

   (A) On a street
   (B) In an office
   (C) At the City Council
   (D) At a theater

45. How does the woman assist the man?

   (A) By giving him a telephone number
   (B) By rescheduling an appointment
   (C) By calling a taxi for him
   (D) By telling him directions

46. What is the man worried about?

   (A) Finding a theater
   (B) Losing his business cards
   (C) Being late for a meeting
   (D) Missing a bus

47. What is going on in the meeting room?

   (A) Some products are being repaired.
   (B) A meeting is being interrupted.
   (C) Lunch is being delivered.
   (D) Some items are being replaced.

48. What does the woman think about the old furniture?

   (A) It is not good enough to use.
   (B) It is broken.
   (C) It is not bad.
   (D) It should be fixed.

49. What does the man hope the new furniture will be like?

   (A) Bigger.
   (B) More stylish.
   (C) More long-lasting.
   (D) More comfortable.

50. What is the dialog mainly about?

   (A) Changing opening hours
   (B) Rebuilding an employee cafeteria
   (C) Choosing a food supplier
   (D) Doing a questionnaire about food

51. What was the woman doing on Tuesday?

   (A) Visiting a customer
   (B) Attending meetings
   (C) Distributing reports
   (D) Cooking some food

52. What advantage does the woman mention about Easygo Food Services?

   (A) It is located in the city.
   (B) Its food is cheap.
   (C) It offers a limited menu.
   (D) It provides a quick delivery service.

53. What is the woman's problem?

   (A) Her working hours are too short.
   (B) Her computer is not working.
   (C) Her password has been lost.
   (D) Her timesheet has been deleted.

54. How long ago did the woman probably get to the office?

   (A) 10 minutes ago
   (B) 20 minutes ago
   (C) 30 minutes ago
   (D) Two hours ago

55. What does the man recommend?

   (A) Calling a delivery worker
   (B) Changing a username
   (C) Resubmitting a report
   (D) Talking to a supervisor

56. Why is the order late?

   (A) Some parts were out of stock.
   (B) Some fees had not been paid.
   (C) The order was canceled.
   (D) It was shipped to the wrong location.

57. What will the supplier give?

   (A) Two free parts
   (B) A discount
   (C) More time to fix the parts
   (D) Free delivery

58. According to the woman, what will probably happen?

   (A) An item will be returned.
   (B) Alternative parts will be used.
   (C) Another order will be placed.
   (D) Repairs will be completed.

59. What was recently received?

   (A) A computer
   (B) A projector
   (C) A printer
   (D) A copier

60. Why does the man need to hurry?

   (A) He needs to check some equipment.
   (B) The e-mail system is malfunctioning.
   (C) The woman needs some of his materials.
   (D) He is late for an appointment.

61. What does the woman advise the man to do?

   (A) Check a computer
   (B) Install some software
   (C) Buy a new printer
   (D) E-mail some files to her

62. What does the woman ask the man to do?

   (A) Decrease the testing of a product
   (B) Review some sales figures
   (C) Offer her some ideas
   (D) Celebrate the launch of a new item

63. What was wrong with the product?

   (A) It was too big.
   (B) It did not appeal to women.
   (C) Customers did not like its price.
   (D) People felt its scent was too strong.

64. What does the man offer to do?

   (A) Create a new product
   (B) Revise a proposal
   (C) Purchase a projector
   (D) Share some data

Go on to the next page ➜

65. What is the topic of the conversation?

    (A) An essay
    (B) An anniversary party
    (C) A charity event
    (D) A restaurant opening

66. What is the man concerned about?

    (A) Overcrowding
    (B) Research costs
    (C) Accommodation
    (D) Customer response

67. What will the speakers most likely do next?

    (A) Reschedule a team event
    (B) Book a larger room
    (C) Prepare a list
    (D) Start some research

68. Why is the man calling the woman?

    (A) To advertise a new center
    (B) To ask for some opinions
    (C) To talk about a sports game
    (D) To postpone an event

69. What does the woman like about the community center?

    (A) It offers various programs.
    (B) It has a program for winter sports.
    (C) It has a nice receptionist.
    (D) Its programs are adequately priced.

70. What does the woman suggest?

    (A) Offering a new service
    (B) Renewing some old facilities
    (C) Extending opening hours
    (D) Decreasing prices

This is the end of Part 3.

Look at the next page to start Part 4 →

PART 4: TALKS

> **Directions:** You will hear several talks, each with one speaker. Then you will answer three questions about the talk. Listen and select the best response to each question. Mark the corresponding letter (A), (B), (C), or (D) on the answer sheet.

71. What is the topic of the message?

   (A) Neighborhood concerns
   (B) Garden landscaping
   (C) Garage sales
   (D) Work satisfaction

72. Why does the speaker talk about her neighbor?

   (A) He removed some trees.
   (B) He made a painting.
   (C) He created a patio.
   (D) He recommended the company.

73. What does the woman ask the listener to do?

   (A) Give her a price
   (B) Buy her a painting
   (C) Come to her neighbor's property
   (D) Evaluate the quality of her work

74. What is being advertised?

   (A) An event
   (B) Exhibitors
   (C) A change of location
   (D) Fair organizers

75. How does the speaker describe the career advisors?

   (A) They move across the region.
   (B) They are volunteers.
   (C) They live in the city.
   (D) They are renowned.

76. When are the listeners asked to visit the fair?

   (A) On Thursday
   (B) On Friday
   (C) On Saturday
   (D) On Sunday

77. What is the purpose of the message?

   (A) To schedule vehicle repair
   (B) To transfer a worker
   (C) To post a job advertisement
   (D) To schedule a visit

78. What time can the man leave his office?

   (A) At 4:30
   (B) At 5:00
   (C) At 6:00
   (D) At 7:00

79. Why does the man want the woman to call him back?

   (A) To get an address
   (B) To make a payment
   (C) To arrange an appointment
   (D) To decide on a meeting venue

80. Who is the man talking to?

   (A) High school students
   (B) Accounting department employees
   (C) Catering workers
   (D) Parking lot guards

81. Where is the group probably going to meet before the training course?

   (A) At a subway station
   (B) At a sports stadium
   (C) In a lobby
   (D) In a parking lot

82. According to the speaker, what is the best way to get to the training venue?

   (A) On foot
   (B) By bus
   (C) By subway
   (D) By taxi

83. Who most likely is the speaker?

(A) A screenwriter

(B) A book critic

(C) An author

(D) A musician

84. What kind of novel is *Into the Forest*?

(A) Tragedy

(B) Romance

(C) Horror

(D) Comedy

85. What does the speaker encourage fans of Oyama to do?

(A) Get a signed copy of a book

(B) Wait for another year

(C) Go to a movie theater

(D) Return a product

86. What is the topic of Rebecca Lung's lecture?

(A) Marketing

(B) Publishing

(C) Fashion

(D) Eye problems

87. What did Rebecca Lung do recently?

(A) She wrote a book.

(B) She moved jobs.

(C) She designed luxury items.

(D) She worked in publishing.

88. What does the speaker encourage the listeners to do after the talk?

(A) Go on a vacation

(B) Buy a book

(C) Listen to a presentation

(D) Invite a guest

89. Where is the announcement taking place?

(A) At a company celebration

(B) At the opening of a craft center

(C) At a movie theater

(D) At a sports field

90. What has been altered?

(A) The time of a party

(B) The weather forecast

(C) The entertainment program

(D) The location of a sale

91. What is the reason for the change?

(A) Bad weather is due to start.

(B) All tickets are sold.

(C) Programs were printed with errors.

(D) Procedures were not implemented.

92. Who most likely are the listeners?

(A) Staff at a sports center

(B) Employees of an advertising company

(C) Managers at an accounting firm

(D) Workers at an automobile repair store

93. What does Smart Cars wish to do?

(A) Appeal to different customers

(B) Invent new products

(C) Become more conventional

(D) Share production equipment

94. What does the speaker want the listeners to do?

(A) Hold meetings

(B) Work longer hours

(C) Stand up

(D) Develop ideas

95. Why did the speaker leave the message?

(A) To ask about food for takeout

(B) To make payment for a service

(C) To provide feedback on an inspection

(D) To give information about a process

96. What will a license allow Mr. Franklin to do?

(A) Manage a restaurant

(B) Open a shop

(C) Close a business

(D) Inspect a product

97. What does the speaker mention about licenses?

(A) They can be bought with a grant.

(B) They must be checked every year.

(C) They are not permanent.

(D) They are granted free of charge.

98. What is the purpose of the talk?

(A) To introduce local artists

(B) To present a tour schedule

(C) To arrange a visit

(D) To talk about a town's history

99. According to the speaker, what can be found in the Old Town?

(A) Art museums

(B) Historic buildings

(C) Well-known stores

(D) A seafront

100. What will happen in the afternoon?

(A) A late lunch at an art museum

(B) A visit to the seafront

(C) A boat tour

(D) An art sale

This is the end of Part 4.

Go on to the next page to start Part 5 ➜

Test 3: Reading

The Reading section evaluates how well you understand written English. The Reading test has three sections and will take approximately 75 minutes. You must mark your answers on the answer sheet not in the test book.

PART 5: INCOMPLETE SENTENCES

Directions: One or more words is missing from each of the following sentences. Choose the best answer choice to complete the sentence. Mark the corresponding letter (A), (B), (C), or (D) on the answer sheet.

101. It is taking the bank _____ longer than predicted to offload its property assets in North America.

    (A) consider
    (B) consideration
    (C) considerable
    (D) considerably

102. Managers _____ team members do not meet the required standards must tackle the issue and not simply deny its existence.

    (A) who
    (B) which
    (C) whose
    (D) that

103. The company decided to create _____ own microchips instead of continuing to have them created by overseas suppliers.

    (A) themselves
    (B) them
    (C) their
    (D) they're

104. All invoices should go to accounts by the 25th _____ reimbursement can be made in the next month's pay run.

    (A) however so
    (B) so as to
    (C) so much so
    (D) so that

105. I have composed three letters of complaint to the Customer Service Department, but I never receive any _____.

    (A) reply
    (B) replying
    (C) replied
    (D) replication

106. _____ the resignation last year of our marketing director, our marketing strategy has struggled with a lack of direction of late.

    (A) In spite of
    (B) Because of
    (C) Instead of
    (D) Nevertheless

107. _____ recent developments, we will not be hiring a new head of Human Resources.

    (A) So much so
    (B) Nonetheless
    (C) In addition to
    (D) In light of

108. The company is thinking of creating private parking spaces for executives, as there are often no _____ spots in the parking lot.

    (A) empty
    (B) emptiness
    (C) emptily
    (D) emptier

109. We could enhance our _____ if we clarified who does what in each department, thereby preventing situations where the same task is done twice by two different people.

(A) carefulness

(B) efficiency

(C) accountability

(D) decision

110. While we have accomplished considerable sales tractions in the east of the country, we have not been as successful _____ the west.

(A) at

(B) into

(C) in

(D) than

111. Staff are required _____ helmets at all times within the warehouse and surrounding facilities.

(A) putting on

(B) to put on

(C) put on

(D) to have put on

112. I sat in the meeting room for _____ 30 minutes, but no one attended the meeting.

(A) despite

(B) more than

(C) not only

(D) so that

113. The advantage of our product as opposed to the competition's products is that it is less _____ to use.

(A) complexity

(B) complication

(C) complex

(D) as complex

114. Staff working late may have dinner _____ they like, as long as the cost does not go beyond the permitted amount.

(A) whatever

(B) wherever

(C) anyway

(D) regardless

115. Our specialized gardening soil guarantees that all water held in the soil is made _____ available to plants.

(A) ready

(B) readied

(C) readily

(D) readiness

116. Please reply to the invitation, _____ or not you can come.

(A) whether

(B) either

(C) in total

(D) until

117. As _____ before, we do not aim to revisit issues that we have already covered in previous meetings.

(A) discuss

(B) discussing

(C) discussed

(D) discussion

118. The firm is achieving a budget _____, but the Board of Trustees is still expecting a tough year.

(A) renewal

(B) facility

(C) surplus

(D) prize

Go on to the next page ➔

119. We should consider providing _____ benefits to employees aside from salary in order to boost morale.

    (A) reassured
    (B) additional
    (C) desired
    (D) approved

120. We are upgrading a number of _____ facilities for our staff to use in their free time.

    (A) renovated
    (B) important
    (C) entertainer
    (D) recreational

121. The new president has _____ to complete the work begun by the former CEO.

    (A) done
    (B) succeeded
    (C) reunited
    (D) attempted

122. The company _____ launched an updated version of its flagship Smartphone operating system.

    (A) recent
    (B) recently
    (C) recentness
    (D) most recent

123. The Annual General Meeting _____ Shareholders is taking place next week in the events hall on the 18th floor.

    (A) at
    (B) of
    (C) from
    (D) into

124. Mr. Gambetta is _____ with checking that all windows are closed and locked at the end of the working day.

    (A) required
    (B) tasked
    (C) allowed
    (D) forced

125. Our product range is wider _____ our competitors'.

    (A) at
    (B) than
    (C) of
    (D) with

126. We are one of the world's biggest _____ of professional services.

    (A) supplies
    (B) supply
    (C) supplied
    (D) suppliers

127. Any occurrences _____ to employee discipline should be reported directly to your department's contact in Human Resources.

    (A) causing
    (B) pertaining
    (C) counting
    (D) rising

128. Our logistics costs have _____ due to fuel price rises.

    (A) increased
    (B) stayed
    (C) contented
    (D) consumed

129. The government is _____ monitoring global financial markets amid the current crisis.

    (A) about
    (B) nearly
    (C) closely
    (D) narrowly

130. Customers are increasingly wanting to decrease the _____ of calories they consume each day.

    (A) assortment
    (B) amount
    (C) summary
    (D) demand

131. Passengers with special dietary requirements must communicate their meal _____ online before traveling.

    (A) prefers
    (B) preferences
    (C) preferential
    (D) preferred

132. The payment was not issued because the _____ was missing from the invoice.

    (A) title
    (B) cancellation
    (C) accompaniment
    (D) signature

133. I wish to thank Ms. Kim for the excellent _____ she gave our team when we began our new project last month.

    (A) supporter
    (B) supported
    (C) supporting
    (D) support

134. The Human Resources officer saw the department managers to talk about the _____ criteria for candidates ahead of the graduate interviews.

    (A) selection
    (B) reference
    (C) writing
    (D) recruit

135. Resourcing for the project has been scaled up, with both Mr. Morrill _____ Ms. Webb being made responsible for working on it.

    (A) either
    (B) or
    (C) neither
    (D) and

136. Let me know _____ you have completed the report, as I want to take a look at it before it's circulated.

    (A) as long as
    (B) as soon as
    (C) as well as
    (D) as far as

137. New recruits are advised to read the company induction manual _____ and to follow up on anything that they find unclear with their managers.

    (A) helpfully
    (B) carefully
    (C) excessively
    (D) badly

138. The Human Resources Department is now receiving _____ from managers for staff promotions.

    (A) proposals
    (B) information
    (C) sources
    (D) approvals

139. Sadly, many current members of staff have neither the _____ nor the aptitude necessary to perform well in their roles.

    (A) qualify
    (B) qualified
    (C) qualifiers
    (D) qualifications

140. We are reducing the price of our household products by 20% for a _____ period in order to observe the impact of lower pricing.

    (A) shorter
    (B) shortage
    (C) shorten
    (D) short

Go on to the next page ➜

PART 6: TEXT COMPLETION

> **Directions:** The following texts have sentences with some words and phrases missing. Read the answer choices given to complete the sentences. Choose the best answer choice to complete the sentence. Mark the corresponding letter (A), (B), (C), or (D) on the answer sheet.

Questions 141–143 refer to the following e-mail.

From: stacey.tan@interiorarts.net
To: sonia@mailme.us
Date: Friday, July 9 11:05 a.m.
Subject: Renovation plan

Dear Sonia,

It was very nice to meet you yesterday. I am now pleased to _____

      141. (A) sent
          (B) send
          (C) sending
          (D) to send

you my plan for your house renovation.

As you requested, I have tried to include both old and new elements in the design, achieving, I hope, a contemporary yet also traditional feel. I have also attempted to make _____ use of space, producing multi-purpose areas that can

      142. (A) versatile
          (B) different
          (C) stylish
          (D) particular

be used for a variety of functions.

Along with the design, I have _____ attached a listing of suppliers

      143. (A) however
          (B) yet
          (C) often
          (D) also

from which you can select the required materials and furnishings.

Please give me a call at 555-3821 if you have any suggestions or questions about the design. Otherwise, please confirm your acceptance of the design, and I can then start scheduling the renovation project with you.

Best regards,
Stacey

Stacey Tan
Head Designer
Interior Arts

Questions 144–146 refer to the following letter.

Dear Mr. Jones,

I am writing in response to your job advertisement in *The Tribune* for a sales manager at Newton Sugar. I believe that I have the necessary _____ and experience to excel as a sales manager

144. (A) skillfully
(B) skilled
(C) skillful
(D) skills

at your company.

I have worked for three years in a similar role at Unique Sugar, where my chief area of responsibility has been supermarket accounts. At Unique Sugar, I have gained an extensive network of trade contacts, which would undoubtedly be of use were I to work at Newton Sugar. _____ to my direct

145. (A) In addition
(B) According
(C) Following
(D) In contract

involvement in managing client relationships, I have also developed leadership skills as manager of the Business Sales Team for the last two years. This role has included people management, as well as strategy and financial planning.

My _____ in working at Newton Sugar is also motivated

146. (A) enthusiasm
(B) interest
(C) development
(D) neutrality

by my desire to transfer to the Newton area in order to be close to my family.

I attach my résumé for your reference. Please do contact me should you require any further details.

Kind regards,
Larry Barnes
Enc.

Go on to the next page →

Questions 147–149 refer to the following information.

Economy class travelers on Victoria Airways will _____ be

147. (A) soon
(B) the other day
(C) gradually
(D) recently

provided complimentary cosmetic treatments on selected routes.

The Beauty Service, already available to first and business class travelers, will be extended to economy class passengers beginning in November. Beauty Service provides a series of treatments, _____ are conducted by

148. (A) where
(B) which
(C) what
(D) who

specially trained members of the flight crew.

We offer face and head massage, manicure, face masks, and other skin treatments. Beauty Service treatment _____ are

149. (A) shows
(B) briefings
(C) sessions
(D) classes

approximately ten minutes long, and are performed in a specially designed section of the aircraft. The Victoria Airlines Beauty Service guarantees that you arrive at your destination refreshed, relaxed, and ready to go!

Questions 150–152 refer to the following letter.

MANSFIELD STREET AUTOS

Mansfield St., Honolulu

Robert Garcia
Ala Wai Avenue
Honolulu
January 14

Dear Mr. Garcia,

As you may know, Mansfield Street Autos this year _____ its

150. (A) celebrates
(B) names
(C) calls
(D) launches

15th anniversary. To mark these 15 years of providing excellent value and service to our customers throughout Honolulu and beyond, we are organizing a number of events and special deals.

To thank you for your loyal support, we invite you to join us at our Mansfield Street showroom on February 17 for a special Customer Appreciation Day—an afternoon of driving-inspired fun, beginning at 3 o'clock. Curious about the new Primus 8 sport utility vehicle? You are welcome to test drive it _____ on February 17!

151. (A) your
(B) your
(C) yourself
(D) yourselves

We will offer five advance release vehicles ready for customers to drive.

The Customer Appreciation Day will also feature a speech by the mayor, noting the _____ contribution that Mansfield Street Autos has made to

152. (A) significance
(B) significant
(C) signaling
(D) signing the

the local economy over the last 15 years.

We very much look forward to seeing you on February 17.

Best wishes,

Stanley Wong
Director of Sales
Mansfield Street Autos

Go on to the next page ➜

PART 7: READING COMPREHENSION

> **Directions:** This section includes a variety of texts. You will read each one and answer questions about it. Choose the best answer and mark the corresponding letter (A), (B), (C), or (D) on the answer sheet.

Questions 153–154 refer to the following announcement.

INTERCITY BUS COMPANY

BIG STAR Intercity Bus Company is excited to announce a number of new routes beginning May 20, as follows:

☆ An additional ten buses per day on the Austin-Dallas route.

☆ Increased morning and evening services on all commuter routes.

☆ Upgraded vehicle fleet with air-conditioning on all buses.

☆ Free Wi-Fi Internet for travelers on all routes.

In spite of this substantial investment in improving the customer experience, we also announce that fares will stay unchanged throughout this year.

Updated schedules will be available on our website and at bus terminals by the beginning of May.

Thank you for your continued support.

---

153. What is the main subject of the announcement?

(A) A transportation service

(B) An intercity highway

(C) A new range of Internet services

(D) The cancellation of catering deliveries

154. What is NOT mentioned in the announcement?

(A) The company intends to increase prices.

(B) The company has spent money.

(C) The company will offer a free service to customers.

(D) There is a website.

Questions 155–156 refer to the following announcement.

ANNOUNCEMENT

Evergreen Fashion

A new fashion destination
12 Georgia Boulevard

We provide you with the finest in designer fashion,
from 9:30 a.m. to 5:30 p.m., Monday through Saturday,
and 11:00 a.m. to 5:00 p.m. on Sundays.

Our specialties are casual and formal womenswear, shoes,
and accessories. We give you the latest styles, direct from the
designer collections.

As a special gift to celebrate our new store, please bring this
announcement for a 10% discount on your purchases. Valid July only.

155. What is being advertised?

(A) A fashion walk

(B) A new store opening

(C) A seasonal sale

(D) A change of business hours

156. What time does Evergreen Fashion close on Thursdays?

(A) 9:00 a.m.

(B) 11:00 a.m.

(C) 5:30 p.m.

(D) 5:00 p.m.

Go on to the next page ➜

Questions 157–159 refer to the following information.

HOBBES

Shipping and Returns

We deliver our top brand cosmetics to all international addresses. Free shipping, and overnight and two-day delivery are available for continental US destinations only. Express delivery (5–7 days) is offered for international customers. Please contact Customer Service for further information. Please also remember that you may be charged for customs charges on international orders and such charges are your responsibility.

We accept returns within 30 days of purchase, on the condition that items are unused and returned in their original packaging. Because of health and safety and the nature of cosmetics products, we cannot accept returns of opened items unless faulty. Purchases made by phone or online can be returned to any of our stores, or by mailing them to the returns address provided. Customers are responsible for shipping costs on returns, but these will be refunded in the case of faulty items.

---

157. What is Hobbes's business?

(A) It offers delivery services.

(B) It provides packaging.

(C) It manufactures safety clothing.

(D) It sells cosmetics products.

158. What delivery option is NOT available?

(A) Free shipping

(B) Same-day shipping

(C) Overnight shipping

(D) Two-day shipping

159. What is indicated in Hobbes's returns policy?

(A) Unwanted products may only be returned if they are unopened.

(B) Customers need to return items to a store.

(C) Return delivery is always free.

(D) No cosmetic products can be returned for reasons of health and safety.

Questions 160–161 refer to the following notice.

Renovations

Our hotel is currently undergoing renovations, which will create an even better environment for our guests. As a result, we will need to make numerous changes over the course of this month. The first floor lobby and cafe will be closed from October 5 through October 15. During this time, front desk services will move to the second floor, where a temporary reception area will be available. We will continue to provide guests with the highest quality of customer service from the second floor. Also, the hotel elevators will be out of service on October 8 for required maintenance work and upgrading. On this day, guests will be asked to use the stairs. Any guests staying on upper floors who have difficulty with stairs should contact reception to transfer to a room on a lower floor.

We thank guests for their patience and understanding as we embark on our ambitious plans to improve our hotel. We will do everything we can to give you a pleasant stay despite these inconveniences. All guests should direct any concerns to staff members who will be happy to provide assistance.

160. What is the aim of the notice?

(A) To advertise new facilities in the hotel

(B) To notify guests of changes created by renovation work

(C) To promote free services offered by the hotel

(D) To ask guests to move rooms

161. What will always be available in October?

(A) The stairs

(B) The cafeteria

(C) The elevators

(D) The first floor lobby

Go on to the next page →

Questions 162–164 refer to the following e-mail.

To: Mary Brandon (mbrandon@uroffice.net)
From: James Moray (jmoray@uroffice.net)
Date: Tuesday, August 14 3:09 p.m.
Subject: ATTENTION: Order AKB571948
Attachments: AKB571948.pdf

Dear Mary,

I am writing to inform you that, as discussed in our phone conversation this morning, your team mishandled order number AKB571948. This order, for a number of tables, microphones, and drawers for the new offices of Morgan Pitts on the fourth floor of Hobson Tower, Federal Street, was placed on August 5. Drawers were delivered to the customer's premises on August 7. However, as has now been confirmed, these were not the right model that the client ordered. The drawers remain, still packaged, at Morgan Pitts, and need to be picked up by your staff and returned to the storehouse. Also, the correct drawers need to be delivered.

Furthermore, the tables and microphones that are part of the order have still not been delivered to the customer. I called the warehouse directly and was told that these were in fact dispatched on August 9. The shipping department's electronic records also verify this. The tracking number is AKB32949. Would you please trace this order and let me know its whereabouts immediately? The customer's offices are now meant to be functioning, but the absence of furniture has made this impossible. Morgan Pitts is an esteemed client, and this is now a matter of urgency.

I am enclosing a copy of the original order for your convenience.

Best regards,
James Moray
Senior Account Manager

---

162. What is the purpose of the e-mail?

(A) To outline a delivery procedure

(B) To describe an office transfer process

(C) To arrange a meeting

(D) To detail issues with an order

163. According to the e-mail, where are the delivered drawers?

(A) In the storehouse

(B) In Morgan Pitts's offices

(C) At the building's reception

(D) In the delivery department

164. What does Mr. Moray request that Ms. Brandon do?

(A) Call Morgan Pitts

(B) Send a copy of an order form

(C) Enter some electronic records

(D) Trace some items

Questions 165–168 refer to the following advertisement.

Commuters, are you tired of the painful traffic hold-ups and the overcrowded, expensive trains? Do you remember the happy days when you went everywhere by bicycle? Why not do it again?

Now is the perfect time to return to the bicycle with Easy Cycles. Throughout June, we are offering reductions of up to 25% on all bicycles in our stores. In addition, we are offering up to 30% off accessories, and up to 35% off cycling attire. Finally, safety equipment such as helmets and reflectors is reduced by up to 50%!

And remember, Easy Cycles partners with local government to give you a range of competitive financing deals on your purchases.

Easy Cycles was created ten years ago with the goal of making lives better through cycling. We sell bicycles of all kinds, from mountain bikes and road bikes, to commuter bikes that are perfect for those desiring a comfortable ride to and from work each day.

Easy Cycles: Our Passion, Your Bike

165. What benefits of cycling are implied in the advertisement?

(A) It is good for commuters' health.

(B) It is better than taking the train during the summer months.

(C) It is less expensive than other forms of transportation.

(D) It makes people feel more energetic.

166. The word "hold-ups" in paragraph 1 is closest in meaning to

(A) automobiles

(B) road construction

(C) reasons

(D) delays

167. What discount is provided on clothing?

(A) 25%

(B) 30%

(C) 35%

(D) 50%

168. What is stated about Easy Cycles?

(A) It recently started business.

(B) It cooperates with government.

(C) It focuses on commuter bicycles.

(D) Its staff all commute by bike.

Go on to the next page ➔

Questions 169–171 refer to the following letter.

Camden Publishing Inc.

Mr. B. Carlisle
54 Rice Street
Indianapolis, IN

July 11

Dear Mr. Carlisle:

Many thanks for your recent application for the position of Junior Editor. The managers have looked at your résumé and cover letter, and were very pleased with your credentials and references.

Unfortunately, I am sorry to inform you that you have not been selected for interview on this occasion. This was because the managers all felt that you were overqualified for the position. We would therefore like to recommend that you apply for the position of Senior Editor, within the same department. For this position, we are looking for candidates with extensive experience in publishing, particularly in managing editorial workflows, which you appear to have. If you are interested in being considered for this role, please call me as soon as possible and I will arrange an interview for you. In the case that you are interested in this, please send us your résumé again, this time including a list of key projects that you have worked on in your previous employment.

I am enclosing a copy of the Senior Editor job advertisement and the related job description. Please contact me if you have any questions.

I look forward to hearing from you soon.

Sincerely,
Jayne Willis
Personnel Officer

---

169. What position did Mr. Carlisle apply for?

(A) Personnel officer

(B) Junior Editor

(C) Manager

(D) Senior Editor

170. What is implied about Mr. Carlisle?

(A) He has experience in publishing.

(B) He knows Ms. Willis.

(C) His résumé did not please the managers.

(D) He went to an interview at Camden Publishing Inc.

171. According to the letter, what did Mr. Carlisle NOT enclose in his application?

(A) A covering letter

(B) References

(C) A résumé

(D) The names of past projects

Questions 172–175 refer to the following e-mail.

From: Mabel Kirkpatrick m.kirkpatrick@maxrealestate.co.uk
To: Ung-hee Kim Ung-hee86@mailme.net
Date: January 23

Dear Mr. Kim,

Thank you for your e-mail notifying me of your intention to vacate your apartment at 66 Lake Avenue when your lease ends on February 11. I'll explain the procedures for moving out.

I will meet you at the property on the morning that your lease ends to conduct an inspection, as provided for in your tenant agreement. I will confirm that the items listed on the property's inventory are still present and in good order, and that the property in general is in good condition and clean. Please do not forget that according to the terms of the tenant agreement, you are supposed to thoroughly clean the property before you vacate.

If the inspection finds that the property and its contents are in an acceptable condition, we will then reimburse your security deposit. If, on the other hand, some damage has occurred, or if extra cleaning is necessary, the cost of this will be deducted from your deposit before it is given back to you. Supposing we reach agreement on any deductions, the deposit money will be transferred back to you before the afternoon of February 12.

In the meantime, I want to take this opportunity to wish you the best of luck with your return to your home country, and to express to you my congratulations on your new job there.

Best regards,

Mabel Kirkpatrick
Apartment Rentals Agent
Max Real Estate

---

172. Why was the e-mail written?

(A) To terminate the tenant's agreement

(B) To ask the tenant to vacate the property

(C) To arrange a viewing by new tenants

(D) To explain how the tenant can leave

173. When will Ms. Kirkpatrick visit the apartment?

(A) January 22

(B) January 23

(C) February 11

(D) February 12

174. According to the e-mail, in what situation will the tenant's full deposit not be returned?

(A) If the apartment is dirty

(B) If the tenant fails to vacate on time

(C) If the tenant doesn't pay the rent

(D) If the tenant prevents new tenants from viewing the property

175. What is implied about Mr. Kim?

(A) He is leaving the country.

(B) He would not like to leave the apartment.

(C) He deals with real estate.

(D) He has been a student.

Go on to the next page ➜

Questions 176–180 refer to the following advertisement.

Mowby International Real Estate

One of the world's top real estate companies, Mowby International Real Estate has been offering buyers and sellers outstanding service for over 20 years. From our foundation specializing in high-end luxury property in southern Portugal and the Mediterranean, we have grown to supply sales and property management services in all significant high-value property markets around the world. Our international network of agents has won many industry awards, including *International Realty Magazine*'s International Realtor of the Year Award in 2007, 2008, and 2010.

We have received these awards because our agents have consistently remained at the top of the business. They are ready and waiting to offer you the knowledge of the local market that you need, whether you are purchasing a home or investing in the property market. We are always conducting local, national, and transnational research to inform your buying decisions.

For further information, and to contact us, please visit your local office,
or check out our website at www.mowbyIRE.com

176. What is the purpose of the advertisement?

(A) To recruit for international job vacancies

(B) To market properties in Europe

(C) To advertise job opportunities in one country

(D) To promote a company's services

177. What is stated about Mowby International Real Estate?

(A) It has expanded overseas.

(B) It deals in affordable housing.

(C) It publishes an industry magazine.

(D) It gives training to its staff.

178. The word "conducting" in paragraph 2 is closest in meaning to

(A) hiring

(B) creating

(C) performing

(D) choosing

179. What is NOT one of Mowby International Real Estate's services?

(A) House sales

(B) Property management

(C) Market research

(D) Magazine publishing

180. What are the readers advised to do?

(A) Apply for a job

(B) Sign up for a publication

(C) Contribute to market research

(D) Access information online

Questions 181–185 refer to the following memo and e-mail.

For the attention of: All tenants, Crompton Tower
Circulation: To be posted on all office boards and distributed to all floor managers
Date: April 18

Dear Tenants,

As you may already know, Battersea Property recently purchased Crompton Tower. As a result, we have now assumed responsibility for the management of the building. We believe that you will find Battersea a capable and efficient partner. Please see below a list of important contacts in the various offices of our Buildings Management Division:

Cleaning Services:
Robert Hughes
rhughes@battproperty.com

Parking Lot Maintenance:
Stephanie Atkinson
satkinson@battproperty.com

Elevator Maintenance:
Charles Redmayne
credmayne@battproperty.com

General Building Maintenance (including security):
William Lang
wlang@battproperty.com

Telephones/Internet/Satellite:
Penelope Romero
promero@battproperty.com

Finance/Contracts:
Laura McBride
lmcbride@battproperty.com

Thank you.

Battersea Property
149 Melbourne Road
Adelaide
Tel: 08-7015-5510

From: Meghan Eccles mceccles@fawcettlaw.co.au
To: William Lang gwcleveley@battproperty.com
Date: April 23
Subject: 10th floor access

Dear Mr. Lang,

My name is Meghan Eccles and I am the Office Manager at Fawcett Law, located on the 10th floor of Crompton Tower. I was engaged in ongoing discussions with your predecessor concerning the access control to our office, which we regard as insufficient. We wish to upgrade the access control to our office to a tamperproof fingerprint access system. The previous management company had reached agreement with us to share the costs of this installation, but we had yet to reach an agreement on the details of this cost-sharing. I would be grateful if you could call me to discuss this matter at your earliest convenience, as we would like the system to be operational as soon as possible.

Kind regards,
Meghan Eccles

Questions on next page ➜

181. What kind of business is Battersea Property?

    (A) A road construction company

    (B) A property investment company

    (C) An escalator maker

    (D) An Internet service provider

182. What is noted in the memo?

    (A) New employees have been appointed.

    (B) Tenants have moved out.

    (C) A company department has been reformed.

    (D) A change of ownership has taken place.

183. To which office did Ms. Eccles send the e-mail?

    (A) Telephones/Internet/Satellite

    (B) Cleaning services

    (C) Finance/contracts

    (D) Building maintenance

184. What is the purpose of Ms. Eccles' e-mail?

    (A) To request advice on office security

    (B) To overturn an agreement

    (C) To raise issues about office cleaning

    (D) To discuss financial arrangements

185. In the e-mail, the word "insufficient" in paragraph 1 is closest in meaning to

    (A) unworthy

    (B) passive

    (C) inadequate

    (D) distrusted

Questions 186–190 refer to the following e-mails.

To: Michael Morrell michael@morrelleditorial.com
From: Cordelia Sanders cordelia.sanders@highgatepub.com
Subject: Freelance Agreement
Date: January 10

Dear Michael,

Many thanks for agreeing to offer us your freelance editorial services. As agreed earlier today during our telephone conversation, we would like you to conduct the following projects over the coming months, within the given deadlines:

Project details / hours / total fee / deadline
History of Modern Greece editing / 150 hours / $7,500 / April 10
Calculus and Management proofreading / 20 hours / $1,000 / February 3
Science Now review / 30 hours / $1,500 / March 24
Political Philosophy edit / 100 hours / $5,000 / August 15

As we discussed, you will receive payment for your work at the end of the month in which we receive your invoice, on the condition that we have your invoice by the 10th of the month and that the bank details you provide us are correct.

I am enclosing a Freelance Services Agreement for you. I would appreciate it if you could sign it and return it to me. This Agreement will cover you for all the work you do for us from now on.

I want to thank you again for agreeing to work with us. Freelancers have played a crucial role in the ten-year history of our company, and we hope to continue this success by fostering good relationships with our freelancers. We look forward to developing a mutually beneficial working relationship with you.

Please do contact me if you have any queries at any point. Otherwise, you will hear from the editors managing your various projects soon.

Best wishes,

Cordelia

Cordelia Sanders
Freelance Services Coordinator
Highgate Publishing
Tel: (366) 555-5893

To: Cordelia Sanders cordelia.sanders@highgatepub.com
From: Michael Morrell michael@morrelleditorial.com
Subject: Delayed payment
Date: May 6

Dear Cordelia,
I am sorry to inform you that there are once again problems with your Accounts Department. I have not received payment for my most recent project, despite finishing the work by the agreed deadline of March 24, and e-mailing my invoice before April 9. Please could you check this for me?

Thanks and best wishes,
Michael

Questions on next page ➜

186. What does Mr. Morrell receive from Ms. Sanders?

(A) An invoice

(B) A contract

(C) Some textbooks

(D) Some conference dates

187. What is stated about Highgate Publishing?

(A) It never misses it deadlines.

(B) It focuses on books about science.

(C) It has changed its contract for freelance workers.

(D) It was founded ten years ago.

188. In the first e-mail, the word "work" in paragraph 5 is closest in meaning to

(A) deal

(B) collaborate

(C) thank

(D) determine

189. What is the purpose of the second e-mail?

(A) To apologize for a missed deadline

(B) To deal with a complaint

(C) To ask for a delayed payment

(D) To extend a deadline

190. How much money is due to Mr. Morrell?

(A) $1,000

(B) $1,500

(C) $5,000

(D) $7,500

Questions 191–195 refer to the following business card and e-mail.

Hudson Financial

Jake Yung
Partner, Actuaries

Hudson Financial, Inc., 29th floor Tower Building, Baltimore, MD, USA
E-mail: j.yung@hudson-financial.com
Office phone: +1 956-555-0192
Cell phone: 238-555-4448
www.hudson-financial.com

To: Jake Yung j.yung@hudson-financial.com
From: Heather Hwang hhwang@correofirst.com
Subject: Actuarial position
Date: July 20

Dear Mr. Yung,

It was my pleasure to meet you at the Actuaries Colloquium in Canada two weeks ago. I hope you had a nice journey home. I was very interested to hear about the opening you mentioned you currently have for a Senior Actuarial Consultant. As we discussed briefly at the conference, I believe that I have the required background for the role.

In my current job at Jenkins, UK, I have been involved in a variety of projects, such as monthly and quarterly reporting based on relationship database analysis, financial studies on investment simulation and asset allocation, and revenue and expense forecasting. Also from this role, and from my previous position at Cyrus Inc., Australia, I have extensive experience in claims and risk adjustment analysis, using a variety of industry-specific software packages.

Aside from my actuarial skills, I am also multilingual. In addition to an accounting degree, I have a degree in modern European languages. I am fluent in Spanish and French, and also have a working knowledge of Italian. These languages have been extremely useful to me in my career so far, and I am certain that they would also be a great bonus to me within the international environment of your company. Moreover, I am a team player, and also good at leading others.

I have enclosed my résumé for your reference. Please contact me if you need any further information. I would be delighted to attend any meeting or interview at your offices upon your request.

I look forward to hearing from you.

Sincerely,

Heather Hwang

Questions on next page ➜

191. What is indicated about Mr. Yung?

    (A) He doesn't know Ms. Hwang.
    (B) He has been at his company for a long time.
    (C) He ran a seminar.
    (D) He recently went to Canada.

192. What is the purpose of the e-mail?

    (A) To request an address
    (B) To follow up on a previous discussion
    (C) To arrange a conference presentation
    (D) To suggest someone for a job

193. What does Ms. Hwang want to do?

    (A) Take part in a simulation
    (B) Get a job at Hudson Financial
    (C) Present at a conference
    (D) Master a foreign language

194. What is NOT stated as one of Ms. Hwang's abilities?

    (A) Leadership
    (B) Working in a team
    (C) Risk taking
    (D) Speaking more than one language

195. Where does Ms. Hwang suggest meeting Mr. Yung?

    (A) In Canada
    (B) In the UK
    (C) In Australia
    (D) In the USA

Questions 196–200 refer to the following memo and table.

MEMO

To: All employees, Marketing
From: Laura Morton
Date: August 11
Re: Departmental Meeting next month

The main item on the agenda for next month's Departmental Meeting is going to be our press advertising. In particular, we have to decide which consumer segments— and therefore which publication—to focus our advertising spend on. Please take some time over the weeks leading up to the meeting to think about this, referring to the enclosed list of publications. Kevin has composed the list from our original selection of 20 titles based on his market research, which helped him eliminate titles that are too far removed from our customer base, or that cost too much for advertising space.

Please remember when looking at the list that Kevin has already suggested that we select the cheapest option, not only because of cost, but also because that magazine has the second largest circulation, and also the smallest number of competing advertisements. This appears sensible, as we would save money while also guaranteeing that we achieve maximum impact on the reader. All other opinions will be welcome at the meeting, however.

	A	B	C	D
1	Publication	Rate	Circulation	Max. No. of Ads
2	*Men's Monthly*	$60,000	490,000	No limit
3	*Watch Now!*	$72,000	400,000	No limit
4	*Luxury Weekly*	$52,000	480,000	34
5	*Healthy Life*	$90,000	320,000	40

Questions on next page ➔

196. What does the memo discuss?

(A) Placing advertisements

(B) Signing up for magazine subscriptions

(C) Postponing a meeting

(D) Raising the marketing budget

197. How many magazines were initially discussed?

(A) 4

(B) 10

(C) 15

(D) 20

198. Why were some magazines eliminated?

(A) They are not based on sufficient research.

(B) They contain too many advertisements.

(C) They are not read by target customers.

(D) They have sold out.

199. Which magazine does Kevin recommend choosing?

(A) *Men's Monthly*

(B) *Watch Now!*

(C) *Luxury Weekly*

(D) *Healthy Life*

200. What is indicated about *Men's Monthly* magazine?

(A) It does not include advertising.

(B) It is only purchased by men.

(C) It has the largest number of readers.

(D) It targets middle-aged men.

This is the end of the Reading Test.

Look at the next page to start the Speaking Test ➜

Test 3: Speaking

This speaking test includes 11 questions that evaluate your ability to speak English. This test will take approximately 20 minutes.

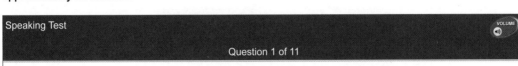

Speaking Test | VOLUME

Questions 1–2: Read a text aloud

Directions: In this part of the test, you will read aloud the text on the page. You will have 45 seconds to prepare. Then you will have 45 seconds to read the text aloud.

> Gartner and Associates is seeking an Executive Assistant to support the Managing Director. This position will require some backup support for three analysts as well. The ideal candidate will have strong communication and organizational skills. The candidate should also have 2 years' experience related to administrative and/or managerial office work. Duties include managing the director's calendar, making travel arrangements, and prioritizing items. A four-year college degree is preferred. Working hours are 8:00 a.m. to 4:00 p.m., and the assistant can expect a salary of about $35,000 with full benefits.

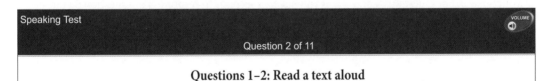

Speaking Test | VOLUME

Questions 1–2: Read a text aloud

Directions: In this part of the test, you will read aloud the text on the page. You will have 45 seconds to prepare. Then you will have 45 seconds to read the text aloud.

> I'd like to inform everyone that the employee cafeteria will be closed next week for renovations. The work will begin this Saturday and continue until next Saturday. The purpose of the renovation is to upgrade the kitchen, redecorate the dining area, and provide a more pleasant dining atmosphere for our employees. In addition, the kitchen staff will be expanding the menu with more delicious and healthy dishes. The new menu will be available starting on Monday, May 15. We apologize for any inconvenience this work may cause.

Go on to the next page ➜

Question 3: Describe a picture

Directions: You will describe a photograph as completely as you can. The photograph is in the test book. You will have 30 seconds to prepare what you will say, and then you will have 45 seconds to describe the picture in as much detail as possible.

Questions 4–6: Respond to questions

Directions: You will be asked three questions. After each question you will hear a beep. Begin speaking your answer immediately after the beep. You will not have any time to prepare your answer. For Questions 4 and 5 you will have 15 seconds to respond. For Question 6 you will have 30 seconds.

Imagine that an American marketing firm is doing research in your country. You have agreed to participate in a telephone interview about cleaning.

Question 4: How often do you clean your room or home, and when was the last time you did it?

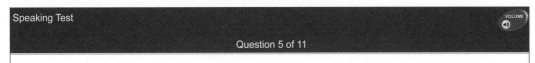

Questions 4–6: Respond to questions

Directions: You will be asked three questions. After each question you will hear a beep. Begin speaking your answer immediately after the beep. You will not have any time to prepare your answer. For Questions 4 and 5 you will have 15 seconds to respond. For Question 6 you will have 30 seconds.

———————————————

Imagine that an American marketing firm is doing research in your country. You have agreed to participate in a telephone interview about cleaning.

Question 5: What kind of equipment do you use when you clean your room or home?

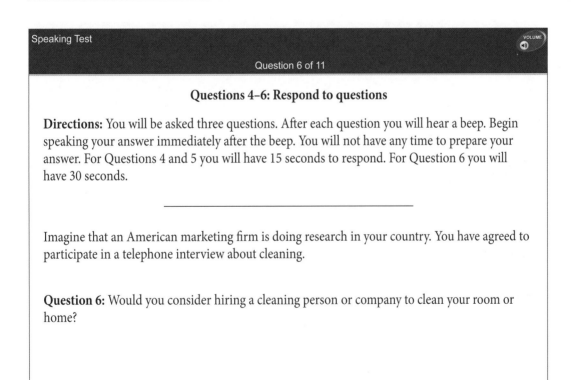

Questions 4–6: Respond to questions

Directions: You will be asked three questions. After each question you will hear a beep. Begin speaking your answer immediately after the beep. You will not have any time to prepare your answer. For Questions 4 and 5 you will have 15 seconds to respond. For Question 6 you will have 30 seconds.

———————————————

Imagine that an American marketing firm is doing research in your country. You have agreed to participate in a telephone interview about cleaning.

Question 6: Would you consider hiring a cleaning person or company to clean your room or home?

Go on to the next page ➜

Speaking Test

Questions 7–9: Respond to questions using information provided

Directions: You will read a short text and then answer three questions based on the information in the text. You will have 30 seconds to read the text before the first question. After each question you will hear a beep. Begin speaking immediately after the beep. You will not have any extra time to prepare your answer. For Questions 7 and 8 you will have 15 seconds to respond. For Question 9 you will have 30 seconds.

Speaking Test

City Office Supplies, Ltd.
6842 Dunlop Road, Oakville
1-777-555-7635

Invoice No: 625-7890
Date: October 27
Customer: Knowledge Publishing Company
Customer Number: 9631

Purchase Details

Product	Quantity	Price
1. L-Tech Wireless Keyboard	4	$ 89.16
2. Prism Desk Lamp	3	11.49
3. HQ A-4 Paper	200 boxes	1,147.70
4. Stick-'em Notes (large)	70	79.80
5. Color Staples	50 boxes	131.68
	TOTAL	$1,459.83

Our payment policy is as follows:
The total amount of an order must be paid within 30 days of the date stated on the invoice.
A 3% discount will be given for payment within seven days of the stated date.
Payments can be made by bank transfer, credit card, or check. If paying by check, make it payable to City Office Supplies.

Thank you for your business.

Question 10: Propose a solution

Directions: You will hear about a problem and be asked to propose a solution. You will have 30 seconds to prepare your solution, and then 60 seconds to speak.

Respond as if you work at the bank.

In your response, make sure to

• show that you recognize the problem, and

• propose a way of dealing with the problem.

Now listen to the voice message.

Question 11: Express an opinion

Directions: You will hear about a specific topic and then give your opinion about it. Make sure you say as much as you can about the topic in the time allowed. You will have 15 seconds to prepare, and then 60 seconds to speak.

This is the end of the Speaking Test.

Go on to the next page to start the Writing Test ➔

Test 3: Writing

This writing test includes 8 questions that evaluate your ability to write English. This test will take approximately 1 hour.

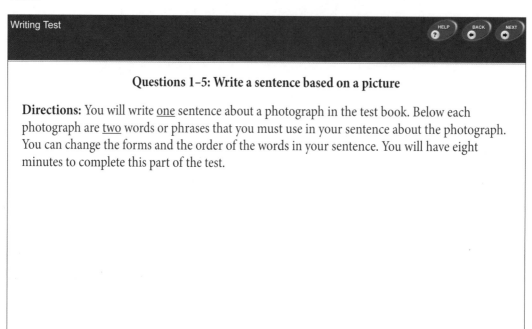

Questions 1–5: Write a sentence based on a picture

Directions: You will write <u>one</u> sentence about a photograph in the test book. Below each photograph are <u>two</u> words or phrases that you must use in your sentence about the photograph. You can change the forms and the order of the words in your sentence. You will have eight minutes to complete this part of the test.

doctor, stand

_____

lunch, enjoy

_____

book, glasses

_____

Go on to the next page ➔

presentation, business

directions, ask

Questions 6–7: Respond to a written request

Directions: You will write responses to two e-mails. Your essay will be evaluated on

- sentence quality
- grammar
- vocabulary
- organization

You will have 10 minutes to read and respond to each e-mail.

Directions: Read the e-mail.

From: Classified Ads Dept.
To: Customer placing an ad
Subject: Your advertisement
Sent: November 4, 9:34 a.m.

Thank you for your e-mail. I will be more than happy to answer any questions and make sure your advertisement is placed in a prominent position. I do have a couple of requests. First, you said in your initial message that you wanted your company logo placed in your ad. Please send me a scan of this so I can pass it on to the designer.

The next thing is the size and duration of your advertisement. We offer three sizes:

30mm x 90mm ($1.25), 1/4 page ($2.20), full page ($6.75)

Please choose a size and a method of payment (check, credit card, bank transfer, etc).

Finally, would you like to keep the text of the advertisement you sent me in exactly the same style or would you prefer our expert design team to make your ad as professional as it can be? The cost for this is an extra $15 per ad. And later if you decide to renew your ad, it is, of course, free to resubmit.

Directions: Write a reply to the e-mail. Write as if you are the person placing the ad. In your reply explain that you are attaching a scan of the company's logo. Also choose the size of the ad, the duration, the payment method, and whether you want the design team to work on the ad.

Write your response here or on a computer.

_____
_____
_____
_____
_____
_____
_____
_____
_____

Go on to the next page ➜

Directions: Read the e-mail.

From: Terry Pinn
To: Nana's Restaurant
Subject: reservation june 2
Sent: May 27, 5:41 p.m.

Dear Nana's Restaurant,

We have a dinner reservation for the above day but we need directions to your restaurant. We tried looking for it online but your website doesn't have directions or a map. Can you help?

Terry Pinn

Directions: Write a reply to the e-mail. Write as if you are responding to the customer. In your reply explain why there is not a map or directions on your website. Also, explain how to get to the restaurant by car or bus.

Write your response here or on a computer.

_____
_____
_____
_____
_____
_____
_____
_____
_____
_____

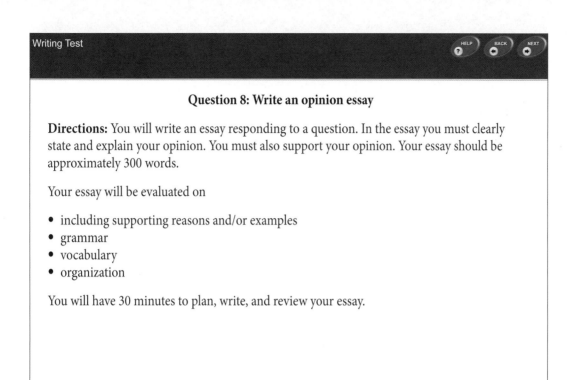

Question 8: Write an opinion essay

Directions: You will write an essay responding to a question. In the essay you must clearly state and explain your opinion. You must also support your opinion. Your essay should be approximately 300 words.

Your essay will be evaluated on

- including supporting reasons and/or examples
- grammar
- vocabulary
- organization

You will have 30 minutes to plan, write, and review your essay.

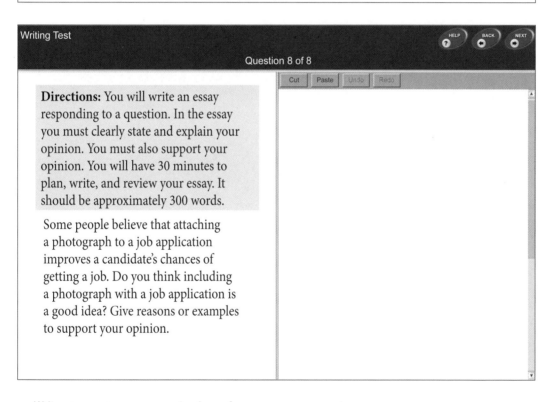

Cut   Paste   Undo   Redo

Directions: You will write an essay responding to a question. In the essay you must clearly state and explain your opinion. You must also support your opinion. You will have 30 minutes to plan, write, and review your essay. It should be approximately 300 words.

Some people believe that attaching a photograph to a job application improves a candidate's chances of getting a job. Do you think including a photograph with a job application is a good idea? Give reasons or examples to support your opinion.

Write your essay on a separate piece of paper or on a computer.

This is the end of Test 3.

TOEIC® TEST 4

Listening Answer Sheet

1. Ⓐ Ⓑ Ⓒ Ⓓ	26. Ⓐ Ⓑ Ⓒ	51. Ⓐ Ⓑ Ⓒ Ⓓ	76. Ⓐ Ⓑ Ⓒ Ⓓ
2. Ⓐ Ⓑ Ⓒ Ⓓ	27. Ⓐ Ⓑ Ⓒ	52. Ⓐ Ⓑ Ⓒ Ⓓ	77. Ⓐ Ⓑ Ⓒ Ⓓ
3. Ⓐ Ⓑ Ⓒ Ⓓ	28. Ⓐ Ⓑ Ⓒ	53. Ⓐ Ⓑ Ⓒ Ⓓ	78. Ⓐ Ⓑ Ⓒ Ⓓ
4. Ⓐ Ⓑ Ⓒ Ⓓ	29. Ⓐ Ⓑ Ⓒ	54. Ⓐ Ⓑ Ⓒ Ⓓ	79. Ⓐ Ⓑ Ⓒ Ⓓ
5. Ⓐ Ⓑ Ⓒ Ⓓ	30. Ⓐ Ⓑ Ⓒ	55. Ⓐ Ⓑ Ⓒ Ⓓ	80. Ⓐ Ⓑ Ⓒ Ⓓ
6. Ⓐ Ⓑ Ⓒ Ⓓ	31. Ⓐ Ⓑ Ⓒ	56. Ⓐ Ⓑ Ⓒ Ⓓ	81. Ⓐ Ⓑ Ⓒ Ⓓ
7. Ⓐ Ⓑ Ⓒ Ⓓ	32. Ⓐ Ⓑ Ⓒ	57. Ⓐ Ⓑ Ⓒ Ⓓ	82. Ⓐ Ⓑ Ⓒ Ⓓ
8. Ⓐ Ⓑ Ⓒ Ⓓ	33. Ⓐ Ⓑ Ⓒ	58. Ⓐ Ⓑ Ⓒ Ⓓ	83. Ⓐ Ⓑ Ⓒ Ⓓ
9. Ⓐ Ⓑ Ⓒ Ⓓ	34. Ⓐ Ⓑ Ⓒ	59. Ⓐ Ⓑ Ⓒ Ⓓ	84. Ⓐ Ⓑ Ⓒ Ⓓ
10. Ⓐ Ⓑ Ⓒ Ⓓ	35. Ⓐ Ⓑ Ⓒ	60. Ⓐ Ⓑ Ⓒ Ⓓ	85. Ⓐ Ⓑ Ⓒ Ⓓ
11. Ⓐ Ⓑ Ⓒ	36. Ⓐ Ⓑ Ⓒ	61. Ⓐ Ⓑ Ⓒ Ⓓ	86. Ⓐ Ⓑ Ⓒ Ⓓ
12. Ⓐ Ⓑ Ⓒ	37. Ⓐ Ⓑ Ⓒ	62. Ⓐ Ⓑ Ⓒ Ⓓ	87. Ⓐ Ⓑ Ⓒ Ⓓ
13. Ⓐ Ⓑ Ⓒ	38. Ⓐ Ⓑ Ⓒ	63. Ⓐ Ⓑ Ⓒ Ⓓ	88. Ⓐ Ⓑ Ⓒ Ⓓ
14. Ⓐ Ⓑ Ⓒ	39. Ⓐ Ⓑ Ⓒ	64. Ⓐ Ⓑ Ⓒ Ⓓ	89. Ⓐ Ⓑ Ⓒ Ⓓ
15. Ⓐ Ⓑ Ⓒ	40. Ⓐ Ⓑ Ⓒ	65. Ⓐ Ⓑ Ⓒ Ⓓ	90. Ⓐ Ⓑ Ⓒ Ⓓ
16. Ⓐ Ⓑ Ⓒ	41. Ⓐ Ⓑ Ⓒ Ⓓ	66. Ⓐ Ⓑ Ⓒ Ⓓ	91. Ⓐ Ⓑ Ⓒ Ⓓ
17. Ⓐ Ⓑ Ⓒ	42. Ⓐ Ⓑ Ⓒ Ⓓ	67. Ⓐ Ⓑ Ⓒ Ⓓ	92. Ⓐ Ⓑ Ⓒ Ⓓ
18. Ⓐ Ⓑ Ⓒ	43. Ⓐ Ⓑ Ⓒ Ⓓ	68. Ⓐ Ⓑ Ⓒ Ⓓ	93. Ⓐ Ⓑ Ⓒ Ⓓ
19. Ⓐ Ⓑ Ⓒ	44. Ⓐ Ⓑ Ⓒ Ⓓ	69. Ⓐ Ⓑ Ⓒ Ⓓ	94. Ⓐ Ⓑ Ⓒ Ⓓ
20. Ⓐ Ⓑ Ⓒ	45. Ⓐ Ⓑ Ⓒ Ⓓ	70. Ⓐ Ⓑ Ⓒ Ⓓ	95. Ⓐ Ⓑ Ⓒ Ⓓ
21. Ⓐ Ⓑ Ⓒ	46. Ⓐ Ⓑ Ⓒ Ⓓ	71. Ⓐ Ⓑ Ⓒ Ⓓ	96. Ⓐ Ⓑ Ⓒ Ⓓ
22. Ⓐ Ⓑ Ⓒ	47. Ⓐ Ⓑ Ⓒ Ⓓ	72. Ⓐ Ⓑ Ⓒ Ⓓ	97. Ⓐ Ⓑ Ⓒ Ⓓ
23. Ⓐ Ⓑ Ⓒ	48. Ⓐ Ⓑ Ⓒ Ⓓ	73. Ⓐ Ⓑ Ⓒ Ⓓ	98. Ⓐ Ⓑ Ⓒ Ⓓ
24. Ⓐ Ⓑ Ⓒ	49. Ⓐ Ⓑ Ⓒ Ⓓ	74. Ⓐ Ⓑ Ⓒ Ⓓ	99. Ⓐ Ⓑ Ⓒ Ⓓ
25. Ⓐ Ⓑ Ⓒ	50. Ⓐ Ⓑ Ⓒ Ⓓ	75. Ⓐ Ⓑ Ⓒ Ⓓ	100. Ⓐ Ⓑ Ⓒ Ⓓ

Reading Answer Sheet

101. Ⓐ Ⓑ Ⓒ Ⓓ	126. Ⓐ Ⓑ Ⓒ Ⓓ	151. Ⓐ Ⓑ Ⓒ Ⓓ	176. Ⓐ Ⓑ Ⓒ Ⓓ
102. Ⓐ Ⓑ Ⓒ Ⓓ	127. Ⓐ Ⓑ Ⓒ Ⓓ	152. Ⓐ Ⓑ Ⓒ Ⓓ	177. Ⓐ Ⓑ Ⓒ Ⓓ
103. Ⓐ Ⓑ Ⓒ Ⓓ	128. Ⓐ Ⓑ Ⓒ Ⓓ	153. Ⓐ Ⓑ Ⓒ Ⓓ	178. Ⓐ Ⓑ Ⓒ Ⓓ
104. Ⓐ Ⓑ Ⓒ Ⓓ	129. Ⓐ Ⓑ Ⓒ Ⓓ	154. Ⓐ Ⓑ Ⓒ Ⓓ	179. Ⓐ Ⓑ Ⓒ Ⓓ
105. Ⓐ Ⓑ Ⓒ Ⓓ	130. Ⓐ Ⓑ Ⓒ Ⓓ	155. Ⓐ Ⓑ Ⓒ Ⓓ	180. Ⓐ Ⓑ Ⓒ Ⓓ
106. Ⓐ Ⓑ Ⓒ Ⓓ	131. Ⓐ Ⓑ Ⓒ Ⓓ	156. Ⓐ Ⓑ Ⓒ Ⓓ	181. Ⓐ Ⓑ Ⓒ Ⓓ
107. Ⓐ Ⓑ Ⓒ Ⓓ	132. Ⓐ Ⓑ Ⓒ Ⓓ	157. Ⓐ Ⓑ Ⓒ Ⓓ	182. Ⓐ Ⓑ Ⓒ Ⓓ
108. Ⓐ Ⓑ Ⓒ Ⓓ	133. Ⓐ Ⓑ Ⓒ Ⓓ	158. Ⓐ Ⓑ Ⓒ Ⓓ	183. Ⓐ Ⓑ Ⓒ Ⓓ
109. Ⓐ Ⓑ Ⓒ Ⓓ	134. Ⓐ Ⓑ Ⓒ Ⓓ	159. Ⓐ Ⓑ Ⓒ Ⓓ	184. Ⓐ Ⓑ Ⓒ Ⓓ
110. Ⓐ Ⓑ Ⓒ Ⓓ	135. Ⓐ Ⓑ Ⓒ Ⓓ	160. Ⓐ Ⓑ Ⓒ Ⓓ	185. Ⓐ Ⓑ Ⓒ Ⓓ
111. Ⓐ Ⓑ Ⓒ Ⓓ	136. Ⓐ Ⓑ Ⓒ Ⓓ	161. Ⓐ Ⓑ Ⓒ Ⓓ	186. Ⓐ Ⓑ Ⓒ Ⓓ
112. Ⓐ Ⓑ Ⓒ Ⓓ	137. Ⓐ Ⓑ Ⓒ Ⓓ	162. Ⓐ Ⓑ Ⓒ Ⓓ	187. Ⓐ Ⓑ Ⓒ Ⓓ
113. Ⓐ Ⓑ Ⓒ Ⓓ	138. Ⓐ Ⓑ Ⓒ Ⓓ	163. Ⓐ Ⓑ Ⓒ Ⓓ	188. Ⓐ Ⓑ Ⓒ Ⓓ
114. Ⓐ Ⓑ Ⓒ Ⓓ	139. Ⓐ Ⓑ Ⓒ Ⓓ	164. Ⓐ Ⓑ Ⓒ Ⓓ	189. Ⓐ Ⓑ Ⓒ Ⓓ
115. Ⓐ Ⓑ Ⓒ Ⓓ	140. Ⓐ Ⓑ Ⓒ Ⓓ	165. Ⓐ Ⓑ Ⓒ Ⓓ	190. Ⓐ Ⓑ Ⓒ Ⓓ
116. Ⓐ Ⓑ Ⓒ Ⓓ	141. Ⓐ Ⓑ Ⓒ Ⓓ	166. Ⓐ Ⓑ Ⓒ Ⓓ	191. Ⓐ Ⓑ Ⓒ Ⓓ
117. Ⓐ Ⓑ Ⓒ Ⓓ	142. Ⓐ Ⓑ Ⓒ Ⓓ	167. Ⓐ Ⓑ Ⓒ Ⓓ	192. Ⓐ Ⓑ Ⓒ Ⓓ
118. Ⓐ Ⓑ Ⓒ Ⓓ	143. Ⓐ Ⓑ Ⓒ Ⓓ	168. Ⓐ Ⓑ Ⓒ Ⓓ	193. Ⓐ Ⓑ Ⓒ Ⓓ
119. Ⓐ Ⓑ Ⓒ Ⓓ	144. Ⓐ Ⓑ Ⓒ Ⓓ	169. Ⓐ Ⓑ Ⓒ Ⓓ	194. Ⓐ Ⓑ Ⓒ Ⓓ
120. Ⓐ Ⓑ Ⓒ Ⓓ	145. Ⓐ Ⓑ Ⓒ Ⓓ	170. Ⓐ Ⓑ Ⓒ Ⓓ	195. Ⓐ Ⓑ Ⓒ Ⓓ
121. Ⓐ Ⓑ Ⓒ Ⓓ	146. Ⓐ Ⓑ Ⓒ Ⓓ	171. Ⓐ Ⓑ Ⓒ Ⓓ	196. Ⓐ Ⓑ Ⓒ Ⓓ
122. Ⓐ Ⓑ Ⓒ Ⓓ	147. Ⓐ Ⓑ Ⓒ Ⓓ	172. Ⓐ Ⓑ Ⓒ Ⓓ	197. Ⓐ Ⓑ Ⓒ Ⓓ
123. Ⓐ Ⓑ Ⓒ Ⓓ	148. Ⓐ Ⓑ Ⓒ Ⓓ	173. Ⓐ Ⓑ Ⓒ Ⓓ	198. Ⓐ Ⓑ Ⓒ Ⓓ
124. Ⓐ Ⓑ Ⓒ Ⓓ	149. Ⓐ Ⓑ Ⓒ Ⓓ	174. Ⓐ Ⓑ Ⓒ Ⓓ	199. Ⓐ Ⓑ Ⓒ Ⓓ
125. Ⓐ Ⓑ Ⓒ Ⓓ	150. Ⓐ Ⓑ Ⓒ Ⓓ	175. Ⓐ Ⓑ Ⓒ Ⓓ	200. Ⓐ Ⓑ Ⓒ Ⓓ

Test 4: Listening

The Listening section evaluates how well you understand spoken English. The Listening test has four sections and will take approximately 45 minutes. You <u>must</u> mark your answers on the answer sheet not in the test book.

🎧 PART 1: PHOTOGRAPHS
40

> **Directions:** For each item in Part 1, you will hear four statements about a photograph in the test book. You must listen carefully to the statements in order to select the statement that best describes the photograph. Mark the corresponding letter (A), (B), (C), or (D) on the answer sheet.

Example

Listen to the statements and select the one that best describes the picture.

(A) They're drinking orange juice.
(B) They're turning on a computer.
(C) They're looking at a screen.
(D) They're putting on formal clothes.

Statement **(C), "They're looking at a screen."** best describes the picture, so you should choose answer (C) and mark it on your answer sheet.

Sample Answer

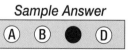

Go on to the next page ➜

🎧
41

1.

2.

3.

4.

Go on to the next page ➜

5.

6.

7.

8.

Go on to the next page ➔

9.

10.

This is the end of Part 1.

Look at the next page to start Part 2 ➔

PART 2: QUESTION–RESPONSE

42

Directions: For each item in Part 2, you will hear a statement or a question followed by three responses. Listen and choose the best response. Then mark the corresponding letter (A), (B), or (C) on the answer sheet.

Example

Have you met the new Managing Director?

(A) Actually I talked with him in the lobby just now.
(B) Yes, I took the call.
(C) No, he takes the subway to work.

The best response to the question "Have you met the new Managing Director?" is answer choice **(A), "Actually I talked with him in the lobby just now."** You should mark answer (A) on your answer sheet.

Sample Answer

● Ⓑ Ⓒ

43

11. Listen and choose the best response.

12. Listen and choose the best response.

13. Listen and choose the best response.

14. Listen and choose the best response.

15. Listen and choose the best response.

16. Listen and choose the best response.

17. Listen and choose the best response.

18. Listen and choose the best response.

19. Listen and choose the best response.

20. Listen and choose the best response.

21. Listen and choose the best response.

22. Listen and choose the best response.

23. Listen and choose the best response.

24. Listen and choose the best response.

25. Listen and choose the best response.

26. Listen and choose the best response.

27. Listen and choose the best response.

28. Listen and choose the best response.

29. Listen and choose the best response.

30. Listen and choose the best response.

31. Listen and choose the best response.

32. Listen and choose the best response.

33. Listen and choose the best response.

34. Listen and choose the best response.

35. Listen and choose the best response.

36. Listen and choose the best response.

37. Listen and choose the best response.

38. Listen and choose the best response.

39. Listen and choose the best response.

40. Listen and choose the best response.

This is the end of Part 2.

Go on to the next page to start Part 3 ➔

🎧 PART 3: CONVERSATIONS
44

> **Directions:** You will hear conversations with two speakers. Then you will answer three questions about each conversation. Listen and select the best response to each question. Mark the corresponding letter (A), (B), (C), or (D) on the answer sheet.

41. Where most likely are the speakers?

    (A) At a station

    (B) In a taxi line

    (C) In an office

    (D) At an airport terminal

42. What is the man concerned about?

    (A) Getting a taxi

    (B) Missing a meeting

    (C) Giving a presentation

    (D) Losing a ticket

43. What does the woman recommend?

    (A) Taking another flight

    (B) Rescheduling a meeting time

    (C) Waiting longer

    (D) Finding a driver

44. What subjects does the woman want to study?

    (A) Computer programming

    (B) Web design

    (C) Creative writing

    (D) Advertising

45. What is the woman concerned about?

    (A) An assignment deadline

    (B) A class schedule

    (C) Job availability

    (D) Course fees

46. What does the man say he will do?

    (A) Return the woman's application

    (B) Suggest different classes

    (C) Send the woman more information

    (D) Hire the woman

47. Where does the dialog probably take place?

    (A) In a field

    (B) At a café

    (C) At a delivery company

    (D) At a supermarket

48. What does the woman say about deliveries?

    (A) They have been destroyed.

    (B) They have gone bad.

    (C) They have been small.

    (D) They have been late.

49. What will the man probably do next?

    (A) Buy an umbrella

    (B) Go to the vegetable section

    (C) Go home

    (D) Make some soup

50. Where does the conversation take place?

    (A) At a bookstore

    (B) At a jewelry shop

    (C) At a printing company

    (D) At a school

51. What does the woman need to do to get some information?

    (A) Attend a party

    (B) Visit an office

    (C) Return to school

    (D) Fill out a form

52. What will the woman get by signing up for the card?

    (A) A free ticket

    (B) Weekly magazines

    (C) Details about discounts

    (D) Invitations to celebrations

53. Why is the man concerned?

(A) He has lost his card.

(B) He has not received any instructions.

(C) He is going to try something new.

(D) He missed an important meeting.

54. What does the man want the woman to do?

(A) Schedule a conference

(B) Show him some calculations

(C) Arrange a reservation

(D) Help him with a telephone call

55. Why is the man going to his drawer?

(A) To tidy it up

(B) To move it outside

(C) To get some information

(D) To look for a calculator

56. According to the woman, what is the problem?

(A) A client was not punctual for a meeting.

(B) A purchased item was not received.

(C) A user's manual is incorrect.

(D) A computer is out of order.

57. What does the man suggest doing?

(A) Returning to the store

(B) Ordering an additional item

(C) Contacting the manufacturer

(D) Looking at a receipt

58. What time does the store close this week?

(A) At 5:00 p.m.

(B) At 6:00 p.m.

(C) At 7:00 p.m.

(D) At 9:00 p.m.

59. What are the speakers discussing?

(A) The title of a book

(B) The number of employees

(C) The venue of a team meeting

(D) The expected sales numbers for next year

60. How do the speakers resolve the issue?

(A) By calling a manager

(B) By looking at a schedule

(C) By asking a librarian

(D) By printing more copies

61. What will the woman probably do next?

(A) Check an electronic calendar

(B) Repair a computer

(C) Make a reservation

(D) Make a phone call

62. What does the woman say about Crystal Blackman?

(A) She is interested in a full-time position.

(B) She does not want to move abroad.

(C) She has more experience than expected.

(D) She previously taught marketing at a university.

63. According to the woman, what will happen in Jakarta next month?

(A) An old shopping mall will be reopened.

(B) A new store will open.

(C) The company will transfer to a smaller building.

(D) A marketing system will be revised.

64. What will the man probably do next?

(A) Call a supervisor

(B) Read a résumé

(C) Make a job offer

(D) Talk to an applicant

Go on to the next page →

65. What event is the man planning to attend?

(A) A business presentation

(B) A theater production

(C) A sports game

(D) An acting class

66. What is the woman doing this week?

(A) Planning a trip to Italy

(B) Finishing a report

(C) Cooking for her sister

(D) Meeting a family member

67. What does the man advise the woman to do?

(A) Get tickets from him

(B) Check a website

(C) Swap seats

(D) Invite a friend

68. What are the speakers mainly discussing?

(A) Printing invitations

(B) Having an office renovated

(C) Ordering color printers

(D) Purchasing office supplies

69. What does the woman want the man to consider?

(A) The cost of a printer

(B) The color of invitations

(C) The method of shipment

(D) The size of air conditioners

70. Why have company sales dropped?

(A) A production line was upgraded.

(B) A product range was reduced.

(C) The weather was cool.

(D) Delivery fees were high.

This is the end of Part 3.

Look at the next page to start Part 4 ➔

PART 4: TALKS

45

Directions: You will hear several talks, each with one speaker. Then you will answer three questions about the talk. Listen and select the best response to each question. Mark the corresponding letter (A), (B), (C), or (D) on the answer sheet.

71. What did Ms. Sanchez apply for?

   (A) A bank account
   (B) A university course
   (C) A debit card
   (D) A mortgage

72. What does the speaker say about Ms. Sanchez's application?

   (A) It is being finished.
   (B) It is being evaluated.
   (C) It didn't meet the deadline.
   (D) It has been turned down.

73. How can Ms. Sanchez check the status of her application?

   (A) By stopping by an office
   (B) By checking a website
   (C) By responding to an e-mail
   (D) By calling an office

74. What was approved by City Hall?

   (A) A building project
   (B) A new strategy
   (C) A revised bus service
   (D) An entertainment event

75. What are some businesspeople worried about?

   (A) Project management problems
   (B) Intense competition
   (C) Worsened traffic congestion
   (D) Delayed construction work

76. What will happen next month?

   (A) A construction project will start.
   (B) Traffic calming measures will be implemented.
   (C) A new schedule will be created.
   (D) A public meeting will take place.

77. What area does Martin Vermont work in?

   (A) Finance
   (B) Creating writing
   (C) Journalism
   (D) Advertising

78. What accomplishment of Martin Vermont is mentioned?

   (A) He started a university.
   (B) He moved offices.
   (C) He developed new products.
   (D) He founded a company.

79. What is Martin Vermont going to do?

   (A) Start teaching at a university
   (B) Host a television program
   (C) Work in advertising
   (D) Hold an event

80. Where is the talk being held?

   (A) In a shopping center
   (B) In an art museum
   (C) In a gym
   (D) In a movie theater

81. According to the speaker, what is new this year?

   (A) Discounts will be offered.
   (B) Argentinean movies will be shown.
   (C) Two venues will be used.
   (D) A reception will take place.

82. Who is Pedro Gonzalez?

   (A) An artist
   (B) A sports instructor
   (C) A shop owner
   (D) A film director

83. What is the purpose of the call?

    (A) To get an estimate
    (B) To ask for advice
    (C) To arrange a meeting
    (D) To offer a solution

84. What does the client want to do?

    (A) Come to a meeting
    (B) Change an agreement
    (C) Set up a new company
    (D) Decrease costs

85. What does the woman want the listener to do?

    (A) See her client
    (B) Review a budget
    (C) Give her a call back
    (D) Run an audit

86. What is the subject of the message?

    (A) A job advertisement
    (B) A reimbursement
    (C) An inspection
    (D) A food order

87. What does the caller want the listener to do?

    (A) Ship a missing item
    (B) Display correct signs
    (C) Organize a schedule
    (D) Change a rule

88. What does the caller say about Ms. Totsby?

    (A) She wants to go back to a restaurant.
    (B) She will meet a candidate.
    (C) She has moved jobs.
    (D) She will telephone again.

89. What did Mr. Kim order?

    (A) A book
    (B) A ship
    (C) Computer equipment
    (D) Office stationery

90. When will the order arrive?

    (A) On Monday
    (B) On Wednesday
    (C) On Thursday
    (D) On Friday

91. What does the speaker offer Mr. Kim?

    (A) A charge-free telephone line
    (B) A special discount
    (C) Free delivery
    (D) Full compensation

92. Who most likely is the speaker?

    (A) An event host
    (B) A company founder
    (C) A cabin crew member
    (D) A news presenter

93. According to the talk, what is Budget Air going to do?

    (A) Recruit employees
    (B) Reduce ticket prices
    (C) Expand airport lounges
    (D) Purchase additional airplanes

94. Where is Budget Air's headquarters?

    (A) In San Francisco
    (B) In Seattle
    (C) In Mumbai
    (D) In New Delhi

95. In what kind of company is the talk most likely taking place?

(A) A software developer
(B) A financial advisory service
(C) An electronics manufacturer
(D) A beverage producer

96. What does the speaker offer the listeners?

(A) Consulting reports
(B) Engineering help
(C) A free gift
(D) A reduced price

97. How can the listeners get further information?

(A) By contacting the speaker
(B) By talking to a customer
(C) By calling a developer
(D) By going to an Internet site

98. What is the purpose of the talk?

(A) To announce a speaker
(B) To welcome conference delegates
(C) To make changes at a hotel
(D) To greet tour participants

99. What does the speaker advise the listeners to do?

(A) Obtain information packs
(B) Sign up for a conference
(C) Buy books
(D) Make copies of a schedule

100. Where will tonight's event take place?

(A) In a local restaurant
(B) In the Barney Room
(C) On the second floor
(D) In the foyer

This is the end of Part 4.

Go on to the next page to start Part 5 ➜

Test 4: Reading

The Reading section evaluates how well you understand written English. The Reading test has three sections and will take approximately 75 minutes. You must mark your answers on the answer sheet not in the test book.

PART 5: INCOMPLETE SENTENCES

Directions: One or more words is missing from each of the following sentences. Choose the best answer choice to complete the sentence. Mark the corresponding letter (A), (B), (C), or (D) on the answer sheet.

101. Our customers value our products more _____ than they do those of our competitors.

    (A) highly
    (B) higher
    (C) high
    (D) highest

102. Global Communications has _____ raised its stake in Star Telecom above 35% by buying V-Network, a Star Telecom shareholder.

    (A) accidentally
    (B) indirectly
    (C) statistically
    (D) chiefly

103. Morale _____ staff is particularly high at the moment because of the company's outstanding successes last year and the accompanying staff bonuses.

    (A) with
    (B) along
    (C) between
    (D) among

104. We offer _____ outsourcing solutions to streamline companies' operations.

    (A) invent
    (B) inventive
    (C) invention
    (D) inventing

105. Our presentation met _____ the client's full approval.

    (A) before
    (B) by
    (C) with
    (D) to

106. Because no company cars were available, the sales team _____ the express train to the seminar.

    (A) board
    (B) took
    (C) came
    (D) ran

107. Anyone parking their car in the company parking lot needs to _____ a valid parking permit in the window of the car.

    (A) publish
    (B) produce
    (C) display
    (D) note

108. Please get there on time so that we can start the meeting _____ at 9:00 a.m.

    (A) shortly
    (B) promptly
    (C) currently
    (D) anytime

109. She is interested _____ in the salary, but also in the job itself.

(A) both

(B) as well as

(C) either

(D) not only

110. The analyst found that interdepartmental communication within the company was _____ poor.

(A) excess

(B) exceed

(C) excessive

(D) excessively

111. The Advertising Department thinks that the new product is highly _____ and should achieve our sales expectations.

(A) market

(B) marketing

(C) marketable

(D) marketed

112. Your application _____ the Marketing Department has been received and will be considered shortly.

(A) into

(B) to

(C) from

(D) on

113. During the meeting, it was agreed that the product would be _____ in time for re-launch ahead of the holiday period.

(A) upgrading

(B) upgrade

(C) upgraded

(D) upgrades

114. The reduced gym membership _____ for company employees includes unlimited entry and complimentary towels on each visit.

(A) status

(B) qualification

(C) fee

(D) annuity

115. Ms. Burns has been Deputy Manager in the Research and Development Department _____ 2009.

(A) since

(B) within

(C) at

(D) from

116. Following the first round of interviews for the graduate program, 200 candidates were _____ from the recruitment process.

(A) eliminated

(B) dissatisfied

(C) resigned

(D) managed

117. Most of the presentations went over time, but Mr. Weiner finished _____ early.

(A) him

(B) his

(C) himself

(D) he

118. The sales plan for the following year was presented _____ by the executives at the conference.

(A) passionate

(B) passion

(C) impassioned

(D) passionately

Go on to the next page ➜

119. The company's standard employment contracts state that employees must give three months' _____ if they wish to terminate their contract.

(A) letter
(B) degree
(C) notice
(D) employment

120. Access to the Customer Relationship Management System _____ made available to all staff when they start working at the company.

(A) is
(B) was
(C) has been
(D) was being

121. Ms. Norris and Mr. Stacey celebrated _____ promotions by buying dinner for the whole team.

(A) they
(B) them
(C) their
(D) theirs

122. I'd like to _____ the main conference room, but the online room reservation function is malfunctioning.

(A) reserve
(B) reserved
(C) reserving
(D) reserves

123. _____ sales are currently below our estimates, we are optimistic that the situation will improve in the next quarter.

(A) Although
(B) Nevertheless
(C) In spite of
(D) Regardless

124. We cannot give _____ on discounted items purchased during sale periods.

(A) advantages
(B) statistics
(C) refunds
(D) credits

125. One of our most _____ accomplishments last year was the launch of the new sports coupe.

(A) remark
(B) remarks
(C) remarkable
(D) remarking

126. Some employees believe that their projects do not have to be evaluated, _____ we should always assess and question project outcomes.

(A) but
(B) that
(C) either
(D) otherwise

127. Faulty items can only be fixed, not replaced, unless returned to retail outlets _____ 28 days of delivery.

(A) between
(B) within
(C) by
(D) from

128. Use of public transportation for company business must be _____ in advance with your manager.

(A) picked up
(B) assigned
(C) manipulated
(D) arranged

129. We intend to focus on emerging markets, which have a _____ need for water.

(A) causing
(B) scheduled
(C) regular
(D) growing

130. Sales to India have increased 10%, demonstrating the _____ effects of targeting marketing spend on the Indian market last year.

(A) easy
(B) beneficial
(C) negotiable
(D) hesitant

131. Please register at the front desk _____ arrival at the banquet hall.

    (A) to
    (B) on
    (C) as
    (D) from

132. We have enhanced our _____ to customer complaints, as shown in our better ranking in recent customer satisfaction surveys.

    (A) respond
    (B) responding
    (C) responsive
    (D) responsiveness

133. Our research shows that our rivals are seen as charging more _____ prices than we do.

    (A) producible
    (B) reasonable
    (C) important
    (D) purchasing

134. In order to be _____ onto the Executive MBA program, applicants must have at least two years' work experience at an executive level.

    (A) acceptance
    (B) accept
    (C) accepting
    (D) accepted

135. The Chief Financial Officer has every _____ of coming to next week's Annual General Meeting in Washington, D.C.

    (A) intend
    (B) intending
    (C) intention
    (D) intentional

136. We have succeeded in raising _____ in our factories by 8% in order to meet growing demand for our products.

    (A) creation
    (B) output
    (C) figures
    (D) shipping

137. I'd like to _____ that we explain the roles and responsibilities of those working in this department.

    (A) suggestion
    (B) suggested
    (C) suggesting
    (D) suggest

138. We set up _____ meetings to insure that all aspects of the project are adequately coordinated.

    (A) frequent
    (B) frequency
    (C) frequents
    (D) frequently

139. The way in which the editor _____ negotiations with freelance workers resulted in many freelancers no longer wishing to work with the company.

    (A) openness
    (B) opened
    (C) opener
    (D) opening

140. New strategic investment funds have been increasing in popularity as investors _____ new sources of income.

    (A) seek
    (B) purchase
    (C) benefit
    (D) beg

Go on to the next page ➜

PART 6: TEXT COMPLETION

> **Directions:** The following texts have sentences with some words and phrases missing. Read the answer choices given to complete the sentences. Choose the best answer choice to complete the sentence. Mark the corresponding letter (A), (B), (C), or (D) on the answer sheet.

Questions 141–143 refer to the following e-mail.

From: Amy Cather acather@gcentral.gov
To: All employees mailer@gcentral.gov
Subject: PC maintenance
Date: January 15

Dear all,

The IT Team _____ new operating systems on all computers

> **141.** (A) have installed
> (B) to install
> (C) installs
> (D) will be installing

after 5:00 p.m. on Friday, March 10. We expect to finish the installation process on all terminals by midday on Sunday, March 12.

In order to help us with this, we ask all staff to switch off their terminals by 4:45 p.m. on Friday, March 10. Company laptops may still be used after this time, but we ask that these also are turned off _____ you leave for the weekend on

> **142.** (A) before
> (B) after
> (C) until
> (D) anytime

March 10. Laptops must remain in the office that weekend so that they can also be upgraded by IT staff.

The installation of the new operating system is not _____ to

> **143.** (A) recommended
> (B) expected
> (C) helped
> (D) needed

cause loss of or damage to existing files. Nevertheless, we suggest that you back up all your files beforehand. As is our general practice, files should be saved on the central server, and not on individual computer drives.

Best regards,

Amy Cather
Head, IT Support

Questions 144–146 refer to the following letter.

Kristen Barsky
13 Kansas Avenue
Detroit, MI 48220

September 6

Dear Ms. Barsky,

Many thanks for your telephone call of September 3 regarding an item on
your credit card statement that had been charged twice. We got in touch with
the merchant in question and this error has _____

                  144. (A) because
                           (B) to
                           (C) now
                           (D) yet

been rectified.

The amount overcharged last month will now be credited to your account and
_____ on your statement for October.

145. (A) will appear
      (B) appeared
      (C) have appeared
      (D) had appeared

We would like to take this opportunity to apologize for the trouble that this error
has caused you. Regrettably, the problem was _____

                    146. (A) below
                           (B) up
                           (C) out of
                           (D) underneath

our control, and caused by an error on the part of the merchant from whom you
made the purchase. Please feel free to contact us again in the future in the
event of any further problems with your credit card billing.

Yours sincerely,

Jonathan Zeldin
Fraud Investigation Dept.
Smart Card

Go on to the next page →

Questions 147–149 refer to the following letter.

Calway Inc.

CALWAY CENTER • TUS KOWLOON • HONG KONG

August 15

Dear Ms. Simms,

It is my pleasure to let you know that we would like to offer you the position
of Project Manager at Calway Inc. Could you please call me back anytime
_____ business hours to confirm that you wish to accept

147. (A) during
(B) throughout
(C) until
(D) below

the position.

As explained at interview, as a new employee you will receive a _____

148. (A) busy
(B) lengthy
(C) temporary
(D) period

contract for the first six months of your employment with us. After this time, a decision
will be made, in light of your performance over the six-month period, as to whether
_____ you as a permanent employee.

149. (A) hire
(B) to hire
(C) hiring
(D) hired

I look forward to hearing from you soon.

Kind regards,

Lakshmi Batra
Head of Human Resources

Questions 150–152 refer to the following article.

Growing your business
THROUGH SALES

By Jeremy Nigh

Your start-up company is in its early stages, and your client base still mainly comprises your own personal contacts. Now, you want to develop the company by employing your first salesperson.

You may expect the salesperson you get to adequately create and manage a sales plan for your business. However, you could not be more _____ because the skills required for

150. (A) wrong
(B) wronged
(C) wrongly
(D) wrongs

being a great salesperson are considerably different from those needed to be an effective sales manager. The fact of the matter is that having a great sales record does not make someone a capable manager, and that not everyone is management _____.

151. (A) materially
(B) materialize
(C) materials
(D) material

As a small business owner, it is your responsibility to plan your sales strategy before you employ your first salesperson. If you do this, you will know exactly what _____ of

152. (A) item
(B) type
(C) part
(D) post

salesperson you need to help you realize your strategy, and that person will know what is expected of them. Just as you plan every other aspect of your business, so too must you plan your sales strategy if you want your company to fulfill its potential.

Go on to the next page ➔

PART 7: READING COMPREHENSION

Directions: This section includes a variety of texts. You will read each one and answer questions about it. Choose the best answer and mark the corresponding letter (A), (B), (C), or (D) on the answer sheet.

Questions 153–154 refer to the following e-mail.

To: Harold Song
From: Kimberly Kent
Subject: Malibu Optical Convention
Date: April 10

Dear Harold,

I am now attaching my presentation for the Malibu Optical Convention next month. As discussed, I'd be very grateful if you could read it and tell me your thoughts. Especially, I wonder if you could help me make it more succinct, as I am concerned that it is a little too long. Any suggestions would be greatly appreciated. Also, please can you double check that the company logo on page one is in the right format—as you know, I am not good with design!

If you are happy to, could we meet tomorrow or the day after to talk about it? I want to hear your feedback in person. Afternoons anytime after 2 work for me, so please let me know when would suit you best.

Best,
Kim

153. Why is the woman e-mailing the man?

(A) To inform him of a design change
(B) To arrange a conference
(C) To express gratitude
(D) To get help with a presentation

154. What does Ms. Kent ask Mr. Song to do?

(A) Give a presentation on her behalf
(B) Check a proposal
(C) Meet with her one afternoon
(D) Complete a conference schedule

Questions 155–156 refer to the following letter.

Tenpil Pharma

November 11

Patricia Darnley
Sales Manager
Butler Henderson
342 Milan Avenue
Arlington, VA 43245

Dear Ms. Darnley,

We are writing to inform you that as of December 1, we will be transferring our headquarters to Mildmay Business Park, Axton Boulevard, Baltimore, MD. You should use this address for all written correspondence with customer service effective December 1. Customer service telephone numbers will be the same. Our Product Development Team will stay at our current address in Arlington, VA.

I am also taking this opportunity to send you our new product brochure, which may be of interest to you.

Thank you for your valued support. We hope to continue offering excellent service from our new premises.

Sincerely,

Peter Freeman
Customer Relations Officer
Tenpil Pharma

Enc.

155. What is the purpose of the letter?

(A) To advertise new products

(B) To arrange a business meeting

(C) To reply to a customer

(D) To communicate a change of address

156. What is being sent with the letter?

(A) A business agreement

(B) An invoice for purchased items

(C) A list of phone numbers

(D) Information about products

Go on to the next page ➔

Questions 157–159 refer to the following e-mail.

From: Debra Langley dlangley@food_direct.com
To: All employees employees@food_direct.com
Date: May 5
Subject: New policy

The updated leave policy will take effect on May 6.

To summarize the revised policy, which was e-mailed to you all on April 16, all employees will now have to request leave at least two calendar weeks before the date upon which the proposed leave starts. Requests must be submitted through the company intranet by clicking on "Absence Management" and then "Submit Leave Request." Once entered into the system, request forms will be sent automatically to your line manager and department manager (where these differ).

We hope that these arrangements are clear. If not, please get in touch with your Human Resources contact.

---

157. Why was the e-mail written?

(A) To explain an office move

(B) To ask about new computer software

(C) To give feedback on customer service

(D) To sum up a new policy

158. When will the change occur?

(A) Today

(B) Tomorrow

(C) In one week

(D) In two weeks

159. What do staff have to do to submit a request?

(A) Consult their managers

(B) Speak to staff in Human Resources

(C) Fill out an online form

(D) Make their own appointments

Questions 160–161 refer to the following article.

Chime Music
Announces Digital Strategy

Chime Music, whose Downtown label hosts some of the best up-and-coming artists in popular music, announced Friday its plan to invest in digital sales over the coming quarter. Chime, which reported a significant drop in profits for the third consecutive quarter last month, has had its revenues squeezed by illegal MP3 downloads and competitors' more innovative offerings in digital sales. Following its competitors, Chime will now seek to produce value-added digital content, for instance offering exclusive video and multimedia content to customers buying albums and singles digitally. In this way, the company expects to increase sales, and thereby maintain its stable of exciting new artists. The company's biggest star, Jessica Saunders, won a record four awards at last month's Music Association Awards, and has had three number one hits this year. However, she is also presumed to be the most illegally downloaded artist, something that Chime aims to address with its new strategy.

160. How does Chime Music plan to raise sales?

(A) By expanding into new countries

(B) By selling electronic content

(C) By attracting the best artists

(D) By selling more albums

161. What is mentioned about Jessica Saunders?

(A) She is the company's best known artist.

(B) She is the number one musician this year.

(C) She served as a presenter at a ceremony.

(D) She purchased some MP3s.

Go on to the next page ➔

Questions 162–165 refer to the following schedule.

National Association of Electrical Engineers (NAEE)

JOB FAIR

Socrates Conference Center, Joles Science Park, Cambridge CB14 7NP

SCHEDULE

8:00–9:30 a.m. Registration
Delegates register for the event, and receive conference packs.
Location: Conference center front desk

9:30–10:00 a.m. Opening Address
Jonathan Hope, President of the NAEE, will give the opening speech on
emerging trends in aeronautical engineering.
Location: Crescent Room

10:00–10:30 a.m. Break
Complimentary tea and coffee break. Delegates will have the chance to
chat informally with recruiters and company representatives.
Location: Exhibition Center

10:30 a.m.–4:30 p.m. Employer Exhibition
Delegates can meet representatives of various companies about job openings.
Job seekers are encouraged to bring copies of their résumé to distribute to employers
of interest. Some companies will be hosting official interviews on the day of the fair.
Location: Exhibition Center

4:30–5:30 p.m. Keynote Lecture
"Modeling and Performance Verification Tools in Electronics" by Dr. Linda Finn.
Location: Crescent Room

10:30 a.m.–5:30 p.m. Career Guidance
Professional career advisers will be on hand throughout the event to give delegates
advice on their résumés and job hunting tips.
Location: Fisher Room

---

162. For whom is this event mostly likely intended?

(A) Math teachers

(B) Engineering professionals

(C) Careers consultants

(D) Event managers

163. What will the president of the association talk about?

(A) New developments in the field

(B) The opening of a new research center

(C) The growth of global markets

(D) Advice on gardening

164. What will happen during the break?

(A) An opening address will be given.

(B) Interviews will be held.

(C) Free refreshments will be offered.

(D) Talks will be given by staff.

165. What will be available in the Fisher Room?

(A) Family counseling

(B) Job interviews

(C) Presentations of new products

(D) Assistance for job seekers

Questions 166–168 refer to the following letter.

Jump Travel

165, Rue de Temple
Lille, France
Tel: 02 48 90 48 12
Fax: 02 48 56 11 48

Ms. Julie Mathieson
Av. du Nuremberg
Lille, France

September 26

Dear Ms. Mathieson,

Many thanks for using Jump Travel's English language service. Your request has been processed successfully, and I can now confirm your reservation and itinerary. I'm afraid there are no direct flights to your destination, so you will have to transfer in Paris. Please see your itinerary below and contact us if anything is incorrect. Changes can be made until October 5.

Outbound	**Inbound**
Departure date: October 16	Departure date: November 1
From: Lille Nord Airport	From: Lyon International
To: Lyon International	To: Lille Nord Airport
Departure time: 07:05 a.m.	Departure time: 20:15 p.m.
Arrival at destination: 13:35 p.m.	Arrival at destination: 01:25 a.m. (November 2)

Your tickets for these flights will be e-mailed to you within 24 hours. Should you need to speak to us about anything, please call us at 02 48 90 48 12, e-mail jump-lille@jumptravel.fr, or visit any of our branches.

Best wishes for an enjoyable journey,

Margot Thibauld
Manager
Jump Travel, Lille

---

166. What is the purpose of the letter?

(A) To confirm journey plans

(B) To make a payment for a flight

(C) To announce a change of destination

(D) To reserve a vacation package

167. What is suggested about Ms. Mathieson?

(A) She knows French.

(B) She wanted a direct flight.

(C) She is busy.

(D) She will visit friends in Paris.

168. When will Ms. Mathieson return to Lille?

(A) October 5

(B) October 16

(C) November 1

(D) November 2

Go on to the next page ➜

Questions 169–171 refer to the following flyer.

SuperClean Office Cleaning Solutions
Coming to Columbus

SuperClean Office Cleaning Solutions will be starting its operations in Columbus, OH, in July. Already successful on the East Coast, SuperClean is every office's favorite partner when it comes to office cleaning. Why? Because we offer free quotes, use only the most thoughtful and reliable employees, and include no hidden costs in our charges—we have only two, clearly defined packages that cater to all your office cleaning needs:

Our Standard Cleaning Package includes:
* *daily disposal of trash from trash cans*
* *daily floor wiping/vacuuming*
* *daily bathroom cleaning*
* *weekly desk tidying*

Our Free Choice Cleaning Package offers all of the above, plus:
* *monthly window cleaning*
* *monthly thorough office cleaning*
* *bimonthly carpet washing / floor waxing*

In addition, companies with multiple sites can receive up to **20% off** our standard prices. Please contact us for a quote.

To mark our expansion into Columbus, we are giving clients in the area a special 10% discount on our Standard Cleaning Package, and 10% off our Free Choice Cleaning Package, for a short time only.

To take advantage of these wonderful deals, and to experience our fantastic cleaning and customer service, contact us now.
Telephone: 875-555-1991
E-mail: customercare@superclean-columbus.com

---

169. What is the purpose of the advertisement?

(A) To offer discounts on printing services

(B) To publicize the expansion of a business

(C) To recruit office cleaners

(D) To announce changes to a package

170. What service is NOT offered in the Standard Cleaning Package?

(A) Trash removal

(B) Restroom cleaning

(C) Floor shining

(D) Desk tidying

171. Who can get the largest discount?

(A) Companies with more than one office

(B) Firms choosing the basic package

(C) New offices in the area

(D) Current clients

Questions 172–175 refer to the following notice.

SALEM AUTOMOTIVE

Date: June 6   **Subject:** Charity event

Salem Automotive will be hosting its annual charity event on July 7, to which all staff are cordially invited. This year's nominated charity, selected by staff, is the Junior Community Choir. As usual, the event will be held in the Mortimer Center, where a buffet lunch will be served. Entertainment will be provided by local comedian Bobby Mortimer and the Cardinal Jazz Trio.

Chairman Harry Peterson will be present, and will give a speech at the end of the event. Harry has been the driving force behind the company's engagement with the local community, and wishes to take the opportunity to thank staff members for their contribution over the years.

Tickets for the event cost $30 and will be sold on a first come, first served basis starting June 15. Various employees will be selling tickets. Please refer to staff notice boards for details of your closest ticket seller. Needless to say, all proceeds from ticket sales will be donated to the Junior Community Choir. To thank us for our support, the Choir will be visiting our site at lunchtime on August 18 to give a special performance in the staff lunchroom.

172. Who is the notice for?

(A) Employees

(B) Interns

(C) Choir singers

(D) Corporate caterers

173. What is the purpose of the event?

(A) To support a community charity

(B) To hire new employees

(C) To recruit volunteers

(D) To motivate staff

174. When will tickets become available?

(A) June 6

(B) June 15

(C) July 7

(D) August 18

175. What is NOT true about Harry Peterson?

(A) He is a company employee.

(B) He has directed the company's work with the community.

(C) He is thankful to staff members.

(D) He is responsible for the event.

Go on to the next page ➜

Questions 176–180 refer to the following information.

Newport Shipping Co. FAQs

➤ Where do I find my local Newport Shipping representative?
Newport Shipping has a wide network of branches throughout North and South America, Oceania, and Europe. We also have more than 400 branches in Africa run by our partner, Newport Transportation Co. You can find your closest store using our online store locator at www.newportshipping.com/storefinder. Alternatively, you may call our international customer service at 1-800-555-2121. At all our stores, you will find friendly and helpful staff, as well as items for all your shipping needs, such as packaging solutions, wrapping, and labels.

➤ Does Newport Shipping offer package pick-up?
Yes, Newport Shipping will collect packages from business or private addresses in most locations. To check your location, please use our online address checker at www.newportshipping.com/addresscheck. The address checker can also show you the operating hours of your local collection service. Same-day pick-ups are available at most city locations, except in South America, and 24-hour collection is available from most branches in Europe.

➤ How can I track my delivery?
Newport Shipping owns an industry-leading shipment tracking system that enables you to monitor your shipment at every stage of the process. To track your shipment, simply log on to our website at www.newportshipping.com and click on "Track." Then, type in the unique shipment number that you received when your order was processed. We also have a mobile application that enables you to track your shipment while you are on the move. The application is available for most popular platforms and can be downloaded from app stores in the usual way, for free.

➤ What happens if my package is damaged?
Newport Shipping very rarely damages a package. However, there are times when, due to circumstances beyond our control, a shipment is mishandled. If you believe for any reason that your delivery has been mistreated, please contact our Customer Service Department immediately at 1-800-555-4939. We guarantee that our operators will do everything possible to resolve the issue. In the event that the item has been damaged, you will benefit from Newport Shipping's free replacement policy on most shipped items.

176. Who most likely is the audience for the information?

(A) Customers
(B) New employees
(C) Store managers
(D) Delivery drivers

177. What is stated about branches in Africa?

(A) They are operated by an associate company.
(B) They are newly launched.
(C) They have a same-day pick up service.
(D) They offer 24-hour collection.

178. The word "unique" in paragraph 3 is closest in meaning to

(A) unreal
(B) individual
(C) electronic
(D) special

179. How can shipments be traced?

(A) By checking a website
(B) By purchasing insurance
(C) By going to a store
(D) By calling a customer representative

180. What should the customer do first if a package is damaged?

(A) Visit the website
(B) Make a phone call
(C) Send an e-mail
(D) Pay for insurance

Questions 181–185 refer to the following article and e-mail.

Sinaloa Property News

Phase 1 of Rawlinson Court Development Now Complete

Holmes Developments announced in May that the first phase of the landmark Rawlinson Court development off Haigh Street was finished. The completion of Phase 1 is a remarkable achievement for the house builder, who encountered various problems with planning regulations in securing permission for the build. The development, whose total projected cost is $30 million, will feature more than 100 dwellings, including 50 affordable homes—20 more than originally planned. Phase 1 comprises 15 homes, all of which have already been sold.

"Holmes has worked with the neighborhood authorities and community to complete Phase 1 of the build on time," Holmes' Public Relations Manager Bella Walker told *Sinaloa Property News*. "While local figures at first raised concerns about the development, we believe that our inclusion of affordable homes in the project will help allay their fears, and insure that local residents are able to purchase property in the area, thanks to Rawlinson Court and Holmes Developments."

Walker announced that the company will be hosting a street party in the development on July 15 to welcome new owners and tenants, and to thank builders and other workers for their efforts.

The choice of the Haigh Street district for the development surprised many when it was first announced. However, the latest announcement of plans for a high-speed railway with a station on Haigh Street, as well as the construction of Highway 15, has drawn the attention of many in the real estate business. Two other developers are now rumored to be considering making bids to redevelop other sites in the neighborhood.

To: Mark Parker m.parker@holmesdev.co.uk
From: Margaret Russell russell.m@thepr.biz
Date: June 22
Subject: Rawlinson Court opening party

Dear Mark,

I'm writing to update you on preparations for the upcoming event at your company's Rawlinson Court development.

We have now organized all catering, for which you will be invoiced directly prior to the event. Costs are well within our approved budget. I would like to draw your attention to a matter that was raised during our event planning meeting here yesterday. This concerns the weather. As you know, the present plan, as requested by your company, is to hold the event outdoors in the central courtyard area. However, we think it would be better to develop a contingency plan in case of inclement weather on the day. Perhaps a large tent would be a good alternative, and we would be able to order one within the stipulated budget. Please let me know what you think.

On another note, we have successfully generated some media attention for the event. Local radio have asked us if they can broadcast a piece live from the event, and we have been told that reporters from both local newspapers will attend. Please could you put me in touch with your Public Relations Manager so that we can make preparations for this?

Best wishes,

Margaret Russell
Events Management Assistant

Questions on next page ➔

181. What is the main topic of the article?

(A) A court trial

(B) Public transportation

(C) New regulations

(D) A housing development

182. What is implied in the article?

(A) The area has become a popular place for construction.

(B) Costs are higher than expected.

(C) Local residents oppose the building of the train station.

(D) A welcome party for future residents has been postponed.

183. Who most likely is Mark Parker?

(A) A resident of Rawlinson Court

(B) A newspaper reporter

(C) A relative of Margaret Russell

(D) A colleague of Bella Walker

184. What is suggested in the e-mail?

(A) Looking at a weather forecast

(B) Decreasing a budget

(C) Making alternative arrangements

(D) Purchasing less food

185. What will Mark Parker probably do?

(A) Introduce Margaret Russell to Bella Walker

(B) Call another catering service

(C) Go to a meeting with Margaret Russell

(D) Contact local media reporters

Questions 186–190 refer to the following advertisement and e-mail.

ASIAN KITCHEN

Asian Kitchen is the largest importer and distributor of Korean, Japanese, and Chinese food products on the East Coast. Our company was founded over ten years ago, and has since become established as the market leader, supplying fresh meats, vegetables, and processed products to stores and restaurants throughout the region. We operate a delivery fleet of more than 300 refrigerated vehicles, and have a central warehouse with a storage capacity of 130,000 square feet.

As we intend to expand our network of satisfied customers, we are currently offering discounted delivery charges of up to 15% for new customers buying a minimum of $2,500 of produce per month.*

For further information about purchasing from us, and for a product price list, please e-mail our customer account staff at customers@a-kitchen-suppliers.com.

*terms and conditions apply

To: customers@a-kitchen-suppliers.com
From: Maggie Lee maggie@maggieseoul.com
Subject: Korean food supplies
Date: December 5

Dear Sir/Madam,

I am in the process of launching a restaurant in Raleigh, North Carolina. As we will be specializing in Korean cuisine, we are seeking suppliers of Korean ingredients, primarily vegetables, meats, and beverages. We will likely purchase somewhere within the region of $5,000–$10,000 of supplies per month. We are also intending to expand our business by opening a number of other restaurants in surrounding areas over the coming years. We have been given an estimate by Kwak Wholesale, but we are dissatisfied with that company's delivery charges. They could not offer us a discount, even though we are a business with strong future growth potential. I'd greatly appreciate it if you could give me a call to discuss our requirements and to give me an estimate.

I look forward to hearing from you.

Best,
Maggie Lee

Questions on next page ➜

186. What is NOT stated about Asian Kitchen?

(A) It owns a number of restaurants.

(B) It delivers on the East Coast.

(C) It provides chilled products.

(D) It offers discounts to new customers.

187. What is the purpose of Ms. Lee's message?

(A) To find out about doing business with Asian Kitchen

(B) To comment on a supplier

(C) To change a food order

(D) To apply for a position at Asian Kitchen

188. What is stated about Ms. Lee?

(A) She has a background in the restaurant trade.

(B) She is dissatisfied with her business partner.

(C) She will attempt to grow her business.

(D) She runs a food market.

189. What can be assumed about Kwak Wholesale?

(A) It has more growth potential than Asian Kitchen.

(B) It charges extra for delivery.

(C) It has a larger supply network than Asian Kitchen.

(D) It was unhappy with Ms. Lee.

190. What most likely will Ms. Lee receive from Asian Kitchen?

(A) A job offer

(B) A 15% discount on delivery charges

(C) A price list

(D) Item samples

Questions 191–195 refer to the following form and e-mail.

ELECTRONICS WEEKLY

✔ Yes, please sign me up for six weekly issues of *Electronics Weekly*, at the special introductory rate of $2 per issue. After that, I'd like six more issues at the regular price of $4.99.

Customer Details		Payment Information	
Name:	Arthur Whitney	Credit card:	Visa
Address:	45 Lincoln Street, Montreal, Canada	Name on card:	Arthur Whitney
E-mail:	awhitney@plusmail.com	Card number:	4541 1991 72352 1978 CVS 285

Two complimentary items courtesy of *Electronics Weekly*:

Item	Code	Quantity
Desk lamp	PH31G	
Smartphone headphones	GP23L	1
Electric kettle	GO33P	
Universal electric converter	MG12P	1

Comments
Although I understand I can only have two free items from the list above, could I possibly buy item GO33P and so receive this as well as the two other items I have chosen?

To: Arthur Whitney awhitney@plusmail.com
From: Francesca Stanton f.stanton@elecsweekly.org
Subject: *Electronics Weekly* subscription

Dear Mr. Whitney,

Many thanks for subscribing to *Electronics Weekly*. You will be getting your first discounted issue shortly.

I am sorry to inform you that one of the free items that you chose, MG12P, is out of stock at the moment. We will ship the item to you as soon as it is available. I am afraid that at present I cannot inform you when this will be. The other free item that you chose, GP23L, is available and will be delivered to you along with your first issue of the magazine.

In response to your question regarding the possibility of purchasing an additional item, I am sorry that we are not able to sell any of the products on our free items list. I apologize for any disappointment that this may cause you. I am certain that you would be able to source the item from a vendor who does sell such products.

Thank you again for your subscription.

Yours sincerely,

Francesca Stanton
Promotions Dept.
Weekly Magazines

Questions on next page ➜

191. Why did Mr. Whitney complete the form?

(A) To purchase a subscription

(B) To ask for a credit card refund

(C) To make an additional order

(D) To stop receiving a magazine

192. What is the total cost of Mr. Whitney's order?

(A) $2

(B) $4.99

(C) $41.94

(D) $119.88

193. What does Mr. Whitney indicate on the form?

(A) He ordered the wrong product by mistake.

(B) He has a new address.

(C) He was overcharged for an item.

(D) He wants to purchase an additional item.

194. According to the e-mail, which item is not available at present?

(A) Smartphone headphones

(B) Desk lamp

(C) Electric kettle

(D) Universal electric converter

195. What does Ms. Stanton advise Mr. Whitney to do?

(A) Select a different item

(B) Wait for a full refund

(C) Find an alternative seller

(D) Re-subscribe to the newsletter

Questions 196–200 refer to the following e-mails.

To: Nancy Levine nlevine@socpol.edu
From: Adam Wooding awooding@marlboropub.com
Date: April 17
Subject: Social Policy Conference

Dear Prof. Levine,

I work as Senior Editor for Health and Social Sciences at Marlboro Books in New Hampshire. I am currently looking for authors for a series of new titles in the fields of economics and sociology. I would therefore very much like to attend your conference in London on June 18.

I note from your tentative schedule that many of the speakers whose talks I would like to attend are presenting on Friday. Due to other work commitments, I am regrettably not able to attend the conference until Saturday. I will be traveling back from a work trip to Shanghai on that Friday. A colleague of mine told me that, when faced with a similar situation in the past, she was able to view the conference talks online. I wonder if you have similar arrangements this year to put the presentations on your website? I'd appreciate it if you could let me know. I am most interested in viewing the following talks:

Prof. John Whitaker: European economic crisis
Dr. Kevin Sharpe: The new social economy of regional politics
Prof. Maria Dominguez: Social welfare in post-war African states
Prof. Douglas Swann: International development theory—A case study

Thank you very much for any advice on this.

Kind regards,

Adam Wooding
Senior Editor
Marlboro Publishing

To: Adam Wooding awooding@marlboropub.com
From: Nancy Levine nlevine@socpol.edu
Date: April 20
Subject: Social Policy Conference

Dear Mr. Wooding,

Thank you very much for your message, and for your interest in our conference. You'll be relieved to know that we do indeed plan to make many of our presentations available for on-demand viewing. We will also be showing all presentations live on our website during the event. To access the live stream and the videos after the event, please follow these steps:

1. Visit our website, www.socpol.edu
2. Click either on "Streaming" (accessible during the conference), or "Filmed Lectures" (available 24 hours after the conference ends).
3. When prompted, enter your membership username. Note that only members are able to access video content.

Due to rights issues, we cannot offer on-demand video of all the lectures. I'm sorry to let you know that the third of the lectures that you are interested in will not be available on-demand. It will, nevertheless, be streamed live on the Friday of the conference.

Please e-mail me if you have any further queries, or call us at our London office.

Best,

Prof. Nancy Levine
Social Policy Society

Questions on next page →

196. In which industry does Mr. Wooding most likely work?

(A) Academia

(B) Publishing

(C) Law

(D) Event management

197. Where will the conference be held?

(A) In Shanghai

(B) In London

(C) In New Hampshire

(D) In Rome

198. In the first e-mail, the word "tentative" in paragraph 2 is closest in meaning to

(A) temporary

(B) draft

(C) amended

(D) printed

199. What should Mr. Wooding do to be able to watch the presentations?

(A) Get a password.

(B) Contact the society's office.

(C) Become a member of the society.

(D) Postpone a conference

200. Which presentation will Mr. Wooding probably not be able to watch?

(A) European economic crisis

(B) Social welfare in post-war African states

(C) The new social economy of regional politics

(D) None

This is the end of the Reading Test.

Look at the next page to start the Speaking Test ➔

Test 4: Speaking

This speaking test includes 11 questions that evaluate your ability to speak English. This test will take approximately 20 minutes.

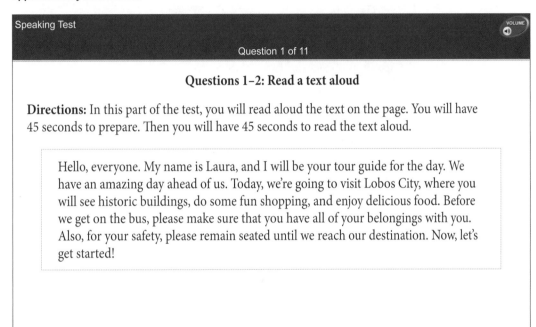

Speaking Test

VOLUME

Questions 1–2: Read a text aloud

Directions: In this part of the test, you will read aloud the text on the page. You will have 45 seconds to prepare. Then you will have 45 seconds to read the text aloud.

> Hello, everyone. My name is Laura, and I will be your tour guide for the day. We have an amazing day ahead of us. Today, we're going to visit Lobos City, where you will see historic buildings, do some fun shopping, and enjoy delicious food. Before we get on the bus, please make sure that you have all of your belongings with you. Also, for your safety, please remain seated until we reach our destination. Now, let's get started!

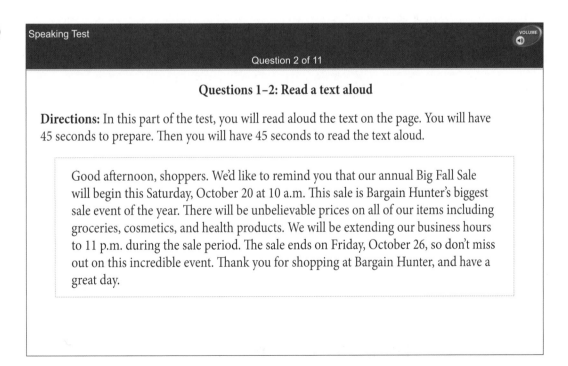

Speaking Test

VOLUME

Questions 1–2: Read a text aloud

Directions: In this part of the test, you will read aloud the text on the page. You will have 45 seconds to prepare. Then you will have 45 seconds to read the text aloud.

> Good afternoon, shoppers. We'd like to remind you that our annual Big Fall Sale will begin this Saturday, October 20 at 10 a.m. This sale is Bargain Hunter's biggest sale event of the year. There will be unbelievable prices on all of our items including groceries, cosmetics, and health products. We will be extending our business hours to 11 p.m. during the sale period. The sale ends on Friday, October 26, so don't miss out on this incredible event. Thank you for shopping at Bargain Hunter, and have a great day.

Go on to the next page ➔

Question 3: Describe a picture

Directions: You will describe a photograph as completely as you can. The photograph is in the test book. You will have 30 seconds to prepare what you will say, and then you will have 45 seconds to describe the picture in as much detail as possible.

Questions 4–6: Respond to questions

Directions: You will be asked three questions. After each question you will hear a beep. Begin speaking your answer immediately after the beep. You will not have any time to prepare your answer. For Questions 4 and 5 you will have 15 seconds to respond. For Question 6 you will have 30 seconds.

———————————

Imagine that an Australian marketing firm is doing research in your country. You have agreed to participate in a telephone interview about job interviews.

Question 4: When was the last time you had a job interview, and was it successful?

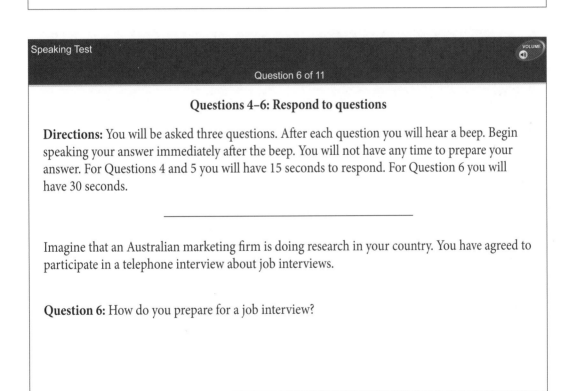

Questions 4–6: Respond to questions

Directions: You will be asked three questions. After each question you will hear a beep. Begin speaking your answer immediately after the beep. You will not have any time to prepare your answer. For Questions 4 and 5 you will have 15 seconds to respond. For Question 6 you will have 30 seconds.

_____

Imagine that an Australian marketing firm is doing research in your country. You have agreed to participate in a telephone interview about job interviews.

Question 5: What do you usually wear to a job interview?

Questions 4–6: Respond to questions

Directions: You will be asked three questions. After each question you will hear a beep. Begin speaking your answer immediately after the beep. You will not have any time to prepare your answer. For Questions 4 and 5 you will have 15 seconds to respond. For Question 6 you will have 30 seconds.

_____

Imagine that an Australian marketing firm is doing research in your country. You have agreed to participate in a telephone interview about job interviews.

Question 6: How do you prepare for a job interview?

Go on to the next page ➔

Questions 7–9: Respond to questions using information provided

Directions: You will read a short text and then answer three questions based on the information in the text. You will have 30 seconds to read the text before the first question. After each question you will hear a beep. Begin speaking immediately after the beep. You will not have any extra time to prepare your answer. For Questions 7 and 8 you will have 15 seconds to respond. For Question 9 you will have 30 seconds.

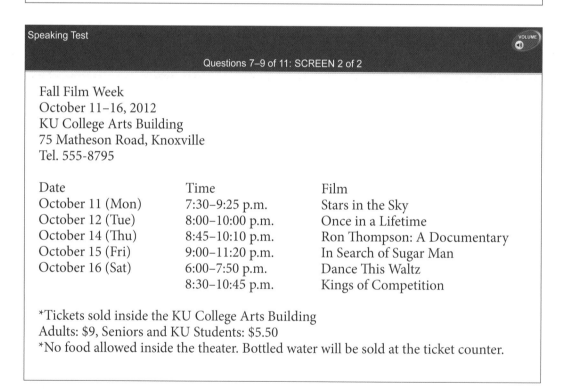

Fall Film Week
October 11–16, 2012
KU College Arts Building
75 Matheson Road, Knoxville
Tel. 555-8795

Date	Time	Film
October 11 (Mon)	7:30–9:25 p.m.	Stars in the Sky
October 12 (Tue)	8:00–10:00 p.m.	Once in a Lifetime
October 14 (Thu)	8:45–10:10 p.m.	Ron Thompson: A Documentary
October 15 (Fri)	9:00–11:20 p.m.	In Search of Sugar Man
October 16 (Sat)	6:00–7:50 p.m.	Dance This Waltz
	8:30–10:45 p.m.	Kings of Competition

*Tickets sold inside the KU College Arts Building
Adults: $9, Seniors and KU Students: $5.50
*No food allowed inside the theater. Bottled water will be sold at the ticket counter.

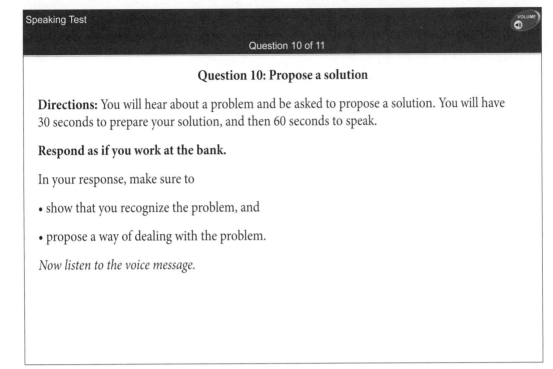

51

Speaking Test

VOLUME

Question 10 of 11

Question 10: Propose a solution

Directions: You will hear about a problem and be asked to propose a solution. You will have 30 seconds to prepare your solution, and then 60 seconds to speak.

Respond as if you work at the bank.

In your response, make sure to

• show that you recognize the problem, and

• propose a way of dealing with the problem.

Now listen to the voice message.

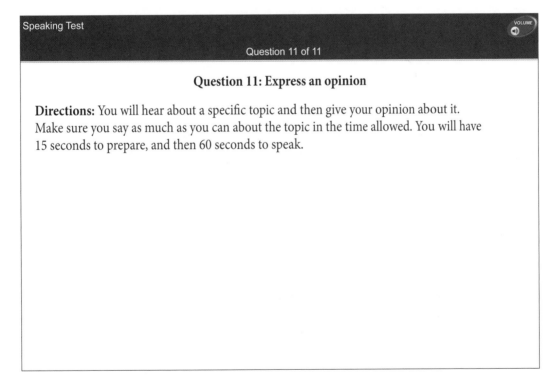

52

Speaking Test

VOLUME

Question 11 of 11

Question 11: Express an opinion

Directions: You will hear about a specific topic and then give your opinion about it. Make sure you say as much as you can about the topic in the time allowed. You will have 15 seconds to prepare, and then 60 seconds to speak.

This is the end of the Speaking Test.

Go on to the next page to start the Writing Test ➔

Test 4: Writing

This writing test includes 8 questions that evaluate your ability to write English. This test will take approximately 1 hour.

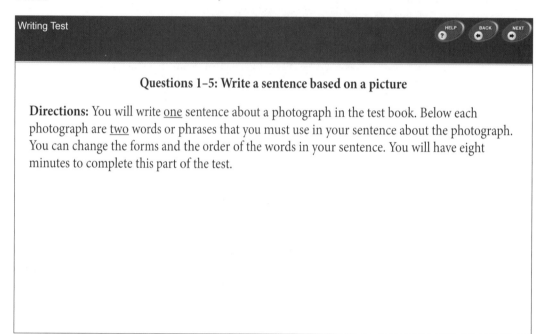

Questions 1–5: Write a sentence based on a picture

Directions: You will write one sentence about a photograph in the test book. Below each photograph are two words or phrases that you must use in your sentence about the photograph. You can change the forms and the order of the words in your sentence. You will have eight minutes to complete this part of the test.

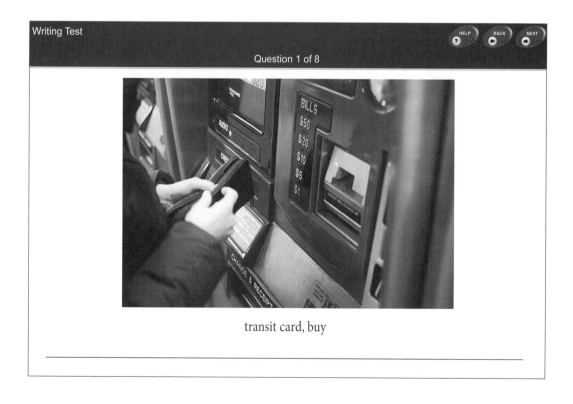

transit card, buy

Writing Test

play, soccer

Writing Test

recycle, trash can

Go on to the next page ➔

play, guitar

_____

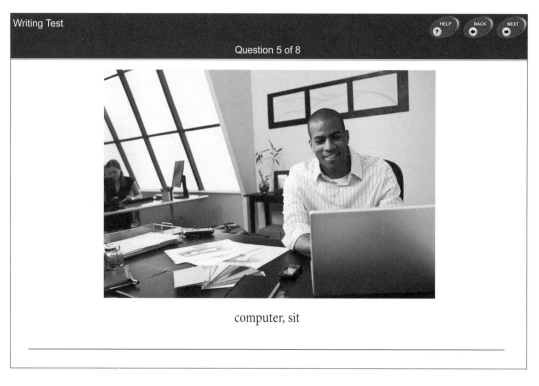

computer, sit

_____

Questions 6–7: Respond to a written request

Directions: You will write responses to two e-mails. Your essay will be evaluated on

- sentence quality
- vocabulary
- grammar
- organization

You will have 10 minutes to read and respond to each e-mail.

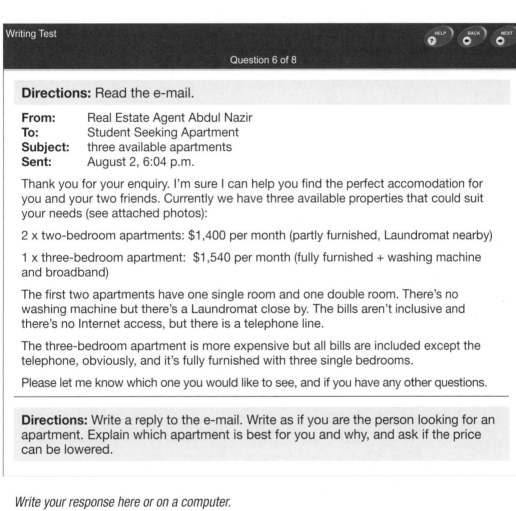

Directions: Read the e-mail.

From: Real Estate Agent Abdul Nazir
To: Student Seeking Apartment
Subject: three available apartments
Sent: August 2, 6:04 p.m.

Thank you for your enquiry. I'm sure I can help you find the perfect accomodation for you and your two friends. Currently we have three available properties that could suit your needs (see attached photos):

2 x two-bedroom apartments: $1,400 per month (partly furnished, Laundromat nearby)

1 x three-bedroom apartment: $1,540 per month (fully furnished + washing machine and broadband)

The first two apartments have one single room and one double room. There's no washing machine but there's a Laundromat close by. The bills aren't inclusive and there's no Internet access, but there is a telephone line.

The three-bedroom apartment is more expensive but all bills are included except the telephone, obviously, and it's fully furnished with three single bedrooms.

Please let me know which one you would like to see, and if you have any other questions.

Directions: Write a reply to the e-mail. Write as if you are the person looking for an apartment. Explain which apartment is best for you and why, and ask if the price can be lowered.

Write your response here or on a computer.

_____

_____

_____

_____

_____

_____

_____

_____

Go on to the next page ➔

Writing Test

Question 7 of 8

Directions: Read the e-mail.

From: Kids' Birthday Party Fun Company
To: Sam's Dad
Subject: Sam's birthday party
Sent: March 12, 4:04 p.m.

Thank you for contacting us regarding your son Sam's upcoming birthday party. Yes, we have a range of services and products for every budget. We do all kinds of birthday parties with good food and fun entertainment.

As you can see by our attached brochure, we have three menus: pizza, barbecue, and fried chicken. The cake choices are ice cream cake, chocolate cake, or strawberries and cream cake.

Our entertainment options include clowns, magicians, inflatable jumping structures, and even a merry-go-round! Again, each one is always the highlight of our parties and will fit any budget.

Glance through our brochure and let me know which options you prefer.

Directions: Write a reply to the e-mail. Write as if you are the person planning the party. In your reply write which menu and services you want for the party. Suggest a convenient time for someone from the party company to come to your house and do the paperwork for the order.

Write your response here or on a computer.

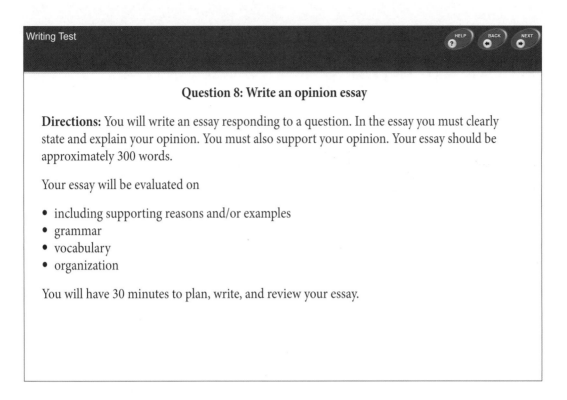

Question 8: Write an opinion essay

Directions: You will write an essay responding to a question. In the essay you must clearly state and explain your opinion. You must also support your opinion. Your essay should be approximately 300 words.

Your essay will be evaluated on

- including supporting reasons and/or examples
- grammar
- vocabulary
- organization

You will have 30 minutes to plan, write, and review your essay.

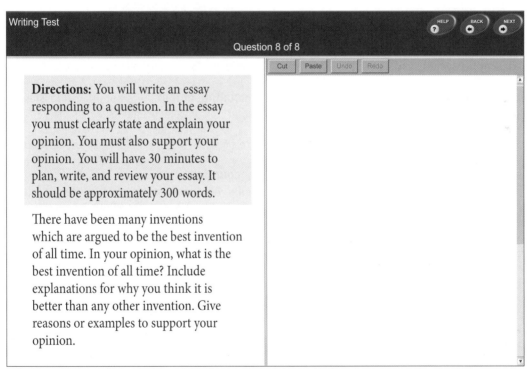

Cut | Paste | Undo | Redo

Directions: You will write an essay responding to a question. In the essay you must clearly state and explain your opinion. You must also support your opinion. You will have 30 minutes to plan, write, and review your essay. It should be approximately 300 words.

There have been many inventions which are argued to be the best invention of all time. In your opinion, what is the best invention of all time? Include explanations for why you think it is better than any other invention. Give reasons or examples to support your opinion.

Write your essay on a separate piece of paper or on a computer.

This is the end of Test 4.

Mini-Dictionary

Some of the more difficult words from each of the Reading and Listening passages are defined here in this mini-dictionary. The definitions focus on the meanings of the words in the context in which they appear in the text. Definitions and examples are from *Collins COBUILD Key Words for the TOEIC*.

ability /əbɪlɪti/ (abilities)
NOUN Your **ability to** do something is the fact that you can do it. ○ *The public never had faith in his ability to do the job.*

absence /æbsᵊns/ (absences)
1 NOUN Someone's **absence** from a place is the fact that they are not there. ○ *the problem of high employee absence in the public sector*
2 NOUN The **absence** of something from a place is the fact that it is not there or does not exist. ○ *In the absence of a will the courts decide who the guardian is.*

absorb /əbsɔrb, -zɔrb/ (absorbs, absorbing or absorbed)
VERB To **absorb** something, such as a liquid or gas, is to take it in. ○ *Dust dries air because it absorbs moisture.*

accept /æksɛpt/ (accepts, accepting or accepted)
VERB If you **accept** something that you have been offered, you say yes to it or agree to take it. ○ *students who have accepted an offer of admission from the university*

acceptable /æksɛptəbᵊl/
ADJECTIVE **Acceptable** activities and situations are those that most people approve of or consider to be normal. ○ *The air pollution exceeds most acceptable levels by 10 times or more.*

acceptance /æksɛptəns/ (acceptances)
NOUN **Acceptance of** an offer or a proposal is the act of saying yes to it or agreeing to it. ○ *a letter of acceptance*

access /æksɛs/ (accesses, accessing or accessed)
1 NOUN If you have **access to** a building or other place, you are able or allowed to go into it. ○ *Does the school have wheelchair access?*
2 NOUN If you have **access to** something such as information or equipment, you have the opportunity or right to see it or use it. ○ *households with Internet access*
3 VERB If you **access** something, especially information held on a computer, you succeed in finding or obtaining it. ○ *a service that allows users to access the Internet on their phones*
4 NOUN An **access** code is a set of numbers or letters that allows you to do something such as join a conference call or see information on a computer. ○ *Do not leave any security information, such as passwords or access codes, on the system.*

accommodate /əkɒmədeɪt/ (accommodates, accommodating or accommodated)
VERB To **accommodate** someone or **accommodate** their needs means to provide them with what they want or need. ○ *The staff were very helpful and did everything they could do accommodate us.*

accomplish /əkɒmplɪʃ/ (accomplishes, accomplishing or accomplished)
VERB If you **accomplish** something, you succeed in doing it. ○ *We accomplished our goal.*

accomplished /əkɒmplɪʃt/
ADJECTIVE If someone is **accomplished** at something, they are very good at it. ○ *She is an accomplished painter.*

accomplishment /əkɒmplɪʃmənt/ (accomplishments)
NOUN Your **accomplishments** are the things that you can do well or the important things that you have done. ○ *appreciation for each person's special efforts and accomplishments*

accounting /əkaʊntɪŋ/
NOUN **Accounting** is the activity of keeping detailed records of the amounts of money a business or person receives and spends. ○ *the accounting firm of Leventhal & Horwath*

accurate /ækyərɪt/
ADJECTIVE **Accurate** information, measurements, and statistics are correct to a very detailed level. An **accurate** instrument is able to give you information of this kind. ○ *a quick and accurate way of monitoring the amount of carbon dioxide in the air*

achievement /ətʃivmənt/ (achievements)
NOUN An **achievement** is something that you succeed in doing or causing to happen, usually after a lot of effort. ○ *Only the achievement of these goals will bring lasting peace.*

acquire /əkwaɪər/ (acquires, acquiring or acquired)
VERB If you **acquire** something such as a skill or a habit, you learn it, or develop it through your daily life or experience. ○ *Piaget was convinced that children acquire knowledge and abilities in stages.*

adequately /ˈædɪkwɪtli/

ADVERB If something is **adequately** done, it is done well enough according to what is required. ○ *Many students are not adequately prepared for higher education.*

adjustment /əˈdʒʌstmənt/ (adjustments)

NOUN Risk **adjustment** is the process of taking into account the risks involved when providing insurance or investing money. ○ *The objective of risk adjustment is to help ensure that budgetary allocations take into account the morbidity of individual patients.*

advance /ædˈvæns/

1 ADJECTIVE An **advance** copy or screening is one that is shown or made available to a small group of people before being shown or made available to the general public. ○ *The press were invited to a special advance screening of the movie.*

2 PHRASE **in advance** If you do something **in advance**, you do it before a particular date or event. ○ *The subject of the talk is announced a week in advance.*

advanced /ædˈvænst/

1 ADJECTIVE Someone who is **advanced** has already learned the basic facts or skills and is doing more difficult work. ○ *The course is suitable for intermediate and advanced students.*

2 ADJECTIVE **Advanced** booking is done before an event happens. ○ *Advanced booking is recommended.*

advancement /ædˈvænsmənt/

NOUN **Advancement** is progress in your job or in your social position. ○ *He did it to help us and not in the hope of any advancement.*

advantage /ædˈvæntɪdʒ/ (advantages)

1 NOUN An **advantage** is a way in which one thing is better than another. ○ *The great advantage of this technique is the cost.*

2 PHRASE **take advantage of** If you **take advantage of** something, you make good use of it while it is available. ○ *Take advantage of this unique opportunity to see behind the scenes of a famous theater.*

advice /ædˈvaɪs/

NOUN If you give someone **advice**, you tell them what you think they should do. ○ *Don't be afraid to ask for advice about the course.*

affect /əˈfɛkt/ (affects, affecting or affected)

VERB If something **affects** a person or thing, it influences them or causes them to change in some way. ○ *The new law will directly affect thousands of people.*

affordable /əˈfɔrdəbəl/

ADJECTIVE If something is **affordable**, most people have enough money to buy it. ○ *the availability of affordable housing*

agent /ˈeɪdʒənt/ (agents)

NOUN An **agent** is a person who looks after someone else's business affairs or does business on their behalf. ○ *You are buying direct, rather than through an agent.*

agreement /əˈgrimənt/ (agreements)

1 NOUN An **agreement** is a formal decision about future action that is made between two or more people, groups, or countries. ○ *Management and unions have reached an agreement on overtime.*

2 NOUN In grammar, **agreement** refers to the way that a word has a form appropriate to the number or gender of the noun or pronoun it relates to. ○ *There has to be agreement between the subject (which is plural) and the verb.*

allow /əˈlaʊ/ (allows, allowing or allowed)

1 VERB If you **allow** someone **to** do something, you give them permission to do it. If you **allow** something, you give permission for people to do or have it. ○ *The government will allow them to advertise on radio and television.*

2 VERB If one thing **allows** another thing **to** happen, it creates the opportunity for the second thing to happen. ○ *She said this would allow more effective planning.*

ample /ˈæmpəl/

ADJECTIVE If there is an **ample** amount of something, there is enough of it and usually some extra. ○ *The navy had ample opportunity to intercept them at sea.*

analysis /əˈnælɪsɪs/ (analyses)

NOUN **Analysis** is the process of studying information or statistics in order to understand or explain something. ○ *This involves mathematical analysis of data from astronomy.*

annual /ˈænyuəl/

1 ADJECTIVE **Annual** events happen once every year. ○ *the society's annual conference*

2 ADJECTIVE **Annual** quantities or rates relate to a period of one year. ○ *The electronic and printing unit has annual sales of about $80 million.*

anxious /ˈæŋkʃəs/

1 ADJECTIVE If someone is **anxious**, they are feeling nervous or worried about something. ○ *I felt very anxious about my presentation.*

2 ADJECTIVE If you are **anxious to** do something, you are eager to do it. ○ *We were all anxious to meet her.*

apologize /əˈpɒlədʒaɪz/ (apologizes, apologizing or apologized)

VERB When you **apologize**, you say that you are sorry. ○ *He apologized for being late.*

appealing /əˈpilɪŋ/

ADJECTIVE Someone or something that is **appealing** is pleasing and attractive. ○ *There was a sense of humor to what he did that I found very appealing.*

applicant /ˈæplɪkənt/ (applicants)

NOUN An **applicant** is someone who formally asks to have

something, such as permission to do something, a visa, or a job. ○ *The firm recently had fifty applicants for one job.*

application /ˌæplɪˈkeɪʃᵊn/ (applications)

1 NOUN An **application for** something is a formal written request for it. ○ *His application for a student loan was rejected.*

2 NOUN An **application** is a piece of software for a computer or cellphone that does a particular thing. ○ *If you are running too many applications your laptop may slow down.*

3 NOUN An **application form** is a written list of questions that you have to answer when you apply for a job. ○ *I enclose my completed application form for the position of Administrative Assistant.*

apply /əˈplaɪ/ (applies, applying or applied)

1 VERB If you **apply for** something such as a job or membership in an organization, you write a letter or fill in a form in order to ask formally for it. ○ *I am continuing to apply for jobs.*

2 VERB If something such as a rule or a remark **applies to** a person or in a situation, it is relevant to the person or the situation. ○ *The convention does not apply to us.*

3 VERB If charges or fees **apply**, they must be paid. ○ *If your account becomes overdrawn, transaction charges will apply.*

appreciate /əˈpriʃieɪt/ (appreciates, appreciating or appreciated)

1 VERB If you **appreciate** something, you are grateful for it. ○ *I would appreciate it if you could give me a call to discuss this.*

2 VERB If you **appreciate** something, you like it. ○ *The audience clearly appreciated his performance.*

approval /əˈpruːvᵊl/

NOUN **Approval** is a formal or official statement that something is acceptable. ○ *The testing and approval of new drugs will be speeded up.*

approve /əˈpruːv/ (approves, approving or approved)

VERB If someone in a position of authority **approves** a plan or idea, they formally agree to it and say that it can happen. ○ *The Russian Parliament has approved a program of radical economic reforms.*

approximately /əˈprɒksɪmɪtli/

ADVERB **Approximately** is used to say that a number, time, or position is close but not exact. ○ *Approximately $150 million is to be spent on improvements.*

arrangement /əˈreɪndʒmənt/ (arrangements)

NOUN **Arrangements** are plans and preparations which you make so that something will happen or be possible. ○ *The staff is working on final arrangements for the conference.*

assessment /əˈsɛsmənt/ (assessments)

NOUN **Assessment** is the process of testing or studying someone or something in order to make a judgement about them. ○ *Everything from course learning materials to final assessment is completed via the Web.*

asset /ˈæsɛt/ (assets)

NOUN The **assets** of a company or a person are all the things that they own. ○ *By the end of 1989 the group had assets of 3.5 billion francs.*

assist /əˈsɪst/ (assists, assisting or assisted)

1 VERB If you **assist** someone, you help them to do a job or task by doing part of the work for them. ○ *Dr. Amid was assisted by a young Asian nurse.*

2 VERB If you **assist** someone, you give them information, advice, or money. ○ *The public is urgently requested to assist police in tracing this man.*

assistance /əˈsɪstəns/

NOUN If you give someone **assistance**, you give them information or advice. ○ *Employees are being offered assistance in finding new jobs.*

assume /əˈsuːm/ (assumes, assuming or assumed)

1 VERB If you **assume that** something is true, you imagine that it is true, sometimes wrongly. ○ *It is a misconception to assume that the two continents are similar.*

2 VERB If someone **assumes** power or responsibility, they take it. ○ *Mr. Cross will assume the role of Chief Executive with a team of four directors.*

assumption /əˈsʌmpʃᵊn/ (assumptions)

NOUN If you make an **assumption that** something is true or will happen, you accept that it is true or will happen, often without any real proof. ○ *Dr. Subroto questioned the scientific assumption on which the global warming theory is based.*

assure /əˈʃʊər/ (assures, assuring or assured)

VERB If you **assure** someone **that** something is true or will happen, you tell them that it is definitely true or will definitely happen, often in order to make them less worried. ○ *The government has assured us that it maintains robust command and control arrangements for its nuclear weapons.*

attach /əˈtætʃ/ (attaches, attaching or attached)

1 VERB If you **attach** something **to** an object, you join it or fasten it to the object. ○ *The gadget can be attached to any vertical surface.*

2 VERB In computing, if you **attach** a file **to** a message that you send to someone, you send it with the message but separate from it. ○ *It is possible to attach executable program files to email.*

attendance /əˈtɛndəns/ (attendances)

NOUN Someone's **attendance** at an event or an institution is the fact that they are present at the event or go regularly to the institution. ○ *Her attendance at school was sporadic.*

attraction /əˈtrækʃᵊn/ (attractions)

NOUN An **attraction** is a feature that makes something interesting or desirable. ○ *the attractions of living on the waterfront*

auditorium /ɔdɪtɔriəm/ (**auditoriums** or **auditoria**)

NOUN An **auditorium** is a large room, hall, or building that is used for events such as meetings and concerts. ○ *a high school auditorium*

available /əveɪləbᵊl/

1 ADJECTIVE If something you want or need is **available**, you can get it. ○ *The studio is available for private use.*

2 ADJECTIVE Someone who is **available** is not busy and is therefore free to talk or to do a particular task. ○ *No one at the company was available for comment.*

awareness /əwɛərnəs/

NOUN **Awareness** of something is knowing about it. ○ *We need to raise public awareness of the disease.*

background /bækgraʊnd/ (**backgrounds**)

1 NOUN A person's **background** is the kind of life, education, and work experience they have had. ○ *His background was in engineering.*

2 NOUN The **background** of a picture consists of the things that are shown as being behind the main subject of the picture, and less noticeable or important. ○ *It's a painting of a lake, with forests and mountains in the background.*

baggage /bægɪdʒ/

NOUN Your **baggage** is all the bags that you take with you when you travel. ○ *Justin's baggage arrived at his parents home.*

basis /beɪsɪs/ (**bases**)

NOUN If something is done **on** a particular **basis**, it is done according to that method, system, or principle. ○ *These judges dealt with questions of law on a day-to-day basis.*

beforehand /bɪfɔrhænd/

ADVERB If something happens **beforehand**, it happens before a particular event. ○ *How did she know beforehand that I was going to go out?*

belong /bɪlɔŋ/ (**belongs, belonging** or **belonged**)

VERB If someone **belongs to** a particular group, they are a member of that group. ○ *I used to belong to a youth club.*

belongings /bɪlɔŋɪŋz/

NOUN Your **belongings** are the things that you own, especially things that are small enough to be carried. ○ *I collected my belongings and left.*

benefit /bɛnɪfɪt/ (**benefits, benefiting, benefitting, benefited** or **benefitted**)

VERB If you **benefit from** something or if it **benefits** you, it helps you or improves your life. ○ *a variety of government programs benefiting children*

beverage /bɛvərɪdʒ, bɛvrɪdʒ/ (**beverages**)

NOUN A **beverage** is a drink. [FORMAL] ○ *hot beverages*

borrow /bɒroʊ/ (**borrows, borrowing** or **borrowed**)

1 VERB If you **borrow** something that belongs to someone else, you use it for a period of time and then return it. ○ *Can I borrow a pen please?*

2 VERB If you **borrow** money **from** someone or **from** a bank, they give it to you and you agree to pay it back at some time in the future. ○ *Morgan borrowed $5,000 from his father to form the company 20 years ago.*

brand /brænd/ (**brands**)

NOUN A **brand** of a product is the version of it that is made by one particular manufacturer. ○ *another brand of cola*

brand name /brænd neɪm/ (**brand names**)

NOUN A **brand name** is the name that a manufacturer gives to a product that it sells. ○ *The drug is marketed under the brand name Viramune.*

brochure /broʊʃʊər/ (**brochures**)

NOUN A **brochure** is a thin magazine with pictures that gives you information about a product or a service. ○ *travel brochures*

campaign /kæmpeɪn/ (**campaigns**)

NOUN A **campaign** is a planned set of activities carried out over a period of time in order to achieve something, for example to sell a product or bring about political change. ○ *The new product will be launched with an exciting marketing campaign.*

capability /keɪpəbɪliti/ (**capabilities**)

NOUN If you have the **capability** or the **capabilities** to do something, you have the ability or the qualities that are necessary to do it. ○ *People experience differences in physical and mental capability depending on the time of day.*

capable /keɪpəbᵊl/

1 ADJECTIVE If someone is **capable**, they have the skill or qualities necessary to do a particular thing well, or to do most things well. ○ *She's a very capable organizer.*

2 ADJECTIVE If a person or thing is **capable of** doing something, they have the ability to do it. ○ *The kitchen is capable of catering for several hundred people.*

capacity /kəpæsiti/ (**capacities**)

NOUN The **capacity** of a piece of equipment or a building is its size, power, or volume. ○ *Each stadium had a seating capacity of about 50,000.*

capital /kæpɪtᵊl/ (**capitals**)

1 NOUN The **capital** of a country is the city or town where its government or legislature meets. ○ *Kathmandu, the capital of Nepal*

2 ADJECTIVE A **capital** letter is written or printed in the form that is used at the beginning of sentences or names. ○ *Each word in the title should start with a capital letter.*

category /kætɪgɔri/ (**categories**)

NOUN If people or things are divided into **categories**, they are divided into groups in such a way that the members of each group are similar to each other in some way. ○ *This book clearly falls into the category of fictionalized autobiography.*

certificate /sərtɪfɪkɪt/ (**certificates**)
NOUN A **certificate** is an official document that you receive when you have completed a course of study or training. ○ *He recently obtained a teaching certificate.*

challenging /tʃælɪndʒɪŋ/
ADJECTIVE A **challenging** task or job requires great effort and determination. ○ *I like my job, but I'd really like to do something more challenging.*

characteristic /kærɪktərɪstɪk/ (**characteristics**)
NOUN The **characteristics** of a person or thing are the qualities or features that belong to them and make them recognizable. ○ *their physical characteristics*

charge /tʃɑrdʒ/ (**charges, charging** or **charged**)
1 VERB If you **charge** someone an amount of money, you ask them to pay that amount for something that you have sold to them or done for them. ○ *Even local daycare centers charge $150 a week.*
2 NOUN A **charge** is an amount of money that you have to pay for a service. ○ *When users choose to play games, a monthly charge of $2.50 or less shows up on their phone bill.*
3 PHRASE **take/be in charge of** If you **take charge of** something, you become responsible for it and in control of it. If you are **in charge of** something, you are responsible for it and control it. ○ *I am in charge of rewriting our company's brochure.*

chronic /krɒnɪk/
ADJECTIVE A **chronic** situation or problem is very severe and unpleasant. ○ *There is a chronic shortage of patrol cars in this police district.*

circulation /sɜrkyəleɪʃ°n/
NOUN The **circulation** of a magazine or newspaper is the number of copies that are sold each time it is produced. ○ *As people are reading more online, the circulation of many newspapers has fallen considerably.*

circumstance /sɜrkəmstæns/ (**circumstances**)
1 NOUN The **circumstances** of a particular situation are the conditions which affect what happens. ○ *Recent opinion polls show that 60 percent favor abortion under certain circumstances.*
2 NOUN The **circumstances** of an event are the way it happened or the causes of it. ○ *I'm making inquiries about the circumstances of Mary Dean's murder.*
3 NOUN Your **circumstances** are the conditions of your life, for example, how much money you have, who you live with, etc. ○ *The amount that you can borrow with a loan will depend upon your personal circumstances.*

claim /kleɪm/ (**claims, claiming** or **claimed**)
1 VERB If you say that someone **claims that** something is true, you mean they say that it is true but you are not sure whether or not they are telling the truth. ○ *He claimed that it was all a conspiracy against him.*
2 NOUN A **claim** is a request for money that someone makes to an insurance company or other organization. ○ *Claims for property damage following the storms are likely to run to millions of dollars.*

classify /klæsɪfaɪ/ (**classifies, classifying** or **classified**)
VERB To **classify** things means to divide them into groups or types so that things with similar characteristics are in the same group. ○ *Rocks can be classified according to their mode of origin.*

collection /kəlɛkʃ°n/ (**collections**)
NOUN **Collection** is the act of collecting something from a place or from people. ○ *Money can be sent to any one of 22,000 agents worldwide for collection.* A fashion designer's new **collection** consists of the new clothes he or she has designed for the next season. ○ *Her latest collection will be modeled at the Paris fashion show.*

combine /kəmbaɪn/ (**combines, combining** or **combined**)
1 VERB If you **combine** two or more things or if they **combine**, they exist together. ○ *If improved education is combined with other factors, dramatic results can be achieved.*
2 VERB If you **combine** two or more things or if they **combine**, they join together to make a single thing. ○ *Combined with other compounds, they created a massive dynamite-type bomb.*

comment /kɒmɛnt/ (**comments**)
NOUN A **comment** is something that you say which expresses your opinion of something or which gives an explanation of it. ○ *He made his comments at a news conference in Amsterdam.*

commercial /kəmɜrʃ°l/
1 ADJECTIVE **Commercial** means involving or relating to the buying and selling of goods. ○ *Attacks were reported on police, vehicles, and commercial premises.*
2 NOUN A **commercial** is an advertisement that is broadcast on television or radio. ○ *The song has also been used in TV commercials for Royal Caribbean Cruise Lines.*

commitment /kəmɪtmənt/ (**commitments**)
NOUN If you make a **commitment to** do something, you promise that you will do it. [FORMAL] ○ *We made a commitment to keep working together.*

committee /kəmɪti/ (**committees**)
NOUN A **committee** is a group of people who meet to make decisions or plans for a larger group. ○ *The report was given to the ethics committee for review.*

commute /kəmyut/ (**commutes, commuting** or **commuted**)
1 VERB If you **commute**, you travel a long distance every day

between your home and your place of work. ○ *He's going to commute.*

2 NOUN A **commute** is the journey that you make every day between your home and your place of work. ○ *If you have a long commute, good gas mileage is a top priority.*

commuter /kəmyut/ (**commuters**)

NOUN A **commuter** is someone who travels a long distance every day between their home and their place of work. ○ *The number of commuters has dropped by 100,000.*

compare /kəmpɛər/ (**compares, comparing** or **compared**)

VERB When you **compare** things, you consider them and discover the differences or similarities between them. ○ *Compare the two illustrations in Fig. 60.*

compatible /kəmpætɪbəl/

ADJECTIVE If a brand of computer or equipment is **compatible with** another brand, they can be used together and can use the same software. ○ *iTunes is only compatible with the iPod while Microsoft and Sony are offering rival technologies.*

competition /kɒmpɪtɪʃən/

1 NOUN **Competition** is an activity involving two or more companies, in which each company tries to get people to buy its own goods in preference to the other companies' goods. ○ *Clothing stores also face heavy competition from factory outlets.*

2 NOUN A **competition** is an event in which many people take part to find out who is best at a particular activity. ○ *I'm taking part in a surfing competition.*

comply /kəmplaɪ/ (**complies, complying** or **complied**)

VERB If someone or something **complies with** an order or set of rules, they are in accordance with what is required or expected. ○ *Some beaches had failed to comply with water quality standards.*

compose /kəmpoʊz/ (**composes, composing** or **composed**)

VERB If someone **composes** something such as a letter, poem, or speech they write it. [FORMAL] ○ *He started to compose a reply to Anna.*

concept /kɒnsɛpt/ (**concepts**)

NOUN A **concept** is an idea or abstract principle. ○ *She added that the concept of arranged marriages is misunderstood in the west.*

concern /kənsɜrn/ (**concerns, concerning** or **concerned**)

1 VERB If something such as a book or a piece of information **concerns** a particular subject, it is about that subject. ○ *The bulk of the book concerns Sandy's two middle-aged children.*

2 VERB If a situation, event, or activity **concerns** you, it affects or involves you. ○ *It doesn't concern you at all.*

3 VERB If something **concerns** you, it worries you. ○ *It concerns me that we were not told about this.*

4 NOUN A **concern** is a fact or situation that worries you. ○ *My concern is that we won't have enough time.*

concerning /kənsɜrnɪŋ/

PREPOSITION You use **concerning** to indicate what a question or piece of information is about. [FORMAL] ○ *a large body of research concerning the relationship between anger and health*

conclusion /kənkluʒən/ (**conclusions**)

1 NOUN When you come to a **conclusion**, you decide that something is true after you have thought about it carefully and have considered all the relevant facts. ○ *Over the years I've come to the conclusion that she's a very great musician.*

2 in conclusion PHRASE You say **in conclusion** to indicate that what you are about to say is the last thing that you want to say. ○ *In conclusion, walking is a cheap, safe, enjoyable and readily available form of exercise.*

condition /kəndɪʃən/ (**conditions**)

1 NOUN The **condition** of someone or something is the state they are in. ○ *He remains in a critical condition in a California hospital.*

2 NOUN The **conditions** in which people live or do things are the factors that affect their comfort, safety, or success. ○ *This change has been timed under laboratory conditions.*

3 NOUN A **condition** is something which must happen or be done in order for something else to be possible, especially when this is written into a contract or law. ○ *Egypt had agreed to a summit subject to certain conditions.*

4 NOUN In grammar **condition** is the use of words such as "if" or "unless," which show that a particular situation must exist before something else is possible. ○ *Condition can be shown by the phrase "even if."*

conduct /kəndʌkt/ (**conducts, conducting** or **conducted**)

VERB When you **conduct** an activity or task, you organize it and carry it out. ○ *I decided to conduct an experiment.*

conference /kɒnfərəns, -frəns/ (**conferences**)

1 NOUN A **conference** is a meeting, often lasting a few days, which is organized on a particular subject or to bring together people who have a common interest. ○ *The president summoned all the state governors to a conference on education.*

2 NOUN A **conference call** is a phone call with more than two people. ○ *Officials scheduled a conference call for 5 pm Sunday.*

confusing /kənfyuzɪŋ/

ADJECTIVE **Confusing** means difficult to understand because information is not clear. ○ *The financial regulations are really confusing.*

congratulations /kəngrætʃəleɪʃənz/

CONVENTION You say "**Congratulations**" to someone in order to congratulate them. ○ *The organizers of the Games deserve the warmest congratulations.*

connect /kənɛkt/ (**connects, connecting** or **connected**)

1 VERB If something or someone **connects** one thing **to** another, or if one thing **connects to** another, the two things are joined together. ○ *You can connect the machine to your hi-fi.*

2 VERB If a piece of equipment or a place **is connected to** a source of power or water, it is joined to that source so that it has power or water. ○ *These appliances should not be connected to power supplies.*

3 VERB If one plane or train **connects with** another, it arrives at a time which allows passengers to change to the other one in order to continue their journey. ○ *My connecting flight didn't depart for another two hours.*

connection /kənɛkʃ°n/ **(connections)**

1 NOUN If there is a **connection** between a piece of equipment and a source of power or water, the piece of equipment is joined to the source so that it receives power or water. ○ *a high-speed Internet connection*

2 NOUN If you get a **connection** at an airport or station, you catch a plane, train, or bus after getting off another plan, train, or bus. ○ *I missed my connection and had to wait another hour.*

consecutive /kənsɛkyətɪv/

ADJECTIVE Consecutive periods of time or events happen one after the other without interruption. ○ *This is the third consecutive year that these countries achieved economic growth.*

consequence /kɒnsɪkwɛns, -kwəns/ **(consequences)**

in consequence, as a consequence PHRASE If one thing happens and then another thing happens **in consequence** or **as a consequence**, the second thing happens as a result of the first. ○ *people who are suffering and dying as a consequence of the civil war*

consequently /kɒnsɪkwɛntli, -kwəntli/

ADVERB Consequently means as a result. [FORMAL] ○ *Apprehension and stress had made him depressed and consequently irritable with his family.*

considerably /kənsɪdərəbli/

ADVERB Considerably means much or a lot. ○ *Children vary considerably in the rate at which they learn.*

consideration /kənsɪdəreɪʃ°n/

1 NOUN Consideration is careful thought about something. ○ *There should be careful consideration about the use of such toxic chemicals.*

2 NOUN A **consideration** is something that should be thought about when you are planning or deciding something. ○ *Price is an important consideration for shoppers.*

consistently /kənsɪstəntli/

ADVERB Consistently means in a way that stays the same and does not change. ○ *Jones and Armstrong maintain a consistently high standard.*

consultant /kənsʌltənt/ **(consultants)**

NOUN A **consultant** is a person who gives expert advice to a person or organization on a particular subject. ○ *a team of management consultants sent in to reorganize the department*

consultation /kɒnsəlteɪʃ°n/ **(consultations)**

NOUN A **consultation**, or a **consultation with** someone, is a meeting which is held to discuss something. **Consultation** is discussion about something. ○ *The plans were drawn up in consultation with the World Health Organization.*

contact /kɒntækt/ **(contacts)**

NOUN Your **contacts** are the people you know in an organization or profession who help you or give you information. ○ *I have some business contacts who might be able to help you.*

continental /kɒntɪnɛnt°l/

ADJECTIVE Continental is used to refer to something that belongs to or relates to a continent. ○ *The most ancient parts of the continental crust are 400 billion years old.*

contract /kɒntrækt/ **(contracts)**

NOUN A **contract** is a legal agreement, usually between two companies or between an employer and employee, which involves doing work for a stated sum of money. ○ *He was given a seven-year contract with an annual salary of $150,000.*

contribute /kəntrɪbyut/ **(contributes, contributing** or **contributed)**

1 VERB If you **contribute to** something, you say or do things to help to make it successful. ○ *He believes he has something to contribute to a discussion concerning the uprising.*

2 VERB If something **contributes to** an event or situation, it is one of the causes of it. ○ *The report says design faults in both the vessels contributed to the tragedy.*

contribution /kɒntrɪbyuʃ°n/ **(contributions)**

NOUN If you make a **contribution to** something, you do something to help make it successful or to produce it. ○ *He was awarded a prize for his contribution to world peace.*

conventional /kənvɛnʃ°n°l/

ADJECTIVE Someone who is **conventional** has behavior or opinions that are ordinary and normal. ○ *a respectable married woman with conventional opinions*

convince /kənvɪns/ **(convinces, convincing** or **convinced)**

VERB If someone or something **convinces** you **of** something, they make you believe that it is true or that it exists. ○ *The waste disposal industry is finding it difficult to convince the public that its operations are safe.*

cooperate /koʊɒpəreɪt/ **(cooperates, cooperating** or **cooperated)**

VERB If you **cooperate with** someone, you work with them or help them for a particular purpose. You can also say that two people **cooperate**. ○ *It was agreed that the two leaders should cooperate in a joint enterprise.*

corporate /kɔrpərɪt, -prɪt/

ADJECTIVE Corporate means relating to business corporations or to a particular business corporation. ○ *This established a strong corporate image.*

corporation /kɔrpəreɪʃᵊn/ (corporations)

NOUN A **corporation** is a large business or company.
○ *multinational corporations*

corresponding /kɔrispɒndɪŋ/

ADJECTIVE **Corresponding** things have a close similarity or connection between them. ○ *March and April sales this year were up 8 percent on the corresponding period in 2012.*

creative /krieɪtɪv/

ADJECTIVE **Creative** means including or using ideas that are new and unusual or interesting. ○ *A designer should take risks with creative designs that stand out from the rest.*

critical /krɪtɪkᵊl/

ADJECTIVE If someone or something receives **critical acclaim**, critics say that they are very good. ○ *His novel has received much critical acclaim around the world.*

crucial /kruʃᵊl/

ADJECTIVE If you describe something as **crucial**, you mean it is extremely important. ○ *He had administrators under him but made the crucial decisions himself.*

current /kɜrənt/

ADJECTIVE **Current** means happening, being used, being valid, or being done at the present time. ○ *The current situation is very different to that in 2010.*

customize /kʌstəmaɪz/ (customizes, customizing or customized)

VERB If you **customize** something, you change its appearance or features to suit your tastes or needs. ○ *a control that allows photographers to customize the camera's basic settings*

damage /dæmɪdʒ/ (damages, damaging or damaged)

1 VERB To **damage** an object means to break it, spoil it physically, or stop it from working properly. ○ *He maliciously damaged a car with a baseball bat.*

2 NOUN **Damage** is harm that is caused to an object or person. ○ *The blast caused extensive damage to the house.*

deadline /dɛdlaɪn/ (deadlines)

NOUN A **deadline** is a time or date before which a particular task must be finished or a particular thing must be done. ○ *We were not able to meet the deadline because of manufacturing delays.*

deal /dil/ (deals, dealing or dealt)

1 NOUN A **deal** is an agreement or arrangement, especially in business. ○ *They made a deal to share the money between them.*

2 VERB If a person, company, or store **deals in** a particular type of goods, their business involves buying or selling those goods. ○ *They deal in antiques.*

3 VERB When you **deal with** someone or something that needs your attention, you give your attention to them, and often solve a problem or make a decision about them. ○ *The bank needs to improve the way that it deals with complaints.*

4 VERB If a book, speech, or movie **deals with** a particular thing, it has that thing as its subject. ○ *The first part of the book deals with his early life in Beijing.*

5 VERB If you **deal with** a particular person or organization, you have business relations with them. ○ *Part of my job is to deal with suppliers.*

decide /dɪsaɪd/ (decides, deciding or decided)

1 VERB If you **decide** to do something, you choose to do it, usually after you have thought carefully about the other possibilities. ○ *She decided to take a course in philosophy.*

2 VERB If you **decide** that something is true, you form that opinion about it after considering the facts. ○ *The government decided that the company represented a security risk.*

decision /dɪsɪʒᵊn/ (decisions)

1 NOUN When you make a **decision**, you choose what should be done or which is the best of various possible actions. ○ *A decision was made to discipline Marshall.*

2 NOUN **Decision** is the act of deciding something or the need to decide something. ○ *The growing pressures of the crisis may mean that the moment of decision can't be too long delayed.*

deduct /dɪdʌkt/ (deducts, deducting or deducted)

VERB When you **deduct** an amount from a total, you subtract it from the total. ○ *The company deducted this payment from his compensation.*

degree /dɪgri/ (degrees)

NOUN A **degree** at a university or college is a title or qualification that you get when you have completed a course of study there. ○ *He earned a master's degree in economics at Yale.*

delay /dɪleɪ/ (delays, delaying or delayed)

1 VERB If you **delay** doing something, you do not do it immediately or at the planned or expected time, but you leave it until later. ○ *The disclosures forced it to delay publication of its annual report.*

2 VERB To **delay** someone or something means to make them late or to slow them down. ○ *Various setbacks and problems delayed production.*

3 NOUN If there is a **delay**, something does not happen until later than planned or expected. ○ *Although the tests have caused some delay, flights should be back to normal soon.*

4 NOUN **Delay** is a failure to do something immediately or in the required or usual time. ○ *Any errors should be reported to us without delay.*

delegate /dɛlɪgɪt/ (delegates)

NOUN A **delegate** is a person who is chosen to vote or make decisions on behalf of a group of other people, especially at a conference or a meeting. ○ *a meeting attended by delegates from 35 countries*

delighted /dɪlaɪtɪd/

1 ADJECTIVE If you are **delighted**, you are extremely pleased and excited about something. ○ *I know Frank will be delighted to see you.*

2 ADJECTIVE If someone invites or asks you to do something, you can say that you would be **delighted** to do it, as a way of showing that you are very willing to do it. ○ *"You have to come to Todd's graduation party."—"I'd be delighted."*

deliver /dɪlɪvər/ (**delivers, delivering** or **delivered**)
VERB If you **deliver** something somewhere, you take it there. ○ *Only 90% of first-class mail is delivered on time.*

delivery /dɪlɪvəri/ (**deliveries**)
NOUN A **delivery** is an occasion when goods or mail are delivered. ○ *We are waiting for a delivery of new parts.*

demonstrate /dɛmənstreɪt/ (**demonstrates, demonstrating** or **demonstrated**)
1 VERB If you **demonstrate** something, you show people how it works or how to do it. ○ *He demonstrated the prototype to a group of senior officers.*
2 VERB If you **demonstrate** a particular skill, quality, or feeling, you show by your actions that you have it. ○ *They have demonstrated their ability to work together.*

department /dɪpɑrtmənt/ (**departments**)
NOUN A **department** is one of the sections in an organization such as a government, business, or school. ○ *He moved to the sales department.*

deposit /dɪpɒzɪt/ (**deposits, depositing** or **deposited**)
1 NOUN A **deposit** is a sum of money which is part of the full price of something, and which you pay when you agree to buy it. ○ *A $50 deposit is required when ordering, and the balance is due upon delivery.*
2 VERB To **deposit** a sum of money is to pay it into a bank account. ○ *Bank customers are able to deposit and withdraw money 24 hours a day.*

describe /dɪskraɪb/ (**describes, describing** or **described**)
VERB If you **describe** a person, object, event, or situation, you say what they are like or what happened. ○ *She read a poem by Carver which describes their life together.*

description /dɪskrɪpʃn/ (**descriptions**)
NOUN A **description** of someone or something is an account which explains what they are or what they look like. ○ *Police have issued a description of the man who was aged between fifty and sixty.*

detail /diteɪl, dɪteɪl/ (**details, detailing** or **detailed**)
1 NOUN The **details of** something are its individual features or elements. ○ *I recall every detail of the party.*
2 NOUN **Details** about someone or something are facts or pieces of information about them. ○ *See the bottom of this page for details of how to apply for this exciting offer.*
3 NOUN If you examine or discuss something **in detail**, you do it thoroughly and carefully. ○ *Read the contract in detail before signing it.*
4 VERB If you **detail** things, you list them or give information

about them. ○ *The report detailed the mistakes that were made.*

deteriorate /dɪtɪəriəreɪt/ (**deteriorates, deteriorating** or **deteriorated**)
VERB If something **deteriorates**, it becomes worse in some way. ○ *Relations between the two countries steadily deteriorated.*

develop /dɪvɛləp/ (**develops, developing** or **developed**)
1 VERB If you say that a country **develops**, you mean that it changes from being a poor agricultural country to being a rich industrial country.
2 VERB To **develop** something is to make it grow or change over a period of time and become more advanced, complete, or successful. ○ *She won a grant to develop her own business.*
3 VERB If someone **develops** a new product, they design it and produce it. ○ *Companies need to develop new products to stay ahead of the competition.*

device /dɪvaɪs/ (**devices**)
NOUN A **device** is an object that has been invented for a particular purpose, for example, for recording or measuring something. ○ *an electronic device that protects your vehicle 24 hours a day*

direct /dɪrɛkt, daɪ-/ (**directs, directing** or **directed**)
1 ADJECTIVE **Direct** means moving toward a place or object, without changing direction and without stopping, for example, in a trip. ○ *They'd come on a direct flight from Athens.*
2 ADJECTIVE You use **direct** to describe an experience, activity, or system which only involves the people, actions, or things that are necessary to make it happen. ○ *the advantage of farmers selling direct to consumers*
3 ADJECTIVE You use **direct** to emphasize the closeness of a connection between two things. ○ *They were unable to prove that she died as a direct result of his injection.*
4 VERB When someone **directs** a project, they are responsible for organizing it. ○ *Mrs. Clarkson will be directing our move into the Japanese market.*
5 VERB If you **direct** a remark, question, etc. **at** someone, you say it to them. ○ *You should direct any complaints to the customer service manager.*

disappointment /dɪsəpɔɪntmənt/ (**disappointments**)
NOUN **Disappointment** is the feeling of being slightly sad because something has not happened or because something is not as good as you hoped. ○ *Business leaders have expressed disappointment with the slow pace of progress.*

discount /dɪskaʊnt/ (**discounts, discounting** or **discounted**)
1 NOUN A **discount** is a reduction in the usual price of something. ○ *This voucher entitles you to a 10% discount on your next purchase.*
2 VERB If a product or service is **discounted**, it is being sold for a lower price than usual. ○ *The store does not offer refunds on discounted items.*

disposal /dɪspoʊzəl/

1 NOUN **Disposal** is the act of getting rid of something that is no longer needed or wanted. ○ *They are investigating new methods for the permanent disposal of radioactive wastes.*

2 NOUN If you have something **at** your **disposal**, you can use it whenever you want. ○ *Guests have a swimming pool, spa, and golf course at their disposal.*

disrupt /dɪsrʌpt/ **(disrupts, disrupting** or **disrupted)**

VERB If someone or something **disrupts** an event, system, or process, they cause difficulties that prevent it from continuing or operating in a normal way. ○ *Antiwar protesters disrupted the debate.*

distribute /dɪstrɪbyut/ **(distributes, distributing** or **distributed)**

VERB If you **distribute** things, you hand them or deliver them to a number of people. ○ *Students shouted slogans and distributed leaflets.*

distribution /dɪstrɪbyuʃən/

NOUN **Distribution** is when a company supplies goods to the stores or businesses that sell them. ○ *Companies need good distribution networks.*

district /dɪstrɪkt/ **(districts)**

NOUN A **district** is a particular area of a city or country. ○ *I drove around the business district.*

domestic /dəmɛstɪk/

ADJECTIVE **Domestic** political activities, events, and situations happen or exist within one particular country. ○ *over 100 domestic flights a day to 15 UK destinations*

drastic /dræstɪk/

ADJECTIVE A **drastic** change is a very great change that has a sudden or serious effect. ○ *Drastic budget cuts will affect all areas of education.*

due /du/

1 PHRASE If an event is **due to** something, it happens or exists as a direct result of that thing. ○ *The country's economic problems are largely due to the weakness of the recovery.*

2 ADJECTIVE If something is **due** at a particular time, it is expected to happen, be done, or arrive at that time. ○ *The report is due at the end of this week.*

3 ADJECTIVE Something that is **due** to someone is owed to them either as a debt or because they have a right to it. ○ *No further payments are due until next month.*

duration /dʊəreɪʃən/

NOUN The **duration of** an event or state is the time during which it happens or exists. ○ *Courses are of two years' duration.*

economy /ɪkɒnəmi/ **(economies)**

1 NOUN The **economy** of a country or region is the system by which money, industry, and trade are organized. ○ *The Japanese economy grew at an annual rate of more than 10 percent.*

2 NOUN **Economy** is the cheapest class of travel on a plane or train. ○ *If you travel in economy class, there is usually less legroom.*

effect /ɪfɛkt/ **(effects)**

1 NOUN The **effect of** one thing **on** another is the change that the first thing causes in the second thing. ○ *The Internet could have a significant effect on trade in the next few years.*

2 PHRASE If a law or policy **takes effect** at a particular time, it officially begins to apply or be valid from that time. ○ *The new rules take effect on January 1.*

effective /ɪfɛktɪv/

ADJECTIVE Something that is **effective** works well and produces the results that were intended. ○ *Simple antibiotics are effective against this organism.*

efficient /ɪfɪʃənt/

ADJECTIVE If something or someone is **efficient**, they are able to do tasks successfully, without wasting time or energy. ○ *With today's more efficient transportation, people can commute longer distances in shorter periods of time.*

element /ɛlɪmənt/ **(elements)**

NOUN The different **elements** of a situation, activity, or process are the different parts of it. ○ *The plot has all the elements not only of romance but of high drama.*

eliminate /ɪlɪmɪneɪt/ **(eliminates, eliminating** or **eliminated)**

VERB To **eliminate** something, especially something you do not want or need, means to remove it completely. [FORMAL] ○ *The Sex Discrimination Act has not eliminated discrimination in employment.*

emerge /ɪmɜrdʒ/ **(emerges, emerging** or **emerged)**

1 VERB If a fact or result **emerges** from a period of thought, discussion, or investigation, it becomes known as a result of it. ○ *the growing corruption that has emerged in the past few years*

2 NOUN An **emerging market** is a financial or consumer market in a newly developing country or former communist country. ○ *Many emerging markets have outpaced more mature markets, such as the US and Japan.*

enclose /ɪnkloʊz/ **(encloses, enclosing** or **enclosed)**

VERB If you **enclose** something with a letter, you put it in the same envelope as the letter. ○ *I have enclosed a check for $100.*

encounter /ɪnkaʊntər/ **(encounters, encountering** or **encountered)**

VERB If you **encounter** a situation or problem you experience it. ○ *Environmental problems they found were among the worst they encountered.*

encourage /ɪnkɜ́rɪdʒ/ **(encourages, encouraging** or **encouraged)**

VERB If you **encourage** someone **to** do something, you try to persuade them to do it. ○ *The plan is to encourage people to sell their assets and pay taxes at the lower rate.*

engage /ɪngéɪdʒ/ **(engages, engaging** or **engaged)**

VERB If you **engage in** an activity, you do it. [FORMAL] ○ *He has never engaged in criminal activities.*

engineer /ɛ́ndʒɪnɪ́ər/ **(engineers)**

NOUN An **engineer** is a person who uses scientific knowledge to design, construct, and maintain engines and machines or structures such as roads, railroads, and bridges. ○ *one of the engineers who designed the railroad*

equipment /ɪkwɪ́pmənt/

NOUN **Equipment** consists of the things which are used for a particular purpose, for example, a hobby or job. ○ *a shortage of medical equipment and medicine*

essential /ɪsɛ́nʃəl/

ADJECTIVE The **essential** aspects of something are its most basic or important aspects. ○ *Most authorities agree that play is an essential part of a child's development.*

evaluate /ɪvǽlyueɪt/ **(evaluates, evaluating** or **evaluated)**

VERB If you **evaluate** something or someone, you consider them in order to make a judgment about them, for example about how good or bad they are. ○ *They will first send in trained nurses to evaluate the needs of the individual situation.*

eventually /ɪvɛ́ntʃuəli/

1 ADVERB **Eventually** means in the end, especially after a lot of delays, problems, or arguments. ○ *Eventually, the army caught up with him in Latvia.*
2 ADVERB **Eventually** means at the end of a situation or process or as the final result of it. ○ *Dehydration eventually leads to death.*

examine /ɪgzǽmɪn/ **(examines, examining** or **examined)**

VERB If you **examine** something, you look at it carefully. ○ *Forensic scientists are examining the bombers' car.*

example /ɪgzǽmpəl/ **(examples)**

1 NOUN An **example of** something is a particular situation, object, or person which shows that what is being claimed is true. ○ *The doctors gave numerous examples of patients being expelled from the hospital.*
2 **for example** PHRASE You use **for example** to introduce and emphasize something which shows that something is true. The abbreviation e.g. is used in written notes. ○ *A few simple precautions can be taken, for example, ensuring that desks are the right height.*

exceed /ɪksíd/ **(exceeds, exceeding** or **exceeded)**

VERB If something **exceeds** a particular amount or number, it is greater or larger than that amount or number. [FORMAL] ○ *Its research budget exceeds $700 million a year.*

except /ɪksɛ́pt/

PREPOSITION You use **except** to introduce the only thing or person that a statement does not apply to, or a fact that prevents a statement from being completely true. ○ *No illness, except malaria, has caused as much death as smallpox.*

exceptional /ɪksɛ́pʃənəl/

ADJECTIVE You use **exceptional** to describe someone or something that has a particular quality, usually a good quality, to an unusually high degree. ○ *children with exceptional ability*

exclusive /ɪksklúsɪv/

ADJECTIVE Something that is **exclusive** is owned or used by only one person or organization and not shared with anyone else. ○ *This information will remain the exclusive property of the employer.*

exhibit /ɪgzɪ́bɪt/ **(exhibits)**

NOUN An **exhibit** is an object that is displayed in a museum or art gallery. ○ *The Egyptian exhibits will be on display until May 24.*

exhibition /ɛ̀ksəbɪ́ʃən/ **(exhibitions)**

NOUN An **exhibition** is a public event at which pictures, sculptures, or other objects of interest are displayed, for example at a museum or art gallery. ○ *an exhibition of expressionist art*

expansion /ɪkspǽnd/

NOUN **Expansion** is the process of becoming greater in size, number, or amount. ○ *The company has abandoned plans for further expansion.*

expect /ɪkspɛ́kt/ **(expects, expecting** or **expected)**

VERB If you **expect** something **to** happen, you believe that it will happen. ○ *They expect a gradual improvement in sales of new cars.*

experience /ɪkspɪ́əriəns/ **(experiences, experiencing** or **experienced)**

1 NOUN **Experience** is knowledge or skill in a particular job or activity, which you have gained because you have done that job or activity for a long time. ○ *He has also had managerial experience on every level.*
2 NOUN An **experience** is something that you do or that happens to you, especially something important that affects you. ○ *Many of his clients are very nervous, usually because of a bad experience in the past.*
3 VERB If you **experience** a particular situation, you are in that situation or it happens to you. ○ *I have experienced the full range of treatments offered.*

expert /ɛ́kspɜrt/ **(experts)**

1 NOUN An **expert** is a person who is very skilled at doing something or who knows a lot about a particular subject.

○ *Health experts warn that the issue is a global problem.*

2 ADJECTIVE **Expert** describes someone who is very skilled at doing something or who knows a lot about a particular subject. ○ *Our expert kitchen designers will create the look you want.*

expertise /ɛkspɜrtiz/

NOUN **Expertise** is special skill or knowledge that is acquired by training, study, or practice. ○ *students with expertise in forensics*

express /ɪksprɛs/ **(expresses, expressing** or **expressed)**

1 VERB When you **express** an idea or feeling, or **express yourself**, you show what you think or feel. ○ *He expressed grave concern at American attitudes.*

2 ADJECTIVE An **express** service is one in which things are sent or done faster than usual. ○ *If you want your order quickly, choose express delivery.*

3 ADJECTIVE An **express** train or bus is a fast one that stops at very few places. ○ *The express train only takes an hour.*

extend /ɪkstɛnd/ **(extends, extending** or **extended)**

1 VERB If you **extend** something, you make it longer or bigger. ○ *This year they have introduced three new products to extend their range.*

2 VERB If you **extend** something, you make it last longer than before or end at a later date. ○ *They have extended the deadline by twenty-four hours.*

3 VERB If you **extend** something to other people, you make it available to more people or make it include more people. ○ *These screening tests will be extended to women over 70 from next year.*

extensive /ɪkstɛnsɪv/

ADJECTIVE Something that is **extensive** covers a wide range of details, ideas, or items. ○ *The security forces have extensive powers of search and arrest.*

extra /ɛkstrə/

1 ADJECTIVE An **extra** amount, person, or thing is more than is usual, necessary or expected. ○ *The company now has a chance to sell an extra 40,000 cars a year.*

2 ADVERB You can use **extra** before adjectives and adverbs to emphasize the quality that they are describing. ○ *You need to be extra careful when handling glass.*

3 PRONOUN If something costs **extra** or if you pay **extra**, you have to pay more money for it in addition to what you are already paying. ○ *You have to pay extra for performances after 6 p.m.*

extreme /ɪkstrim/

ADJECTIVE **Extreme** means very great in degree or intensity. ○ *the author's extreme reluctance to generalize*

extremely /ɪkstrimli/

ADVERB You use **extremely** in front of adjectives and adverbs to emphasize that the specified quality is present to a very great degree. ○ *These headaches are extremely common.*

facility /fəsɪlɪti/ **(facilities)**

NOUN A **facility** is a room, building, or piece of equipment that is used for a particular purpose. ○ *The hotel has no conference facilities.*

familiar /fəmɪlyər/

1 ADJECTIVE If someone or something is **familiar**, you have seem them or heard of them before. ○ *His face looks familiar.*

2 ADJECTIVE If you are **familiar with** something, you know or understand it well. ○ *You will gain confidence as you use and become familiar with the software.*

fare /fɛər/ **(fares)**

NOUN A **fare** is the money that you pay for a trip on a bus, plane, train, etc. ○ *He could not afford the fare.*

feature /fitʃər/ **(features)**

1 NOUN A **feature of** something is an interesting or important part or characteristic of it. ○ *The ships have built-in safety features including specially-strengthened hulls.*

2 VERB If something such as an event, product, or magazine **features** something or someone, they are an important part of it. ○ *The exhibition also features objects and photos from private collections.*

feedback /fidbæk/

NOUN **Feedback** is written or spoken remarks on how well you do something. ○ *He said the company was encouraged by feedback it received from selected customers.*

figure /fɪgyər/ **(figures)**

NOUN A **figure** is a particular amount expressed as a number, especially a statistic. ○ *Norway is a peaceful place with low crime figures.*

file /faɪl/ **(files)**

NOUN In computing, a **file** is a set of related data that has its own name. ○ *Now that you have loaded WordPerfect, it's easy to create a file.*

finance /faɪnæns, fɪnæns/

NOUN **Finance** is the management of money. ○ *the principles of corporate finance*

financial /faɪnænʃl, fɪn-/

ADJECTIVE **Financial** means relating to or involving money. ○ *The company is in financial difficulties.*

forecast /fɔrkæst/ **(forecasts)**

NOUN A **forecast** is a statement of what is expected to happen in the future, especially in relation to a particular event or situation. ○ *The weather forecast is better for today.*

forecasting /fɔrkæstɪŋ/

NOUN **Forecasting** is when you say what you think is going to happen in the future. ○ *She has a background in audience profiling and social trend forecasting.*

form /fɔrm/ (**forms, forming** or **formed**)

1 NOUN A **form of** something is a type or kind of it. ○ *He contracted a rare form of cancer.*

2 NOUN A **form** is a paper with questions on it and spaces marked where you should write the answers. ○ *You will be asked to fill in a form stating your name, date of birth, and occupation.*

3 NOUN In grammar, a **form** is a way of writing or saying a word that shows its tense, number, etc. ○ *"Caught" is a past form of the verb "catch."*

4 VERB If something consists of particular things, people, or features, you can say that they **form** that thing. ○ *Cereals form the staple diet of an enormous number of people around the world.*

5 VERB If you **form** something such as a relationship or plan, you make it start to exist and develop. ○ *A plan was formed to tackle the problem.*

formal /fɔrmᵊl/

ADJECTIVE **Formal** clothes are clothes that are suitable for special or important occasions. ○ *More formal evening dresses are entirely appropriate for evening weddings.*

format /fɔrmæt/ (**formats**)

NOUN The **format** of something is the way or order in which it is arranged and presented. ○ *music available in a digital format*

former /fɔrmər/

ADJECTIVE **Former** is used to describe what someone or something used to be in the past. ○ *He pleaded not guilty to murdering his former wife.*

forward /fɔrwərd/

1 ADVERB You use **forward** to show that something progresses or improves. ○ *We are excited to move forward into a new era with our new company name.*

2 PHRASE If you **look forward to** something that is going to happen, you want it to happen because you think you will enjoy it. ○ *I am looking forward to working with you.*

frequently /frɪkwəntli/

ADVERB If something happens **frequently**, it happens often. ○ *the most frequently asked question*

function /fʌŋkʃᵊn/ (**functions, functioning** or **functioned**)

VERB If a machine, system, or office **is functioning**, it is working or operating. ○ *The authorities say the prison is now functioning normally.*

gather /gæðər/ (**gathers, gathering** or **gathered**)

VERB If people **gather** somewhere, they come together in a group. ○ *A small crowd had gathered to watch what was happening.*

generate /dʒɛnəreɪt/ (**generates, generating** or **generated**)

VERB To **generate** something means to cause it to begin and develop. ○ *the excitement generated by the changes in Eastern Europe*

graphics /græfɪks/

NOUN **Graphics** are drawings, pictures, or symbols, especially when they are produced by a computer. ○ *when enlarging pixel graphics the dots get larger and the image becomes rough*

hazardous /hæzərdəs/

ADJECTIVE Something that is **hazardous** is dangerous, especially to people's health or safety. ○ *The pollution of ground water by hazardous wastes has resulted in the closing of wells.*

host /hoʊst/ (**hosts, hosting** or **hosted**)

1 VERB If you **host** a party or other event, you invite the guests and provide the food, drink, and entertainment. ○ *Monty is hosting a dinner party at his home Saturday evening.*

2 NOUN The **host** of a party or other event, is the person who has invited the guests and provided the food, drink, and entertainment. ○ *We were greeted warmly by our hosts.*

3 VERB The person who **hosts** a television or radio show introduces it and talks to the guests who appear in it. ○ *She hosted the television talk show "True-Life."*

4 NOUN The **host** of a television or radio show is the person who introduces it and talks to the guests who appear in it. ○ *American talk-show host, Oprah Winfrey, interviewed the disgraced cyclist.*

impact /ɪmpækt/ (**impacts**)

NOUN The **impact** that something has **on** a situation, process, or person is a sudden and powerful effect that it has on them. ○ *an area where technology can make a real impact*

implement /ɪmplɪmɛnt, -mənt/ (**implements, implementing** or **implemented**)

VERB If you **implement** something such as a plan, you ensure that what has been planned is done. ○ *The government promised to implement a new system to control financial loan institutions.*

imply /ɪmplaɪ/ (**implies, implying** or **implied**)

VERB If an event or situation **implies** that something is the case, it makes you think it likely that it is the case. ○ *Exports in June rose 1.5%, implying that the economy was stronger than many investors had realized.*

improve /ɪmpruv/ (**improves, improving** or **improved**)

VERB If something **improves** or if you **improve** it, it gets better. ○ *Both the texture and condition of your hair should improve.*

increase (**increases, increasing** or **increased**)

1 VERB /ɪnkris/ If something **increases** or you **increase** it, it becomes greater in number, level, or amount. ○ *The population continues to increase.*

2 NOUN /ɪnkris/ If there is an **increase in** the number, level, or amount of something, it becomes greater. ○ *a sharp increase in productivity*

indeed /ɪndid/

ADVERB You use **indeed** at the end of a clause to give extra force to the word "very," or to emphasize a particular word. ○ *We are very pleased indeed.*

indicate /ˈɪndɪkeɪt/ **(indicates, indicating** or **indicated)**
VERB If one thing **indicates** another thing, the first thing shows that the second is true. ○ *The report indicates that most people agree.*

individual /ˌɪndɪˈvɪdʒuəl/
ADJECTIVE **Individual** means relating to one person or thing, rather than to a large group. ○ *They wait for the group to decide rather than making individual decisions.*

inform /ɪnˈfɔrm/ **(informs, informing** or **informed)**
1 VERB If you **inform** someone **of** something, you tell them about it. ○ *They would inform him of any progress they had made.*
2 VERB To **inform** someone's decision or choice is to influence it by providing facts or information. ○ *The report provided important insights that would help inform our decision-making.*

initially /ɪˈnɪʃəli/
ADVERB **Initially** means soon after the beginning of a process or situation, rather than in the middle or at the end of it. ○ *Forecasters say the gales may not be as bad as they initially predicted.*

innovative /ˈɪnəveɪtɪv/
1 ADJECTIVE Someone who is **innovative** introduces changes and new ideas. ○ *He was one of the most creative and innovative engineers of his generation.*
2 ADJECTIVE Something that is **innovative** is new and original. ○ *The company has won a prestigious industry prize for the innovative design of its kitchen tools.*

input /ˈɪnpʊt/
NOUN **Input** is the ideas, information, effort, or other resources that are given to a group or project to help them succeed. ○ *The committee welcomes the input of any members wishing to contribute.*

inquire /ɪnˈkwaɪər/ **(inquires, inquiring** or **inquired)**
VERB [FORMAL] If you **inquire** about something, you ask for information about it. ○ *He called them several times to inquire about job possibilities.*

inquiry /ɪnˈkwaɪəri, ˈɪnkwɪri/ **(inquiries) also enquiry**
NOUN An **inquiry** is a question you ask in order to get some information. ○ *He made some inquiries and discovered she had gone to Connecticut.*

inspection /ɪnˈspɛkʃən/ **(inspections)**
NOUN If you do an **inspection of** something, you look at every part of it carefully in order to find out about it or check that it is all right. ○ *Officers doing a routine inspection of the vessel found fifty kilograms of the drug.*

instance /ˈɪnstəns/ **(instances)**
1 PHRASE You use **for instance** to introduce a particular event, situation, or person that is an example of what you are talking about. ○ *TB is an infinitely bigger problem than, for instance, AIDS.*
2 NOUN An **instance** is a particular example or occurrence of something. ○ *The committee reported numerous instances where key information was not shared.*

institute /ˈɪnstɪtut/ **(institutes)**
NOUN An **institute** is an organization set up to do a particular type of work, especially research or teaching. You can also use **institute** to refer to the building the organization occupies. ○ *the National Cancer Institute* ○ *an elite research institute devoted to computer software*

insufficient /ˌɪnsəˈfɪʃənt/
ADJECTIVE Something that is **insufficient** is not large enough in amount or degree for a particular purpose. [FORMAL] ○ *He decided there was insufficient evidence to justify criminal proceedings.* ○ *These efforts were insufficient to contain the crisis.*

insurance /ɪnˈʃʊərəns/
NOUN **Insurance** is an arrangement in which you pay money to a company, and they pay money to you if something unpleasant happens to you, for example if your property is stolen or damaged, or if you get a serious illness. ○ *The insurance company paid out for the stolen jewelry and silver.* ○ *We recommend that you take out travel insurance on all vacations.* ○ *regulation of the insurance industry*

intend /ɪnˈtɛnd/ **(intends, intending** or **intended)**
1 VERB If you **intend** to do something, you have decided or planned to do it. ○ *an opinion poll on how people intend to vote*
2 VERB If something **is intended** for a particular purpose, it has been planned to fulfill that purpose. If something **is intended** for a particular person, it has been planned to be used by that person or to affect them in some way. ○ *This money is intended for the development of the tourist industry.*

interest /ˈɪntrɪst, -tərɪst/ **(interests, interesting** or **interested)**
1 NOUN If you have an **interest in** something, you want to learn or hear more about it. ○ *There has been a lively interest in the elections in the last two weeks.*
2 VERB If something **interests** you, it attracts your attention so that you want to learn or hear more about it or continue doing it. ○ *It may interest you to know that Miss Woods, the housekeeper, witnessed the attack.*
3 NOUN If something is in the **interests** of a particular person or group, it will benefit them in some way. ○ *The media were required to act in the public interest.*
4 NOUN If a person, country, or organization has an **interest in** a possible event or situation, they want that event or situation to happen because they are likely to benefit from it. ○ *The West has an interest in promoting democratic forces in Eastern Europe.*

5 NOUN **Interest** is extra money that you receive if you have invested a sum of money. **Interest** is also the extra money that you pay if you have borrowed money or are buying something on credit. ○ *a current account which pays interest*

6 PHRASE If you do something **in the interests of** a particular result or situation, you do it in order to achieve that result or maintain that situation. ○ *a call for all businessmen to work together in the interests of national stability*

7 NOUN The **interest rate** is the amount of interest that must be paid on a loan or investment, expressed as a percentage of the amount that is borrowed or gained as profit. ○ *The Federal Reserve lowered interest rates by half a point.*

interview /ɪntərvyu/ (**interviews, interviewing** or **interviewed**)

1 NOUN An **interview** is a formal meeting at which someone is asked questions in order to find out information about them. ○ *The three-year study is based on interviews with judges, lawyers, and parents.*

2 VERB If you **are interviewed**, someone asks you questions about yourself to find out information about you. ○ *The resident doctor interviewed her and prepared a case history.*

introductory /ɪntrədʌktəri/

ADJECTIVE An **introductory** offer or price on a new product is something such as a free gift or a low price that is meant to attract new customers. ○ *a special introductory offer*

inventory /ɪnvəntɔri/ (**inventories**)

NOUN An **inventory** is a written list of all the objects in a particular place. ○ *The apartment comes fully furnished with kitchen equipment, as listed on the inventory.*

invest /ɪnvɛst/ (**invests, investing** or **invested**)

1 VERB If you **invest in** something, or if you **invest** a sum of money, you use your money in a way that you hope will increase its value, for example, by paying it into a bank, or buying stocks or property. ○ *He invested all our profits in gold stocks.*

2 VERB When a government or organization **invests in** something, it gives or lends money for a purpose that it considers useful or profitable. ○ *Why does Japan invest, on average, twice as much capital per worker per year than the United States?*

investment /ɪnvɛstmənt/ (**investments**)

1 NOUN **Investment** is the activity of investing money. ○ *The government must introduce tax incentives to encourage investment.*

2 NOUN An **investment** is an amount of money that you invest, or the thing that you invest it in. ○ *an investment of twenty-eight million dollars*

investor /ɪnvɛstər/ (**investors**)

NOUN An **investor** is a person or organization that buys stocks or bonds, or pays money into a bank in order to receive a profit. ○ *The main investor in the project is the French bank Credit National.*

label /leɪbᵊl/ (**labels**)

1 NOUN A **label** is a piece of paper or plastic, that is attached to an object in order to give information about it. ○ *Check the label on the bottle.*

2 NOUN A record **label** is a company that sells recorded music. ○ *Her new album is out now on the PMR label.*

lack /læk/ (**lacks, lacking** or **lacked**)

1 NOUN If there is a **lack of** something, there is not enough of it or it does not exist at all. ○ *Despite his lack of experience, he got the job.*

2 VERB If you say that someone or something **lacks** a particular quality or that a particular quality **is lacking** in them, you mean that they do not have any or enough of it. ○ *He seems to lack the ability to work as part of a team.*

launch /lɔntʃ/ (**launches, launching** or **launched**)

1 VERB If a company **launches** a new product, it makes it available to the public. ○ *Crabtree & Evelyn has just launched a new jam, Worcesterberry Preserve.*

2 NOUN The **launch** of a new product is the action of making it available to the public for the first time, or an event when this happens. ○ *The company's spending has also risen following the launch of a new Sunday magazine.*

leadership /lidərʃɪp/ (**leaderships**)

NOUN **Leadership** refers to the qualities that make someone a good leader, or the methods a leader uses to do his or her job. ○ *She showed excellent leadership during a difficult time for the company.* Someone's **leadership** is their position of being in control of something or being the leader in something. ○ *The group's market leadership could be under threat.*

lengthy /lɛŋθi/

ADJECTIVE **Lengthy** means lasting for a long time. ○ *After lengthy meetings, a decision has still not been reached.*

license /laɪsᵊns/ (**licenses**)

NOUN A **license** is an official document which gives you permission to do, use, sell, or own something. ○ *You need a license to operate a pharmacy.*

limit /lɪmɪt/ (**limits**)

NOUN A **limit** is the greatest amount, extent, or degree of something that is possible or allowed. ○ *There is no limit to how much fresh fruit you can eat in a day.*

limited /lɪmɪtɪd/

ADJECTIVE Something that is **limited** is not very great in amount, range, or degree. ○ *The bike will be produced in extremely limited quantities.*

lobby /lɒbi/ (**lobbies**)

NOUN A **lobby** is the large area that is just inside the entrance of a public building or office block. ○ *I met her in the lobby of the hotel.*

logo /loʊgoʊ/ (logos)

NOUN The **logo** of a company or organization is the special design or way of writing its name that it puts on all its products, stationery, or advertisements. ○ *Staff should wear uniforms, and vehicles should bear company logos.*

maintain /meɪnteɪn/ (maintains, maintaining or maintained)

VERB If you **maintain** something, you continue to have it and do not let it stop or grow weaker. ○ *The department maintains close contacts with the chemical industry.*

maintenance /meɪntɪnəns/

NOUN The **maintenance** of a building, vehicle, or machine is the process of keeping it in good condition by regularly checking it and repairing it when necessary. ○ *The window was jammed so I called the maintenance company.*

manage /mænɪdʒ/ (manages, managing or managed)

VERB If someone **manages** an organization, system, team, or project, they are responsible for organizing and controlling it. ○ *Within two years she was managing her own team of salespeople.*

management /mænɪdʒmənt/ (managements)

1 NOUN **Management** is the control and organizing of a business, system, team, or project, or the methods involved in this. ○ *She has extensive experience in project management.*
2 NOUN You can refer to the people who control and organize a business or other organization as the **management**. ○ *The management is doing its best to improve the situation.*

managerial /mænɪdʒɪəriəl/

ADJECTIVE **Managerial** means relating to the management of something such as a business or project. ○ *his managerial skills*

manual /mænyuəl/ (manuals)

NOUN A **manual** is a book or set of instructions that tells you how to do something or how a piece of machinery works. ○ *The camera comes with an instruction manual.*

manufacturer /mænyəfæktʃərər/ (manufacturers)

NOUN A **manufacturer** is a business or company that makes goods in large quantities to sell. ○ *the world's largest doll manufacturer*

market /mɑrkɪt/ (markets, marketing or marketed)

1 NOUN The **market** for a particular type of thing is the number of people who want to buy it, or the area of the world in which it is sold. ○ *the Russian market for personal computers* A **market** is a place where goods are bought and sold, often outdoors. ○ *Boston has a famous food market.*
2 VERB To **market** a product means to organize its sale, by deciding on its price, where it should be sold, and how it should be advertised. ○ *the company that markets the drug*

marketing /mɑrkɪtɪŋ/

NOUN **Marketing** is the organization of the sale of a product, by deciding on its price, where it should be sold, and how it should be advertised. ○ *They launched a multi-million-dollar marketing campaign for the new phones.*

materials /mətɪəriəlz/

NOUN **Materials** are the things that you need for a particular activity. ○ *The builders ran out of materials two months into the project.*

maximum /mæksɪməm/

ADJECTIVE You use **maximum** to describe an amount which is the largest that is possible, allowed, or required. ○ *A personal trainer can help you get the maximum benefit out of your exercise regime.*

meantime /mintaɪm/

in the meantime PHRASE **In the meantime** is used for talking about the period of time between two events. ○ *The director will be here shortly. Can I offer you some tea or coffee in the meantime?*

media /midiə/

1 NOUN You can refer to television, radio, newspapers, and magazines as **the media**. ○ *The trial generated a huge amount of interest in the media.*
2 NOUN **Media** are means of expressing ideas or of communicating with other people, including television, newspapers, and the Internet. ○ *Companies are increasingly looking to new media to market their products and services.*

memo /mɛmoʊ/ (memos)

NOUN A **memo** is a short note that you send to a person who works with you. ○ *He sent a memo to everyone in his department.*

mention /mɛnʃ°n/ (mentions, mentioning or mentioned)

VERB If you **mention** something, you say or write something about it, usually briefly. ○ *The article did not mention his first film, made while he was still a student.*

merchant /mɜrtʃənt/ (merchants)

NOUN A **merchant** is a person or company that buys or sells goods. ○ *A large proportion of record sales now comes through online merchants.*

merger /mɜrdʒər/ (mergers)

NOUN A **merger** is the joining together of two separate companies or organizations so that they become one. ○ *the proposed merger of two Japanese banks*

method /mɛθəd/ (methods)

NOUN A **method** is a particular way of doing something. ○ *We use the most advanced production methods.*

minimum /mɪnɪməm/

ADJECTIVE You use **minimum** to describe an amount which is the smallest that is possible, allowed, or required. ○ *The minimum cost to produce something like this would be around $2 per unit.*

mobile /moʊbᵊl/

ADJECTIVE You use **mobile** to describe something that relates to or is designed for cellphones or similar devices. ○ *There has been a huge growth in e-commerce for mobile devices.* You use **mobile** to describe something that can be moved easily from place to place. ○ *mobile laboratories in six-wheel-drive vehicles*

model /mɒdᵊl/ (**models**)

NOUN A particular **model** is a particular version of a machine or product produced by a company. ○ *To keep the cost down, opt for a basic model.*

modernized /mɒdərnaɪzd/

ADJECTIVE A **modernized** system or building has been changed by replacing old equipment or methods with new ones. ○ *The plant has been extensively modernized.*

monitor /mɒnɪtər/ (**monitors, monitoring** or **monitored**)

1 VERB If you **monitor** something, you regularly check its development or progress. ○ *Senior managers can then use the budget as a control document to monitor progress against the agreed actions.*

2 NOUN A **monitor** is a screen that is used to display information, for example in an airport or as part of a desktop computer. ○ *My computer monitor suddenly went blank.*

mortgage /mɔrgɪdʒ/ (**mortgages**)

NOUN A **mortgage** is a loan of money which you get from a bank or savings and loan association in order to buy a house. ○ *His application for a mortgage was rejected.*

motivated /moʊtɪveɪtɪd/

ADJECTIVE Someone who is **motivated** is very determined and willing to work hard in order to achieve things. ○ *We are looking for a highly motivated professional.*

multinational /mʌltɪnæʃᵊnᵊl/ **also multi-national**

ADJECTIVE A **multinational** company has offices or owns companies in many different countries. ○ *The multinational company is increasingly becoming a worldwide phenomenon.*

multiple /mʌltɪpᵊl/

ADJECTIVE **Multiple** things, occasions, or places means many things, occasions, or places. ○ *He had traveled to Europe on multiple occasions.*

necessarily /nɛsɪsɛərɪli/

ADVERB If you say that something is **not necessarily** the case, you mean that it may not be the case or is not always the case. ○ *Anger is not necessarily the most useful or acceptable reaction to such events.*

necessary /nɛsɪsɛri/

ADJECTIVE If something is **necessary**, it is needed in order for something else to happen. ○ *Certain skills are necessary for running a business.*

negotiate /nɪgoʊʃieɪt/ (**negotiates, negotiating** or **negotiated**)

VERB If people **negotiate with** each other or **negotiate** an agreement, they talk about a problem or a situation such as a business arrangement in order to solve the problem or complete the arrangement. ○ *Three companies were negotiating to market the drug.*

negotiation /nɪgoʊʃieɪʃᵊn/ (**negotiations**)

NOUN **Negotiations** are formal discussions between people in business or politics, during which they try to reach an agreement. ○ *We have had meaningful negotiations, and I believe we are very close to a deal.*

network /nɛtwɜrk/ (**networks**)

NOUN A **network of** people or institutions is a large number of them that have a connection with each other and work together as a system. ○ *He had developed a powerful network of contacts.*

notice /noʊtɪs/ (**notices, noticing** or **noticed**)

1 NOUN A **notice** is a written announcement in a public place or in a newspaper or magazine. ○ *A notice had been put on the door saying "Closed due to circumstances beyond our control."* If you give **notice** about something that is going to happen, you give a warning in advance that it is going to happen. ○ *Three months' notice is required for withdrawals.*

2 VERB If you **notice** something or someone, you become aware of them. ○ *Did you notice anything unusual about him?*

numerous /numərəs/

ADJECTIVE **Numerous** things, occasions, or reasons means many things, occasions, or reasons. ○ *Numerous tests had been made, but no physical cause for her symptoms could be found.*

object /ɔbdʒɛkt/ (**objects**)

NOUN An **object** is anything that has a fixed shape or form, that you can touch or see, and that is not alive. ○ *household objects such as lamps and ornaments*

objective /əbdʒɛktɪv/ (**objectives**)

NOUN An **objective** is something that you are trying to achieve. ○ *Our objective is to become the number one digital corporation.*

occasion /əkeɪʒᵊn/ (**occasions**)

NOUN An **occasion** is a time when something happens, or a case of it happening. ○ *The team repeated the experiment on three separate occasions with the same results.* An **occasion** is an important event, ceremony, or celebration. ○ *We generally wear dark suits and ties for formal occasions.*

occur /əkɜr/ **(occurs, occurring** or **occurred)**
VERB When something **occurs**, it happens. ○ *The crash occurred when the crew shut down the wrong engine.*

odd /ɒd/
ADJECTIVE If something is **odd**, it is strange. ○ *He didn't come, which was odd because he had promised he would.*

offer /ɔfər/ **(offers, offering** or **offered)**
1 VERB If you **offer** something to someone, you ask them if they would like to have it. ○ *Patients are offered dietary advice.*
2 VERB If you **offer to** do something, you say that you are willing to do it. ○ *They offered to buy the company for $110 a share.*
3 VERB If you **offer** goods, you present them for sale. ○ *All our books are offered at a discount of 25%.*
4 VERB If you **offer** something, you propose to give it as payment. ○ *They offered $21.50 a share in cash for 49.5 million shares.*
5 NOUN An **offer** is something that someone says they will give you or do for you. ○ *He accepted their offer of a part-time job.*

official /əfɪʃˀl/ **(officials)**
NOUN An **official** is a person who holds a position of authority in an organization or government department. ○ *Local officials say the shortage of water restricts the kind of businesses they can attract.*

ongoing /ɒngoʊɪŋ/
ADJECTIVE An **ongoing** situation has been happening for quite a long time and seems likely to continue for some time in the future. ○ *There is an ongoing debate on the issue.*

operate /ɒpəreɪt/ **(operates, operating** or **operated)**
VERB If you **operate** a business or organization, you work to keep it running properly. If a business or organization **operates**, it carries out its work. ○ *The law was changed to allow commercial banks to operate in the country.*

operational /ɒpəreɪʃˀnˀl/
ADJECTIVE **Operational** means in use or ready for use. ○ *The whole system will be fully operational by December.*

opportunity /ɒpərtunɪti/ **(opportunities)**
NOUN An **opportunity** is a situation in which it is possible for you to do something that you want to do. ○ *Participants must have the opportunity to take part in the discussion.*

opposed /əpoʊzd/
as opposed to PHRASE You use **as opposed to** when you want to make it clear that you are talking about one particular thing and not something else. ○ *We ate in the restaurant, as opposed to the bistro.*

option /ɒpʃˀn/ **(options)**
NOUN An **option** is something that you can choose to do in preference to one or more alternatives. ○ *The company offers various payment options including an installment plan.*

optional /ɒpʃənˀl/
ADJECTIVE If something is **optional**, you can choose whether or not you do it or have it. ○ *It becomes economical to offer the customer optional extras.*

organization /ɔrgənɪzeɪʃˀn/ **(organizations)**
NOUN An **organization** is an official group of people, for example a political party, a business, a charity, or a club. ○ *She works for an organization that matches interns with companies that use them.* The **organization** of something is the way in which its different parts are arranged. ○ *Poor organization makes an essay difficult to follow.*

original /ərɪdʒɪnˀl/
ADJECTIVE You use **original** when referring to something that existed at the beginning of a process or activity, or the characteristics that something had when it began or was made. ○ *The original plan was to hold an indefinite stoppage.* An **original** document is not a copy. ○ *an original movie poster*

outstanding /aʊtstændɪŋ/
ADJECTIVE **Outstanding** means extremely good. ○ *She is an outstanding athlete.*

overcharge /oʊvərtʃɑrdʒ/ **(overcharges, overcharging** or **overcharged)**
VERB If someone **overcharges** you, they charge you too much for their goods or services. ○ *The dispute involved allegations that the law firm had grossly overcharged its client.*

overqualified /oʊvərkwɒlɪfaɪd/
ADJECTIVE If you are **overqualified** for a job, you have more experience or qualifications than are needed for that job. ○ *Many of those employed in India's remote-services business would be deemed overqualified in the West.*

package /pækɪdʒ/ **(packages)**
NOUN A **package** is a set of goods or services that are sold together for one price. ○ *Hotel accommodation, flights, and airport transfers are included as part of the package.* A **package** is something wrapped in paper, or in a box or an envelope in order to be sent somewhere. ○ *A package arrived for you.*

participate /pɑrtɪsɪpeɪt/ **(participates, participating** or **participated)**
VERB If you **participate in** an activity, you take part in it. ○ *Over half the population of this country participate in sports.*

particular /pərtɪkyələr/
1 ADJECTIVE You use **particular** to emphasize that you are talking about one thing or one kind of thing rather than other similar ones. ○ *I have to know exactly why it is I'm doing a particular job.*
2 **in particular** PHRASE You use **in particular** to indicate that what you are saying applies especially to one thing or person. ○ *The situation in North Africa in particular is worrying.*

particularly /pərtɪkyələrli/

1 ADVERB **Particularly** means more than usual or more than other things. ○ *Progress this month has been particularly disappointing.*

2 ADVERB You use **particularly** to indicate that what you are saying applies especially to one thing or situation. ○ *More local employment will be created, particularly in service industries.*

partner /pɑrtnər/ (**partners, partnering** or **partnered**)

1 NOUN A **partner** is another person or organization that you do something with, for example, running a business or playing a sport. ○ *One business partner can insure the life of the other partner.*

2 NOUN The **partners** in a firm or business are the people who share the ownership of it. ○ *He's a partner in a Chicago law firm.*

3 VERB If you **partner** with someone to do something, you agree to do it together. ○ *Local businesses are partnering with schools to offer students work experience.*

party /pɑrti/ (**parties**)

1 NOUN A **party** is a social event at which people enjoy themselves doing things such as eating, drinking, dancing, and talking. ○ *We threw a huge birthday party.*

2 NOUN A **party** of people is a group of people who are doing something together, for example traveling together. ○ *He became separated from the rest of his party.*

3 NOUN One of the people involved in a legal agreement or dispute can be referred to as a **party**. ○ *Any change to the terms must be agreed by both parties.*

patent /pætᵊnt/ (**patents**)

NOUN A **patent** is an official right to be the only person or company allowed to make or sell a new product for a certain period of time. ○ *P&G applied for a patent on its cookies.*

permanent /pɜrmənənt/

1 ADJECTIVE Something that is **permanent** lasts forever. ○ *The ban is intended to be permanent.*

2 ADJECTIVE A **permanent** employee is one who is employed for an unlimited length of time. ○ *At the end of the probationary period you will become a permanent employee.*

permission /pərmɪʃᵊn/

NOUN If someone who has authority over you gives you **permission to** do something, they say that they will allow you to do it. ○ *He asked permission to leave the room.*

permit /pɜrmɪt, pərmɪt/ (**permits, permitting** or **permitted**)

1 VERB If someone **permits** something, they allow it to happen. If they **permit** you **to** do something, they allow you to do it. [FORMAL] ○ *Employees are permitted to use the golf course during their free hours.*

2 NOUN A **permit** is an official document which says that you may do something. For example you usually need a **permit** to work in a foreign country. ○ *The majority of foreign nationals working here have work permits.*

phase /feɪz/ (**phases**)

NOUN A **phase** is a particular stage in a process or in the gradual development of something. ○ *This autumn, 6,000 residents will participate in the first phase of the project.*

platform /plætfɔrm/ (**platforms**)

NOUN A **platform** is one particular system for running software, for example a particular computer operating system or type of smart phone. ○ *Information in this form can be communicated to all team members, regardless of the software platforms they use.*

policy /pɒlɪsi/ (**policies**)

1 NOUN A **policy** is a set of ideas or plans that is used as a basis for making decisions, especially in politics, economics, or business. ○ *What is the school's policy on unauthorized absences?*

2 NOUN An insurance **policy** is an agreement with an insurance company to protect against a particular risk. ○ *Check whether your policy covers problems caused by flight delays.*

position /pəzɪʃᵊn/ (**positions**)

1 NOUN A **position** in a company or organization is a job. [FORMAL] ○ *He left a career in teaching to take up a position with the Arts Council.*

2 NOUN The **position** of someone or something is the place where they are in relation to other things. ○ *The notice was displayed in a highly visible position at the front entrance to the building.*

potential /pətɛnʃᵊl/

1 NOUN If you say that someone or something has **potential**, you mean that they have the necessary abilities or qualities to become successful or useful in the future. ○ *Analysts try to identify those startup companies with the potential to succeed.*

2 ADJECTIVE You use **potential** to say that someone or something is capable of developing into the kind of person or thing mentioned. ○ *The firm has identified 60 potential customers at home and abroad.*

practical /præktɪkᵊl/

ADJECTIVE **Practical** things involve real situations rather than ideas or theories. ○ *practical suggestions on how to increase the fiber in your diet*

predecessor /prɛdɪsɛsər/ (**predecessors**)

NOUN Your **predecessor** is the person who had your job before you. ○ *He learned everything he knew from his predecessor.*

prediction /prɪdɪkʃᵊn/ (**predictions**)

NOUN If you make a **prediction**, you say what you think will happen in the future. ○ *He was unwilling to make a prediction about which books would sell in the coming year.*

preparation /prɛpəreɪʃᵊn/ (**preparations**)

1 NOUN **Preparation** is the process of getting something ready for use or for a particular purpose or making arrangements for

something. ○ *Behind any successful event lay months of preparation.*

2 NOUN **Preparations** are all the arrangements that are made for a future event. ○ *Final preparations are underway for celebrations to mark the company's 50 years in business.*

presence /prɛzᵊns/

NOUN The **presence** of someone or something in a place is the fact that they are there. ○ *The organization has an administrative office in St. Louis to maintain a Midwest presence.*

present /prɛzənt, prɪzɛnt/ (presents, presenting or presented)

1 VERB When you **present** information or **present** to a group, you give or show information to people in a formal way. ○ *He recently presented the results of his research at an international conference.*

2 VERB If you **present** an official document, you show it to someone in authority. ○ *Please present your identification at the gate.*

3 ADJECTIVE If someone is **present** at an event, they are there. ○ *Will the chief executive himself be present?*

4 ADJECTIVE You use **present** to describe things and people that exist now, rather than those that existed in the past or those that may exist in the future. ○ *The present situation in the region is highly worrying.*

5 PHRASE **at present** At present means now, at the present time. ○ *We have no further information at present.*

6 NOUN A **present** is a gift. ○ *The book was a present to me from one of my students.*

presume /prɪzum/ (presumes, presuming or presumed)

VERB If you **presume that** something is the case, you think that it is the case, although you are not certain. ○ *areas that have been presumed to be safe*

previous /priviəs/

ADJECTIVE A **previous** event or thing is one that happened or existed before the one that you are talking about. ○ *She has a teenage daughter from a previous marriage.*

priority /praɪɔrɪti, -ɑr-/

ADJECTIVE You can use **priority** to describe something that is considered more important or urgent than other similar things. ○ *Most of the funds are directed towards priority projects.*

procedure /prəsidʒər/ (procedures)

NOUN A **procedure** is a way of doing something, especially the usual or correct way. ○ *Police insist that Michael did not follow the correct procedure in applying for a visa.*

proceeds /prousidz/

NOUN The **proceeds** of an activity or the sale of something are the money that is made from it. ○ *He uses the proceeds from his photographs to finance his productions.*

process /prɒsɛs/ (processes, processing or processed)

1 NOUN A **process** is a series of actions which are carried out in order to achieve a particular result. ○ *Quality checks are made at every stage of the process.*

2 VERB If you **process** something, you put it through a system in order to deal with it. ○ *Your invoice is currently being processed and will be paid shortly.*

produce /prədus/ (produces, producing or produced)

VERB If you **produce** something, you make or create it. ○ *The company produced circuitry for communications systems.*

production /prədʌkʃᵊn/

1 NOUN **Production** is the process of manufacturing or producing something in large quantities. ○ *That model won't go into production before late 2014.*

2 NOUN **Production** is the amount of goods manufactured or produced by a company or country. ○ *We needed to increase the volume of production.*

program /prougræm, -grəm/ (programs, programming or programmed)

1 NOUN A **program** is a set of planned activities, classes, or events that people can take part in. ○ *The organization implemented a broad range of training programs to meet the needs of small businesses.*

2 NOUN A television or radio **program** is a show that is broadcast on television or radio. ○ *local news programs*

3 NOUN A **program** is a small book or sheet of paper that gives information about an entertainment such as a play or concert. ○ *Her name was spelled incorrectly in the program.*

4 NOUN A **program** is a set of instructions that a computer follows in order to perform a particular task. ○ *The chances of an error occurring in a computer program increase with the size of the program.*

5 VERB When you **program** a computer or other device, you give it a set of instructions to make it able to perform a particular task. ○ *He programmed his computer to compare all the possible combinations.*

project /prɒdʒɛkt, -dʒɪkt/ (projects)

NOUN A **project** is a task that requires a lot of time and effort. ○ *a research project on alternative medicine*

projected /prədʒɛktɪd/

ADJECTIVE You can use **projected** to say what something is planned or expected to be. ○ *The projected deficit will be more than $1.5 million.*

promote /prəmout/ (promotes, promoting or promoted)

1 VERB If a firm **promotes** a product, it tries to increase the sales or popularity of that product. ○ *He has announced a national tour to promote his second solo album.*

2 VERB If someone **is promoted**, they are given a more important job or rank in the organization that they work for. ○ *I was promoted to editor and then editorial director.*

promotion /prəmouʃ°n/ (promotions)

1 NOUN If you are given **promotion** or a **promotion**, you are given a more important job or rank in the organization that you work for. ○ *Consider changing jobs or trying for a promotion.*

2 NOUN A **promotion** is an attempt to make a product or event popular or successful, often by advertising or by offering special prices. ○ *We often run special promotions in our stores on Saturdays.*

prompt /prɒmpt/ (prompts, prompting or prompted)

1 VERB If you **are prompted** to do something on a computer screen, a message or window appears asking you to type or click something. ○ *To claim your discount, enter your discount code when prompted.*

2 NOUN A **prompt** is something such as a question or computer message that asks you to do something, usually to type, write, or say a word or phrase. ○ *Type your command at the prompt, then press Enter.*

proposal /prəpouz°l/ (proposals)

NOUN A **proposal** is a plan or an idea, often a formal or written one, which is suggested for people to think about and decide upon. ○ *The board has put forward proposals for relocating the firm's head office.*

provide /prəvaɪd/ (provides, providing or provided)

VERB If you **provide** something that someone needs or wants, or if you **provide** them **with** it, you give it to them or make it available to them. ○ *I'll be glad to provide a copy of this.*

publication /pʌblɪkeɪʃ°n/ (publications)

1 NOUN The **publication** of a book or magazine is the act of printing it and sending it to stores to be sold. ○ *the publication of an article in a physics journal*

2 NOUN A **publication** is a book or magazine that has been published. ○ *the ease of access to scientific publications on the Internet*

purchase /pɜrtʃɪs/ (purchases, purchasing or purchased)

1 VERB When you **purchase** something, you buy it. [FORMAL] ○ *Nearly three out of every 10 new car buyers are purchasing their vehicles online.*

2 NOUN A **purchase** is something that you buy or the act of buying something. [FORMAL] ○ *When you make a purchase you are entitled to return the goods if they are unsatisfactory.*

qualification /kwɒlɪfɪkeɪʃ°n/ (qualifications)

NOUN Your **qualifications** are the examinations that you have passed or the skills that you have. ○ *What qualifications do you need to be a pharmacist?*

quality /kwɒlɪti/ (qualities)

1 NOUN The **quality** of something is how good or bad it is. ○ *high quality paper and plywood*

2 NOUN Something of **quality** is of a high standard. ○ *In our work, quality is paramount.*

3 NOUN Someone's **qualities** are the characteristics that they have, especially the good ones. ○ *He wanted to introduce mature people with leadership qualities.*

quarter /kwɔrtər/ (quarters)

NOUN A **quarter** is a fixed period of three months. Companies often divide their financial year into four quarters. ○ *The group said results for the third quarter are due on October 29.*

quarterly /kwɔrtərli/

ADJECTIVE **Quarterly** means happening every three months or relating to a period of three months. ○ *The software group last night announced record quarterly profits of $1.98 billion.*

quote /kwout/ (quotes, quoting or quoted)

1 NOUN A **quote** for a piece of work is the price that someone says they will charge you to do the work. ○ *Always get more than one quote for construction work.*

2 VERB If you **quote** a word or reference number, you mention it in something such as a letter or email. ○ *Please quote your booking number in all correspondence.*

raise /reɪz/ (raises, raising or raised)

1 VERB If you **raise** the rate or level of something, you increase it. ○ *We have been left with no option but to raise prices.*

2 VERB If you **raise** an issue or a question, you mention it or bring it to someone's attention. ○ *Some raised concerns about the high cost of complying with the regulations.*

3 NOUN A pay **raise** is an increase in the amount of money someone is paid for doing their job. ○ *I haven't had a raise in three years.*

range /reɪndʒ/ (ranges, ranging or ranged)

1 NOUN A **range of** things is a number of different things of the same general kind. ○ *We sell a wide range of office supplies and stationery.*

2 NOUN A **range** is the complete group that is included between two points on a scale of measurement or quality. ○ *products available in this price range*

3 VERB If things **range between** two points or **range from** one point **to** another, they vary within these points on a scale of measurement or quality. ○ *They range in price from $3 to $15.*

rapidly /ræpɪdli/

ADVERB **Rapidly** means fast. ○ *Operating profit is rising more rapidly.*

rare /rɛər/

ADJECTIVE An event or situation that is **rare** does not occur very often. ○ *This kind of problem is extremely rare, he said.*

rate /reɪt/ (rates, rating or rated)

1 NOUN A **rate** is the amount of money that is charged for goods or services. ○ *There are reduced rates for college students and seniors.*

2 NOUN The **rate** of taxation or interest is the amount of tax or interest that needs to be paid. It is expressed as a percentage of the amount that is earned, gained as profit, or borrowed.

○ *The card has a fixed annual rate of 9.9% and no annual fee.*

3 NOUN The **rate** at which something happens is the number of times it happens over a period of time. ○ *They measured volunteers' heart rates to assess their fitness levels.*

4 VERB If something or someone **is rated** at a particular rank or score, they are given that rank or score. ○ *The product was recently rated 10/10 by a leading consumer magazine.*

rather /ˈræðər/

1 CONJUNCTION **Rather than** means "instead of." ○ *The new advertisements will focus on product and features, rather than image.*

2 ADVERB You can use **rather** to say what is actually the case instead of something else that has been suggested. [FORMAL] ○ *I do not think she positively chose this option; rather, it was the only option made available to her.*

reach /riːtʃ/ (reaches, reaching or reached)

1 VERB When someone or something **reaches** a place, they arrive there. ○ *He reached Cambridge shortly before three o'clock.*

2 VERB When people **reach** an agreement or a decision, they succeed in achieving it. ○ *The Senate has failed to reach agreement in the fiscal budget crisis.*

3 VERB If you **reach** someone on the telephone, you succeed in contacting them. ○ *Do you have a number where I can reach you while you're away?*

realize /ˈriːəlaɪz/ (realizes, realizing or realized)

1 VERB If you **realize** something, you become aware of it or understand it. ○ *People don't realize how serious the situation is.*

2 VERB If you **realize** a plan or an idea, you make it happen. ○ *This enabled him to realize his dream of owning a home.*

reasonable /ˈriːzᵊnəbᵊl/

1 ADJECTIVE If you say that a decision or idea is **reasonable**, you mean that it is fair and sensible. ○ *a perfectly reasonable argument*

2 ADJECTIVE If you say that a price is **reasonable**, you mean that it is fair and not too high. ○ *You get an interesting meal for a reasonable price.*

reasoning /ˈriːzənɪŋ/

NOUN **Reasoning** is the process by which you reach a conclusion after thinking about all the facts. ○ *the reasoning behind the decision*

receipt /rɪˈsiːt/ (receipts)

1 NOUN A **receipt** is a piece of paper that shows that you have received goods or money. ○ *You can return the goods for a refund if you still have the receipt.*

2 NOUN **Receipt of** something is the act of receiving it. [FORMAL] ○ *Your tickets will be sent to you on receipt of your payment.*

recent /ˈriːsᵊnt/

ADJECTIVE A **recent** event or period of time happened not long before the present time. ○ *Sales have fallen by more than 75 percent in recent years.*

recognition /ˌrɛkəgˈnɪʃᵊn/

NOUN If something is done **in recognition of** someone's achievements, it is done as a way of showing official appreciation for them. ○ *The company was selected as Dairy Processor of the Year in recognition of its contribution to the industry.*

recommend /ˌrɛkəˈmɛnd/ (recommends, recommending or recommended)

1 VERB If you **recommend** that something is done, you suggest that it should be done. ○ *We strongly recommend reporting the incident to the police.*

2 VERB If someone **recommends** a person or thing to you, they suggest that you would find that person or thing good or useful. ○ *Brenda came highly recommended as a hard-working manager.*

recover /rɪˈkʌvər/ (recovers, recovering or recovered)

VERB If you **recover** something, you are able to get it back after it has been lost or apparently destroyed. ○ *The data can probably be recovered from the hard disk.*

recreation /ˌrɛkriˈeɪʃən/

NOUN **Recreation** is things that you do in your spare time to relax. ○ *Saturday afternoon is for recreation.*

recruit /rɪˈkruːt/ (recruits, recruiting or recruited)

1 VERB If you **recruit** people for an organization, you ask them to join it. ○ *We need to recruit and train more skilled workers.*

2 NOUN A **recruit** is someone who has been asked to join or has recently joined an organization. ○ *There will be a training day for new recruits.*

reduce /rɪˈduːs/ (reduces, reducing or reduced)

1 VERB If you **reduce** something, you make it smaller in size or amount, or less in degree. ○ *We are working hard to reduce costs across the company.*

2 VERB If you **reduce** something that is for sale, you cut its price. ○ *Everything in the store is reduced.*

refer /rɪˈfɜr/ (refers, referring or referred)

1 VERB If someone or something **refers to** a particular subject or person, they say something relating to them. ○ *The article referred to a study done recently in Canada.*

2 VERB If a word **refers to** a particular thing, situation, or idea, it describes it in some way. ○ *The term electronics refers to electrically-induced action.*

reference /ˈrɛfərəns, ˈrɛfrəns/ (references, referencing or referenced)

1 NOUN A **reference** is a letter written by someone who know you, that describes your character and abilities. When you apply for a job, an employer might ask for **references**. ○ *The firm offered to give her a reference.*

2 NOUN **Reference** is the act of consulting something for information or advice. ○ *Please keep this sheet in a safe place for reference.*

3 VERB If you **reference** something, you say something relating to it. ○ *The report referenced similar cases that had happened in the past.*

4 PHRASE **with reference to** You use **with reference to** in order to indicate what something relates to. ○ *I am writing with reference to your article on salaries for scientists.*

regard /rɪgɑrd/ (**regards, regarding** or **regarded**)

1 VERB If you **regard** someone or something **as** being a particular thing or **as** having a particular quality, you believe that they are that thing or have that quality. ○ *I regard creativity both as a gift and as a skill.*

2 NOUN You can write **regards** or an expression such as **best regards** or **with kind regards** before your name as a friendly way of ending a letter or email. ○ *I hope you will find this helpful. Best regards, Lisa Holden.*

regarding /rɪgɑrdɪŋ/

PREPOSITION You can use **regarding** to indicate the subject that is being talked or written about. ○ *I wrote to them regarding problems with waste collection.*

region /ridʒ°n/ (**regions**)

1 NOUN A **region** is a large area of land that is different from other areas of land, for example because it is one of the different parts of a country with its own customs and characteristics, or because it has a particular geographical feature. ○ *Barcelona, capital of the autonomous region of Catalonia*

2 PHRASE **in the region of** You say **in the region of** to indicate that an amount is approximate. ○ *The program will cost in the region of six million dollars.*

register /rɛdʒɪstər/ (**registers, registering** or **registered**)

VERB If you **register** for something, you put your name on an official list. ○ *Many students register for these courses to widen skills for use in their current job.*

registration /rɛdʒɪstreɪʃ°n/

NOUN **Registration** is the act of putting your name or someone's name on an official list. ○ *If you are interested in this training day, fill in the registration forms.*

regular /rɛgyələr/

1 ADJECTIVE **Regular** events happen fairly often, with equal amounts of time between them. ○ *We're going to be meeting there on a regular basis.*

2 ADJECTIVE **Regular** means "normal." ○ *Speedy delivery is 24 hours, regular delivery is 2–3 working days.*

3 ADJECTIVE A **regular** customer or visitor is one who often buys from a particular company or visits a particular place. ○ *Regular customers will know what's good on the menu.*

regularly /rɛgyələrli/

ADVERB If an event happens **regularly**, it happens fairly often and with equal amounts of time between each event. ○ *He also writes regularly for "International Management" magazine.*

regulation /rɛgyəleɪʃən/ (**regulations**)

NOUN **Regulations** are rules made by a government or other authority in order to control the way something is done. ○ *Any new construction must conform to building regulations.*

relate /rɪleɪt/ (**relates, relating** or **related**)

VERB If something **relates to** a particular subject or **is related to** it, it concerns that subject. ○ *Other recommendations relate to the details of how such data is stored.*

relationship /rɪleɪʃ°nʃɪp/ (**relationships**)

NOUN The **relationship** between two people or groups is the way in which they feel and behave toward each other. ○ *He and his manager had always had a good working relationship.*

release /rɪlis/ (**releases, releasing** or **released**)

1 VERB If a company or performer **releases** a new product such as a CD, they make it available for people to buy. ○ *The movie will be released on DVD on March 21.*

2 VERB If someone **releases** information, they make it available. ○ *They're not releasing any more details yet.*

3 NOUN A **release** is a new product that has been made available to buy. ○ *We are working hard preparing for the software release at the end of this month.*

4 NOUN A press **release** is a written statement given to the media by an organization. ○ *The departure of the company chairman was announced today in a press release.*

reliable /rɪlaɪəb°l/

ADJECTIVE People or things that are **reliable** can be trusted to work well or to behave in the way that you want them to. ○ *Japanese cars are so reliable.*

relieved /rɪlivd/

ADJECTIVE If you are **relieved**, you are feeling happy because something unpleasant has stopped or not happened. ○ *Officials are relieved that the rise in prices has slowed.*

remain /rɪmeɪn/ (**remains, remaining** or **remained**)

1 VERB If someone or something **remains** in a particular place, they stay there. ○ *He went to work in New York while his family remained in Mumbai.*

2 VERB If someone or something **remains** in a particular state or condition, they stay in that state or condition and do not change. ○ *The situation remains extremely unstable.*

remarkable /rɪmɑrkəb°l/

ADJECTIVE If something is **remarkable**, it is very unusual or surprising in a good way. ○ *They encouraged the growth of private businesses, with remarkable success.*

remove /rɪmuv/ (**removes, removing** or **removed**)

VERB If you **remove** something from a place, you take it away. [WRITTEN] ○ *A tree was removed from the yard because it was blocking light.*

renewal /rɪnu̲əl/ (renewals)

NOUN The **renewal of** something such as a license or contract is an official increase in the period of time for which it remains valid. ○ *They will discuss the possible renewal of his contract.*

replace /rɪpleɪs/ (replaces, replacing or replaced)

1 VERB To **replace** a person or thing means to put another person or thing in their place. ○ *They were planning to pull down the building and replace it with shops and offices.*

2 VERB If you **replace** something that has been lost, damaged, or broken, you get or give someone a new one to use instead. ○ *If you have any problems with your new computer, we will repair or replace it free of charge.*

replacement /rɪpleɪsmənt/ (replacements)

1 NOUN A **replacement** is a new thing or person that takes the place of something that has been lost or broken, or someone who has left. ○ *A math teacher is leaving and we haven't yet found a replacement.*

2 NOUN The **replacement** of something is the act of putting something new in its place. ○ *the replacement of damaged or lost books*

representative /rɛprɪzɛntətɪv/ (representatives)

1 NOUN A **representative** is a person whose job is to sell a company's products or services, especially by visiting other companies. ○ *One of our representatives will be happy to call on you.*

2 ADJECTIVE Something that is **representative** of a particular group or type of thing is typical of it. ○ *This is in no way representative of the kind of behavior we expect from students.*

request /rɪkwɛst/ (requests, requesting or requested)

1 VERB If you **request** something, you ask for it politely or formally. [FORMAL] ○ *A customer called requesting a copy of our brochure.*

2 NOUN If you make a **request**, you politely or formally ask someone to do something. ○ *I just have one small request: could we start at 9:30 tomorrow rather than 9?*

require /rɪkwaɪər/ (requires, requiring or required)

1 VERB If you **require** something or if something **is required**, you need it or it is necessary. [FORMAL] ○ *If you require further information, you should consult the registrar.*

2 VERB If a law or rule **requires** you **to** do something, you have to do it. [FORMAL] ○ *The rules also require employers to provide safety training.*

reschedule /riʃkɛdʒul, -dʒuəl/ (reschedules, rescheduling or rescheduled)

VERB If someone **reschedules** an event, they change the time at which it is supposed to happen. ○ *Since I'll be away, I'd like to reschedule the meeting.*

research /rɪsɜrtʃ, risɜrtʃ/

NOUN **Research** is work that involves studying something and trying to discover facts about it. ○ *The new design is the product of months of research.*

reserve /rɪzɜrv/ (reserves, reserving or reserved)

VERB If you **reserve** something such as a table, room, or ticket, you arrange for it to be kept for you to use. ○ *I've reserved the meeting room for 2:30 this afternoon.*

resident /rɛzɪdənt/ (residents)

NOUN The **residents** of an area or building are the people who live there. ○ *He called on the city to build more low-cost homes for local residents.*

residential /rɛzɪdɛnʃᵊl/

ADJECTIVE A **residential** course or conference is one in which people stay overnight at the place where the course or conference takes place. ○ *My company is sending me on a three-day residential training course.*

resource /risɔrs/ (resources)

NOUN A **resource** is something valuable, such as materials or money, that a person or organization can use to help them achieve something. ○ *This website is a great learning resource.*

responsibility /rɪspɒnsɪbɪlɪti/ (responsibilities)

NOUN If you have **responsibility** for something or someone, or if they are your **responsibility**, it is your job or duty to deal with them and to take decisions relating to them. ○ *Each manager had responsibility for just under 600 properties.*

result /rɪzʌlt/ (results, resulting or resulted)

1 NOUN A **result** is something that happens or exists because of something else that has happened. ○ *This failure is the result of inadequate planning.*

2 PHRASE **as a result** You use **as a result** to introduce an event or situation that has been caused by something else you have mentioned. ○ *We had to extend the project deadline and, as a result, went over budget.*

3 VERB If something **results in** a particular situation or event, it causes that situation or event to happen. ○ *Lengthy admissions procedures have resulted in delays.*

4 VERB If something **results from** a particular event or action, it is caused by that event or action. ○ *Poor productivity could result from low morale among the workforce.*

5 NOUN A company's **results** are the amounts of their sales and profits or loss in a particular period, or a report about this. ○ *The company stated in its results that its US businesses had performed well.*

6 NOUN A **result** is information that you get when you carry out an experiment or a computer search. ○ *I searched for the company name, but got no results.*

retail /riteɪl/

NOUN **Retail** is the activity of selling goods directly to the public, usually in small quantities. ○ *Retail sales grew just 3.8 percent last year.*

retire /rɪtaɪər/ **(retires, retiring** or **retired)**

VERB When older people **retire**, they leave their job and usually stop working completely. ○ *Many said they plan to retire at 50.*

return /rɪtɜrn/ **(returns, returning** or **returned)**

1 VERB When you **return to** a place, you go back there after you have been away. ○ *The president will return to Washington tomorrow.*

2 NOUN Someone's **return** is their arrival back at a place where they were before. ○ *She is looking forward to her return to work next week.*

3 VERB If you **returnto** an activity, you start doing it again. ○ *At that stage he will be 52, young enough to return to politics if he wishes to do so.*

4 VERB If you **return** something **to** someone, you give or send it back to them. ○ *Please fill in the form and return it to us at the above address.*

5 VERB If you **return** someone's call, you call them on the telephone because they called you earlier at a time when you were not available. ○ *I'll ask him to return your call as soon as he gets in.*

6 VERB If you **return** something that you have bought, you take or send it back to the seller because you are not satisfied with it. ○ *If you return unwanted goods in their original condition we will issue you with a credit note.*

7 NOUN A **return** is an item that someone has bought and then returned to the seller because they are not satisfied with it. ○ *When buying online, check the retailer's policy on returns.*

revise /rɪvaɪz/ **(revises, revising** or **revised)**

VERB If you **revise** something, you alter it to make it better or more accurate. ○ *The revised article will be published in our next edition.*

risk /rɪsk/ **(risks)**

1 NOUN **Risk** is the possibility that something unpleasant or damaging could happen, or that someone could lose money. ○ *All investment carries an element of risk.*

2 NOUN If you take a **risk**, you do something that could result in damage or loss. ○ *He took a big risk in hiring her, but it paid off.*

safety /seɪfti/

NOUN **Safety** is the state of not being in danger. ○ *We need to improve safety on our construction sites.*

sample /sæmpəl/ **(samples)**

NOUN A **sample** of something such as a product is a small quantity of it or one example of it, that shows you what it is like. ○ *Register online and receive a free sample.*

satisfaction /sætɪsfækʃən/

NOUN If you feel **satisfaction**, you feel pleased to do or get something. ○ *Customers reported high levels of satisfaction with the service.*

section /sɛkʃən/ **(sections)**

NOUN A **section** of something is one of the parts into which it is divided or from which it is formed. ○ *The first section of the book deals with the background to the conflict.*

secure /sɪkyʊər/ **(secures, securing** or **secured)**

1 ADJECTIVE Something that is **secure** is very well protected, so that there is little risk of crime or damage. ○ *The building has secure undercover parking for 27 vehicles.*

2 VERB If you **secure** something that you want or need, you succeed in obtaining it. [FORMAL] ○ *Graham's achievements helped secure him the job.*

security /sɪkyʊəriti/

NOUN **Security** refers to all the measures that are taken to protect something against crime or damage. ○ *They are now under a great deal of pressure to tighten their airport security.*

segment /sɛgmənt/ **(segments)**

NOUN A **segment** of a market is one part of it, considered separately from the rest. ○ *Three-to-five day cruises are the fastest-growing segment of the market.*

select /sɪlɛkt/ **(selects, selecting** or **selected)**

VERB If you **select** something, you choose it from a number of things of the same kind. ○ *Candidates are selected by interview only.*

selection /sɪlɛkʃən/ **(selections)**

1 NOUN **Selection** is the act of selecting one or more people or things from a group. ○ *We can help you with selection of the right equipment for your needs.*

2 NOUN A **selection** is a set of things or people that have been chosen from a larger group. ○ *this selection of popular songs*

3 NOUN The **selection of** goods available somewhere is the particular range of goods from which you can choose what you want. ○ *It offers the widest selection of antiques of every description in a one day market.*

seminar /sɛminɑr/ **(seminars)**

NOUN A **seminar** is a meeting where a group of people discuss a problem or topic. ○ *a series of half-day seminars to help businessmen get the best value from investing in information technology*

shipment /ʃɪpmənt/ **(shipments)**

NOUN A **shipment** is an amount of goods that is sent to a company or place on a ship, train, airplane, or other vehicle. ○ *We're expecting a new shipment of plastic containers next week.*

signal /sɪgnəl/ **(signals)**

NOUN A **signal** is a series of radio waves, light waves, or changes in electrical current which may carry information. ○ *high-frequency radio signals*

significance /sɪgnɪfɪkəns/

NOUN The **significance** of something is the importance that it has, usually because it will have an effect on a situation or shows something about a situation. ○ *The difference had no statistical significance.*

significant /sɪgnɪfɪkənt/

ADJECTIVE A **significant** amount or effect is large enough to be important or affect a situation to a noticeable degree. ○ *A small but significant number of 11-year-olds are illiterate.*

similar /sɪmɪlər/

ADJECTIVE If one thing is **similar to** another, or if two things are **similar**, they have features that are the same. ○ *The accident was similar to one that happened in 2003.*

simulation /sɪmyəleɪʃ°n/ (simulations)

NOUN **Simulation** or a **simulation** is the process or act of pretending that you are doing something or that something is happening, in a way that is like the real thing. ○ *Training includes realistic simulation of casualty procedures.*

situation /sɪtʃueɪʃ°n/ (situations)

NOUN A **situation** is what is happening in a particular place at a particular time, or what is happening to you. ○ *The family was in a difficult financial situation.*

skill /skɪl/ (skills)

NOUN A **skill** is a type of work or activity which requires special training and knowledge. ○ *an opportunity to learn new computer skills*

solution /səluʃ°n/ (solutions)

NOUN A **solution to** a problem or difficult situation is a way of dealing with it so that the difficulty is removed. ○ *the ability to think of simple, effective solutions to practical problems*

source /sɔrs/ (sources, sourcing or sourced)

1 NOUN The **source of** something is the person, place, or thing that you get it from. ○ *Renewable sources of energy must be used where practical.*

2 VERB If you **source** something, you find a place or company where you can get or buy it. ○ *If you find it difficult to source fresh herbs, use dried ones instead.*

specialize /spɛʃəlaɪz/ (specializes, specializing or specialized)

VERB If you **specialize in** something, you spend most of your time studying it or doing it. ○ *They work for banks or law firms that specialize in business.*

specialized /spɛʃəlaɪzd/

ADJECTIVE Something that is **specialized** is developed especially for a particular purpose. ○ *Specialized equipment is available for working in particularly narrow spaces.*

specialty /spɛʃ°lti/ (specialties)

NOUN Someone's **specialty** is a particular type of work that they do most or do best. ○ *His specialty is international law.*

sponsor /spɒnsər/ (sponsors, sponsoring or sponsored)

VERB If an organization or a person **sponsors** an event, they pay for it. ○ *A local bank is sponsoring the race.*

stable /steɪb°l/ (stables)

NOUN A company's **stable** of artists or brands is the group of artists who sell their work through that company, or brands that are sold by that company. ○ *The agent represents a strong stable of painters.*

standard /stændərd/ (standards)

1 NOUN A **standard** is a level of quality or achievement. ○ *improvements in the general standard of living*

2 NOUN A **standard** is something that you use in order to judge the quality of something else. ○ *We guarantee that all our work will meet the highest standards.*

3 ADJECTIVE You use **standard** to describe things which are usual and normal. ○ *the standard format for a scientific paper*

start-up /stɑrtʌp/

ADJECTIVE A **start-up** company is a small business that has recently been started by someone. ○ *Thousands of start-up firms have entered the computer market.*

statement /steɪtmənt/ (statements)

NOUN A **statement** is something that you say or write which gives information in a formal or definite way. ○ *"Things are moving ahead."—I found that statement vague and unclear.*

stimulating /stɪmyəleɪtɪŋ/

ADJECTIVE If something is **stimulating**, it makes you feel full of ideas and enthusiasm. ○ *The atmosphere at work was always stimulating.*

stipulate /stɪpyleɪt/ (stipulates, stipulating or stipulated)

VERB If a person or rule **stipulates** something, they say clearly that it must be done. ○ *The contract stipulates that three months' notice must be given.*

straightforward /streɪtfɔrwərd/

ADJECTIVE If you describe something as **straightforward**, you approve of it because it is easy to do or understand. ○ *Cost accounting is a relatively straightforward process.*

strategic /strətidʒɪk/

ADJECTIVE **Strategic** means relating to the most important, general aspects of something such as a business plan or military operation, especially when these are decided in advance. ○ *We identify and access new markets by strategic planning and partnerships.*

strategy /strætədʒi/ (strategies)

NOUN A **strategy** is a general plan or set of plans intended to achieve something, especially over a long period. ○ *a customer-led marketing strategy*

struggle /strʌɡᵊl/ (struggles, struggling or struggled)

VERB If you **struggle with** something, you have problems because of it or find it hard to deal with. ○ *Stores are struggling with a lack of consumer confidence.*

submit /səbmɪt/ (submits, submitting or submitted)

VERB If you **submit** a proposal, report, or request **to** someone, you formally send it to them so that they can consider it or decide about it. ○ *They submitted their reports to the board yesterday.*

subscribe /səbskraɪb/ (subscribes, subscribing or subscribed)

VERB If you **subscribe to** a magazine or online service, you arrange to have copies of it or news from it sent to you regularly. ○ *I subscribe to several science blogs.*

substantial /səbstænʃᵊl/

ADJECTIVE **Substantial** means large in amount or degree. [FORMAL] ○ *A substantial number of products will have to change their labels.*

succinct /səksɪŋkt/

ADJECTIVE Something that is **succinct** expresses facts or ideas clearly and in few words. ○ *The book gives an admirably succinct account of the technology and its history.*

suitable /suːtəbᵊl/

ADJECTIVE Someone or something that is **suitable for** a particular purpose or occasion is right or acceptable for it. ○ *Employers usually decide within five minutes whether someone is suitable for the job.*

superior /supɪəriər/

ADJECTIVE Something that is **superior** is very good, and better than other things of the same kind. ○ *A few years ago it was virtually impossible to find superior quality coffee in local stores.*

support /səpɔrt/ (supports, supporting or supported)

1 VERB If you **support** a person or organization, you help them or give them money. ○ *Government should support R&D projects that are too risky to attract private funding.*

2 VERB If you **support** someone or their ideas or aims, you agree with them. ○ *Most business leaders do not support the idea of changing the legislation.*

3 NOUN **Support** is money or help provided to a person or organization. ○ *The candidate thanked his family and his campaign contributors for their support.*

4 VERB If a fact **supports** a statement or a theory, it helps to show that it is true or correct. ○ *Do you have any evidence to support this allegation?*

sustainable /səsteɪnəbᵊl/

ADJECTIVE A **sustainable** plan, method, or system is designed to continue at the same rate or level of activity without failing. ○ *the creation of an efficient and sustainable transportation system*

target /tɑrgɪt/ (targets, targeting, targetting, targeted or targetted)

1 VERB If you **target** a particular group of people, you try to appeal to those people or affect them. ○ *The company has targeted adults as its primary customers.*

2 ADJECTIVE A **target** customer or market is a type of customer or market that a company hopes will buy its products or services. ○ *We decided that we needed to change our target market from the over-45's to the 35–45's.*

task /tæsk/ (tasks)

NOUN A **task** is an activity or piece of work which you have to do, usually as part of a larger project. ○ *She used the day to catch up with administrative tasks.*

temporary /tɛmpəreri/

ADJECTIVE Something that is **temporary** lasts for only a limited time. ○ *His job here is only temporary.*

tentative /tɛntətɪv/

ADJECTIVE **Tentative** agreements, plans, or arrangements are not definite or certain, but have been made as a first step. ○ *Political leaders have reached a tentative agreement to hold a conference next month.*

thorough /θɜroʊ/

ADJECTIVE A **thorough** action or activity is one that is done very carefully and in a detailed way so that nothing is forgotten. ○ *We are making a thorough investigation.*

title /taɪtᵊl/ (titles)

1 NOUN The **title** of a book, play, film, or piece of music is its name. ○ *"Patience and Sarah" was first published in 1969 under the title "A Place for Us."*

2 NOUN A **title** is a book or magazine. ○ *It has become the biggest publisher of poetry in Britain, with 50 new titles a year.*

3 NOUN Someone's **title** is a name that describes their job or status in an organization. ○ *"Could you tell me your official job title?"—"It's Data Processing Manager."*

treatment /tritmənt/ (treatments)

NOUN A **treatment** is a procedure done in order to improve a medical condition or to improve someone's appearance. ○ *an effective treatment for eczema*

trend /trɛnd/ (trends)

NOUN A **trend** is a change or development towards something new or different. ○ *There has been a trend toward part-time employment.*

update /ʌpdeɪt, ʌpdeɪt/ **(updates, updating** or **updated)**

1 **VERB** If you **update** something, you make it more modern, usually by adding new parts to it or giving new information. ○ *an updated edition of the book*

2 **NOUN** An **update** is the most recent information about a particular situation. ○ *Check our website for the latest news updates.*

3 **VERB** If you **update** someone **on** a situation, you give them the latest information about it. ○ *Before we start, I'll update you on what happened yesterday.*

upgrade /ʌpgreɪd, -greɪd/ **(upgrades, upgrading** or **upgraded)**

1 **VERB** If you **upgrade** something, you improve it or replace it with a better one. ○ *I recently upgraded my computer.*

2 **NOUN** An **upgrade** is the action of improving something or replacing it with something better. ○ *Our equipment is outdated and in need of an upgrade.*

vacancy /veɪkənsi/ **(vacancies)**

NOUN A **vacancy** is a job that has not been filled. ○ *We have a vacancy for an assistant.*

vacant /veɪkənt/

ADJECTIVE If something is **vacant**, it is not being used by anyone. ○ *He bought a vacant lot which he planned to develop.*

value /vælyu/ **(values, valuing** or **valued)**

1 **NOUN** The **value** of something is how much money it is worth. ○ *The value of his investment has risen by more than $50,000.*

2 **VERB** If you **value** something or someone, you think that they are important and you appreciate them. ○ *a culture in the workplace which values learning and development*

3 **NOUN** **Value** is the fact that something is worth the money that it costs. ○ *At $20, the set menu offers extremely good value.*

varied /vɛərid/

ADJECTIVE Something that is **varied** consists of things of different types, sizes, or qualities. ○ *It is essential that your diet is varied and balanced.*

various /vɛəriəs/

ADJECTIVE If you say that there are **various** things, you mean there are several different things of the type mentioned. ○ *The company has received various enquiries from customers.*

vehicle /viːkəl/ **(vehicles)**

NOUN A **vehicle** is a machine such as a car, bus, or truck which has an engine and is used to carry people from place to place. ○ *The vehicle would not be able to make the journey on one tank of fuel.*

venue /vɛnyu/ **(venues)**

NOUN A **venue** is the place where an event or activity will happen. ○ *Fenway Park will be used as a venue for the rock concert.*

vibrant /vaɪbrənt/

ADJECTIVE Something that is **vibrant** is attractive and exciting because it is full of life and energy. ○ *The area is popular with young professionals, who enjoy its funky atmosphere and vibrant nightlife.*

warranty /wɔrənti/ **(warranties)**

NOUN A **warranty** is a promise by a company that if you find a fault in something they have sold you, they will repair it or replace it. ○ *The TV comes with a twelve-month warranty.*

Audio Script

This audio script provides an exact record of what you will hear on the CD that accompanies this book.

Track 1 [page 37]

Listening
Part 1: Photographs

> **Directions:** For each item in Part 1, you will hear four statements about a photograph in the test book. You must listen carefully to the statements in order to select the statement that best describes the photograph. Mark the corresponding letter (A), (B), (C), or (D) on the answer sheet.
>
> **Example**
> Listen to the statements and select the one that best describes the picture.
>
> (A) They're drinking orange juice.
> (B) They're turning on a computer.
> (C) They're looking at a screen.
> (D) They're putting on formal clothes.
>
> Statement (C), **"They're looking at a screen."** best describes the picture, so you should choose answer (C) and mark it on your answer sheet.

Track 2 [page 38]

> Listen to the statements and select the one that best describes the picture.

1. Look at photograph number 1 in your test book.
    (A) Some materials are being examined.
    (B) Some products are stacked on the shelves.
    (C) Some shopping carts are being stacked.
    (D) Some boxes are under the cart.

2. Look at photograph number 2 in your test book.
    (A) An engineer is fixing a traffic light.
    (B) There are many tracks on the road.
    (C) Some cars are driving on the street.
    (D) Some people are at a building site.

3. Look at photograph number 3 in your test book.
    (A) A vending machine is being used.
    (B) A door is open.
    (C) All the chairs are empty.
    (D) A table has been placed behind the chairs.

4. Look at photograph number 4 in your test book.
    (A) She is raising her hands.
    (B) She is using some medical equipment.
    (C) She is working at a hospital.
    (D) She is picking up the phone.

5. Look at photograph number 5 in your test book.
    (A) The man is cleaning the desk.
    (B) The man is looking at his laptop.
    (C) The man is tidying a bookshelf.
    (D) The man is opening a book.

6. Look at photograph number 6 in your test book.
    (A) Some people are waiting in line at a counter.
    (B) Some items are being removed.
    (C) Some clothes are displayed in the window.
    (D) Some people are looking at the tables.

7. Look at photograph number 7 in your test book.
    (A) The fruit basket is under the table.
    (B) There are some cushions on the couch.
    (C) Books have been placed on the table.
    (D) The lamp is switched off.

8. Look at photograph number 8 in your test book.
    (A) There are flowers inside the building.
    (B) Some flowers are in a bucket.
    (C) Several pictures are being framed.
    (D) Some vegetables are for sale.

9. Look at photograph number 9 in your test book.
    (A) He is holding a cleaning mop.
    (B) He is cleaning windows.
    (C) He is running on the floor.
    (D) He is wearing a suit.

10. Look at photograph number 10 in your test book.
    (A) He is turning his back.
    (B) He is driving a car.
    (C) He is changing his uniform.
    (D) He is talking to someone.

Track 3 [page 43]

Listening
Part 2: Question-Response

Directions: For each item in Part 2, you will hear a statement or a question followed by three responses. Listen and choose the best response. Then mark the corresponding letter (A), (B), or (C) on the answer sheet.

Example
Have you met the new Managing Director?

(A) Actually I talked with him in the lobby just now.
(B) Yes, I took the call.
(C) No, he takes the subway to work.

The best response to the question "Have you met the new Managing Director?" is answer choice (**A**), **"Actually I talked with him in the lobby just now."** You should mark answer (**A**) on your answer sheet.

Track 4 [page 43]

You will hear a statement or a question followed by three responses. Listen and choose the best response. Then mark the corresponding letter (A), (B), or (C) on the answer sheet.

11. Our flight is delayed by an hour, isn't it?
    (A) To New York.
    (B) Yes, as far as I can see.
    (C) I'm sorry I was late.

12. Did you call me last night?
    (A) I got a cold.
    (B) Yes, didn't you get my voicemail?
    (C) No, I haven't received any calls.

13. How do you like the tea?
    (A) It's very nice.
    (B) Yes, please pass me some milk.
    (C) The copier is switched on.

14. What will be the topic of tomorrow's conference?
    (A) In half an hour.
    (B) Right here.
    (C) A new management strategy.

15. Who answered the client's call?
    (A) Mr. Jones probably did.
    (B) I got the document back.
    (C) At the office.

16. Do you think I need to rewrite my cover letter?
    (A) Yes, you can.
    (B) No, I didn't write it.
    (C) Yes, it's not long enough.

17. What kind of bags did you get?
    (A) They are $50.
    (B) Actually, I didn't buy a bag.
    (C) With my bathing suit.

18. Where do you want me to put these folders?
    (A) Next to the cabinet.
    (B) She didn't stack the boxes.
    (C) That sounds great.

19. We should order a new tire, shouldn't we?
    (A) No, it's not old.
    (B) She's tired today.
    (C) Here's your order.

20. Would you like to walk or take a taxi?
    (A) Every five minutes.
    (B) I'm fine with either.
    (C) Yes, I like them.

21. How did your presentation go?
    (A) Three days ago.
    (B) The present was wonderful.
    (C) Luckily, it went very well.

22. Didn't you think the music was great?
    (A) It is two hours long.
    (B) He will book two seats.
    (C) Yes, it was amazing.

23. Are there any extra pens in the drawer?
    (A) On the left corner.
    (B) The window is broken.
    (C) I haven't seen any lately.

24. I had a great time working with you.
    (A) As soon as I get to work.
    (B) I prefer walking to jogging.
    (C) So did I with you.

25. Can you wait for me to get to work or do you need to leave now?
    (A) What time do you think you can get here?
    (B) You should get off at Central Station.
    (C) On Monday morning.

26. Is she going to leave her job this week?
    (A) Please sign there.
    (B) I have no idea.
    (C) I'm still searching for one.

27. Have you been to the central branch this week?
    (A) Yes, I went there on Monday.
    (B) No, it's not her office.
    (C) I think you need to.

28. Why don't we have breakfast together before work?
    (A) No, the food wasn't good.
    (B) Please leave it at reception.
    (C) That sounds like a good idea.

29. Are you planning to go cycling tomorrow?
    (A) No, I have to stay home.
    (B) Yes, he works in planning.
    (C) She won't be there.

30. When will the rebuilding of the downtown store start?
    (A) In our building.
    (B) I have no clue.
    (C) The refurbishment was really great.

31. Who is going to handle the press release?
    (A) We will prepare for tonight's dinner.
    (B) Ms. Johnson from the PR Department.
    (C) The handle is getting old.

32. When can he finish the sales report?
    (A) It's on sale.
    (B) I think he already completed it.
    (C) He is a TV reporter.

33. It has been much warmer these days.
    (A) I hope it gets even hotter soon.
    (B) This one is shorter than that one.
    (C) He's a weather reporter.

34. How can I switch off the audio?
    (A) That's great.
    (B) Why don't you read the user's guide?
    (C) Turn left.

35. What's the weather going to be like this weekend?
    (A) It will probably snow.
    (B) I am wondering what you think about it.
    (C) Around 11 a.m.

36. Would you mind if I borrowed your card?
    (A) No problem.
    (B) Yes, it looks nice on you.
    (C) No, I don't eat fish.

37. Won't it be more expensive to travel by plane?
    (A) The planning won't last long.
    (B) Yes, by courier.
    (C) I know, but it's much faster.

38. You've never been to London before, have you?
    (A) About five months ago.
    (B) No, this is my first visit.
    (C) Yes, we've met before.

39. Do you know why Alex contacted her?
    (A) Yes, I'm ordering contact lenses.
    (B) No, why don't you ask him directly?
    (C) In the morning.

40. Where should I hand in my job application?
    (A) Yes, I will go on a trip.
    (B) At 5 o'clock.
    (C) Over there.

Track 5 [page 44]

Listening
Part 3: Conversations

> **Directions:** You will hear conversations with two speakers. Then you will answer three questions about each conversation. Listen and select the best response to each question. Mark the corresponding letter (A), (B), (C), or (D) on the answer sheet.

Woman: Hello, I'm calling to book a table for Saturday night at 7:00 p.m.

Man: How many people will be coming?

Woman: There will be four of us. Also, I would like to request a table by the window.

Man: Sure, I'll check our list for Saturday. Luckily, we do have just one more table by the window left at that time. Do you mind giving me your name and phone number so I can keep it for you?

41. What is the woman doing?

42. What is the woman requesting?

43. What should the woman do next?

Man: Excuse me, could you tell me how to get to the modern art exhibit?

Woman: Sure. Walk straight, and then take the elevator to the third floor. Have you been to this gallery before?

Man: No, I've never been to New York before. I came to visit my sister. She's working here.

Woman: Well, I hope you enjoy your time in New York. Why don't you visit the Empire State Building near downtown? It's one of the city's best attractions.

44. Where most likely are the two people?

45. Why is the man in New York?

46. What does the woman recommend the man do?

Man: You've reached Robert at Stonefield Post Office. How may I help you?

Woman: Hello, I was expecting to receive a parcel from Italy last week but it didn't arrive yet.

Man: Actually, there have been some problems at our domestic parcel sorting center. We are experiencing delays of three to five days. Do you have the tracking number for your parcel? You can also track online.

Woman: Thank you. I'll ask my friend for it and check the expected delivery date.

47. Who most likely is the man?

48. What is the purpose of the woman's call?

49. What is the woman going to do?

Man: Hello, I'm wondering if I can open a business account for my company.

Woman: Sure, this is the application form you need. Please fill it out and bring it back to me when you're done.

Man: Actually I want to speak to someone before applying. I have some questions.

Woman: Unfortunately, our business accounts specialist is at a meeting. Then she is going on a business trip this week and will be back next Monday. If you want to see her, you'd better come back again then.

50. What is the man asking for?

51. What does the woman give the man?

52. What should the man do?

Woman: Hello, Sunshine Properties. This is Monica speaking. How may I help you today?

Man: Hi, I just got a job in Boston and I'm looking for an apartment to rent. Ideally, I'd like somewhere near the Financial District. Are there any vacant properties in that area?

Woman: Yes, there are a few apartments available. How soon would you like to move in?

Man: Well, I'm going to be overseas for a business trip until the end of November. So, it would be better if I move in at the beginning of December.

53. Who most likely is the woman?

54. Why is the man calling?

55. What is the woman asking about?

Man: Anna, could you get in touch with the IT Department? I'm having problems with my company cell phone. It's suddenly turned off. I have important numbers on it that I need for a meeting this afternoon.

Woman: OK, I'll call them immediately. I'll also tell them that this is important.

Man: Thanks. I hope it can be up and running again by the meeting.

Woman: It should be fine. I had the same issue with my phone last week and they were able to recover all the numbers.

56. Why is the man calling?

57. When will the woman call the IT Department?

58. What does the woman say about the IT Department?

Woman: I'm really busy until next Monday negotiating a contract with the Alaskan Wood Company. Would you mind writing the sales reports for me? They are due on Friday.

Man: By all means. I'll finish them by the end of Thursday. Are they in your folder?

Woman: Yes, but Samantha has the updated versions. Could you ask her for them? Sorry, I'm rushing to catch a taxi.

Man: Yes, I will. The traffic is very busy today. You'd better go now or you'll miss your flight.

59. What does the woman ask the man to do?

60. When is the man going to complete the work?

61. What is the man's concern?

Woman: Hello, this is Amy Chang. I would like to find out if my car's ready to be picked up this afternoon.

Man: Could you pick it up after Wednesday? We need to do more work on the engine.

Woman: Hmm ... The problem is that I need to go pick up my daughter from college tomorrow.

Man: Then could you drop by this evening? We can lend you a car for free until your car is ready.

62. Why is the woman calling?

63. What is the problem?

64. What is the man's offer?

Man: Hi, Cath. How's your search for a new house going?

Woman: I called a real estate agent and she is trying to find a suitable place near my office in the city.

Man: Most houses in the city are expensive to purchase, and the living expenses are high. Can you afford it?

Woman: Fortunately, I got a pay raise last month. All our team was rewarded for making a very successful deal.

65. What are the speakers mainly talking about?

66. What problem does the man mention?

67. Why is the woman fortunate?

Woman: Hi, Michael. How many people have applied for the two managerial positions?

Man: More than 20 people applied, so we're interviewing the best five. Do you have any time this week to look at the applications?

Woman: I think I'm free on Wednesday afternoon. We can review the applications, and leave out those who don't have a certificate or other qualification in management.

Man: Sure, but remember we should also see if they have practical skills gained from hands-on experience.

68. How many applicants will the speakers interview?

69. What will the speakers do on Wednesday?

70. What does the man think is important?

Track 6 [page 47]

Listening
Part 4: Talks

> **Directions:** You will hear several talks, each with one speaker. Then you will answer three questions about the talk. Listen and select the best response to each question. Mark the corresponding letter (A), (B), (C), or (D) on the answer sheet.

Let's look at the weather. Temperatures have gone down lower than we expect at this time of year, and today it'll snow in most places. Eastern areas will see particularly heavy snow. Many schools and offices have announced closings due to the bad weather and public transportation is experiencing cancellations. Government officials recommend that residents should not travel far away from home. The weather problems will continue until Sunday morning, but I expect the situation to improve late Sunday in time for the beginning of the week. Keep yourself updated by listening for more announcements throughout the day.

71. What does the report say is unusual about the current weather?

72. What does the government advise people to do?

73. When will the weather improve?

You've reached Telecom First. Our Internet services are not working on the west side of the city. We have identified that due to the strong winds a tree has fallen and damaged some of our cables. Our engineers were immediately sent to the scene and have been repairing the cables since 9:00 a.m. We estimate that we will be able to resume Internet service by 1:00 p.m. If your connection is not working by 1:30 p.m., please call again for an updated status report. Thank you for your understanding and patience.

74. Who mostly likely is the speaker?

75. What is the problem?

76. When is the problem going to be resolved?

Hello, Mr. Jones. My name is Jenny Wong from *Health Food Now*. We have received the order you placed on December 15 through our website. I'm calling to confirm which product you wish to order and your order confirmation number. I am sorry but we are currently experiencing technical problems with our online ordering system. As a result, we are asking our customers for order information again. Please call us at 555-7892 to confirm. We apologize for the inconvenience.

77. What is the purpose of the message?

78. What kind of business does the woman probably work for?

79. What does the woman ask Mr. Jones to do?

Good evening, ladies and gentlemen. We are all here to thank one of our most valued employees, Mike Smith, our Regional Marketing Manager in Hong Kong, who is retiring next month. As you may all know, Mike was our first Regional Marketing Rep. After working at the New York headquarters for seven years, Mike was sent to Hong Kong to set up the branch by himself. Thanks to Mike, we have had excellent sales in Hong Kong, and extended our wide network of regional sales offices around East Asia. And now we want to sincerely thank Mike for his 35 years of service and for all his contribution to overseas sales, which have become a central part of our business today.

80. What is the purpose of the speech?

81. What did Mike Smith do?

82. How long has Mike Smith worked at the company?

Welcome to Green Enterprises. My name is Joyce Linn, from the Human Resources Department. We expect you all to get settled into your new jobs as quickly as possible, so please ask me if you have any questions. Today, I'll take you to the manufacturing factory and show you around the building. First, we'll go to the production unit where all of our solar panels are assembled. Please keep your helmet on at all times in the factory. Then I'll take you to the Finishing Department, where you will all be working. Let's start our tour. Please follow me.

83. Who is the audience?

84. What does the speaker say that Green Enterprises produces?

85. What does the speaker ask the listeners to do?

Do you like reading short stories? If you do, stay tuned for *The Book Club* every Tuesday at 3:00 p.m. on ABS FM 98.9. Each week, host Neil Foster discusses the latest releases with a group of well-known authors from all over the world. You may also participate in discussions by phone, and each week we invite one lucky competition winner to join Neil and his guests in the studio. So give us a call during the show at 301-555-8237. Not free at 3:00 p.m. or missed this week's show? No problem! Visit our website to listen again or download the podcast to your phone to listen at your convenience.

86. What is being promoted?

87. How can listeners contribute an opinion?

88. What is available on the website?

Welcome to ASKS Radio's Traffic Update. I'm Gavin Sanders. This morning, there is some bad news. The bus service has been reduced and this is causing significant traffic delays. There is currently a one-hour delay on Highway 5 to Northern Avenue. Please take Highway 35 as an alternative route. We expect this delay to increase until around 9 o'clock. Eventually, cars will be backed up on all the major highways. Please come back for an update. You'll hear more detailed traffic information in fifteen minutes.

89. Who is Gavin Sanders?

90. What is causing a lot of traffic?

91. When is the next traffic report?

Good afternoon everyone and welcome to the Chinatown historic district. My name is George and I'll be your guide today. The district was first founded by Cantonese immigrants around 1920. Later, however, it received immigrants from many other countries looking for work. During the tour, you're allowed to take pictures. We will see many fine examples of Chinese architecture, and many Chinese restaurants and grocery stores. We will also see a Greek church and a Turkish mosque. Please be quiet inside the church and mosque, and please do not take food or beverages inside. Now let's start our tour.

92. What is the main purpose of the talk?

93. What does the speaker say the listeners are permitted to do?

94. What does the speaker ask the audience to do?

Welcome to the Grand Theater. Thank you for coming to tonight's performance of Beethoven's *Piano Concerto*. Before the concert begins tonight, I'd like to ask you to keep in mind some important rules in our theater. First, please switch off all cell phones and pagers. Also, food and drinks are not permitted anywhere but in the lobby. You cannot take them into the auditorium under any circumstances. We are also afraid that no photographs can be taken at any time during the performance. If you are interested in upcoming events at the Grand Theater, please take a brochure at the exit. Thank you very much for your attention and we hope you enjoy the show.

95. Where most likely is the announcement being made?

96. What is the main purpose of the talk?

97. What does the man say the audience may pick up at the exit?

Good morning, passengers. On behalf of Captain Rodriguez and the crew, welcome aboard Mexico Air flight 901 bound for Santiago, Chile. We ask passengers to make sure that your seatbelts are fastened at all times. Our flight time from Mexico City will be 6 hours 55 minutes. Soon after take off, we will provide snacks and drinks. Please remember that passengers connecting to flights to Argentina should go to Terminal 3 after landing. We hope you enjoy the flight.

98. Who is the man talking to?

99. From which country is the flight departing?

100. What does the speaker say will be provided?

Track 7 [page 75]

Speaking
Question 1: Read a text aloud

> **Directions:** In this part of the test, you will read aloud the text on the page. You will have 45 seconds to prepare. Then you will have 45 seconds to read the text aloud.
> Your preparation time begins now.
> Now please read the text aloud.
> Your time is up. Now move on to the next question.

Track 8 [page 75]

Question 2: Read a text aloud

> **Directions:** In this part of the test, you will read aloud the text on the page. You will have 45 seconds to prepare. Then you will have 45 seconds to read the text aloud.
> Your preparation time begins now.
> Now please read the text aloud.
> Your time is up. Now move on to the next question.

Track 9 [page 76]

Question 3: Describe a picture

> **Directions:** You will describe a photograph as completely as you can. The photograph is in the test book. You will have 30 seconds to prepare what you will say, and then you will have 45 seconds to describe the picture in as much detail as possible.
> Your preparation time begins now.
> Now please describe the photograph aloud.
> Your time is up. Now move on to the next question.

Track 10 [page 76]

Questions 4–6: Respond to questions

> **Directions:** You will be asked three questions. After each question you will hear a beep. Begin speaking your answer immediately after the beep. You will not have any time to prepare your answer. For Questions 4 and 5 you will have 15 seconds to respond. For Question 6 you will have 30 seconds.

Imagine that a British marketing firm is doing research in your country. You have agreed to participate in a telephone interview about exercising.

Question 4:   How often do you exercise?

Question 5:   What kinds of exercise do you do?

Question 6:   What do you think are some benefits of exercising?

Track 11 [page 78]

Questions 7–9: Respond to questions using information provided

Directions: You will read a short text and then answer three questions based on the information in the text. You will have 30 seconds to read the text before the first question. After each question you will hear a beep. Begin speaking immediately after the beep. You will not have any extra time to prepare your answer. For Questions 7 and 8 you will have 15 seconds to respond. For Question 9 you will have 30 seconds.

Hello, my name is Jeff Norton, and I'm planning a business trip from New York to Las Vegas from September 10th to the 15th. I'd like to find out some information from you.

Question 7:   Could you tell me what airline options I have?

Question 8:   Which is the least expensive flight?

Question 9:   I'd prefer to take a nonstop flight. Can you give me the details about them?

Track 12 [page 79]

Question 10: Propose a solution

Directions: You will hear about a problem and be asked to propose a solution. You will have 30 seconds to prepare your solution, and then 60 seconds to speak.

Hello, my name is Dean Smith, and I stopped by your store earlier tonight to get some lottery tickets. I think it was around 8:00 p.m. Anyway, the reason I'm calling is that I think I left a folder on the lottery counter. I just realized this now after I got home. It's a red folder, and it contains important files that I need for work tomorrow, so I really hope that it's there. I got your answering machine, so I'm assuming that your store is closed now. But if you're still open, can you call me back as soon as you get this message? I'll come to the store right now to pick it up. If not, can you tell me what time you will open tomorrow morning? You can reach me at 555-3480. Thank you.

Track 13 [page 79]

Speaking
Question 11: Express an opinion

Directions: You will hear about a specific topic and then give your opinion about it. Make sure you say as much as you can about the topic in the time allowed. You will have 15 seconds to prepare, and then 60 seconds to speak.

Some people think it's better to shop online, while others prefer to go to a store to shop. Which do you think is better and why? Give specific reasons and details to support your opinion.

Track 14 [page 89]

Listening
Part 1: Photographs

Directions: For each item in Part 1, you will hear four statements about a photograph in the test book. You must listen carefully to the statements in order to select the statement that best describes the photograph. Mark the corresponding letter (A), (B), (C), or (D) on the answer sheet.

Example
Listen to the statements and select the one that best describes the picture.

(A) They're drinking orange juice.
(B) They're turning on a computer.
(C) They're looking at a screen.
(D) They're putting on formal clothes.

Statement (C), **"They're looking at a screen."** best describes the picture, so you should choose answer (C) and mark it on your answer sheet.

Track 15 [page 90]

Listen to the statements and select the one that best describes the picture.

1.   Look at photograph number 1 in your test book.
    (A) They are holding hands.
    (B) They are sitting near the grass.
    (C) They are climbing a fence.
    (D) They are watering some flowers.

2. Look at photograph number 2 in your test book.
    (A) She is holding a cup.
    (B) She is cleaning the window.
    (C) She is eating.
    (D) She is working at a café.

3. Look at photograph number 3 in your test book.
    (A) Some people are looking at a sculpture.
    (B) Some people are touching the birds.
    (C) A man is purchasing a camera.
    (D) A man is taking a photograph.

4. Look at photograph number 4 in your test book.
    (A) A man is putting on a shirt.
    (B) A man is playing an instrument.
    (C) The street is crowded.
    (D) Some people are surrounding a man.

5. Look at photograph number 5 in your test book.
    (A) People are waiting for a taxi.
    (B) People are crossing a street.
    (C) People are getting on a bus.
    (D) People are stopped at a traffic light.

6. Look at photograph number 6 in your test book.
    (A) People are playing with horses.
    (B) People are riding on a carriage.
    (C) The woman is waving her hand.
    (D) The man is taking off his hat.

7. Look at photograph number 7 in your test book.
    (A) A statue is being cleaned.
    (B) Some buildings are being rebuilt.
    (C) The man is buying a newspaper.
    (D) Some people are sitting near a fountain.

8. Look at photograph number 8 in your test book.
    (A) Some tapestries are on the wall.
    (B) Some people are waiting for food.
    (C) The room has been prepared for a meal.
    (D) The tables are being decorated with flowers.

9. Look at photograph number 9 in your test book.
    (A) Some policemen are on patrol.
    (B) Pedestrians are clapping together.
    (C) Some people are feeding horses.
    (D) The flags are lined up along the street.

10. Look at photograph number 10 in your test book.
    (A) Some people are fishing on the bank.
    (B) Some people are lying on the shore.
    (C) The plants are being watered.
    (D) The boats are in the water.

Track 16 [page 95]

Listening
Part 2: Question–response

Directions: For each item in Part 2, you will hear a statement or a question followed by three responses. Listen and choose the best response. Then mark the corresponding letter (A), (B), or (C) on the answer sheet.

Example
Have you met the new Managing Director?

(A) Actually I talked with him in the lobby just now.
(B) Yes, I took the call.
(C) No, he takes the subway to work.

The best response to the question "Have you met the new Managing Director?" is answer choice **(A)**, **"Actually I talked with him in the lobby just now."** You should mark answer **(A)** on your answer sheet.

Track 17 [page 95]

You will hear a statement or a question followed by three responses. Listen and choose the best response. Then mark the corresponding letter (A), (B), or (C) on the answer sheet.

11. Who's going to meet you at the airport?
    (A) At 9:00 p.m.
    (B) Of course, I will.
    (C) I thought Mr. Hamilton would.

12. Have you spoken to Mr. Knight recently?
    (A) No, he's out of the country.
    (B) $20 and 95 cents.
    (C) He's our assistant.

13. Isn't there an auto repair shop on Saragossa Street?
    (A) I repaired a new car.
    (B) There are two pairs of socks.
    (C) Not that I can think of.

14. Why are you staying at work tonight?
    (A) I need to finish a sales report.
    (B) I'm sorry I'm late.
    (C) I arrived here just now.

15. Who should you ask when you take a day off?
    (A) Don't switch off the light.
    (B) David's the person you need.
    (C) Maybe next week.

16. When will the sales report be done?
    (A) In a few days.
    (B) It's not on sale.
    (C) It's five pages long.

17. How many chairs did you request?
    (A) As many as possible.
    (B) She's the chairman's daughter.
    (C) More or less.

18. Do you have time to check my report?
    (A) Of course, send it to me.
    (B) Yes, it's 5 o'clock.
    (C) I appreciate your help.

19. Where's the occupational health clinic?
    (A) I often go to the gym.
    (B) I commute by bus.
    (C) A block away from here.

20. What do you think of the new branch?
    (A) Two minutes' walk.
    (B) It's no better than the old one.
    (C) I've never felt like that.

21. Are you going to stop by the bank?
    (A) The bank will be renovated.
    (B) Yes, after lunch.
    (C) To Toronto.

22. Would you mind if I switched off the air conditioner?
    (A) You should make a left turn.
    (B) No, no problem.
    (C) I feel all right.

23. Did you think the workshop was helpful?
    (A) The shop is not open.
    (B) Not really.
    (C) Yes, I totally understand it.

24. Have you noticed that the new employee is never on time?
    (A) We've known each other for a while.
    (B) Yes, he's always late.
    (C) We'll wait for you.

25. Do you know what time he will come to my office?
    (A) Around 4.
    (B) Yes, here is for newcomers.
    (C) Show me around your office.

26. Do you need my home address or office address?
    (A) I need both.
    (B) No, this dress isn't big enough.
    (C) Yes, that'll be better.

27. Are you going to take a walk or ride your bicycle?
    (A) OK. I will drive you home.
    (B) I'm fine with either.
    (C) Yes, it's good exercise.

28. Should I meet the supervisor before I leave?
    (A) Yes, I enjoyed the first one.
    (B) No, I don't live in Seattle.
    (C) I don't think you need to.

29. Is the apartment still available to rent?
    (A) Yes, do you want to take a look?
    (B) I will be able to finish it.
    (C) In the design department.

30. The printer is out of order, isn't it?
    (A) No, it's working.
    (B) Yes, I'm happy to order.
    (C) I don't like computers at all.

31. How about having coffee before we start the meeting?
    (A) Sure, dinner today would be great.
    (B) In the afternoon.
    (C) That sounds great.

32. Which hotel are we going to sleep at on the trip?
    (A) Three nights and four days.
    (B) Yes, I stayed at many places.
    (C) The one near the city.

33. Why did you call her yesterday?
    (A) I have no idea where to go.
    (B) In the evening.
    (C) I just wanted to say hi.

34. What are you going to do this weekend?
    (A) It will be quick.
    (B) I'm going home.
    (C) Tomorrow is Saturday.

35. Can you show me how to install the software on my laptop?
    (A) I'm very tall, too.
    (B) I like to wear a tie.
    (C) Yes, but maybe later.

36. Can I borrow your calculator?
   (A) Sure, no problem.
   (B) The price is very high.
   (C) Yes, please calculate it.

37. When will the rain stop?
   (A) I don't know.
   (B) Three more stops from the library.
   (C) It was three days ago.

38. How's your job hunting going?
   (A) It's hard.
   (B) Can you send me your resume?
   (C) In the conference room.

39. Aren't you going to the theater tonight?
   (A) No, I don't think I can.
   (B) I would think about it.
   (C) It was wonderful.

40. Where should we go for coffee?
   (A) No, we don't like tea.
   (B) There's a drink menu for you.
   (C) Downstairs.

Track 18 [page 96]

Listening
Part 3: Conversations

> **Directions:** You will hear conversations with two speakers. Then you will answer three questions about each conversation. Listen and select the best response to each question. Mark the corresponding letter (A), (B), (C), or (D) on the answer sheet.

Woman: Hi, this is Victoria Gibbon from JSF Corporation. I'm calling to find out the status of our order for eight copy machines.

Man: Hi, Victoria. It has not been dispatched yet. We only have a few left in stock at the moment. I was just about to request the rest from our main manufacturing center.

Woman: Oh, great. Actually, can we add two more copiers to our order?

Man: OK, I'll talk to the factory manager and then call you right back.

41. What is the purpose of the call?

42. What items are the speakers talking about?

43. What does the woman want to do?

Man: Can you give me a ride to the post office on your way to the office this afternoon?

Woman: Actually, I'm not going. I'm attending an important meeting with a client after lunch. Why don't you ask John to drive? He needs to get some new fabric samples.

Man: That's a great idea. What's his phone number?

Woman: I don't know. It should be on the staff list online.

44. What does the man ask the woman to do?

45. What is the woman's plan in the afternoon?

46. What is the man going to do next?

Woman: Don't you think the office is colder than usual? Why don't we switch on the heater?

Man: It's not working at the moment. I called the maintenance department and someone is coming to fix it tomorrow morning. So, it should start working again tomorrow.

Woman: Well, I've got a sore throat and this temperature isn't good for it. Could you close the window to keep the heat inside?

47. Where are the speakers?

48. When most likely will the machine start working?

49. What does the woman want the man to do?

Woman: Hi, Brian. Are you coming to Mike's Halloween party this Friday?

Man: I'm afraid I'm not. I'll have to work late to finish the weekly sales report. It's due in next Monday.

Woman: Well ... I finished the new advertising project I was working on yesterday. I think I can help you with the report if you'd like.

Man: Sounds great. Can you come to my office in an hour? I'll see what you can do to help.

50. When is the party?

51. What does the man need to do?

52. What is the woman going to do later?

Man: How's the renovation of our new office in Pine Valley going?

Woman: They say it's going quite well. In fact, the office will be ready one week earlier than we planned. We have received and set up all of the new office furniture.

Man: One week ahead of schedule? I'm not available that week. I have to do the second safety training course for new employees.

Woman: Please pack up your stuff before we move and leave it to me. Someone will take it there for you.

53. What is the topic of discussion?

54. How far ahead of schedule is the renovation?

55. What does the woman ask the man to do?

Man: Hello, I want to borrow some money for my small business. Can you help me?

Woman: I'm sorry. The Loan Manager who deals with business loans is having a lunch break right now. He'll be back at 2 o'clock. Do you mind coming back then?

Man: Unfortunately, I'm going to be on a train to Detroit at 2 o'clock. I'll be staying there on business for the rest of the week.

Woman: Oh. Then could you leave your name and a phone number that we can call you at? I'll ask the manager to contact you sometime next week to help you.

56. What is the man's request?

57. What is the problem?

58. What does the woman ask the man to do?

Man: Hi, Katy. Don't you have to be in Tokyo for the marketing conference this week? I thought you already left this morning.

Woman: Yes, but the marketing manager called yesterday and told me that they canceled it because of a typhoon there.

Man: So will they reschedule the conference? If my schedule allows, I also would like to participate in it.

Woman: I don't think they decided yet. If you want to know for sure, you should contact the manager and ask her about it.

59. What is the main topic of the conversation?

60. What is the problem?

61. What does the woman advise the man to do?

Woman: Alex, do you see a yellow folder in the filing cabinet? It has the applicants' resumes for the new managerial position. I have to go through them before I start the interviews tomorrow.

Man: I don't see it in here. Have you asked Mr. Ramsey? He might have it. He also said he would read the resumes before the interviews.

Woman: I already went to his office, but his secretary told me he'd gone to see a doctor because of a headache.

Man: Well, my computer has all the resumes on it as well. So I'll e-mail them to you as soon as I'm back in the office.

62. What is the woman searching for?

63. Who is the woman going to meet tomorrow?

64. What is the man going to do?

Woman: Good morning, I want to open a checking account. What do I need?

Man: You need to present some identification with a picture—a driver's license or a passport, for example.

Woman: OK, I have my driver's license. How long will you need to process my application?

Man: We need about 20 minutes. Would you mind filling out this application form while I go photocopy your driver's license?

65. Where most likely are the speakers?

66. What does the woman show the man?

67. What is the man going to do next?

Man: Do you know how many people have registered for the sales seminar next Tuesday?

Woman: 150 participants had registered as of last night. We were expecting a lot fewer. There will be enough chairs and tables, but I'm worried that we may not have enough food for everyone.

Man: I know some caterers who have quite good and fast service. I hired them for our company's Christmas party last year. They can usually deliver fresh food within a day.

Woman: They sound great. Do you have their phone number? I'll call them to make arrangements.

68. What are the speakers discussing?

69. What is the woman concerned about?

70. What does the woman ask for?

Track 19 [page 99]

Listening
Part 4: Talks

> **Directions:** You will hear several talks, each with one speaker. Then you will answer three questions about the talk. Listen and select the best response to each question. Mark the corresponding letter (A), (B), (C), or (D) on the answer sheet.

Good morning everyone. This is Joe Griffin with your latest KODO Radio traffic report. Commuters will be delighted to hear that traffic is flowing quickly on all expressways north of the city today, despite an accident. However, the Henderson Freeway is moving slowly due to the closure of one lane. This is due to the construction of the new railroad connecting Henderson County with Central Station. Also, there will be delays for traffic heading in the direction of the city because the roads around City Hall are being repaired. They have also closed both Parry's Boulevard and Eighth Avenue. But Eighth Avenue will be open by tomorrow morning. That's all from me for now. Stay tuned for Tom Maletti's interview with classical music sensation Jocelyn Tan, coming up next.

71. What is the main content of the report?

72. What is causing problems near City Hall?

73. What is the next program?

This message is for Margaret Gernin at Crowther and Associates. My name is Paul Romero, from JJT Office Supplies. Thank you for the order you made yesterday for five new toner cartridges for your photocopiers. I'm afraid the model that you ordered is out of stock at the moment. A new shipment will arrive next week. We are wondering if you'd like to wait for this shipment, or if you'd like us to send you an alternative model now. Our own brand X56S cartridges can be used for your model of photocopier without any problems. Please could call us back at 555-1667 to let us know how you wish to proceed. I will be out of the office this afternoon, but my colleague Adam Boyle will be happy to receive your call.

74. What is the message about?

75. Why is the speaker calling?

76. What does the caller want Ms. Gernin to do?

Ladies and gentlemen, attention please. It's almost 1:00 p.m. so we will shortly stop over in Alcala de Henares for lunch. The restaurant where we'll eat is famous among locals for its excellent menu. I encourage you to try one of the traditional chicken dishes. After lunch, there will be approximately four hours to enjoy sightseeing at your leisure. The bus will then depart and continue our journey on to Seville. Please insure that you return to the tour bus by 7:00 p.m. so that we can leave on time. Thank you very much and see you later.

77. Who most likely is making the announcement?

78. What does the speaker recommend the listeners do?

79. When are the listeners supposed to leave the city?

Hello passengers, and welcome aboard this Apollo Airways flight from London. My name is Richard Blackman, and we are heading to Los Angeles today. Valerie Anderson and her team of flight attendants will be looking after you in the cabin during the flight. Our flight time today will be approximately 11 hours. The weather conditions seem generally good, although please be prepared for some turbulence caused by strong winds when flying over the Atlantic. We are departing slightly later than scheduled due to problems processing the baggage in the terminal, but we expect to take off within the next 30 minutes or so. In the meantime, our flight attendants will be serving you some complimentary refreshments. I apologize for the delay, and I hope you have a comfortable flight.

80. Who most likely are the listeners?

81. What weather conditions does the speaker mention?

82. According to the speaker, what will happen next?

With the news where you are, this is Chuck Langdon. Local government officials decided Friday to open a new recreation center for Littlefield. The recreation center will be equipped with a swimming pool, tennis courts, football and baseball fields, an all-weather soccer field, and a high-tech gym. Local residents were delighted with the news. Right now, they have to travel over 30 miles from downtown on the expressway to their closest sports center in Kirkland. The Littlefield center, which will be located in the city's northern suburbs, will open in two years. The budget set aside to cover to cost of the project is around $5 million. Now, for a look at the weather forecast, let's hear from Lauren.

83. Who most likely is the speaker?

84. When will the new building open?

85. What will the listeners hear next?

Before we begin today's meeting, let me introduce our new sales manager, Barbara Tenison. Barbara has worked at one of our main competitors, Pasos Press. Barbara spent over ten years at Pasos, and led many of their most successful sales campaigns. Before moving into sales, Barbara began her career as a teacher, so I believe she will be a great addition to the educational products team. She will first review our sales strategies and develop a plan for the coming year. I'm very excited to have Barbara working with us. OK, let's get started. I believe the head of human resources is going to speak first.

86. Where is the speech taking place?

87. According to the speaker, what was Ms. Tenison's first job?

88. What will happen after the speech?

Don't miss Hudson department store's famous summer event! There will be huge reductions on all items throughout all our stores across the country. It's true—reductions on all items, including sportswear, men's and ladies' fashions, cosmetics and jewelry. And for the very first time, we will offer up to 30% off all electrical items. Check labels in store for individual prices. Also, don't forget there is still time for you to get further discounts if you sign up for a Hudson storecard by Thursday. So, don't miss out. Visit your closest Hudson department store from Friday to take part in this fantastic once-a-year event. Offer ends Sunday.

89. What kind of event is being advertised?

90. What will be 30% cheaper?

91. When will the event start?

Hi and welcome to the CP Automobiles manufacturing plant. Today this tour for recent recruits will first visit the testing facility. There our engineers insure the quality and safety of all our models. Today, a trial version of a new model will be examined. Please keep in mind that everything you see here is confidential and should not be disclosed to anyone outside the company. Before we begin the tour, there are a few points that I need to cover. For your safety, it's important to put on your hardhats and safety goggles before you go inside the plant. Also, please turn off your cell phones, as they can disrupt some of our operations. Now, please follow me.

92. What does the company make?

93. Who are the listeners?

94. What does the speaker ask the listeners to do?

Good evening, everyone, and many thanks for coming to today's celebration. Before we eat, I'd like to say a few words about Mandi Peterson. As you know, Mandi is leaving us today after 20 years at our company. Mandi was selected for our accountant training program immediately after graduating from American University. She then joined first the tax department, and later the auditing team, where she later worked as department manager. Mandi became a partner in 1992 and contributed greatly to growing our business. She won the Businesswoman of the Year award in 1995, in recognition of her excellent achievements. Mandi is now writing an autobiography to be published next year. Let's wish her the best of luck for a bright future.

95. What industry does Ms. Peterson work in?

96. What was Ms. Peterson's first position in the company?

97. What is Ms. Peterson going to do next?

Are you interested in temporary work over the summer? Do you like meeting people from different cultures and working on a team? If your answer to these questions is "yes", why don't you apply to work at an Excite Summer Camp? Excite receives thousands of teenagers from around the world every summer. We're looking for staff to fill a number of positions, such as activity leaders and camp counselors. Applicants must be between the ages of 17 and 25, and must provide references from a teacher or previous employer. If you are interested, please visit www.excitecamps.com for more information. Application closing date: Friday, May 14.

98. What is being advertised?

99. Who is the advertisement for?

100. According to the advertisement, where is information available?

Track 20 [page 127]

Speaking
Question 1: Read a text aloud

Directions: In this part of the test, you will read aloud the text on the page. You will have 45 seconds to prepare. Then you will have 45 seconds to read the text aloud.

Your preparation time begins now.

Now please read the text aloud.

Your time is up. Now move on to the next question.

Track 21 [page 127]

Question 2: Read a text aloud

Directions: In this part of the test, you will read aloud the text on the page. You will have 45 seconds to prepare. Then you will have 45 seconds to read the text aloud.

Your preparation time begins now.

Now please read the text aloud.

Your time is up. Now move on to the next question.

Track 22 [page 128]

Question 3: Describe a picture

Directions: You will describe a photograph as completely as you can. The photograph is in the test book. You will have 30 seconds to prepare what you will say, and then you will have 45 seconds to describe the picture in as much detail as possible.

Your preparation time begins now.

Now please describe the photograph aloud.

Your time is up. Now move on to the next question.

Track 23 [page 128]

Questions 4–6: Respond to questions

Directions: You will be asked three questions. After each question you will hear a beep. Begin speaking your answer immediately after the beep. You will not have any time to prepare your answer. For Questions 4 and 5 you will have 15 seconds to respond. For Question 6 you will have 30 seconds.

Imagine that a Canadian marketing firm is doing research in your country. You have agreed to participate in a telephone interview about going to the movies.

Question 4: How often do you go to the movies, and who do you go with?

Question 5: What kind of food or snacks do you get when you go to the movies?

Question 6: What was the most interesting movie you've watched recently, and why did you like it?

Track 24 [page 130]

Speaking
Questions 7–9: Respond to questions using information provided

Directions: You will read a short text and then answer three questions based on the information in the text. You will have 30 seconds to read the text before the first question. After each question you will hear a beep. Begin speaking immediately after the beep. You will not have any extra time to prepare your answer. For Questions 7 and 8 you will have 15 seconds to respond. For Question 9 you will have 30 seconds.

Woman: Hello, my name is Diane Carter, and I'm calling to get some information about the upcoming marketing seminar at your convention center. I've got a few questions I'd like to ask about it.

Question 7: When is the seminar, and what is the first scheduled session?

Question 8: How much is the registration fee?

Question 9: Can you tell me about the afternoon sessions in detail?

Track 25 [page 131]

Speaking
Question 10: Propose a solution

Directions: You will hear about a problem and be asked to propose a solution. You will have 30 seconds to prepare your solution, and then 60 seconds to speak.

Hi, my name is Gina Arquette. I purchased a 40-inch 3D television from your store yesterday. It was delivered to my home today, and the delivery person set it up in my living room. However, I'm having a little bit of a problem with the television. When I try to program the channels on the TV, a few of the channels do not work. They're regular channels that worked fine on my old television, but for some reason, I just get a blank screen on the new TV. I've read the user's manual several times, but I just can't figure out what the problem is. I'm planning on having some friends over tonight to watch a football game, so I would like this to be fixed as soon as possible. Please call me back when you get this message. My phone number is 555-3426. Thank you.

Track 26 [page 131]

Speaking
Question 11: Express an opinion

> **Directions:** You will hear about a specific topic and then give your opinion about it. Make sure you say as much as you can about the topic in the time allowed. You will have 15 seconds to prepare, and then 60 seconds to speak.

What kind of qualities do you think a good manager should have? Use specific details and examples to explain why these qualities are important.

Track 27 [page 141]

Listening
Part 1: Photographs

> **Directions:** For each item in Part 1, you will hear four statements about a photograph in the test book. You must listen carefully to the statements in order to select the statement that best describes the photograph. Mark the corresponding letter (A), (B), (C), or (D) on the answer sheet.
>
> **Example**
> Listen to the statements and select the one that best describes the picture.
>
> (A) They're drinking orange juice.
> (B) They're turning on a computer.
> (C) They're looking at a screen.
> (D) They're putting on formal clothes.
>
> Statement (C), **"They're looking at a screen."** best describes the picture, so you should choose answer (C) and mark it on your answer sheet.

Track 28 [page 142]

> Listen to the statements and select the one that best describes the picture.

1. Look at photograph number 1 in your test book.
   (A) The parking lot is empty.
   (B) The building is two stories high.
   (C) Some cars have been left near the building.
   (D) The window of the building is being cleaned.

2. Look at photograph number 2 in your test book.
   (A) He is drying his uniform.
   (B) He is preparing some food.
   (C) He is tasting a dish.
   (D) He is wiping his hands.

3. Look at photograph number 3 in your test book.
   (A) The man is looking up at a screen.
   (B) Some CDs are stored in a cabinet.
   (C) There are paintings attached to the wall.
   (D) The store is filled with customers.

4. Look at photograph number 4 in your test book.
   (A) Some people are walking into a restaurant.
   (B) Some people are sitting at the table eating.
   (C) Some people are checking the menu.
   (D) Some people are serving food onto plates.

5. Look at photograph number 5 in your test book.
   (A) Some people are jogging on the field.
   (B) Some people are mowing the grass.
   (C) Some people are cheering at a soccer game.
   (D) Some people are lined up.

6. Look at photograph number 6 in your test book.
   (A) They are taking pictures.
   (B) They are reaching for buckets.
   (C) They are putting on T-shirts.
   (D) They are painting the wall.

7. Look at photograph number 7 in your test book.
   (A) They are facing each other.
   (B) They are having a discussion at a table.
   (C) They are looking in different directions.
   (D) They are standing in line to use a public telephone.

8. Look at photograph number 8 in your test book.
   (A) The woman is putting her hair in a ponytail.
   (B) The woman is cleaning the desk.
   (C) The woman is looking through the microscope.
   (D) The woman is writing with a pen.

9. Look at photograph number 9 in your test book.
   (A) Two men are pointing at something.
   (B) A woman is raising her hands.
   (C) A man is selling a pair of binoculars.
   (D) A man is looking at the woman.

10. Look at photograph number 10 in your test book.
    (A) A woman is talking on a stage.
    (B) A young man is giving a presentation.
    (C) The people are listening to the woman.
    (D) Some people are standing up.

Track 29 [page 147]

Listening
Part 2: Question–response

> **Directions:** For each item in Part 2, you will hear a statement or a question followed by three responses. Listen and choose the best response. Then mark the corresponding letter (A), (B), or (C) on the answer sheet.
>
> **Example**
> Have you met the new Managing Director?
>
> (A) Actually I talked with him in the lobby just now.
> (B) Yes, I took the call.
> (C) No, he takes the subway to work.
>
> The best response to the question "Have you met the new Managing Director?" is answer choice **(A)**, **"Actually I talked with him in the lobby just now."** You should mark answer (A) on your answer sheet.

Track 30 [page 147]

> You will hear a statement or a question followed by three responses. Listen and choose the best response. Then mark the corresponding letter (A), (B), or (C) on the answer sheet.

11. I want it served with sliced lemons, please.
    (A) OK, try mine.
    (B) I prefer rice to noodles.
    (C) Sure, and do you want anything else?

12. Do you know when the flight arrives?
    (A) There are a few departing for Seoul.
    (B) It should get here by 4 o'clock.
    (C) At Gate 2.

13. What are the opening hours of that new grocery store down the street?
    (A) Four hours per day.
    (B) They're open from 9 a.m. to 11 p.m.
    (C) Yes, we should review the products on the market.

14. Why don't we meet at the outdoor café after work?
    (A) That sounds great.
    (B) Please open the door.
    (C) Without milk, please.

15. I thought you'd already departed for Minnesota.
    (A) Turn left there.
    (B) My plan has changed.
    (C) Just three things.

16. You've read the article on health in *Family Magazine*, haven't you?
    (A) In fact, I wrote it.
    (B) I don't suppose he will read it.
    (C) I meet my grandparents often.

17. Isn't our office stationery order due today?
    (A) Yes, but not until the afternoon.
    (B) Take them in any order.
    (C) I didn't apply for the post.

18. I'm thankful to you for helping me on such short notice, Ms. Gao.
    (A) There was a notice last week.
    (B) I'm happy you appreciate it.
    (C) You could've thanked me.

19. When will the president come?
    (A) It's a present for you.
    (B) I haven't been told yet.
    (C) In the main lobby.

20. Please lend me your phone.
    (A) I wish to rent this room.
    (B) Sorry, it's out of order.
    (C) In the maintenance office.

21. How are we going to get to the supermarket?
    (A) I have a lot of things to get.
    (B) I'll call a cab.
    (C) It's $10.

22. Would you let Mrs. Davis know that I visited while she was out?
    (A) No problem, I'll let her know.
    (B) In aisle three.
    (C) Yes, she has a lot of talent.

23. Will Scott be dropping by our office this weekend?
    (A) To meet his co-workers.
    (B) I hope so.
    (C) He didn't get anything.

24. Why don't you check the meeting time with Ms. Robins?
    (A) Thanks for the reminder.
    (B) Down the steps.
    (C) A bit earlier than that.

25. Who is in charge of safety inspections for this building?
    (A) He never replied to my questions.
    (B) That would be Mr. White.
    (C) It doesn't seem safe.

26. Didn't you get the secretary's signature to authorize this payment?
    (A) Yes, she is the author of this textbook.
    (B) Thanks, I will pay you back.
    (C) No, she's been away on a business trip.

27. Do you know who's responsible for the conference?
    (A) Yes, it's next Thursday.
    (B) Yes, Mr. Warner is.
    (C) No, we don't want any more references.

28. Will you tell me when this report is due?
    (A) Not until the end of this week.
    (B) I can't report this.
    (C) No, it's too short.

29. What color do you want for the new water fountain?
    (A) May I get some water?
    (B) I think gray.
    (C) Yes, it's the most popular model.

30. Did you call the construction company?
    (A) I'll go with you.
    (B) I would like your company.
    (C) No, I had no time.

31. The new manager will have the office next to mine.
    (A) Who's the next candidate?
    (B) Have you met him yet?
    (C) I found some new ones.

32. Why was their tour postponed?
    (A) Because of severe weather.
    (B) At 6 tomorrow morning.
    (C) To India.

33. Have you seen the keys to the warehouse?
    (A) You've discussed the key issue.

(B) Ask Ms. Moore. She had them right before.
(C) You have to take a break.

34. Are we getting ballpoint pens or pencils?
    (A) She took the point.
    (B) I'll pencil that in.
    (C) Let's get both.

35. Where do these dishes go?
    (A) It is mine.
    (B) The side dishes were fine.
    (C) Over here, on the shelf in this cupboard.

36. It's too late to call the doctor's office, isn't it?
    (A) Yes, you should call before 8.
    (B) I got two calls.
    (C) He's in the accountant's office.

37. Are you expecting to have a meeting with Mr. Martinez today or tomorrow?
    (A) Yes, at lunch.
    (B) In Meeting Room 4.
    (C) It has been postponed to next Monday.

38. Does Mr. Harris prefer tea or coffee?
    (A) I dislike that green color.
    (B) Either one will be good for him.
    (C) The printer is new.

39. How do you switch on this fax machine?
    (A) The date for the meeting has been confirmed.
    (B) The machine in the corridor.
    (C) Press the green button.

40. Where can I purchase tickets for Saturday's show?
    (A) You can book them online.
    (B) On the weekend.
    (C) Yes, I need VIP seats.

Track 31 [page 148]

Listening
Part 3: Conversations

> **Directions:** You will hear conversations with two speakers. Then you will answer three questions about each conversation. Listen and select the best response to each question. Mark the corresponding letter (A), (B), (C), or (D) on the answer sheet.

Man: Hi, I'm calling to book a room for August 16 through 20. I'm scheduled to participate in the International Geographic Association conference at your hotel.

Woman: Absolutely, sir. We have a special package for all conference attendees. A room will be $120 per night, and that includes complimentary drinks in the room, and free coupons for breakfast in our restaurant.

Man: Oh, that sounds great. And by the way, is there any park to go running in near the hotel? I like to jog in the fresh air.

Woman: Yes, sir. There is a public park nearby. You can find further information about the park on our website.

41. What is the purpose of the call?

42. What does the woman offer the man?

43. What does the man ask about?

Man: Excuse me, I'm a stranger to the downtown area and I'm searching for the tallest building on Regent Street.

Woman: That's not so far from here. Maybe ten minutes' walk. If you walk two more blocks, you'll reach Regent Street. Turn left and the building is the third one on the left. It's next to the City Council.

Man: I'm glad to hear that. I have an important meeting there in half an hour. I was anxious I'd be late. Thanks for your help.

44. Where does the conversation most likely take place?

45. How does the woman assist the man?

46. What is the man worried about?

Woman: What's happening in the meeting room this morning?

Man: Oh, they're getting rid of the table and some of the chairs from there. The new furniture will be arriving soon.

Woman: I didn't know the furniture was going to be removed. I think the stuff we have now seems OK.

Man: No way. We should've replaced the old office furniture earlier. Some of the older chairs are really hard to sit on. They give me terrible back pain during meetings. The new chairs will be a big relief. I can't wait to go in and try one out!

47. What is going on in the meeting room?

48. What does the woman think about the old furniture?

49. What does the man hope the new furniture will be like?

Man: Hi, Michelle. I received your proposal for changing our catering supplier for the employee cafeteria. I think it is quite convincing.

Woman: I've heard that most of our staff haven't been satisfied with the food for a long time. Employees complain a lot about the food being bland and expensive, and lacking nutrition. It's time to get a new company.

Man: Yes, you're right. You also suggest Easygo Food Services. Why do you believe it would be good to choose them?

Woman: I had meetings with several providers and discussed their services on Tuesday. I found that Easygo offers a varied menu selection at reasonable prices compared with what other suppliers offer.

50. What is the dialogue mainly about?

51. What was the woman doing on Tuesday?

52. What advantage does the woman mention about Easygo Food Services?

Woman: I think there is a problem with my computer. I need to log in when I arrive in the office and log out when I get off each day, right?

Man: Yes, you do. Enter your ID and password twice to log into the company intranet, and your working hours will then be tracked automatically on the online timesheet.

Woman: Yes, that's what I heard in the orientation for new employees. But for some reason, my computer's not working. I've been trying to get it to switch on so that I can log in for the last ten minutes!

Man: Well, maybe your computer has to be checked for viruses. Feel free to use my computer now to log in so you don't waste any more of your time. You should speak to the manager in the technical department about it though.

53. What is the woman's problem?

54. How long ago did the woman probably get to the office?

55. What does the man recommend?

Man: Have you spoken to the engine supplier? Our order hasn't been delivered yet. There are several cars that require replacement engine parts by the beginning of next week.

Woman: Yes. Unfortunately, they said that they dispatched the parts to the wrong address, and they then collected them and took them back three days ago. They offered a 15% discount to apologize for the delay.

Man: When will we receive the parts? We have very little time.

Woman: They will be sent tomorrow morning. Don't worry, we should be able to finish the work this week.

56. Why is the order late?

57. What will the supplier give?

58. According to the woman, what will probably happen?

Man: Tanya, do you know if the printer is down? It seems to be out of order. I have to print some documents for my presentation in 30 minutes.

Woman: Well, we received a new color printer early this morning. But I don't think the software for it has been installed yet.

Man: I need to hurry. I also have to go to the meeting room to check if there is a projector in there.

Woman: Why don't you send me the documents by e-mail? I will call and ask Richard in marketing to print them for you. The printer in his department is probably working OK.

59. What was recently received?

60. Why does the man need to hurry?

61. What does the woman advise the man to do?

Woman: Greg, are you free this afternoon? I'll be doing some test marketing for Skin Energy 2 for Men, and I would like your input.

Man: No problem, that's our new item in male anti-wrinkle products, isn't it? Why are you doing test marketing? Aren't you convinced that the products will appeal to the target customers?

Woman: No, we aren't. They say some men didn't like the strong smell in the original product. So, we made some changes and our test groups gave positive feedback on a lower strength smell. Now, I'm going to try out the product in some real-life buying situations before we release it on a national level.

Man: Luckily, I worked on some similar projects in the first quarter. I can offer you some data for reference.

62. What does the woman ask the man to do?

63. What was wrong with the product?

64. What does the man offer to do?

Woman: Ben, it's time to prepare for mailing out invitations for our charity event. How many do you think we have to send?

Man: Well, we don't want the event to be too busy. However, everyone in our research team is hoping to be invited.

Woman: Right, so I suppose there will be about 200 guests including our own staff and guests from outside.

Man: Maybe. We should make the guest list before we mail out the invitations, and be sure how many people will possibly attend. That'll make it easier to order the right amount of catering.

65. What is the topic of the conversation?

66. What is the man concerned about?

67. What will the speakers most likely do next?

Man: Ms. Rodriguez, my name is Joe, and I'm calling from Taylor Community Center. We are interested in what people in the town think about our services. Our computer records say that you've been a member of the center for three years. Have you been satisfied with our services?

Woman: Yes, of course. You've offered a range of programs for children and adults. I particularly love the baseball games for kids on Saturday afternoons, and the free community lunches on Sundays.

Man: Thank you for your input. I'm pleased to hear that you're happy with us. Is there any way in which you think we can enhance our service?

Woman: Well, I've realized there isn't any daycare for young children. I would appreciate it if the center could provide daycare. Working moms like me who have young children would definitely appreciate that.

68. Why is the man calling the woman?

69. What does the woman like about the community center?

70. What does the woman suggest?

Track 32 [page 151]

Listening
Part 4: Talks

> **Directions:** You will hear several talks, each with one speaker. Then you will answer three questions about the talk. Listen and select the best response to each question. Mark the corresponding letter (A), (B), (C), or (D) on the answer sheet.

Hello, this is Hayley Carroll. My next door neighbor, Peter Moore, gave me your contact information. Your company has been landscaping the Moore's garden over the last few weeks, and they are very satisfied with the quality of the work. We also want some landscaping work done to our garden, and we want someone from your company to come and give us a price quote. We wish to have a new patio laid, and some trees need to be cut down. Our address is 67 Bartholomew Drive, next door to the Moore's house. My number is (382) 555-7937. I look forward to hearing from you soon.

71. What is the topic of the message?

72. Why does the speaker talk about her neighbor?

73. What does the woman ask the listener to do?

Are you searching for a new job? Then visit the city's largest job fair, Great Jobs! This year's Great Job fair has invited more exhibitors and will offer more jobs than ever before. Come along and meet employers from across the region in a friendly and casual atmosphere. In addition, why not come to the fair on Thursday for free one-on-one career advice from our famous team of career advisors for one day only. Whatever job you're searching for, we're here to help. This year's event will be at the Downtown Convention Center from Thursday, June 7 to Sunday, June 10. Admission is free. Doors open 10 a.m.

74. What is being advertised?

75. How does the speaker describe the career advisors?

76. When are the listeners asked to visit the fair?

Good evening, Ms. Cherubini. My name is Harry Hooper. I noticed your advertisement in *The Times and Herald* for the car that you're selling. I'm wondering if I can take a look at it. Could I drop by sometime this week? I finish work at 5, and my office is not far from where your live. I think I can get there by 6 any day this week. Please would you call me back so that we can arrange a suitable day? My number is 235-555-4537. Thank you.

77. What is the purpose of the message?

78. What time can the man leave his office?

79. Why does the man want the woman to call him back?

First of all today, I wish to present to you all some information about next week's training course at the Fawcett Center. The course starts at 10:00 a.m. in the Royal Room, and is for all accounting department staff. Lunch will be offered. I think it'd be best if we all meet before the course at 9:45 a.m. in the lobby. The best way to go to the Fawcett Center is by subway. Parker Station is just a short walk away. If you're going to drive, remember that parking is limited, and you should call the venue in advance to reserve a space in the parking lot. Now, let's start today's meeting.

80. Who is the man talking to?

81. Where is the group probably going to meet before the training course?

82. According to the speaker, what is the best way to get to the training venue?

Good afternoon, everyone. I'm Simon Hopkins, and this is *Books Today*. Today's show features the novel *Into the Forest* by Kentaro Oyama. This novel reintroduces readers to an older Kanako Igawa, who we first met as a younger woman in his previous novel, *Summer Hills*. The older Kanako is a persuasive central character for this novel, and her maturity within the context of the scary and moving plot makes this book particularly terrifying. All Kentaro Oyama fans anxious to read this wonderful new book will have to wait until next month when the book will be sold at bookstores and online retailers. Also, remember you should find out the time and place of your nearest book signing event from Oyama's official website.

83. Who most likely is the speaker?

84. What kind of novel is *Into the Forest*?

85. What does the speaker encourage fans of Oyama to do?

Good morning, all, and thanks for coming to the first in our two-day series of lectures on international sales and marketing. Our first speaker today is Rebecca Lung. She will talk about her views on introducing and developing brands in local markets, with particular focus on sunglasses and optical frames. Rebecca works for one of the biggest importers of fashion items in her country, and has worked in the industry for 15 years. You can also get to know more about her from her recently published book, *Growth Unlimited*, which examines the luxury goods market in East Asia. You may purchase signed copies after the talk.

86. What is the topic of Rebecca Lung's lecture?

87. What did Rebecca Lung do recently?

88. What does the speaker encourage the listeners to do after the talk?

Hello, and welcome to our autumn luncheon. This year is an extremely special occasion as it marks our company's 40th anniversary. As a consequence, we have organized some wonderful entertainment for today. Before the entertainment starts, I want to point out an amendment to the maps in your programs. The maps say that the arts and crafts sale will be held on the football field. However, the weather forecast is not good, so we have moved the arts and crafts sale indoors to the Valenti Building. Please do stop by there, as all proceeds from sales go to some wonderful charities.

89. Where is the announcement taking place?

90. What has been altered?

91. What is the reason for the change?

Next today I wish to discuss the Smart Cars account. Smart Cars are worried about losing market share to their competitors, many of whom have recently set up aggressive marketing campaigns. Smart Cars have requested that we produce a new advertising campaign for them, with a more hard-hitting edge. Instead of stressing the company's conventional image, the new campaign should demonstrate its products in a more youthful light. The aim is to attract a younger audience. As you all know, Smart Cars is one of our most loyal clients, so we have to make every effort to make this new campaign successful. Please come up with some ideas and present some concepts by Friday.

92. Who most likely are the listeners?

93. What does Smart Cars wish to do?

94. What does the speaker want the listeners to do?

Good morning, Mr. Franklin. This is Tricia Milton calling from the Private Business Licensing Division. I just got your message about licensing regulations. Yes, your store will have to be examined by our agents before you open for business. The examination insures that your retail space and back office areas are safe for both the general public and your staff. Examination visits can be scheduled at relatively short notice, and, assuming that your premises pass the examination, you will be granted a license soon after. The fee is $250, and license renewal is necessary every five years. I hope that's been useful in answering your questions. If not, please call me back.

95. Why did the speaker leave the message?

96. What will a license allow Mr. Franklin to do?

97. What does the speaker mention about licenses?

Good morning everyone. Thanks for coming to Acapulco. I'm Oscar, and I'll be your guide today. First, let me talk you through today's itinerary. We'll begin with a visit to Acapulco's famous art gallery where you can see works by some of the area's best-known painters. Next we will stop at the streets of the Old Town, where we will view the various historic monuments and places of interest. After a late lunch at one of the town's nicest restaurants, we'll go to the seafront, where we'll absorb the sea air and look at the famous Acapulco Lighthouse. OK, if you'll follow me, let's start our tour.

98. What is the purpose of the talk?

99. According to the speaker, what can be found in the Old Town?

100. What will happen in the afternoon?

Track 33 [page 179]

Speaking
Question 1: Read a text aloud

> **Directions:** In this part of the test, you will read aloud the text on the page. You will have 45 seconds to prepare. Then you will have 45 seconds to read the text aloud.
>
> Your preparation time begins now.
>
> Now please read the text aloud.
>
> Your time is up. Now move on to the next question.

Track 34 [page 179]

Question 2: Read a text aloud

Directions: In this part of the test, you will read aloud the text on the page. You will have 45 seconds to prepare. Then you will have 45 seconds to read the text aloud.

Your preparation time begins now.

Now please read the text aloud.

Your time is up. Now move on to the next question.

Track 35 [page 180]

Question 3: Describe a picture

Directions: You will describe a photograph as completely as you can. The photograph is in the test book. You will have 30 seconds to prepare what you will say, and then you will have 45 seconds to describe the picture in as much detail as possible.

Your preparation time begins now.

Now please describe the photograph aloud.

Your time is up. Now move on to the next question.

Track 36 [page 180]

Questions 4–6: Respond to questions

Directions: You will be asked three questions. After each question you will hear a beep. Begin speaking your answer immediately after the beep. You will not have any time to prepare your answer. For Questions 4 and 5 you will have 15 seconds to respond. For Question 6 you will have 30 seconds.

Imagine that an American marketing firm is doing research in your country. You have agreed to participate in a telephone interview about cleaning.

Question 4:   How often do you clean your room or home, and when was the last time you did it?

Question 5:   What kind of equipment do you use when you clean your room or home?

Question 6:   Would you consider hiring a cleaning person or company to clean your room or home?

Track 37 [page 182]

Speaking
Questions 7–9: Respond to questions using information provided

Directions: You will read a short text and then answer three questions based on the information in the text. You will have 30 seconds to read the text before the first question. After each question you will hear a beep. Begin speaking immediately after the beep. You will not have any extra time to prepare your answer. For Questions 7 and 8 you will have 15 seconds to respond. For Question 9 you will have 30 seconds.

Hello, I'm an employee at Knowledge Publishing Company, and I ordered some office supplies at your store earlier today. I need to check some details of the order, but I think I lost the invoice on the way back to the office. Can you check a few things for me?

Question 7:   Can you tell me the invoice number, and the total amount of the order?

Question 8:   I'm not sure about this, but I think I ordered 50 medium sized Stick-'em Notes. Is that correct?

Question 9:   OK. Can you tell me about your payment policy?

Track 38 [page 183]

Question 10: Propose a solution

Directions: You will hear about a problem and be asked to propose a solution. You will have 30 seconds to prepare your solution, and then 60 seconds to speak.

Hello, my name is Ken Evans, and I'm calling from an ATM machine at Royal Bank on Vermont Street. I'm calling because I'm having some problems with a machine here. I used the machine to withdraw $20, but no money came out of the machine. The machine didn't print out a receipt, so I don't know if the money has been taken out of my account. Also, my bank card is stuck in the machine, and it won't come out of the slot. I've pressed the cancel button several times, but nothing seems to work. Today is Sunday, so there is no one at the bank, and I don't know what to do. My cell phone number is 555-3356. Please call me back as soon as possible.

Track 39 [page 183]

Question 11: Express an opinion

Directions: You will hear about a specific topic and then give your opinion about it. Make sure you say as much as you can about the topic in the time allowed. You will have 15 seconds to prepare, and then 60 seconds to speak.

Do you agree or disagree with the following statement? Companies should allow employees to wear casual clothes at work. Give specific reasons and details to support your opinion.

Track 40 [page 193]

Listening
Part 1: Photographs

Directions: For each item in Part 1, you will hear four statements about a photograph in the test book. You must listen carefully to the statements in order to select the statement that best describes the photograph. Mark the corresponding letter (A), (B), (C), or (D) on the answer sheet.

Example
Listen to the statements and select the one that best describes the picture.

(A) They're drinking orange juice.
(B) They're turning on a computer.
(C) They're looking at a screen.
(D) They're putting on formal clothes.

Statement (C), **"They're looking at a screen."** best describes the picture, so you should choose answer (C) and mark it on your answer sheet.

Track 41 [page 194]

Listen to the statements and select the one that best describes the picture.

1. Look at photograph number 1 in your test book.
   (A) She is switching on the lamp.
   (B) She is making the bed.
   (C) She is reading a book.
   (D) She is crossing her arms.

2. Look at photograph number 2 in your test book.
   (A) They are holding bags.
   (B) They are sitting on the ground.
   (C) They are moving some rocks.
   (D) They are building a tent.

3. Look at photograph number 3 in your test book.
   (A) A woman is paying a shop assistant.
   (B) A clerk is holding an item.
   (C) A line of customers is waiting near the cashier.
   (D) Two women are shopping in a store.

4. Look at photograph number 4 in your test book.
   (A) All of the boxes are being piled up in a truck.
   (B) Some men are moving furniture.
   (C) Some boxes are stacked up.
   (D) A man is opening a door.

5. Look at photograph number 5 in your test book.
   (A) The men are removing their working clothes.
   (B) The men are wearing safety helmets.
   (C) The men are talking on the phone.
   (D) The men are looking at some construction equipment.

6. Look at photograph number 6 in your test book.
   (A) Some boats are sailing on the river.
   (B) Some people are sitting near the water.
   (C) Some trees are being cut down.
   (D) There is a bridge over the river.

7. Look at photograph number 7 in your test book.
   (A) The women are making the bed.
   (B) The women are lying on the bed.
   (C) The women are taking the bed out of the room.
   (D) The women are removing a light bulb.

8. Look at photograph number 8 in your test book.
   (A) People are cooking some food.
   (B) People are looking at themselves in a window.
   (C) People are taking some food.
   (D) People are leaving dishes on the table.

9. Look at photograph number 9 in your test book.
   (A) The woman has picked up the fruit from the shelf.
   (B) Fruit is displayed in boxes.
   (C) The woman is holding a plastic bag.
   (D) Some fruit is being weighed on a scale.

10. Look at photograph number 10 in your test book.
    (A) Some passengers are getting on the airplane.
    (B) The airplane is landing.
    (C) The airplane is on the runway.
    (D) The airplane is being painted white.

Track 42 [page 199]

Listening
Part 2: Question–response

Directions: For each item in Part 2, you will hear a statement or a question followed by three responses. Listen and choose the best response. Then mark the corresponding letter (A), (B), or (C) on the answer sheet.

Example
Have you met the new Managing Director?

(A) Actually I talked with him in the lobby just now.
(B) Yes, I took the call.
(C) No, he takes the subway to work.

The best response to the question "Have you met the new Managing Director?" is answer choice (A), "**Actually I talked with him in the lobby just now.**" You should mark answer (A) on your answer sheet.

Track 43 [page 199]

You will hear a statement or a question followed by three responses. Listen and choose the best response. Then mark the corresponding letter (A), (B), or (C) on the answer sheet.

11. How can I help you, sir?
   (A) I look forward to meeting you.
   (B) That's the only thing I can help with.
   (C) I'm already being served, thanks.

12. Our sales increased by 30% last year.
   (A) It should be complete this week.
   (B) That's great news.
   (C) No, it's more expensive than $13.

13. Who photocopied the sales report?
   (A) No, the train doesn't go to the airport.
   (B) It's about recent sales statistics.
   (C) I think Jennifer did.

14. Would you make 20 copies of the handout, please?
   (A) No, I don't drink coffee.
   (B) Of course, I'd be happy to.
   (C) The fabric needs to be hand-washed.

15. How do I listen to my phone messages?
   (A) You can leave your message.
   (B) Let me show you in a minute.
   (C) I returned his call.

16. What color would you like to paint the door?
   (A) I received several calls from her.
   (B) Yes, on the wall.
   (C) I just chose blue.

17. Didn't you plan to finish packing these boxes by 6?
   (A) Yes, but I had to do other things.
   (B) No, we need six boxes now.
   (C) Leave them on the top shelf.

18. When's the opening ceremony supposed to begin?
   (A) We don't plan any openings now.
   (B) He was also nominated for best actor.
   (C) Why don't you look at the schedule?

19. Who's taking charge of the medical symposium?
   (A) Please stand at the podium.
   (B) I know hardly anything about it.
   (C) You should go to a doctor.

20. What's the medical clinic over there called?
   (A) Turn left at the end of the street.
   (B) It's Higgs Health Care, I think.
   (C) He's called Ted.

21. Haven't you been to Beijing?
   (A) No, I haven't.
   (B) Yes, I have a few.
   (C) We have two recycle bins.

22. We should take a break now.
   (A) Yes, I'd love to stop for some coffee.
   (B) It should be fixed.
   (C) The more, the merrier.

23. Doesn't the bookstore close at 6 today?
   (A) Not today, only on Sundays.
   (B) 6 out of 12.
   (C) The bus stop is near here.

24. The manual for our new MP3 player is a little complicated.
   (A) The annual fee is cheaper than I expected.
   (B) Yes, when I was young.
   (C) It needs to be modified soon.

25. Why was the shipment delayed this week?
   (A) Yes, on Sunday.
   (B) It will be canceled.
   (C) The shipping address was incorrect.

26. Is Mr. Chang going to attend the conference in Tokyo?
   (A) The application form.
   (B) He's planning to go there, yes.
   (C) I pretend not to see.

27. Would you mind switching off the air conditioner?
   (A) This is the switch.
   (B) Of course not. It's getting chilly in here.
   (C) Sure, I will get the new model.

28. When should we prepare the projector?
   (A) What about half an hour before the meeting starts?
   (B) No, it wasn't a great project.
   (C) In the front seat.

29. Could you go over the budget report after lunch?
   (A) $7 each for lunch.
   (B) I'm sorry, I won't have time then.
   (C) I searched for it everywhere.

30. Why did you repaint the walls in the meeting room?
   (A) They weren't evenly colored.
   (B) Adam will paint them tomorrow.
   (C) Is there more space for me?

31. How much are the theater tickets?
   (A) It will begin at 7 p.m.
   (B) It was quite surprising.
   (C) They're $30 each.

32. Who does this tie belong to?
   (A) It looks like Rob's.
   (B) I would say it's silk.
   (C) The talk wasn't long.

33. Would Mr. Kim prefer to discuss the new business with me today or later in the week?
   (A) I'd like management classes.
   (B) Today would work better for him.
   (C) Yes, it will all be good.

34. We have enough money for today's dinner, don't we?
   (A) No, we should drop by the bank.
   (B) Yes, two more people.
   (C) At 7 o'clock.

35. Do you know where Ms. Green teaches chemistry?
   (A) At a university in Scotland.
   (B) Yes, she is a biology teacher.
   (C) Three days a week.

36. Where should we have dinner tonight?
   (A) Do you have any suggestions?
   (B) At 8 p.m.
   (C) Could you bring the check?

37. You haven't touched the files on my desk, have you?
   (A) It's miles away from here.
   (B) Didn't you move them?
   (C) I haven't met you before.

38. Isn't the optician near the community center?
   (A) As far as I know, it's moved to the shopping mall.
   (B) Yes, it's the central concern.
   (C) I usually use the bus.

39. Are we going to drive to Gettysburg or take the express bus?
   (A) Don't push the button.
   (B) I haven't made up my mind yet.
   (C) It's maybe about three miles.

40. When will Mr. Butler's new CD be released?
   (A) It was not exciting.
   (B) The shop on Boston Street.
   (C) Probably this summer.

Track 44 [page 200]

Listening
Part 3: Conversations

> **Directions:** You will hear conversations with two speakers. Then you will answer three questions about each conversation. Listen and select the best response to each question. Mark the corresponding letter (A), (B), (C), or (D) on the answer sheet.

Man: Hello, may I board the plane now? I hope I still have time. My connecting flight was delayed in Shanghai.

Woman: I'm sorry, sir, but we cannot allow anyone on board now. The doors have already been shut.

Man: Oh, no. If I don't get on this plane, I'll miss an important meeting with a client in Miami.

Woman: I'm sorry but there's nothing I can do to get you on this flight. But there are two more flights this afternoon to Miami. Shall I see if there are any seats available for you on one of those flights?

41. Where most likely are the speakers?

42. What is the man concerned about?

43. What does the woman recommend?

Woman: Hello, I'm calling to inquire about the advertisement I saw in the newspaper this morning. It concerned the Web design classes. Could you give me more information about your program?

Man: Yes, of course. The fall semester starts next Tuesday. The whole program is designed to be completed within one year if you attend full-time day classes. You can finish the program by taking six credits. You should register for three required courses such as Web design theory, computer graphics, and essential Web skills. And then you can pick three elective courses you'd like to take.

Woman: Oh ... I am a full-time assistant editor at a publishing company.

Man: Don't worry about it. We also provide part-time evening classes. So certainly you'll be able to attend the program while also working. Could you give me your home address? I'll mail you a brochure with more detailed information and an application form.

44. What subjects does the woman want to study?

45. What is the woman concerned about?

46. What does the man say he will do?

Man: Excuse me. I'm searching for organic cauliflower and tomatoes. Can you show me where they are?

Woman: Yes, they are in aisle 4, the vegetable section. But we have probably run out of most of the organic food we have today. We'll be receiving new stock tomorrow morning. Because of the cold temperatures this season, shipments have been small.

Man: That's a shame. I'll go and take a look now. If there aren't any, I'll come back tomorrow.

47. Where does the dialog probably take place?

48. What does the woman say about deliveries?

49. What will the man probably do next?

Woman: Hi, I want to buy these two books. They are 20% off, aren't they?

Man: I'm afraid our Back to School Sale ended yesterday. Why don't you sign up for our membership card to be notified of special discounts and receive a 10% discount on your next purchase at the store?

Woman: OK, what information do you want?

Man: Please complete this form and pay $25 for membership. Just fill in your name, phone number, and e-mail address, and then we'll send you an e-mail with information about special offers at the store.

50. Where does the conversation take place?

51. What does the woman need to do to get some information?

52. What will the woman get by signing up for the card?

Man: Hi, Olivia. It seems we have a conference call scheduled for tomorrow with the marketing team at the main office. Actually, I haven't set up a conference call since I joined the company. Can you show me how it works?

Woman: It's not too hard. I've done it twice before. Did you read the manual for conference call procedures?

Man: No, it's in my drawer. Hang on. I'll go get it.

Woman: OK. You'll see it says all callers receive a special phone number and have to enter a common access code. I'll show you what you have to do. Let's go over the instructions together.

53. Why is the man concerned?

54. What does the man want the woman to do?

55. Why is the man going to his drawer?

Woman: Eric, I got the new computer we needed for the VIP client waiting room. But when I opened the box to set up the computer, the wireless mouse I ordered at a 10% discount wasn't there.

Man: Sometimes, some items are accidentally not included in shipments. Why don't you look at the receipt?

Woman: You're right. I don't have the receipt with me. I think I left it on my desk at home. I will look at it as soon as I get home. By the way, have you found a sofa for our office at a good price?

Man: Not yet, but they say that the furniture store across the street is holding a big sale this week. It closes at 7 o'clock during the week of the sale. So I'll drop by the store after work.

56. According to the woman, what is the problem?

57. What does the man suggest doing?

58. What time does the store shut this week?

Man: Excuse me, I think I booked this room for my sales team meeting at 11 o'clock.

Woman: Hmm ... That's odd. I also reserved this room for the next two hours. Let me check the online booking calendar on my computer.

Man: Thank you. That would be fantastic.

Woman: Oh ... You're right. It seems my request for this room didn't go through. Sorry for the trouble. I should check quickly online what room I'm expected to be in now.

59. What are the speakers discussing?

60. How do the speakers resolve the issue?

61. What will the woman probably do next?

Woman: Dick. I've considered the woman we interviewed this morning, Crystal Blackman. She has had experience managing stores for years. She also completed a master's degree in international marketing. I want to hire her, but I suppose she may be overqualified for this part-time position.

Man: Well, I think so, too. Why don't we recommend her for the Area Manager position in Jakarta? She isn't overqualified for that, and we have very few applicants.

Woman: That's a great idea. I wonder if she'd be happy to move there. The position must be filled by the end of the month because our third store is expected to open next month in the new shopping center in Jakarta.

Man: Ok, I will call her and talk about the position. Then, if she's interested, I'll arrange a phone interview with her.

62. What does the woman say about Crystal Blackman?

63. According to the woman, what will happen in Jakarta next month?

64. What will the man probably do next?

Man: Hey, Caroline. I'm going to a theater show at the Grand Auditorium on Market Street on Saturday. Several amateur local actors will be performing. It's a charity event. Are you interested in joining us?

Woman: Oh, that sounds wonderful. My sister who lives in Italy is visiting me this week. I think she'd also like to go to the theater. I imagine the tickets sold out?

Man: I don't know. But I have two free tickets. I purchased the tickets for some friends a few weeks ago. Sadly, they can't go to the theater because of some reports they have to complete by next Monday. You should take my tickets for free if you are interested.

65. What is the woman doing this week?

66. What problem does the man mention?

67. Why is the woman fortunate?

Man: Kate, isn't it time we printed and mailed the invitations for the company's tenth anniversary celebration to all employees? It needs to be done by the end of the week.

Woman: OK. I'll place an order with the publications department after lunch. But there's one important thing we have to consider. Shall we have the invitations printed in color like last year or in black and white?

Man: I see, good point. Color copies are twice as expensive as black and white ones. As you know, because the weather wasn't at all hot over the summer, our air conditioner sales have gone down dramatically. I don't think we can afford to print in color. Let's do them in black and white this year.

68. What are the speakers mainly discussing?

69. What does the woman want the man to consider?

70. Why have company sales dropped?

Track 45 [page 203]

Listening
Part 4: Talks

> **Directions:** You will hear several talks, each with one speaker. Then you will answer three questions about the talk. Listen and select the best response to each question. Mark the corresponding letter (A), (B), (C), or (D) on the answer sheet.

Good morning, Ms. Sanchez. This is Jonathan Smith calling from COB Bank. This is just to confirm that we received your mortgage application on April 4. Your application is now being evaluated by our mortgage team, and you will have our final response within the next seven business days. If you wish to track the progress of your application, please check our website. You will have to enter the application ID number you received when you submitted your application. Thank you.

71. What did Ms. Sanchez apply for?

72. What does the speaker say about Ms. Sanchez's application?

73. How can Ms. Sanchez check the status of her application?

Good afternoon, and welcome to Midwest Local News. I'm Michelle Simms. City Hall gave the approval this morning to the construction of a new retail and entertainment center. The center, to be constructed on the site of the former South Cross Station, is opposed by some local businesspeople who believe that it will worsen the city's already chronic traffic problems in the downtown area. The city mayor, however, remarked that the project will result in the creation of hundreds of new, sustainable jobs in the local economy. She also announced that a series of public meetings will take place beginning next month to consider ways of easing traffic congestion caused by the new center.

74. What was approved by City Hall?

75. What are some businesspeople worried about?

76. What will happen next month?

Good evening to you all. Many thanks for attending our celebration for Martin Vermont, who leaves us this month after a brilliant 20 years to work in academia. All of us who have worked with Martin, and also many who haven't, will be familiar with the excellent work he has done. Martin pioneered our move into new areas, developing the broad range of new financial products that we today provide to our customers.

Martin has also contributed to raising our company's public profile, appearing regularly on current affairs shows as a commentator on economic and financial matters. We can have no doubt that the students at Southern University will benefit greatly from Martin's knowledge and expertise. Let's wish Martin all the best for the future.

77. What area does Martin Vermont work in?

78. What accomplishment of Martin Vermont is mentioned?

79. What is Martin Vermont going to do?

Ladies and gentlemen, may I have your attention please. I'd like to welcome you to the Fox Theater this evening. Tonight we celebrate the opening of this year's South American Film Festival, and it's fantastic to have you all here. As you probably know, this year's Festival is also taking place at a second venue for the first time: at the renovated Zaller Arts Center on Central Avenue. Because of this, we can now give you 30% more movies this year. Now, without further ado, let's begin. I'm happy to welcome the director of our first film, *Heat*, Mr. Pedro Gonzalez. *Heat* is a captivating exposé of life at the Argentinean elite sports institute. After the showing of the movie, Mr. Gonzalez will be responding to your questions. He will also be joining the reception this evening, where you can speak with him more informally.

80. Where is the talk being held?

81. According to the speaker, what is new this year?

82. Who is Pedro Gonzalez?

Hello, Charles. It's Janet. I'm calling to get your advice on a problem we're having at the moment. One of our clients wants us to increase the scope of our audit to include another of their group companies. We have already reached agreement on terms for this audit, and, of course, we really can't agree to the client's request without raising the cost of the audit. The client, though, claims that the audit is already expensive, and expects us to agree to this out of courtesy. We've discussed this in person three times now but have not been able to come to any agreement. I was wondering if you've ever been in this situation and what you'd recommend. Please call me back. Thanks.

83. What is the purpose of the call?

84. What does the client want to do?

85. What does the woman want the listener to do?

Hello. This is a message for the manager of Gerrard's Brasserie. My name is Thomas Hayward and I'm calling from the City Inspection Department. Our inspector, Lisa Totsby, went to see your premises last week and has now submitted her report. Ms. Totsby found that your restaurant generally satisfied health and safety regulations. However, we need to ask you to amend signage in order to demonstrate to staff which route to take in the event of fire or other emergency. Ms. Totsby observed that the evacuation route was clearly indicated within the restaurant itself, but not in the kitchen and food preparation sections. She wishes to return to your premises to check that you have improved this before the end of the month. Please could you call me back at 555-7501 to arrange a suitable time?

86. What is the subject of the message?

87. What does the caller want the listener to do?

88. What does the caller say about Ms. Totsby?

Hello, Mr. Kim. This is Brian Taylor at Stationery Depot. I have just received your message about the order you placed with us last week. I'm very sorry to learn that your computer monitors didn't arrive as expected last Friday. I've looked into this matter and found that, regrettably, this was a mistake on our part as the order was not dispatched. I have now ordered the monitors to be shipped by special delivery, and they will reach your office tomorrow, Wednesday, before midday. To apologize for the trouble, we will waive all handling and delivery charges. In the unlikely event of any further problems with this order, please feel free to contact me directly at 868-555-9111. I'm in the office Monday through Friday, from 9 until 6. Thank you.

89. What did Mr. Kim order?

90. When will the order arrive?

91. What does the speaker offer Mr. Kim?

This is *Global Business Today*, and I'm your host, Natalie Alford. The owner of low-cost airline Budget Air, Kumar Gollapudi, announced yesterday that the company will provide intercontinental routes beginning next quarter. Flights between the airline's New Delhi hub and San Francisco, and between Mumbai and Seattle, will start in July. Gollapudi also stated that Budget Air will hire between 150 and 250 new employees as part of its ambitious growth plans. Over the last ten years, the New Delhi-based carrier has built itself into the leading budget airline for flights within South Asia. This will be the first time that its customers will be able to travel routes outside South Asia.

92. Who most likely is the speaker?

93. According to the talk, what is Budget Air going to do?

94. Where is Budget Air's headquarters?

Good morning. Thank you for coming to this demonstration of our new customer relationship management software. We believe that our software can help all of you here at Vegas Beverages Inc. to streamline your business processes, and, eventually, to understand your customers better. Our software engineers developed this software in consultation with marketing staff at companies around the world, including your own. In this way, we discovered exactly what you need from the software, and have implemented those features. Also, in order to thank your company for helping us, we will offer you a discount on this software of 25%. Please note that the slides from today's demonstration, and details of features that I don't have time to talk about today, will be on our website for you to check out at your leisure.

95. In what kind of company is the talk most likely taking place?

96. What does the speaker offer the listeners?

97. How can the listeners get further information?

Thank you all for attending the inaugural conference of the Global Social Media Association here in beautiful San Jose. You should all have been given your conference packs when you registered this morning. If not, they are available at the information counter in the foyer. Just present your membership card. The pack contains vouchers and details of special offers for delegates at nearby restaurants and stores. One thing I should mention to you is that this evening's seminar on e-book creation has moved. It will now take place in the Hartley Suite, on the second floor, not in the Barney Room as indicated in the printed schedule.

98. What is the purpose of the talk?

99. What does the speaker advise the listeners to do?

100. Where will tonight's event take place?

Track 46 [page 231]

Speaking

Question 1: Read a text aloud

Directions: In this part of the test, you will read aloud the text on the page. You will have 45 seconds to prepare. Then you will have 45 seconds to read the text aloud.

Your preparation time begins now.

Now please read the text aloud.

Your time is up. Now move on to the next question.

Track 47 [page 231]

Question 2: Read a text aloud

Directions: In this part of the test, you will read aloud the text on the page. You will have 45 seconds to prepare. Then you will have 45 seconds to read the text aloud.

Your preparation time begins now.

Now please read the text aloud.

Your time is up. Now move on to the next question.

Track 48 [page 232]

Question 3: Describe a picture

Directions: You will describe a photograph as completely as you can. The photograph is in the test book. You will have 30 seconds to prepare what you will say, and then you will have 45 seconds to describe the picture in as much detail as possible.

Your preparation time begins now.

Now please describe the photograph aloud.

Your time is up. Now move on to the next question.

Track 49 [page 232]

Questions 4–6: Respond to questions

Directions: You will be asked three questions. After each question you will hear a beep. Begin speaking your answer immediately after the beep. You will not have any time to prepare your answer. For Questions 4 and 5 you will have 15 seconds to respond. For Question 6 you will have 30 seconds.

Imagine that an Australian marketing firm is doing research in your country. You have agreed to participate in a telephone interview about job interviews.

Question 4:   When was the last time you had a job interview, and was it successful?

Question 5:   What do you usually wear to a job interview?

Question 6:   How do you prepare for a job interview?

Track 50 [page 234]

Speaking

Questions 7–9: Respond to questions using information provided

Directions: You will read a short text and then answer three questions based on the information in the text. You will have 30 seconds to read the text before the first question. After each question you will hear a beep. Begin speaking immediately after the beep. You will not have any extra time to prepare your answer. For Questions 7 and 8 you will have 15 seconds to respond. For Question 9 you will have 30 seconds.

Man: Hi, I heard that there will be a film week at your college. I'm not a student at the college, so I don't have much information about it. Could I ask a few questions over the phone?

Question 7:   Where is the college located, and how much are the tickets?

Question 8:   I heard that a documentary on Ron Thompson will be shown on the Wednesday of the film week. Is that right?

Question 9:   Can you tell me what films will be shown on Friday and Saturday?

Track 51 [page 235]

Speaking
Question 10: Propose a solution

> **Directions:** You will hear about a problem and be asked to propose a solution. You will have 30 seconds to prepare your solution, and then 60 seconds to speak.

Hello, my name is Deborah Johnson, and I live in apartment 1105 of your building. I've been living at this residence for about three years now, and I've been quite satisfied with everything here. However, there is one concern that I'd like to bring to your attention. There has been a lot of noise coming from the apartment above mine. At first it sounded like little kids running around, so I didn't think much of the noise. However, recently the noise has been getting louder, and it's been happening in the middle of the night when I'm trying to sleep. I don't know who lives upstairs and what's going on in that apartment, but it's gotten to the point that I can't get a good night's rest anymore. I'm calling you because you're the manager of the building, and I'm asking that you do something about this problem. Again, my name is Deborah Johnson, and my number is 555-3420.

Track 52 [page 235]

Speaking
Question 11: Express an opinion

> **Directions:** You will hear about a specific topic and then give your opinion about it. Make sure you say as much as you can about the topic in the time allowed. You will have 15 seconds to prepare, and then 60 seconds to speak.

Some people prefer to take the bus to commute, while others prefer to take the subway. Which do you think is better and why? Give specific reasons and details to support your opinion.

Answer Key

Practice Test 1 – Listening

1.	B	26.	B	51.	D	76.	B
2.	D	27.	A	52.	C	77.	C
3.	C	28.	C	53.	D	78.	B
4.	C	29.	A	54.	B	79.	C
5.	B	30.	B	55.	A	80.	B
6.	C	31.	B	56.	B	81.	A
7.	B	32.	B	57.	A	82.	D
8.	B	33.	A	58.	B	83.	C
9.	A	34.	B	59.	D	84.	D
10.	D	35.	A	60.	B	85.	B
11.	B	36.	A	61.	A	86.	B
12.	B	37.	C	62.	C	87.	D
13.	A	38.	B	63.	B	88.	B
14.	C	39.	B	64.	D	89.	B
15.	A	40.	C	65.	D	90.	D
16.	C	41.	B	66.	D	91.	B
17.	B	42.	C	67.	C	92.	B
18.	A	43.	D	68.	D	93.	C
19.	A	44.	B	69.	A	94.	D
20.	B	45.	D	70.	C	95.	B
21.	C	46.	D	71.	C	96.	D
22.	C	47.	B	72.	D	97.	A
23.	C	48.	D	73.	C	98.	C
24.	C	49.	C	74.	C	99.	D
25.	A	50.	A	75.	A	100.	A

Practice Test 1 – Reading

101.	A	126.	B	151.	A	176.	B
102.	D	127.	D	152.	C	177.	D
103.	D	128.	B	153.	A	178.	C
104.	B	129.	A	154.	B	179.	A
105.	A	130.	D	155.	C	180.	A
106.	A	131.	C	156.	D	181.	C
107.	D	132.	C	157.	D	182.	D
108.	A	133.	B	158.	A	183.	A
109.	C	134.	D	159.	B	184.	B
110.	D	135.	A	160.	A	185.	B
111.	B	136.	D	161.	C	186.	B
112.	B	137.	C	162.	D	187.	C
113.	D	138.	A	163.	B	188.	A
114.	C	139.	D	164.	C	189.	C
115.	A	140.	A	165.	B	190.	A
116.	C	141.	B	166.	B	191.	A
117.	A	142.	B	167.	B	192.	C
118.	C	143.	D	168.	D	193.	A
119.	B	144.	D	169.	C	194.	B
120.	B	145.	B	170.	A	195.	B
121.	B	146.	A	171.	B	196.	D
122.	B	147.	A	172.	A	197.	A
123.	A	148.	A	173.	D	198.	C
124.	C	149.	A	174.	D	199.	D
125.	A	150.	D	175.	B	200.	A

Practice Test 2 – Listening

1.	B	26.	A	51.	A	76.	A
2.	A	27.	B	52.	D	77.	A
3.	D	28.	C	53.	D	78.	D
4.	B	29.	A	54.	A	79.	C
5.	B	30.	A	55.	B	80.	D
6.	B	31.	C	56.	B	81.	B
7.	D	32.	C	57.	C	82.	C
8.	C	33.	C	58.	C	83.	D
9.	D	34.	B	59.	C	84.	A
10.	D	35.	C	60.	D	85.	C
11.	C	36.	A	61.	C	86.	D
12.	A	37.	A	62.	D	87.	A
13.	C	38.	A	63.	C	88.	B
14.	A	39.	A	64.	B	89.	B
15.	B	40.	C	65.	A	90.	A
16.	A	41.	C	66.	D	91.	B
17.	A	42.	D	67.	C	92.	D
18.	A	43.	A	68.	C	93.	A
19.	C	44.	B	69.	A	94.	B
20.	B	45.	C	70.	C	95.	B
21.	B	46.	D	71.	B	96.	A
22.	B	47.	B	72.	D	97.	D
23.	B	48.	C	73.	C	98.	A
24.	B	49.	D	74.	A	99.	A
25.	A	50.	B	75.	B	100.	D

Practice Test 2 – Reading

101.	C	126.	D	151.	A	176.	C
102.	A	127.	A	152.	B	177.	D
103.	A	128.	C	153.	A	178.	A
104.	C	129.	C	154.	B	179.	A
105.	D	130.	A	155.	B	180.	C
106.	B	131.	C	156.	D	181.	A
107.	A	132.	C	157.	C	182.	D
108.	A	133.	B	158.	C	183.	D
109.	A	134.	C	159.	D	184.	C
110.	B	135.	C	160.	B	185.	C
111.	B	136.	D	161.	D	186.	A
112.	D	137.	A	162.	A	187.	B
113.	C	138.	B	163.	D	188.	C
114.	A	139.	B	164.	B	189.	C
115.	D	140.	A	165.	A	190.	D
116.	A	141.	C	166.	D	191.	A
117.	C	142.	A	167.	C	192.	B
118.	A	143.	D	168.	D	193.	D
119.	C	144.	B	169.	C	194.	B
120.	A	145.	C	170.	A	195.	B
121.	C	146.	A	171.	C	196.	D
122.	A	147.	A	172.	B	197.	C
123.	D	148.	C	173.	C	198.	C
124.	D	149.	D	174.	C	199.	B
125.	C	150.	C	175.	B	200.	C

Practice Test 3 – Listening

1.	C	26.	C	51.	B	76.	A
2.	B	27.	B	52.	B	77.	D
3.	A	28.	A	53.	B	78.	B
4.	B	29.	B	54.	A	79.	C
5.	D	30.	C	55.	D	80.	B
6.	D	31.	B	56.	D	81.	C
7.	C	32.	A	57.	B	82.	C
8.	C	33.	B	58.	D	83.	B
9.	A	34.	C	59.	C	84.	C
10.	C	35.	C	60.	A	85.	A
11.	C	36.	A	61.	D	86.	A
12.	B	37.	C	62.	C	87.	A
13.	B	38.	B	63.	D	88.	B
14.	A	39.	C	64.	D	89.	A
15.	B	40.	A	65.	C	90.	D
16.	A	41.	C	66.	A	91.	A
17.	A	42.	C	67.	C	92.	B
18.	B	43.	B	68.	B	93.	A
19.	B	44.	A	69.	A	94.	D
20.	B	45.	D	70.	A	95.	D
21.	B	46.	C	71.	B	96.	B
22.	A	47.	D	72.	D	97.	C
23.	B	48.	C	73.	A	98.	B
24.	A	49.	D	74.	A	99.	B
25.	B	50.	C	75.	D	100.	B

Practice Test 3 – Reading

101.	D	126.	D	151.	C	176.	D
102.	C	127.	B	152.	B	177.	A
103.	C	128.	A	153.	A	178.	C
104.	D	129.	C	154.	A	179.	D
105.	A	130.	B	155.	B	180.	D
106.	B	131.	B	156.	C	181.	B
107.	D	132.	D	157.	D	182.	D
108.	A	133.	D	158.	B	183.	D
109.	B	134.	A	159.	A	184.	D
110.	C	135.	D	160.	B	185.	C
111.	B	136.	B	161.	A	186.	B
112.	B	137.	B	162.	D	187.	D
113.	C	138.	A	163.	B	188.	B
114.	B	139.	D	164.	D	189.	C
115.	C	140.	D	165.	C	190.	B
116.	A	141.	B	166.	D	191.	D
117.	C	142.	A	167.	C	192.	B
118.	C	143.	D	168.	B	193.	B
119.	B	144.	D	169.	B	194.	D
120.	D	145.	A	170.	A	195.	D
121.	D	146.	B	171.	D	196.	A
122.	B	147.	A	172.	D	197.	D
123.	B	148.	B	173.	C	198.	C
124.	B	149.	C	174.	A	199.	C
125.	B	150.	A	175.	A	200.	C

Practice Test 4 – Listening

1.	C	26.	B	51.	D	76.	D
2.	B	27.	B	52.	C	77.	A
3.	A	28.	A	53.	C	78.	C
4.	C	29.	B	54.	D	79.	A
5.	B	30.	A	55.	C	80.	D
6.	D	31.	C	56.	B	81.	C
7.	A	32.	A	57.	D	82.	D
8.	C	33.	B	58.	C	83.	B
9.	B	34.	A	59.	C	84.	B
10.	C	35.	A	60.	B	85.	C
11.	C	36.	A	61.	A	86.	C
12.	B	37.	B	62.	C	87.	B
13.	C	38.	A	63.	B	88.	A
14.	B	39.	B	64.	D	89.	C
15.	B	40.	C	65.	B	90.	B
16.	C	41.	D	66.	D	91.	C
17.	A	42.	B	67.	A	92.	D
18.	C	43.	A	68.	A	93.	A
19.	B	44.	B	69.	B	94.	D
20.	B	45.	B	70.	C	95.	A
21.	A	46.	C	71.	D	96.	D
22.	A	47.	D	72.	B	97.	D
23.	A	48.	C	73.	B	98.	B
24.	C	49.	B	74.	A	99.	A
25.	C	50.	A	75.	C	100.	C

Practice Test 4 – Reading

101.	A	126.	A	151.	D	176.	A
102.	B	127.	B	152.	B	177.	A
103.	D	128.	D	153.	D	178.	B
104.	B	129.	D	154.	C	179.	A
105.	C	130.	B	155.	D	180.	B
106.	B	131.	B	156.	D	181.	D
107.	C	132.	D	157.	D	182.	A
108.	B	133.	B	158.	B	183.	D
109.	D	134.	D	159.	C	184.	C
110.	D	135.	C	160.	B	185.	A
111.	C	136.	B	161.	A	186.	A
112.	B	137.	D	162.	B	187.	A
113.	C	138.	A	163.	A	188.	C
114.	C	139.	B	164.	C	189.	B
115.	A	140.	A	165.	D	190.	C
116.	A	141.	D	166.	A	191.	A
117.	B	142.	A	167.	B	192.	C
118.	D	143.	B	168.	D	193.	D
119.	C	144.	C	169.	B	194.	D
120.	A	145.	A	170.	C	195.	C
121.	C	146.	C	171.	A	196.	B
122.	A	147.	A	172.	A	197.	B
123.	A	148.	C	173.	A	198.	B
124.	C	149.	B	174.	B	199.	C
125.	C	150.	A	175.	D	200.	B

Test Score Conversion Chart

This score conversion chart will help you *estimate* your TOEIC Listening and Reading test score. Your total score will be *approximate*. It may be higher or lower than the actual TOEIC test score. (If you take the TOEIC test on Monday and then take the TOEIC test again on Tuesday, your score will be different.)

Put the number of your correct answers in the spaces below. Then find the corresponding score on the chart below. Add your Listening and Reading scores. The total will be your *approximate* TOEIC test score.

#	LC	RC	#	LC	RC	#	LC	RC	#	LC	RC
1	5	5	26	105	60	51	250	215	76	405	365
2	5	5	27	110	65	52	255	225	77	410	370
3	5	5	28	115	75	53	260	230	78	415	380
4	5	5	29	120	85	54	265	235	79	420	385
5	5	5	30	125	90	55	270	240	80	430	390
6	5	5	31	130	95	56	280	245	81	435	395
7	10	5	32	135	100	57	285	255	82	440	400
8	15	5	33	140	105	58	295	260	83	445	405
9	20	5	34	145	115	59	300	265	84	450	410
10	25	10	35	150	125	60	310	270	85	460	415
11	30	10	36	155	130	61	315	275	86	465	420
12	35	15	37	165	135	62	320	285	87	470	425
13	40	15	38	170	140	63	325	290	88	475	430
14	45	20	39	175	145	64	330	295	89	480	435
15	50	20	40	180	150	65	340	300	90	485	445
16	55	25	41	185	155	66	345	305	91	490	450
17	60	25	42	190	160	67	350	310	92	490	460
18	65	30	43	195	170	68	360	320	93	495	470
19	70	30	44	200	175	69	365	325	94	495	480
20	75	30	45	210	180	70	370	335	95	495	485
21	80	35	46	215	190	71	375	340	96	495	490
22	85	35	47	220	195	72	380	345	97	495	495
23	90	40	48	230	200	73	390	350	98	495	495
24	95	45	49	235	205	74	395	355	99	495	495
25	100	50	50	240	210	75	400	360	100	495	495

_____ = _____
Listening correct answers   Listening score

_____ = _____
Reading correct answers   Reading score

                              +
Approximate TOEIC Test Score   _____

Sample Answers

Practice Test 1

Speaking Test

Question 3

This is a picture of a family walking in the park. There are four people in the picture. On the left side of the picture, the father is holding his son's hand. The father is wearing a white T-shirt and blue jeans. The son is wearing a yellow T-shirt. On the right side of the picture, the mother is holding her daughter's hand. The mother is wearing a pink top and blue jeans. The daughter is wearing a red top. In the middle of the picture, the son and the daughter are holding each other's hands. In the background of the picture, I can see lots of trees. It looks like the family is enjoying a nice day at the park.

Question 4

I try to exercise at least three days a week. However, these days I don't exercise as much because I've been really busy at work.

Question 5

At the gym where I work out, I use the treadmill and weightlifting machines.

Question 6

There are many benefits of exercising. One benefit is that it makes you more physically fit. When you exercise, you become stronger and have more energy. Also, when you are in shape, your clothes fit better. Another benefit is that exercising makes you feel better, and it is a good way to release stress.

Question 7

Sure. You have four airline options on the dates that you want to travel. They are USA Air, Virgo America, Peak, and Unified Airlines.

Question 8

It's Peak, and it costs $451. It departs at 7:40 p.m. and arrives at 4:26 p.m. But you have to take a connecting flight in Pittsburgh.

Question 9

Sure. There are two nonstop flights. They are Virgo America and Unified Airlines. Virgo costs $593, and it departs New York at 8:00 a.m. and arrives in Las Vegas at 10:50 a.m. Unified costs $610, and it departs New York at 10:00 p.m. and arrives in Las Vegas at 12:45 a.m.

Question 10

Hello, Mr. Smith. I'm calling from Super Convenience. I got your message saying that you were at our store earlier tonight. You said you may have left a folder on the lottery counter at our store. I've checked the counter and you'll be glad to know the folder was there. It sounds like you need the folder as soon as possible, and I guess you have two options. You asked if the store is still open, and we are just getting ready to close up now. But if you can get here in the next 15 minutes, I can wait for you in the store. If you can't make it in that time, you'll have to pick up the folder tomorrow morning. We're open at 7:00 a.m. Please call me back if you can come to the store right now.

Question 11

Personally, I prefer to shop in person at a store. There are a couple of reasons to support my opinion. First, there are certain items that I need to see in person before I can decide to buy them. For example, I would never buy clothes online because you can't try them on. And if the clothes don't fit, you would have to return them and it would be a lot of hassle. But when you shop in a store, you don't have to worry about this. Another reason is that you have to wait a long time to receive items purchased online. When I buy something, I want to bring it home right away, not wait several days to receive it. For these reasons, I think going to a store to shop is better.

Writing Test

Question 1

Someone is using an ATM with their bank card.
Somebody is using a card at the ATM.
This person has a card at the ATM machine.
We can use a bank card to withdraw money from an ATM.
Someone is using a debit card at the ATM.

Question 2

The family are having breakfast.
This family are eating breakfast.
A family are eating breakfast together.
A family are having breakfast together.
A happy family are smiling as they have breakfast.

Question 3

Two tigers are leaping through fire.
The tigers are jumping through fire.
Tigers are leaping through hoops of fire.
The two tigers are jumping through fire.
Two tigers are jumping through rings of fire.

Question 4

The waitress is serving food.
A waitress is serving food.
Food is usually served by a waitress or waiter.
The waitress is smiling as she serves her customers.
The food is about to be served by the waitress.

Question 5

The subway train is full of passengers.
The passenger is trying to get on the subway train.
A female passenger is trying to get on the subway train.
The subway is very crowded and the passenger is getting on
    the train.
There are many passengers on the subway train.

Question 6

Thank you for getting back to me. I lost my transit card last Thursday but I don't know exactly where. The last time I had it was at City Hall station. I then took the train to Manor Park, and I think I must have dropped it on the train. I checked with both stations but they haven't found it, so I guess I'll need a replacement. I can't remember my card number, sorry. My full name is James Anthony Smith, and my address is 198 Winston Boulevard, Coast City.

Could you please let me know where to pick up my replacement card, and when I will be able to get it?

Question 7

Thank you very much for sending me your new catalog. I've spent some time looking through the different Jacuzzis that you offer. I particularly liked the 35-TR model because it has a built in shower. However, the 36-PQ Deluxe model is also good because it has wheels and is therefore mobile. Could you please let me know which of these two models you currently have in stock? Also, it would be good to arrange a time for someone from your firm to come and to give me a quote. I will be away on vacation from tomorrow for two weeks, but any time after that should be fine. The best time for me is in the evenings, after 6 p.m., or, if that isn't possible for you, Saturday mornings are also good. Please let me know when would suit you best.

Question 8

Many students decide to take a year off, or a gap year, before going to college. There are many considerations to these two very important options, and they are as follows.

Firstly, the gap year is very useful if you have spent the past few years living at school away from friends and family. Because you have studied hard to get good grades in order to be accepted to your first choice college, you may need a break, or a year off, for a vacation. A gap year can be great to get back to doing normal things and touch base with those you miss. You can take the pressure off full-time study to see family you may have only seen a few times throughout high school, and friends you have only texted or met occasionally while studying.

Secondly, a gap year means you could get a full-time job and save money that will help finance you through college when you go after you've had your gap year. This makes sense because tuition fees are so expensive now.

However, going straight to college can have its advantages. Most of my friends are going to do this and I can see why they think this way. They want to get their degree earlier so they can get a job much more quickly when they graduate. I've made a few new friends at high school and some are even going to get a part-time job while they study for their degree. Also, if you're studying close to family and friends anyway, there's no reason to have a gap year because you can see them anytime.

In the end, my personal opinion is that I think I'll go straight to college because I can always work for my father at his shop in the evenings, and study when things are quiet. Having said that, if I lived far away from my friends and family, I would probably take a gap year. So it basically comes down to finance and individual situations, and doing what makes you personally more successful and happier in the long run.

Practice Test 2

Speaking Test

Question 3

There are two people in this picture, and they both look like architects. On the left side of the picture is a man. He is sitting at a small round table. He is wearing a blue hard hat and a blue shirt. He is pointing at a blueprint with his left hand. In front of him, a woman is standing at the same table. She is wearing a yellow hard hat. She has long straight hair and is wearing a black outfit. She is pointing at another part of the blueprint with her right hand. She is holding a pen in that hand. It looks like the architects are having a discussion about the blueprint.

Question 4

I go to the cinema to watch a movie once a month. I usually go with my friends, but I also sometimes go with my co-workers.

Question 5

I normally get popcorn and a drink, but I sometimes get a hot dog when I'm really hungry.

Question 6

I recently watched a Korean movie called *Criminals*, and it was really interesting. It was about a group of thieves who try to steal from a museum. I liked it because the plot was very exciting. I also liked it because there were a lot of famous movie stars in it.

Question 7

The seminar is on Saturday, November 2. The first session is The Industry's Past and the Future by Joe Plante. It will start at 9:30 a.m.

Question 8

It's $40 if you register on the day of the event. However, if you register in advance, it's $32. We suggest you register in advance.

Question 9

Sure. After lunch, there will be a talk on campaigns that lead to success at 1:45 p.m. It will be given by Christy Lee. Then Dan Stewart will give a talk on getting ahead of the competition at 3:00 p.m. The final session of the day will be a discussion session, which will start at 5:00 p.m.

Question 10

Hello, my name is Kevin Singh, and I'm a service technician at Power Electronics. I got your message saying that you purchased a television from our store yesterday, but you're having some problems with it. First of all, let me say that I'm sorry for the trouble that you're having. From what you've described in your message, it doesn't sound like it's a problem with the television. Rather, I think there may be something wrong with the connection with the cable box. The reason I say this is that if there was something wrong with the television, you wouldn't be able to program any channels. However, this is not the case in your situation. What I suggest you do is call your local cable company and check that everything is OK with the connection. If they're not able to solve the problem, please call us back. Thank you for your call.

Question 11

In my opinion, a good manager should have the following qualities. Firstly, a manager should have leadership skills. For example, most workers want a manager that they can follow. However, if a manager is not a good leader, then it's very difficult for him or her to lead his or her team in the right direction. Secondly, a manager should be a good listener. The reason for this is that a manager needs to understand his or her workers in order to develop a better relationship with them and make them more productive. Lastly, a good manager should be professional at all times. For instance, a good manager should be responsible for creating a professional environment at work, but if a manager cannot set aside his or her personal feelings, then this cannot be done. Therefore, I believe that a good manager should have leadership ability, good listening skills, and professionalism.

Writing Test

Question 1

People are waiting for a job interview.
Five people are waiting for a job interview.
They are all waiting before a job interview.
Some people are waiting for a job interview.
They are holding their resumes while waiting for a job interview.

Question 2

The street is very crowded.
This is a crowded street.
There is a crowd on the street.
The street is crowded.
The people are crowding the street.

Question 3

The puppy is listening.
The puppy is listening to the headphones.
A puppy has some headphones on and is listening to something.
The puppy is trying to listen through some headphones.
A puppy is listening to music.

Question 4

There is a salesman standing by some cars.
The cars are behind the salesman.
A salesman is selling cars.
The salesman has a lot of cars to sell.
The salesman is standing by some cars.

Question 5

They are on bicycles in the grass.
People are racing on bicycles across the grass.
There's a bicycle race across the grass and hills.
Some people are riding bicycles up a hill covered with grass.
The person is racing on a bicycle up a grassy hill.

Question 6

Hey Stevie!

Yes it's been so long! I'm looking forward to it so much and to seeing everybody again!

Poor first year students, they weren't as friendly as us, were they? You'll have to count me out of their reunion though because I'm working late on the 25th, tell them I would've loved to have come, but can't, sorry.

I'd love to help set up the second year reunion on the 26th. It will be great to get to know everybody again before the party starts! No, I won't forget to bring something along, my husband says I cook a nice chili and tacos, so I'll bring along a big pot and some recyclable bowls and spoons. I'll be there at 6 p.m. to help set up the tables and chairs so I'll see you then.

I'm so looking forward to it!

Sara

Question 7

Dear Mr. Le Rone,

Thank you for your reply. I have two suits, three shirts, and a king size duvet cover to dry clean. That's six articles in total. I don't need them returned quickly, so there is no hurry. I won't have time next week to drop them off at your center so, yes, I would like your express pick-up service, please. My husband will be home all day on Tuesday so you can pick them up at any time after 9:30 a.m.

Could you please tell me what the total price is of the order including the additional charge of the express pick-up service? Also, when will they be ready for pick up, and do you provide delivery?

Patty Sprague

Question 8

As more people are connected to the Internet and more stores offer the option of being able to buy their products online, online sales have increased over the years. However, there are many disadvantages to shopping on the Internet. Here I will explore why I think it is better to shop online nowadays than it is to go out and buy most goods physically.

The first, and perhaps the best reason to shop online, is that purchases are generally delivered to your door, and sometimes it is even free. Whether it is a pizza, or a refrigerator, or a part for your car, online purchasing is far easier and more hassle free. Nowadays, even services such as taxi rides and plumbing can be bought online!

Furthermore, it is safer to shop online than most people think. Paying by using online payment services and cash transfers is very secure today. This beats having cash and small change loose in your pockets which can be annoying. One could, of course, use a debit or other bank card but that takes so long, and you have to be wary of fraud.

On the other hand, a disadvantage of buying online could be that many people prefer to see the products before they buy them, especially for items such as clothes and shoes, which isn't possible to do when you shop on the Internet. However, buying online saves time waiting in line, or calling for assistance if you scan your goods yourself, which is such a waste of time.

Finally, buying online saves money, which is always better. You can save money because some businesses charge extra if you pay in cash or by check. Prices are usually cheaper if you buy online using certain companies, mainly because they don't have to pay extra for retail space and employee wages, etc.

So in conclusion, it is much better to shop online for most things nowadays because it is much cheaper, less hassle with waiting in line, and much safer with modern methods of cash transfers than carrying a wallet with cash and credit cards.

Practice Test 3

Speaking Test

Question 3

This is a picture of a downtown street. In the middle of the picture, I see a yellow cab moving down the street. In the forefront of the picture, there is large steel sewer grate, and there is some steam coming out of it. On the right side of the picture, there are some people crossing the street. On the left side of the picture, there are some people walking up the street. But I can't see them clearly because of the steam. In the background of the picture, I can see buildings on both sides of the street. There is also a very tall building at the end of the street. It looks like an apartment building. It looks like a normal day in a downtown area.

Question 4

I try to clean my house at least once a week because I like coming home to a clean home. The last time I cleaned my home was last Sunday.

Question 5

When I clean my home, I use a vacuum cleaner, a duster, a mop, and paper towels.

Question 6

No, I wouldn't consider hiring a cleaning person or company to clean my home because it is something I can do on my own. Paying another person to clean my home would be a waste of money. Besides, my home is not that big, so it wouldn't be worth hiring someone else to clean it.

Question 7

Let me just check your account. OK, your invoice number is 625-7890, and the total amount of the order is $1,459.83.

Question 8

Actually, that's not correct. It says on the invoice that you ordered 70 Stick-'em Notes. And the size is large, not medium.

Question 9

Certainly. According to our payment policy, the total amount of an order must be paid within 30 days of the date on the invoice. But if you pay within seven days, a 3% discount will be given. You can pay by bank transfer, credit card, or check. If you're paying by check, please make it payable to Knowledge Publishing Company.

Question 10

Hello, Mr. Evans. I'm calling from the Royal Bank customer service center. I just received your message saying that you're having some problems with an ATM machine at our bank on Vermont Street. First, let me apologize for the problems that you're experiencing with our machine. You said that you tried to withdraw some cash from the machine but no money came out. I've just checked the transaction on our system, and no money has been withdrawn from your account. You also said your bank card is stuck in the machine. I'm going to send a technician right away to take care of that for you. The technician should be there within 15 minutes, so please wait at the machine. Again, I'm very sorry for the problems you've experienced. If the technician does not arrive within the next 15 minutes, please call us back.

Question 11

I agree with the statement that companies should allow employees to wear casual clothes at work. First of all, casual clothes are more comfortable to wear. When workers are more comfortable, they can be more productive. Secondly, allowing casual clothes at work can help employees save money. For example, they wouldn't have to keep spending money on dry cleaning and new clothes. Lastly, wearing casual clothes at work can help companies to save energy. For instance, if you allowed workers to wear T-shirts in the summer, you wouldn't have to set the air conditioner to a high setting. For these reasons, I believe that companies should allow employees to wear casual clothes at work.

Writing Test

Question 1

The doctor is standing in the middle.
Standing beside the doctor is a police officer.
A doctor is standing next to a soldier.
There are many people standing near the doctor.
The doctor is standing close to the builder.

Question 2

People are enjoying lunch.
Three friends are having an enjoyable lunch.
Some people are enjoying lunch.
Three people are enjoying their lunch.
Three smiling women are enjoying their lunches.

Question 3

There are some glasses on a book.
Someone has been reading a book with glasses.
Some glasses are on an open book.
Somebody's glasses are on a book.
A book has a pair of glasses on an open page.

Question 4

This is a business meeting with a presentation.
People are in a business meeting where someone is doing a presentation.
A presentation is being given at a business meeting.
The man is giving a presentation at a business meeting.
Someone is giving a presentation at a business meeting.

Question 5

The couple have asked for directions.
Two people are asking someone for directions.
The younger man has been asked for directions.
The man is asking the older people for directions.
The man and woman have asked for directions.

Question 6

Thank you for your email.

I have attached a scanned copy of our company logo so you can give that to your designer.

As to the size and duration of the advertisement, I would prefer a half page if you offer that? I noticed you didn't list this ad size, so, if not, I will go with the full page. I will need the ad to run for three months. Do you have a discount available per quarter?

To begin with, we would prefer to pay by bank transfer. If the advertisement is successful we can switch to direct debit from there, especially if there's a discount.

I'm not bad at designing myself, and as you can see by the attached document, it looks pretty good already, so I'll decline the use of your design team for the extra cost.

Please let me know the details about when the advertisement will appear, or if you need any further information.

Question 7

Dear Mr. Pinn,

Thank you for your email. We are sorry about our website not having clear directions or a map. We are still building the site and I've already called the company who designed it to include these features. However, we are very happy you pointed this out to us because we hadn't noticed this problem. As a thank you we will give you a complimentary appetizer.

To get here is quite easy. If you're coming by car, take the second turn on the right at the end of High Street on to Sears Road. You should see a large blue building on your left and we are directly opposite. The nearest train station is Boston Park Road, turn left out of the station and High Street is at the end of the road. By bus, catch the 147 and that drops you right outside our door, and look for the blue building.

We look forward to serving you and your family on the 2nd.

Yours sincerely,
Arnold Bagsworth, Manager

Question 8

Although there may sometimes be advantages of sending a photograph with a job application, I think it is quite a risky thing to do. Overall, I think trying to use a photograph to help you get a job is a bad idea for the following three reasons.

First, if you attach a photograph to your job application, recruiters may think that you are too desperate for the job. For example, the fact that you included a photograph might make them think that your job history or educational qualifications aren't sufficient, and that this is the reason why you need to add a photograph. If they get this impression about you, they might not even take the time to read your résumé.

Second, you can never know for sure what kind of appearance a company is looking for. It is true that if you are good-looking, a recruiter might be impressed by your appearance. In this case, he or she might be more likely to choose you to come for an interview. At the same time though, it is possible that your look might not be what the company wants, even if you are good-looking. You can never know for sure what kind of appearance a company is looking for in a job candidate.

Finally, photographs can be misleading. Some people attach photographs taken by professional photographers to their job applications. I think this is a really bad idea, because in real life these people often look quite different. This might make an interviewer feel that you are insincere when he or she sees you in person.

For these reasons, I would never attach a photograph to a job application. I would always want the company to consider my educational and professional background, rather than the way I look.

Practice Test 4

Speaking Test

Question 3

This is a picture of a shopping street. On the right side of the picture, there is a young woman standing outside a store. She has long blond hair, and she has her hands in the pockets of her pants. She is wearing a large hoop earring on her left ear. She is looking at a display window of the store. Behind the display window, there is a female mannequin wearing a purple dress. Beside the mannequin is a brown suitcase. In the background of the picture, I can see a man walking down the street in the woman's direction. I can also see a reflection of the man on the window of the store. It looks like a quiet afternoon on a shopping street.

Question 4

The last time I had a job interview was six years ago. It was successful because I got the job, and I'm still working at the company.

Question 5

When I have a job interview, I always wear a formal suit with a shirt and a tie.

Question 6

When I prepare for a job interview, I always try to find out as much information as I can about the company that I'm applying to. By doing this, I can have a better idea of what kind of questions they may ask me during the interview, and this can help me to prepare answers for them.

Question 7

We're located at 75 Matheson Road, Knoxville. Tickets are $9 for adults and $5.50 for seniors and KU students. Tickets will be sold inside the KU College Arts Building.

Question 8

Actually, there will be no film showing on Wednesday. The documentary on Ron Thompson will be shown on Thursday of film week.

Question 9

Sure. On Friday, *In Search of Sugar Man* will be shown from 9 to 11:20 p.m. On Saturday, there will be two movies shown. The first movie is *Dance This Waltz*, and it will be shown from 6 to 7:50 p.m. The second movie is *Kings of Competition*, and it will be shown from 8:30 to 10:45 p.m.

Question 10

Hello, Deborah. This is Larry Robinson, the manager of Diaz Apartments. I got your message saying that there is a problem with noise coming from the apartment upstairs from yours. As the building manager, I'm very sorry to hear that you've been experiencing this kind of problem in my building. I've looked into the situation, and the apartment where the noise is coming from is 1205. I've spoken to the people living there, and it turns out they have been having parties quite frequently. As you know, there is no law against having a party in your own home, but it shouldn't create so much noise that it disturbs other people living in the building. I've given them a warning, and they've promised to keep the noise down. If you hear loud noise coming from that apartment again, let me know immediately. If there is anything else I can do for you, feel free to call me back. Thanks.

Question 1

I prefer to take the subway to commute. First, the subway is more reliable. For instance, even though buses come on a regular basis, they can sometimes run late because of traffic. However, the subway is always on time. Second, the subway is more comfortable to ride on. For example, bus rides are always bumpy, and this makes for a very tiring ride, especially if you have to stand. On the other hand, subway rides are relatively smooth, and you can read a book or play games on your phone even when you're standing. For these reasons, I prefer to take the subway rather than the bus.

Writing Test

Question 1

The woman is buying a transit card.
Someone is buying a transit card.
Somebody is about to buy a transit card.
Someone is about to buy a transit card from a machine.
You can buy a transit card from a machine at the train station.

Question 2

The family are playing soccer.
They are playing soccer in the park.
The children are playing soccer with their dad.
The father is showing his son how to play soccer.
The family are having fun as they play soccer.

Question 3

Someone is recycling cans into a trash can.
A woman is trying to recycle garbage in a trash can.
There are some recycled cans being put into a trash can.
A special trash can is being used to recycle materials.
A woman is using a trash can to recycle materials.

Question 4

A boy is learning to play the guitar.
The boy's brother is teaching him to play the guitar.
The guitar is being played.
The teacher knows how to play the guitar.
The boy can read music and play the guitar.

Question 5

A man is sitting at a computer.
Someone is sitting at a desk using a laptop computer.
The man is sitting down in front of a computer.
Someone is sitting by a computer.
A man is sitting at a desk using a computer.

Question 6

Thanks for your email and the photos. We all looked at them and we like the three-bedroom apartment better than the others because we each want our own room. We would also like to move into an apartment that has Internet and all bills included. Unfortunately, the three-bedroom apartment is a little too expensive for us. Also, this apartment is a bus ride from the nearest train station, so that will cost each of us about $50 extra per month. Since we only have $1,460 between us, could the landlord offer us the apartment at this price? If the landlord agrees to this price, we can sign the lease immediately. Please let me know if this is possible, or if you have any other apartments available that you think would be suitable for us, and which are perhaps closer to the college.

Question 7

Thank you so much for your wonderful brochure! After discussing it with both my wife and the other parents, we have decided to order the pizza and the ice cream cake. Having said that, it has left us with enough money to hire one of your magicians and also your buckaroo mechanical horse because we have a big yard. All this comes to $335 if we calculated right.

Please call me to arrange to come over and deal with the paperwork, and to check out the electricity for your buckaroo ride. My wife will be taking Sam out this Saturday morning to play soccer so this would be an ideal time.

Question 8

There have been many inventions which have helped change the way in which people live and work. There are lots of great inventions but, for me, the best invention of all time has to be the Internet. Its creation has revolutionized the world but here's why it has personally transformed my life.

Professionally, as a businessman, I can't maintain a successful business without the Internet. Most of my meetings and appointments are organized through emails and IMs. Even modern cell phones have the Internet nowadays. I can sift through possible manufacturers on thousands of websites and blogs, order samples, goods and services, set up meetings, book trains, flight and rent cars, to help my business and my employees. I can safely say that with the Internet I have increased the productivity of my company and the profits by at least 50%.

Personally, as a married man with two children, the Internet is a valuable resource that has transformed my family's whole life and our standard of living. I can chat on video messaging to friends, family and colleagues on the other side of the planet. I can order a pizza and a movie from the comfort of our sofa, and download my favorite movies, music, books, at the push of a button. I regularly shop online buying groceries, gifts, even a house—the list is endless. I can even watch my favorite soccer team on a Saturday afternoon with friends through live streaming!

So in conclusion, I personally think the best invention of all time is the Internet. Although many inventions could be suggested as being the most important in history, such as the airplane, the car, or the cell phone, nothing, in my view, has changed the way we live quite so dramatically as the Internet. Now, I couldn't imagine living without it.